ELVIS FOR EVERYONE

The Essential Guide To The
Recorded Music Of Elvis Presley

David Parker

ELVIS FOR EVERYONE

© 2002 Abstract Sounds Publishing
Text Copyright © David Parker 2002

Exclusive distribution in the UK:
Turnaround Distribution
Orders: orders@turnaround.uk.com

Design and art direction: David Parker
Cover artwork: David Parker

First published 2002 by Abstract Sounds Publishing
A division of Abstract Sounds Ltd
2 Elgin Avenue
London W9 3QP

Email: abstractsounds@btclick.com
www.abstractsounds.co.uk

ISBN 0 9535724 5 5

ELVIS FOR EVERYONE

Contents

Introduction

Official RCA/BMG Releases: 1956 – 2001

Photo Feature: The Greatest Hits Compilations

RCA International: The Budget Albums

Follow That Dream: The RCA/BMG Collectors Label

Photo Feature: World Wide Compilation Albums

Unofficial Releases: Studio Recordings & Compilations

Unofficial Releases: Movie Soundtrack Recordings

Unofficial Releases: Live & Rehearsal Recordings

Acknowledgements

ELVIS FOR EVERYONE

INTRODUCTION

This book takes its title from the album "Elvis For Everyone" which was released in 1965 and included eleven previously unreleased masters recorded between 1954 and 1964 amongst it's twelve tracks.
 "Elvis For Everyone" wasn't the only album released during Elvis' lifetime to feature material from a variety of different sources, and in recent years with the advent of the CD upgrade, special edition albums, and collectors boxed sets, I thought the time was right to take another look at the Elvis album discography.

The book is intended as both a reference source for the serious collector, and a guide to the Elvis Presley catalogue for the casual fan who may still be searching for that famous laughing version of "Are You Lonesome Tonight", or simply thinking about which album to buy next.

The first part of this book looks at official album releases from 1956 – 2001, and the track listings refer to both the original version and the most recent CD issue when more than one version of a particular album has been released.

There is also a section on unofficial CD's which doesn't include every bootleg CD, but is intended to provide an overview of the type of material that has been made available unofficially in recent years.

ELVIS PRESLEY (1956)

Original Version:

1. Blue Suede Shoes
2. I'm Counting On You
3. I Got A Woman
4. One Sided Love Affair
5. I Love You Because
6. Just Because
7. Tutti Frutti
8. Trying To Get To You
9. I'm Gonna Sit Right Down And Cry (Over You)
10. I'll Never Let You Go (Little Darlin')
11. Blue Moon
12. Money Honey

CD Re-issue Version:

1. Heartbreak Hotel
2. I Was The One
3. Blue Suede Shoes
4. I'm Counting On You
5. I Got A Woman
6. One Sided Love Affair
7. I Love You Because
8. Just Because
9. Tutti Frutti
10. Trying To Get To You
11. I'm Gonna Sit Right Down And Cry (Over You)
12. I'll Never Let You Go (Little Darlin')
13. Blue Moon
14. Money Honey
15. Shake, Rattle And Roll
16. My Baby Left Me
17. Lawdy Miss Clawdy
18. I Want You, I Need You, I Love You

Recording Information:

Track 5 recorded July 5-6, 1954. Track 10 recorded September 10, 1954.
Track 6 recorded September 1954. Track 11 recorded August 19, 1954.
Track 8 recorded July 11, 1955. Tracks 5, 6, 8, 10, & 11 recorded at Sun Studios, Memphis.
Tracks 3 & 12 recorded January 10, 1956. Track 2 recorded January 11, 1956.
Tracks 2, 3, & 12 recorded at RCA Studios, Nashville.
Tracks 1 & 4 recorded January 30, 1956. Tracks 7 & 9 recorded January 31, 1956.
Tracks 1, 4, 7, & 9 recorded at RCA Studios, New York.
The CD re-issue featured six additional previously released masters.
The original version has also been issued on CD.

ELVIS – ROCK N ROLL NO. 2 (1956)

Original Version:

1. Rip It Up
2. Love Me
3. When My Blue Moon Turns To Gold Again
4. Long Tall Sally
5. First In Line
6. Paralyzed
7. So Glad Your Mine
8. Old Shep
9. Ready Teddy
10. Anyplace Is Paradise
11. How's The World Treating You
12. How Do You Think I Feel

CD Re-issue Version:

1. Hound Dog
2. Don't Be Cruel
3. Any Way You Want Me
4. Rip It Up
5. Love Me
6. When My Blue Moon Turns To Gold Again
7. Long Tall Sally
8. First In Line
9. Paralyzed
10. So Glad Your Mine
11. Old Shep
12. Ready Teddy
13. Anyplace Is Paradise
14. How's The World Treating You
15. How Do You Think I Feel
16. Too Much
17. Playing For Keeps
18. Love Me Tender

Recording Information:

Track 7 recorded January 30, 1956 at RCA Studios, New York.
Tracks 2, 11, & 12 recorded September 1, 1956.
Tracks 3, 4, 6, 8, & 10 recorded September 2, 1956.
Tracks 1, 5, & 9 recorded September 3, 1956.
Tracks 1 – 6 & 8 – 12 recorded at Radio Recorders, Hollywood.
The CD re-issue version featured six additional masters that were originally issued as singles.
The original version has also been issued on CD.

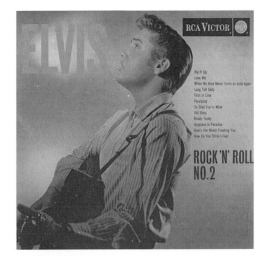

The original back cover art was not included on the first CD issue of this album.

Below: the CD re-issue featured new back cover art, and the original artwork was also included on the reverse of the CD booklet.

Above: The CD re-issue version featured new back cover artwork.

LOVING YOU (1957)

Original Version:

1. Mean Woman Blues
2. (Let Me Be Your) Teddy Bear
3. Loving You
4. Got A Lot O' Livin' To Do
5. Lonesome Cowboy
6. Hot Dog
7. Party
8. Blueberry Hill
9. True Love
10. Don't Leave Me Now
11. Have I Told You Lately That I Love You
12. I Need You So

CD Re-issue Extra Tracks:

13. Tell Me Why
14. Is It So Strange
15. One Night Of Sin
16. When It Rains It Really Pours
17. I Beg Of You (alternate master)
18. Party (alternate master)
19. Loving You (uptempo version)
20. Got A Lot O' Livin' To Do (finale)

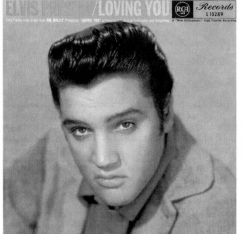

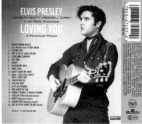

Above: the CD re-issue version featured new back cover artwork, and the original art was included on the reverse of the CD booklet.

Recording Information:

Track 4 recorded January 12, 1957. Track 1 recorded January 13, 1957. Tracks 1 & 4 recorded at Radio Recorders, Hollywood.
Tracks 2, 5, 6, & 7 recorded January 14 – 18, 1957 at the Paramount Scoring Stage, Hollywood.
Track 3 recorded February 24, 1957 at Radio Recorders, Hollywood. Tracks 1 – 7 from the Paramount Motion Picture "Loving You".
Tracks 8 & 11 recorded January 19, 1957. Tracks 9, 10, & 12 recorded February 23, 1957. Tracks 8 – 12 recorded at Radio Recorders, Hollywood.
The CD re-issue version featured an additional 8 previously released performances from the same period .
The original version has also been issued on CD.

JAILHOUSE ROCK & LOVE ME TENDER (CD RELEASE: 1997)

1. Jailhouse Rock
2. Treat Me Nice
3. I Want To Be Free
4. Don't Leave Me Now
5. Young And Beautiful
6. (You're So Square) Baby I Don't Care
7. Jailhouse Rock (movie version)
8. Treat Me Nice (movie version)
9. Young And Beautiful (movie version)
11. Don't Leave Me Now (alternate master)
12. Love Me Tender
13. Poor Boy
14. Let Me
15. We're Gonna Move
16. Love Me Tender (end title version)
17. Let Me (solo)
18. We're Gonna Move (stereo – take 9)
19. Poor Boy (stereo)
20. Love Me Tender (stereo)

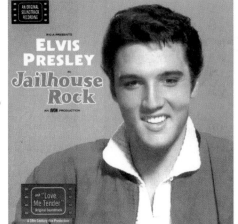

Below:

The original "Jailhouse Rock" EP

Recording Information:

Tracks 12, 13, 15, 18, 19, & 20 recorded August 24, 1956.
Tracks 14 & 17 recorded September 4 – 5, 1956.
Track 16 recorded October 1, 1956.
Tracks 12 – 20 recorded at 20th Century Fox Stage 1, Hollywood.
Tracks 12 – 20 from the 20th Century Fox Motion Picture "Love Me Tender".
Tracks 1, 7, 5, & 10 recorded April 30, 1957.
Tracks 3, 8, & 9 recorded May 3, 1957.
Tracks 1, 3, 5, 7, 8, 9, & 10 recorded at Radio Recorders, Hollywood.
Track 6 recorded May 8, 1957. Tracks 4 & 11 recorded May 9, 1957.
Tracks 4, 6, & 11 recorded at MGM Studios, Hollywood.
Track 2 recorded September 5, 1957 at Radio Recorders, Hollywood.
Tracks 1 – 11 from the MGM Motion Picture "Jailhouse Rock".
Tracks 12 – 15 were first released on the "Love Me Tender" EP in 1956.
Tracks 1, 3, 4, 5, & 6 were first released on the "Jailhouse Rock EP in 1957.

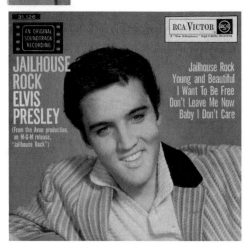

ELVIS' CHRISTMAS ALBUM (1957)

1. Santa Claus Is back In Town
2. White Christmas
3. Here Comes Santa Claus
4. I'll Be Home For Christmas
5. Blue Christmas
6. Santa Bring My Baby Back To Me
7. Oh Little Town Of Bethlehem
8. Silent Night
9. Peace In the Valley
10. I Believe
11. Take My Hand Precious Lord
12. It Is No Secret

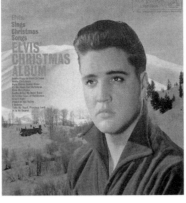

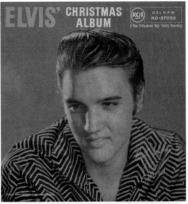

Recording Information:

Track 10 recorded January 12, 1957.
Tracks 9 & 11 recorded January 13, 1957.
Track 12 recorded January 19, 1957.
Track 5 recorded September 5, 1957.
Tracks 2, 3, & 8 recorded September 6, 1957.
Tracks 1, 4, 6, & 7 recorded September 7, 1957.
All selections recorded at Radio Recorders, Hollywood.

Above right: the original British version of the album had a different sleeve design.

Right: the CD version used the cover art from the second issue of the album, which was released in 1958.

This issue also included a gatefold photo album, and this has been reproduced in the CD booklet (left)

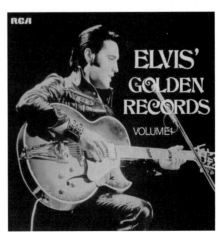

ELVIS GOLDEN RECORDS (1958)

Original Version:

1. Hound Dog
2. Loving You
3. All Shook Up
4. Heartbreak Hotel
5. Jailhouse Rock
6. Love Me
7. Too Much
8. Don't Be Cruel
9. That's When Your Heartaches Begin
10 (Let Me Be Your) Teddy Bear
11. Love Me Tender
12. Treat Me Nice
13. Any Way You Want Me
14. I Want You, I Need You, I Love You

CD Re-issue Extra Tracks:

15. My Baby Left Me
16. I Was The One
17. That's All Right
18. Baby Let's Play House
19. Mystery Train
20. Blue Suede Shoes

Recording Information:

Track 4 recorded January 10, 1956. Track 14 recorded April 14, 1956.
Tracks 4 & 14 recorded at RCA Studios, Nashville.
Tracks 1, 8, & 13 recorded July 2, 1956 at RCA Studios, New York.
Track 11 recorded August 24, 1956 at 20th Century Fox Stage 1, Hollywood.
Track 6 recorded September 1, 1956. Track 7 recorded September 2, 1956.
Track 3 recorded January 12, 1957.
Track 9 recorded January 13, 1957. Tracks 3, 6, 7, & 9 recorded at Radio Recorders, Hollywood.
Track 10 recorded January 14 – 18, 1957 at the Paramount Scoring Stage, Hollywood.
Track 2 recorded February 24, 1957. Track 5 recorded April 30, 1957.
Track 12 recorded September 5, 1957. Tracks 2, 5, & 12 recorded at Radio Recorders, Hollywood.
The CD re-issue version included five additional previously released masters.
The original version has also been issued on CD.

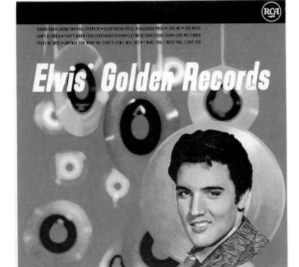

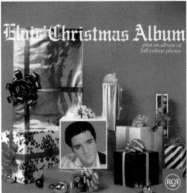

Left: original album art.
Above: a UK re-issue from 1970 featuring a 1968 cover photo from the NBC TV Special.

KING CREOLE (1958)

Original Version:

1. King Creole
2. As Long As I Have You
3. Hard Headed Woman
4. Trouble
5. Dixieland Rock
6. Don't Ask Me Why
7. Lover Doll
8. Crawfish
9. Young Dreams
10. Steadfast, Loyal And True
11. New Orleans

CD Re-issue Extra Tracks:

12. King Creole (take 18)
13. As Long As I Have You
    (movie version – take 4)
14. Danny
15. Lover Doll (undubbed)
16. Steadfast Loyal & True
    (alternate master)
17. As Long As I Have You
    (movie version – take 8)
18. King Creole (take 3)

Recording Information:

Tracks 1, 9, & 10 recorded January 23, 1958.
Tracks 3, 4, 8, & 11 recorded January 15, 1958.
Tracks 2, 5, 6, & 7 recorded January 16, 1958.
All selections recorded at Radio Recorders, Hollywood for the Paramount Motion Picture, "King Creole".
The CD re-issue version featured an additional 7 previously released alternate masters from the same sessions.
The original version has also been issued on CD.

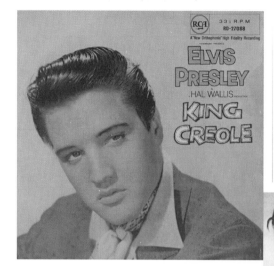

The CD re-issue featured new back cover art and the original artwork was also included on the reverse of the CD booklet.

FOR LP FANS ONLY (1959)

Original Version:

1. That's All Right
2. Lawdy Miss Clawdy
3. Mystery Train
4, Playing For Keeps
5. Poor Boy
6. My Baby Left Me
7. I Was The One
8. Shake Rattle & Roll
9. I'm Left, You're Right, She's Gone
10. You're Heartbreaker

CD Version:

1. That's All Right
2. Lawdy Miss Clawdy
3. Mystery Train
4. Playing For Keeps
5. Poor Boy
6. Money Honey
7. I'm Counting On You
8. My Baby Left Me
9. I Was The One
10. Shake Rattle & Roll
11. I'm Left, You're Right, She's Gone
12. You're A Heartbreaker
13. Trying To Get To You
14. Blue Suede Shoes

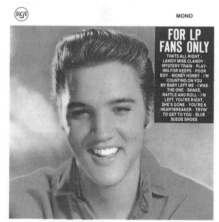

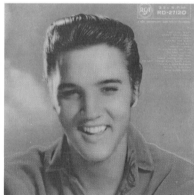

Above left: European CD artwork.

Above right: the original British LP release "Elvis" RD 27120.

Collectors Notes:

The original US release of this album featured 10 previously released performances, and was the first of two albums of previously released material issued whilst Elvis was in the army. The European CD release of this album features the 10 tracks from the original US release, along with four additional tracks, and is effectively a re-issue of the 1959 British album "Elvis" (RD 27120).

A DATE WITH ELVIS (1959)

Original Version:

1. Blue Moon Of Kentucky
2. Young And Beautiful
3. Baby I Don't Care
4. Milkcow Blues Boogie
5. Baby Let's Play House
6. Good Rockin' Tonight
7. Is It So Strange
8. We're Gonna Move
9. I Want To Be Free
10. I Forgot To Remember To Forget

UK LP Version/CD Version:

1. Blue Moon Of Kentucky
2. Milkcow Blues Boogie
3. Baby Let's Play House
4. I Don't Care If The Sun Don't Shine
5. Tutti Frutti
6. I'm Gonna Sit Right Down And Cry Over You
7. I Got A Woman
8. Good Rockin' Tonight
9. Is It So Strange
10. We're Gonna Move
11. Blue Moon
12. Just Because
13. One Sided Love Affair
14. Let Me

Collectors Notes:

The second album of previously released performances issued during Elvis' army service was released in the US with 10 tracks. In the UK a 14 track version of the album was released, and this track listing was also used for the European CD version.

50,000,000 ELVIS FANS CAN'T BE WRONG – ELVIS' GOLD RECORDS VOLUME 2 (1959)

Original Version:

1. I Need Your Love Tonight
2. Don't
3. Wear My Ring Around Your Neck
4. My Wish Came True
5. I Got Stung
6. One Night
7. A Big Hunk O' Love
8. I Beg Of You
9. A Fool Such As I
10. Doncha' Think It's Time

UK LP Version/CD Version:

1. A Big Hunk O' Love
2. My Wish Came True
3. A Fool A Such As I
4. I Need Your Love Tonight
5. Don't
6. I Beg Of You
7. Santa Bring My Baby Back To Me
8. Party
9. Paralyzed
10. One Night
11. I Got Stung
12. King Creole
13. Wear My Ring Around Your Neck
14. Doncha' Think It's Time

CD Re-issue Version:

1. A Big Hunk O' Love
2. My Wish Came True
3. A Fool A Such As I
4. I Need Your Love Tonight
5. Don't
6. I Beg Of You
7. Santa Bring My Baby Back To Me
8. Santa Claus Is Back In Town
9. Party
10. Paralyzed
11. One Night
12. I Got Stung
13. King Creole
14. Wear My Ring Around Your Neck
15. Doncha' Think It's Time
16. Mean Woman Blues
17. Playing For Keeps
18. Hard Headed Woman
19. Got A Lot O' Livin' to Do
20. Peace In The Valley

Recording Information:

Tracks 6 & 8 recorded February 23, 1957.
Tracks 2 & 4 recorded September 5, 1957.
Tracks 3 & 10 recorded February 1, 1958.
Tracks 2, 3, 4, 6, 8, & 10 recorded at Radio Recorders, Hollywood.
Tracks 1, 7, & 9 recorded June 10, 1958.
Track 5 recorded June 11, 1958.
Tracks 1, 5, 7, & 9 recorded at RCA Studio B, Nashville.
The original 10 track album has been issued on CD, and there have been two further CD re-issues featuring additional previously released masters.
The European CD version featured the 14 tracks from the original UK vinyl version, and a second CD re-issue from 1997 featured 10 tracks that were not included on the original album.

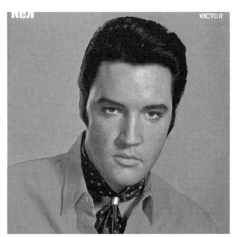

Left: the 14 track CD Version.

Right: a UK re-issue from 1970 featuring a 1968 cover shot.

ELVIS IS BACK (1960)

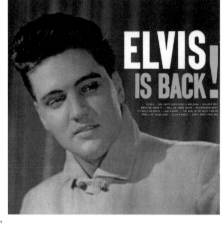

Original Version:

1. Make Me Know It
2. Fever
3. The Girl Of My Best Friend
4. I Will Be Home Again
5. Dirty Dirty Feeling
6. The Thrill Of Your Love
7. Soldier Boy
8. Such A Night
9. It Feels So Right
10. The Girl Next Door Went A Walking
11. Like A Baby
12. Reconsider Baby

Recording Information:

Tracks 1 & 7 recorded March 20, 1960.
Track 9 recorded March 21, 1960.
Tracks 2 & 11 recorded April 3, 1960.
Tracks 3, 4, 5, 6, 8, 10, & 12 recorded April 4, 1960.
All selections recorded at RCA Studio B, Nashville.
The CD re-issue version featured 6 extra tracks from the same sessions that were originally released as singles.
The original version has also been issued on CD

CD Re-issue Version:

1. Stuck On You
2. Fame And Fortune
3. Make Me Know It
4. Fever
5. The Girl Of My Best Friend
6. I Will Be Home Again
7. Dirty Dirty Feeling
8. The Thrill Of Your Love
9. Soldier Boy
10. Such A Night
11. It Feels So Right
12. The Girl Next Door Went A Walking
13. Like A Baby
14. Reconsider Baby
15. Are You Lonesome Tonight?
16. I Gotta Know
17. A Mess Of Blues
18. It's Now Or Never

Left to right:

The CD re-issue version featured slightly different front cover art. The album's original back cover art was included on the reverse of the CD booklet, and a new back cover design was also featured.

G.I. BLUES (1960)

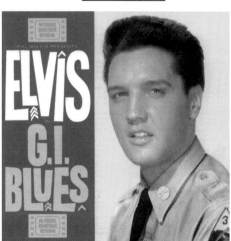

**Above: the original album artwork.
Right: the CD re-issue was also issued as a Collectors Edition digi-pack with new artwork and a 28 page booklet.**

Original Version:

1. Tonight Is So Right For Love
2. What's She Really Like
3. Frankfort Special
4. Wooden Heart
5. GI Blues
6. Pocketful Of Rainbows
7. Shoppin' Around
8. Big Boots
9. Didja Ever
10. Blue Suede Shoes
11. Doin' The Best I Can
12. Tonight's All Right For Love *

CD Re-issue Extra Tracks:

13. Big Boots (fast version)
14. Shoppin' Around (alternate take 11)
15. Frankfort Special (fast version – take 2)
16. Pocketful Of Rainbows (alternate take 2)
17. Didja Ever (alternate take 1)
18. Big Boots (acoustic version)
19. What's She Really Like (alternate take 7)
20. Doin' The Best I Can (alternate take 8)

**Above:
a European release of the album.**

Recording Information:

Tracks 1, 5, 9, & 11 recorded April 27, 1960. Tracks 2, 4, 8, & 10 recorded April 28, 1960.
Tracks 1, 2, 4, 5, 8, 9, 10, & 11 recorded at RCA Studios, Hollywood.
Tracks 3, 6, 7, & 12 recorded May 6, 1960 at Radio Recorders, Hollywood.
All selections recorded for the Paramount Motion Picture "GI Blues".
* "Tonight's All Right for Love" was not included on the original US and UK versions of the album.
It was replaced by "Tonight Is So Right For Love".
By the time the album was released on CD both tracks were included.
The recent CD re-issue of the album featured a further 8 alternate masters from the same sessions.
The original version has also been issued on CD.

HIS HAND IN MINE (1960)

1. His Hand In Mine
2. I'm Gonna Walk Dem Golden Stairs
3. In My Father's House
4. Milky White Way
5. Known Only To Him
6. I Believe In The Man In The Sky
7. Joshua Fit The Battle
8. He Knows Just What I Need
9. Swing Down Sweet Chariot
10. Mansion Over The Hilltop
11. If We Never Meet Again
12. Working On The Building
13. It Is No Secret*
14. You'll Never Walk Alone*
15. Who Am I?*

Recording Information:

Tracks 1, 4, 6, 8, & 10 recorded October 30, 1960.
Tracks 2, 3, 5, 7, 9, 11, & 12 recorded October 31, 1960.
All selections recorded at RCA Studio B, Nashville.
* The original album featured 12 tracks. Three previously released gospel performances were added to the first CD issue of this album.

SOMETHING FOR EVERYBODY (1961)

Original Version:

1. There's Always Me
2. Give Me The Right
3. It's A Sin
4. Sentimental Me
5. Starting Today
6. Gently
7. I'm Coming Home
8. In Your Arms
9. Put The Blame On Me
10. Judy
11. I Want You With Me
12. I Slipped, I Stumbled, I Fell

CD Re-issue Version:

1. Surrender
2. There's Always Me
3. Give Me The Right
4. It's A Sin
5. Sentimental Me
6. Starting Today
7. Gently
8. I'm Coming Home
9. In Your Arms
10. Put The Blame On Me
11. Judy
12. I Want You With Me
13. I Feel So Bad
14. His Latest Flame
15. Little Sister
16. Good Luck Charm
17. Anything That's Part Of You

**Above: the original front and back cover art.
The CD re-issue version featured the original
back cover art on the inside of the CD booklet.**

Left: the CD re-issue version.

Right:

**The CD re-issue version which
featured a slightly different
front cover design and new
back cover artwork.**

Recording Information:

Track 12 recorded November 8, 1960 at Radio Recorders, Hollywood for the 20th Century Fox Motion Picture "Wild In The Country".
Tracks 1, 2, 3, 6, 7, 8, & 11 recorded March 22, 1961.
Tracks 4, 5, 9, & 10 recorded March 23, 1961.
Tracks 1 – 11 recorded at RCA Studio B, Nashville.
The CD re-issue version featured 6 additional masters from the same period that were originally released as singles.
The original version was also issued on CD

BLUE HAWAII (1961)

Original Version:

1. Blue Hawaii
2. Almost Always True
3. Aloha-Oe*
4. No More
5. Can't Help Falling In Love
6. Rock A Hula Baby
7. Moonlight Swim
8. KU-U-I-PO
9. Ito Eats
10. Slicin' Sand
11. Hawaiian Sunset
12. Beach Boy Blues
13. Island Of Love
14. Hawaiian Wedding Song

CD Re-issue Extra Tracks:

15. Steppin' Out Of Line
16. Can't Help Falling In Love (movie version)
17. Slicin' Sand (alternate take 4)
18. No More (alternate take 7)
19. Rock A Hula Baby (alternate take 1)
20. Beach Boy Blues (movie version)
21. Steppin' Out Of Line (movie version)
22. Blue Hawaii (alternate take 3)

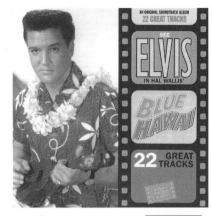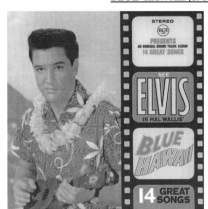

Above: there were slight variations between the original album artwork (left) and the CD re-issue version (right).

Right: the CD re-issue was also issued as a Collectors Edition digi-pack with new artwork and a 28 page booklet.

Recording Information:

Tracks 3, 4, 8, 10, & 11 recorded March 21, 1961.
Tracks 1, 2, 7, 9, 13, & 14 recorded March 22, 1961.
Tracks 5, 6, & 12 recorded March 23, 1961.
All selections recorded at Radio Recorders, Hollywood for the Paramount Motion Picture "Blue Hawaii".
*Elvis' version of "Aloha-Oe" was spliced with an additional version recorded on March 23, 1961 by The Surfers.
The CD re-issue version featured 8 alternate masters from the same sessions.
The original version was also issued on CD.

POT LUCK WITH ELVIS (1962)

Original Version:

1. Kiss Me Quick
2. Just For Old Times Sake
3. Gonna Get Back Home Somehow
4. Such An Easy Question
5. Steppin' Out Of Line
6. I'm Yours
7. Something Blue
8. Suspicion
9. I Feel That I've Known You Forever
10. Night Rider
11. Fountain Of Love
12. That's Someone You Never Forget

CD Re-issue Version:

1. Kiss Me Quick
2. Just For Old Times Sake
3. Gonna Get Back Home Somehow
4. I Met Her Today
5. Such An Easy Question
6. She's Not You
7. I'm Yours
8. You'll Be Gone
9. Something Blue
10. Suspicion
11. I Feel That I've Known You Forever
12. Night Rider
13. For The Millionth And The Last Time
14. Just Tell Her Jim Said Hello
15. Fountain Of Love
16. That's Someone You Never Forget
17. Steppin' Out Of Line

Above: the original album art.

Right: the CD re-issue featured new back cover artwork, and the original back cover artwork was included on the reverse of the CD booklet.

Recording Information:

Track 5 recorded March 22, 1961 at Radio Recorders, Hollywood for the Paramount Motion Picture, "Blue Hawaii".
Tracks 1 & 12 recorded June 25, 1961. Track 6 recorded June 26, 1961.
Track 10 recorded October 16, 1961. Tracks 2, 3, 4, 7, & 11 recorded March 18, 1962.
Tracks 8 & 9 recorded March 19, 1962. Tracks 1 – 4 & 6 – 12 recorded at RCA Studio B, Nashville.
The CD re-issue version featured five additional previously released masters from the same period.
The original version has also been issued on CD.

GIRLS! GIRLS! GIRLS! (1962)

Original Version:

1. Girls! Girls! Girls!
2. I Don't Wanna Be Tied
3. Where Do You Come From?
4. I Don't Want To
5. We'll Be Together
6. A Boy Like Me, A Girl Like You
7. Earth Boy
8. Return To Sender
9. Because Of Love
10. Thanks To The Rolling Sea
11. Song Of The Shrimp
12. The Walls Have Ears
13. We're Coming In Loaded

Recording Information:

Tracks 4, 10, & 13 recorded March 26, 1962.
Tracks 1, 3, 6, 8, 9, 11, & 12 recorded March 27, 1962.
Tracks 2 & 7 recorded March 28, 1962.
Tracks 5 recorded March 29, 1962.
All selections recorded at Radio Recorders, Hollywood for the Paramount Motion Picture "Girls"! Girls! Girls!"
The original album has not been issued on CD in this format.

IT HAPPENED AT THE WORLD'S FAIR (1963)

Original Version:

1. Beyond The Bend
2. Relax
3. Take Me To The Fair
4. They Remind Me Too Much Of You
5. One Broken Heart For Sale
6. I'm Falling In Love Tonight
7. Cotton Candy Land
8. A World Of Our Own
9. How Would You Like To Be
10. Happy Ending

Recording Information:

Tracks 2 & 10 recorded August 30, 1962.
Tracks 1, 3, 4, 5, 6, 7, 8, & 9 recorded September 22, 1962.
All selections recorded at Radio Recorders, Hollywood for the MGM Motion Picture "It Happened At The World's Fair".
The original album has not been issued on CD in this format.

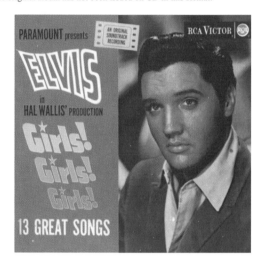

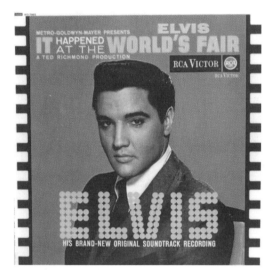

ELVIS GOLDEN RECORDS VOLUME 3 (1963)

Original Version:

1. It's Now Or Never
2. Stuck On You
3. Fame And Fortune
4. I Gotta Know
5. Surrender
6. I Feel So Bad
7. Are You Lonesome Tonight?
8. His Latest Flame
9. Little Sister
10. Good Luck Charm
11. Anything That's Part Of You
12. She's Not You

CD Re-issue Extra Tracks:

13. Wild In The Country
14. Wooden Heart
15. Girl Of My Best Friend
16. Follow That Dream
17. King Of The Whole Wide World
18. Can't Help Falling Love

Recording Information:

Tracks 2 & 3 recorded March 20, 1960.
Track 1 recorded April 3, 1960.
Tracks 4 & 7 recorded April 4, 1960.
Track 5 recorded October 30, 1960.
Track 6 recorded March 12, 1961.
Tracks 8 & 9 recorded June 28, 1961.
Tracks 10 & 11 recorded October 15, 1961.
Track 12 recorded March 16, 1962.
All selections recorded at RCA Studio B, Nashville.

The CD re-issue version featured six additional previously released masters and new back cover art (right)
The original version has also been issued on CD.

FUN IN ACAPULCO (1963)

Original Version:

1. Fun In Acapulco
2. Vino Dinero Y Amor
3. Mexico
4. El Toro
5. Marguerita
6. The Bullfighter Was A Lady
7. There's No Room To Rhumba In A Sports Car
8. I Think I'm Gonna Like It Here
9. Bossa Nova Baby
10. You Can't Say No In Acapulco
11. Guadalajara*
12. Love Me Tonight
13. Slowly But Surely

Recording Information:

Tracks 1, 4, 7, 8, 10, & 11 recorded January 22, 1963.
Tracks 2, 3, 5, 6, & 9 recorded January 23, 1963.
* Elvis overdubbed his vocals on "Guadalajara" on February 27, 1963 at Radio Recorders.
Tracks 1 – 11 recorded at Radio Recorders, Hollywood for the Paramount Motion Picture "Fun In Acapulco".
Track 12 recorded May 27, 1963. Track 13 recorded May 28. 1963.
Tracks 12 & 13 recorded at RCA Studio B, Nashville.
The original album has not been issued on CD in this format.

KISSIN' COUSINS (1964)

Original Version:

1. Kissin' Cousins No. 2
2. Smokey Mountain Boy
3. There's Gold In The Mountains
4. One Boy Two Little Girls
5. Catchin' On Fast
6. Tender Feeling
7. Anyone
8. Barefoot Ballad
9. Once Is Enough
10 Kissin' Cousins
11. Echoes Of Love
12. Long, Lonely Highway

Recording Information:

Track 11 recorded May 26, 1963.
Track 12 recorded May 27, 1963.
Tracks 11 & 12 recorded at RCA Studio B, Nashville.
Tracks 1 – 10 recorded September 30, 1963 at RCA Studio B, Nashville for the MGM Motion Picture "Kissin' Cousins".
Elvis' vocals for these selections were recorded in Hollywood in October 1963.
The original album has not been issued on CD in this format.

ROUSTABOUT (1964)

Original Version:

1. Roustabout
2. Little Egypt
3. Poison Ivy League
4. Hard Knocks
5. It's A Wonderful World
6. Big Love, Big Heartache*
7. One Track Heart*
8. It's Carnival Time
9. Carny Town
10. There's A Brand New Day On The Horizon
11. Wheels On My Heels

Recording Information:

Tracks 2, 3, 4, 5, 6, 7, & 8 recorded March 2, 1964.
Tracks 9, 10, & 11 recorded March 3, 1964.
Track 10 recorded April 29, 1964.
All selections recorded at Radio Recorders, Hollywood for the Paramount Motion Picture "Roustabout".
* Elvis' vocals for "Big Love, Big Heartache" & "One Track Heart" were overdubbed on April 3.
The original album has not been issued on CD in this format.

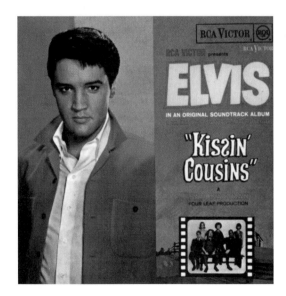

GIRL HAPPY (1965)

Original Version:

1. Girl Happy
2. Spring Fever
3. Fort Lauderdale Chamber Of Commerce
4. Startin' Tonight
5. Wolf Call
6. Do Not Disturb
7. Cross My Heart And Hope To Die
8. The Meanest Girl In Town
9. Do The Clam
10. Puppet On A String
11. I Got To Find My Baby
12. You'll Be Gone

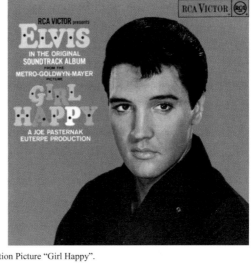

Recording Information:

Track 12 recorded March 12, 1962 at RCA Studio B, Nashville.
Tracks 1, 8, & 10 recorded June 10, 1964.
Tracks 2, 6, & 7 recorded June 11, 1964.
Tracks 3, 4, 5, 9, & 11 recorded June 12, 1964.
Tracks 1 –11 recorded at Radio Recorders, Hollywood for the MGM Motion Picture "Girl Happy".
The original album has not been issued on CD in this format.

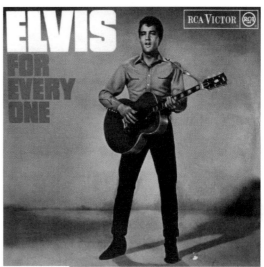

ELVIS FOR EVERYONE (1965)

1. Your Cheatin' Heart
2. Summer Kisses, Winter Tears
3. Finders Keepers, Losers Weepers
4. In My Way
5. Tomorrow Night
6. Memphis, Tennessee
7. For The Millionth And The Last Time
8. Forget Me Never
9. Sound Advice
10. Santa Lucia
11. I Met Her Today
12. When It Rains It Really Pours

Above left:

The original American album artwork which is now used for the CD version.

Above right:

The original UK album from 1965 had a different sleeve design. This can also be found on the back of the booklet in the CD version.

Right:

A UK re-release from the early '70's which also had a different sleeve design.

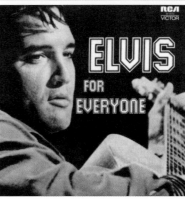

Recording Information:

Track 5 recorded September 10, 1954 at Sun Studios, Memphis. Overdubs added March 18, 1965 at RCA Studio B, Nashville.
Track 12 recorded February 24, 1957 at Radio Recorders, Hollywood.
Track 1 recorded February 1, 1958 at Radio Recorders, Hollywood.
Track 2 recorded August 8, 1960 at Radio Recorders, Hollywood for the 20th Century Fox Motion Picture "Flaming Star".
Tracks 4 & 8 recorded November 7, 1960 at Radio Recorders, Hollywood for the 20th Century Fox Motion Picture "Wild In The Country".
Track 9 recorded July 2, 1961 at RCA Studio B, Nashville for the Mirisch United Artists Motion Picture "Follow That Dream".
Track 7 recorded October 15, 1961 at RCA Studio B, Nashville.
Track 11 recorded October 16, 1961 at RCA Studio B, Nashville.
Tracks 3 & 6 recorded May 27, 1963 at RCA Studio B, Nashville.
Track 10 recorded July 10, 1963 at Radio Recorders, Hollywood for the MGM Motion Picture "Viva Las Vegas".

HARUM SCARUM A.K.A. HAREM HOLIDAY (1965)

Original Version:

1. Harem Holiday
2. My Desert Serenade
3. Go East Young Man
4. Mirage
5. Kismet
6. Shake That Tambourine
7. Hey Little Girl
8. Golden Coins
9. So Close Yet So Far
10. Animal Instinct
11. Wisdom Of The Ages

The title of the movie was changed from "Harum Scarum" to "Harem Holiday" for it's European release. The cover art pictured features a UK version of the album with the title changed to "Harem Holiday". There were no other changes made to the album's cover art.

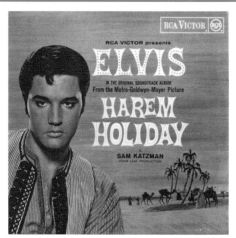

Recording Information:

Track 6 recorded February 24, 1965.
Tracks 2, 5, 7, 8, 9, 10, & 11 recorded February 25, 1965.
Tracks 1, 3, & 4 recorded February 26, 1965.
All selections recorded at RCA Studio B, Nashville for the MGM Motion Picture "Harum Scarum".
Tracks 10 & 11 were not included in the movie. They were added to the album as bonus songs.
The original album has not been issued on CD in this format.

FRANKIE AND JOHNNY (1966)

Original Version:

1. Frankie & Johnny
2. Come Along
3. Petunia The Gardener's Daughter
4. Chesay
5. What Every Woman Lives For
6. Look Out Broadway
7. Beginners Luck
8. Down By The Riverside/
When The Saints Go Marching In
9. Shout It Out
10. Hard Luck
11. Please Don't Stop Loving Me
12. Everybody Come Aboard

Recording Information:

Tracks 1, 3, 4, 6, 9, 11, & 12 recorded May 13, 1965.
Tracks 2, 5, 7, 8, & 10 recorded May 14, 1965.
All selections recorded at Radio Recorders, Hollywood for the United Artists Motion Picture "Frankie And Johnny".
The original album has not been issued on CD in this format.

PARADISE HAWAIIAN STYLE (1966)

Original Version:

1. Paradise Hawaiian Style
2. Queenie Wahine's Papaya
3. Scratch My Back
4. Drums of The Islands
5. Datin'
6. A Dog's Life
7. House Of Sand
8. Stop Where You Are
9. This Is My Heaven
10. Sand Castles

Recording Information:

Tracks 3, 4, & 5 recorded July 26, 1965.
Tracks 1, 2, 6, 7, 8, & 9 recorded July 27, 1965.
Track 10 recorded August 2, 1965.
Elvis' vocals on tracks 1 – 9 were overdubbed in early August, 1965.
All selections recorded at Radio Recorders, Hollywood for the Paramount Motion Picture "Paradise Hawaiian Style".
Track 10 was not included in the movie.
It was added to the album as a bonus song.
The original album has not been issued on CD in this format.

SPINOUT A.K.A. CALIFORNIA HOLIDAY (1966)

Original Version:

1. Stop Look And Listen
2. Adam And Evil
3. All That I Am
4. Never Say Yes
5. Am I Ready
6. Beach Shack
7. Spinout
8. Smorgasbord
9. I'll Be Back
10. Tomorrow Is A Long Time
11. Down In The Alley
12. I'll Remember You

The title of the movie was changed from "Spinout" to "California Holiday" for it's European release. The cover art pictured features a UK version of the album with the title changed to "California Holiday". There were no other changes made to the album's cover art.

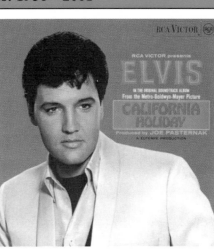

Recording Information:

Tracks 1, 5, 6, & 8 recorded February 16, 1966.
Tracks 2, 3, 4, 7, & 9 recorded February 19, 1966.
Tracks 1 – 9 recorded at Radio Recorders, Hollywood for the MGM Motion Picture "Spinout".
Tracks 10 & 11 recorded May 26, 1966.
Track 12 recorded June 10 – 12, 1966.
Tracks 10 – 12 recorded at RCA, Studio B, Nashville.
The original album has not been issued on CD in this format.

HOW GREAT THOU ART (1967)

1. How Great Thou Art
2. In The Garden
3. Somebody Bigger Than You And I
4. Farther Along
5. Stand By Me
6. Without Him
7. So High
8. Where Could I Go But To The Lord
9. By And By
10. If The Lord Wasn't Walking By My Side
11. Run On
12. Where No One Stands Alone
13. Crying In The Chapel

Recording Information:

Track 13, recorded October 31, 1960.
Tracks 1 & 11 recorded May 25, 1966.
Tracks 5 & 12 recorded May 26, 1966.
Tracks 2, 3, 4, 6, 7, & 9 recorded May 27, 1966.
Tracks 8 & 10 recorded May 28, 1966.
All selections recorded at RCA Studio B, Nashville.

DOUBLE TROUBLE (1967)

Original version:

1. Double Trouble
2. Baby If You'll Give Me All Of Your Love
3. Could I Fall In Love
4. Long Legged Girl
5. City By Night
6. Old Macdonald
7. I Love Only One Girl
8. There's So Much World To See
9. It Won't Be Long
10. Never Ending
11. Blue River
12. What Now, What Next, Where To

Recording Information:

Track 10 recorded May 26, 1963.
Track 12 recorded May 27 1963.
Track 11 recorded May 28, 1963.
Tracks 10 – 12 recorded at RCA Studio B, Nashville.
Tracks 1, 3, 4, & 8 recorded June 28, 1966.
Tracks 2, 5, 6, 7, & 9 recorded June 29, 1966.
Tracks 1 – 9 recorded at MGM Studios, Hollywood for the MGM Motion Picture "Double Trouble".
Track 9 was not included in the movie. It was added to the album as a bonus song.
The original album has not been issued on CD in this format.

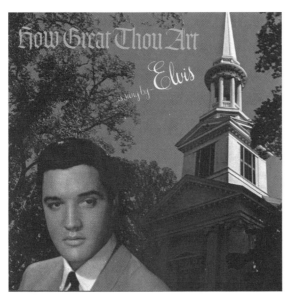

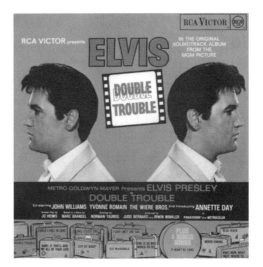

CLAMBAKE (1967)

Original Version:

1. Guitar Man
2. Clambake
3. Who Needs Money
4. A House That Has Everything
5. Confidence
6. Hey, Hey, Hey
7. You Don't Know Me
8. The Girl I Never Loved
9. How Can You Lose What You Never Had
10. Big Boss Man
11. Singing Tree
12. Just Call Me Lonesome

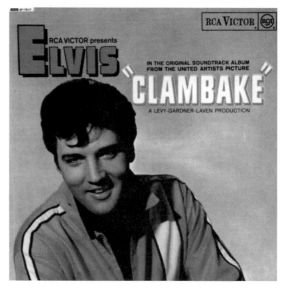

Recording Information:

Tracks 3, 4, 8, & 9 recorded February 21, 1967.
Tracks 5, 6, & 2 recorded February 22, 1967.
Tracks 2 – 6, 8, & 9 recorded at RCA Studio B, Nashville for the United Artists Motion Picture "Clambake".
Tracks 1 & 10 recorded September 10, 1967.
Tracks 7, 11, & 12 recorded September 11, 1967.
Tracks 1, 7, 10, 11, & 12 recorded at RCA Studio B, Nashville
A movie version of "You Don't Know Me" was recorded at the soundtrack session on February 21, 1967, but this was not included on the soundtrack album. RCA used Elvis' re-recording from the September Nashville sessions.
The original album has not been issued on CD in this format.

ELVIS' GOLD RECORDS VOLUME 4 (1968)

Original Version:

1. Love Letters
2. Witchcraft
3. It Hurts Me
4. What'd I Say
5. Please Don't Drag That String Around
6. Indescribably Blue
7. You're The Devil In Disguise
8. Lonely Man
9. A Mess Of Blues
10. Ask Me
11. Ain't That Loving You Baby
12. Just Tell Her Jim Said Hello

CD Re-issue Version:

1. Return To Sender
2. Rock A Hula Baby
3. Love Letters
4. Bossa Nova Baby
5. Witchcraft
6. Kissin' Cousins
7. It Hurts Me
8. Viva Las Vegas
9. What'd I Say
10. Please Don't Drag That String Around
11. Indescribably Blue
12. You're The Devil In Disguise
13. Lonely Man
14. A Mess Of Blues
15. Ask Me
16. Ain't That Loving You Baby
17. Just Tell Her Jim Said Hello
18. Crying In The Chapel

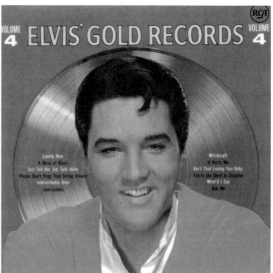

Recording Information:

Track 11 recorded June 10, 1958.
Track 9 recorded March 21, 1960.
Track 12 recorded March 19, 1962.
Tracks 5 & 7 recorded May 26, 1963.
Track 2 recorded May 27, 1963.
Tracks 3 & 10 recorded January 12, 1964.
Track 1 recorded May 26, 1966.
Track 6 recorded June 10 – 12, 1966.
All of the above selections recorded at RCA Studio B, Nashville.
Track 8 recorded November 7, 1960 at Radio Recorders, Hollywood
for the 20th Century Fox Motion Picture "Wild In The Country".
Track 4 recorded August 30, 1963 at Radio Recorders, Hollywood
for the MGM Motion Picture "Viva Las Vegas".
The CD re-issue version featured 6 additional previously released masters
and new back cover art (above right)
The original version has also been issued on CD.

SPEEDWAY (1968)

Original Version:

1. Speedway
2. There Ain't Nothing Like A Song
3. Your Time Hasn't Come Yet Baby
4. Who Are You (Who Am I)
5. He's Your Uncle Not Your Dad
6. Let Yourself Go
7. Your Groovy Self
8. Five Sleepy Heads
9. Western Union
10. Mine
11. Going Home
12. Suppose

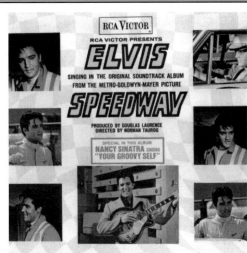

Recording Information:

Tracks 1, 2, 3, 4, 8, & 12 recorded June 20, 1967.
Tracks 5, & 6 recorded June 21, 1967.
Track 7 recorded June 26, 1967.
"There Ain't Nothing Like A Song" was recorded as a duet with   Nancy Sinatra.
Nancy Sinatra also performed "Your Groovy Self". Elvis was not featured on this track
Tracks 1 – 8 and track 12 recorded at MGM Studios, Hollywood for the MGM Motion Picture "Speedway".
Track 12 was not included in the movie. It was added to the album as bonus song.
Track 9 recorded May 27, 1963.
Track 10 recorded September 11, 1967.
Track 11 recorded January 16, 1968.
Tracks 9, 10, & 11 recorded at RCA Studio B, Nashville. Track 11 recorded for the MGM Motion Picture "Stay Away Joe".
The original album has not been issued on CD in this format.

ELVIS – THE 1968 NBC TV SPECIAL (1968)

Original Version:

1. Trouble/Guitar Man
2. Lawdy Miss Clawdy/Baby What You Want Me To Do/Dialogue
3. Medley: Heartbreak Hotel/Hound Dog/All Shook Up/
Can't Help Falling In Love/Jailhouse Rock/Dialogue/Love Me Tender
4. Dialogue/Where Could I Go But To The Lord/Up Above My Head/
Saved
5. Dialogue/Blue Christmas/Dialogue/One Night
6. Memories
7. Medley: Nothingville/Dialogue/Big Boss Man/Guitar Man/
Little Egypt/Trouble/Guitar Man
8. If I Can Dream

CD Version:

1. Trouble/Guitar Man
2. Lawdy Miss Clawdy/Baby What You Want Me To Do/Dialogue
3. Medley: Heartbreak Hotel/Hound Dog/All Shook Up/Can't Help Falling In Love/Jailhouse Rock/Don't Be Cruel*/Blue Suede Shoes*/Dialogue/Love Me Tender
4. Dialogue/Where Could I Go But To The Lord/Up Above My Head/Saved
5. Baby What You Want Me To Do*/That's All Right*/Dialogue/Blue Christmas/Dialogue/One Night/Tiger Man*/Trying To Get To You*
6. Memories
7. Medley: Nothingville/Dialogue/Big Boss Man/let Yourself Go*/It Hurts Me*/Guitar Man/Little Egypt/Trouble/Guitar Man
8. If I Can Dream

Recording Information:

Tracks 1, 4, 6, 7, & 8 recorded June 20 – 23, 1968 at Western Recorders, Los Angeles.
Tracks 2, 3, & 5 recorded June 27 – 29, 1968 at NBC Studios, Burbank, California.
All tracks recorded for the 1968 NBC TV Special "Elvis".
* By the time this album was issued on CD 8 additional performances from the Special had been issued by RCA on other albums, and these were added to the CD version.
A CD version with the original track listing has not been issued in the US or Europe, but some imported versions of the CD, including the Japanese version pictured below right, feature the original track listing.

FROM ELVIS IN MEMPHIS (1969)

Original Version:

1. Wearin' That Loved On Look
2. Only The Strong Survive
3. I'll Hold You In My Heart
4. Long Black Limousine
5. It Keeps Right On A Hurtin'
6. I'm Movin' On
7. Power Of My Love
8. Gentle On My Mind
9. After Loving You
10. True Love Travels On A Gravel Road
11. Any Day Now
12. In The Ghetto

CD Re-issue Extra Tracks:

13. The Fair Is Moving On
14. Suspicious Minds
15. You'll Think Of Me
16. Don't Cry Daddy
17. Kentucky Rain
18. Mama Liked The Roses

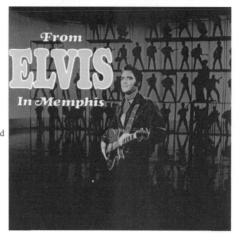

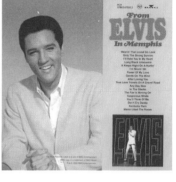

Recording Information:

Tracks 1, & 4 recorded January 13, 1969.
Tracks 6, & 8 recorded January 14, 1969.
Track 12 recorded January 20, 1969.
Track 3 recorded January 22, 1969.
Track 10 recorded February 17, 1969.
Tracks 7, & 9 recorded February 18, 1969.
Track 2 recorded February 19, 1969.
Tracks 5, & 11 recorded February 20, 1969.
All selections recorded at American Sound Studios, Memphis.
The CD re-issue version featured 6 additional previously released masters.
The original version has also been issued on CD.

**Above right: the original back cover
art work.**

**Right: the CD re-issue version featured new
back cover artwork, and the original
back cover artwork was also
included on the reverse of the CD booklet.**

FROM MEMPHIS TO VEGAS FROM VEGAS TO MEMPHIS (1969/1970)

Disc One:

"Elvis In Person"

1. Blue Suede Shoes
2. Johnny B. Goode
3. All Shook up
4. Are You Lonesome Tonight?
5. Hound Dog
6. I Can't Stop Loving You
7. My Babe
8. Medley: Mystery Train/
Tiger Man
9. Words
10. In The Ghetto
11. Suspicious Minds
12. Can't Help Falling In Love

Disc Two:

"Elvis Back In Memphis"

1. Inherit The Wind
2. This Is The Story
3. Stranger In My Own Home Town
4. A Little Bit Of Green
5. And The Grass Won't Pay No Mind
6. Do You Know Who I Am?
7. From A Jack To A King
8. The Fair Is Moving On
9. You'll Think Of Me
10. Without Love (There Is Nothing)

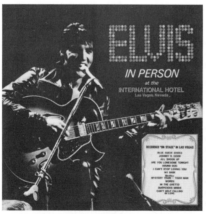

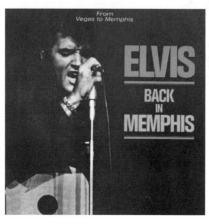

Recording Information – Elvis In Person:

Tracks 2, 3, 4, 7, & 12 recorded August 24, 1969.
Tracks 6, 9, 10, & 11 recorded August 25, 1969.
Tracks 1, 5, & 8 recorded August 26, 1969.
All selections recorded at The International Hotel,
Las Vegas.

Recording Information – Elvis Back In Memphis:

Track 2 recorded January 13, 1969.
Tracks 4, & 9 recorded January 14, 1969.
Track 1 recorded January 15, 1969.
Track 7 recorded January 21, 1969.
Track 10, recorded January 22, 1969.
Tracks 3 & 5 recorded February 17, 1969.
Track 6 recorded February 18, 1969.
Track 8 recorded February 21, 1969.
All selections recorded at American Sound Studios,
Memphis.

Collectors Notes:

These performances were originally issued as a two
record set in 1969.
They were then re-issued as single albums in 1970.
Both albums have only been issued on CD individually.

ELVIS – ON STAGE – FEBRUARY, 1970 (1970)

Original Version:

1. See See Rider
2. Release Me
3. Sweet Caroline
4. Runaway
5. The Wonder Of You
6. Polk Salad Annie
7. Yesterday*
8. Proud Mary
9. Walk A Mile In My Shoes
10. Let It Be Me

CD Re-issue Version:

1. See See Rider
2. Release Me
3. Sweet Caroline
4. Runaway
5. The Wonder Of You
6. Polk Salad Annie
7. Yesterday/Hey Jude
8. Proud Mary
9. Walk A Mile In My Shoes
10. In The Ghetto
11. Don't Cry Daddy
12. Kentucky Rain
13. I Can't Stop Loving You
14. Suspicious Minds
15. Long Tall Sally
16. Let It Be Me

Recording Information:

All tracks recorded at the International Hotel, Las Vegas, Nevada, August 1969 – February 1970.

Original Version:
Tracks 4 & 7 recorded August 25, 1969.
Tracks 3 & 8 recorded February, 16, 1970.
Track 10 recorded February 17, 1970.
Tracks 1, 2, 5, & 6 recorded February 18, 1970.
Track 9 recorded February 19, 1970.
Re-issue Version:
Tracks 10, 14, & 15 recorded February 1970.
Tracks 11, 12, & 16 recorded February 17, 1970.
Track 13 recorded February 19, 1970.

* "Yesterday" was originally performed as a part of a medley with "Hey Jude". The original album omitted the "Hey Jude" ending, but this has now been restored on the CD re-issue version.

Collectors Notes:

The original version was also issued on CD. Whilst the new CD version features extra tracks some of the dialogue from the original album is not included. There are also new dialogue fills on the CD re-issue version which were not included on the original release.

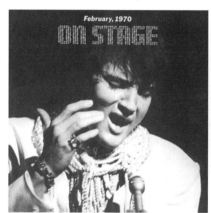

Left: the original front and back covers.
Above: new back cover art from the CD re-issue version

ELVIS – THAT'S THE WAY IT IS (1970)

Original Version:

1. I Just Can't Help Believin'
2. Twenty Days And Twenty Nights
3. How The Web Was Woven
4. Patch It Up
5. Mary In The Morning
6. You Don't Have To Say You Love Me
7. You've Lost That Lovin' Feeling
8. I've Lost You
9. Just Pretend
10. Stranger In The Crowd
11. The Next Step Is Love
12. Bridge Over Troubled Water*

Recording Information:

Track 2 recorded June 4, 1970.
Tracks 3, 5, 10, & 12 recorded June 5, 1970.
Tracks 6 & 9 recorded June 6, 1970.
Track 11 recorded June 11, 1970.
Tracks 2, 3, 5, 6, 9, 10, 11, & 12 recorded at RCA Studio B Nashville.
Tracks 1 & 8 recorded August 11, 1970.
Track 4 recorded August 12, 1970.
Track 7 recorded August 14, 1970
Tracks 1, 4, 7, & 8 recorded live at the International Hotel, Las Vegas.

The original version has been issued on CD with the original artwork (pictured)

However, the original movie has now been re-edited and re-released as "Elvis – That's The Way It Is – Special Edition", and a new three CD set has now been issued.
(See next page)

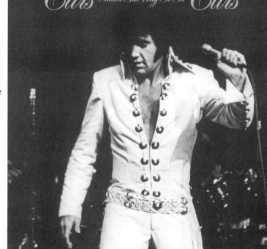

Although regarded as the soundtrack album to the M.G.M. documentary "Elvis – That's The Way It Is", only two of the tracks included here: "I Just Can't Help Believin'" & "Patch It Up" were the movie soundtrack versions.
* The studio master of Bridge Over Troubled Water" had audience applause added at the end of the song.

ELVIS – THAT'S THE WAY IT IS – SPECIAL EDITION (CD RE-ISSUE 2000)

Disc One – Special Edition

1. I Just Can't Help Believin'
2. Twenty Days And Twenty Nights
3. How The Web Was Woven
4. Patch It Up
5. Mary In The Morning
6. You Don't Have To Say You Love Me
7. You've Lost That Lovin' Feeling
8. I've Lost You
9. Just Pretend
10. Stranger In The Crowd
11. The Next Step Is Love
12. Bridge Over Troubled Water
13. Love Letters
14. When I'm Over You
15. Something
16. I'll Never Know
17. Sylvia
18. Cindy Cindy
19. Rags To Riches

Disc Two – The Concert

1. That's All Right
2. Mystery Train/Tiger Man
3. Hound Dog
4. Love Me Tender
5. Just Pretend
6. Walk A Mile in My Shoes
7. There Goes My Everything
8. Words
9. Sweet Caroline
10. You've Lost That Lovin' Feeling
11. Polk Salad Annie
12. Heartbreak Hotel
13. One Night
14. Blue Suede Shoes
15. All Shook Up
16. Little Sister/Get Back
17. I was The One
18. Love Me
19. Are You Lonesome Tonight?
20. Bridge Over Troubled Water
21. Suspicious Minds
22. Can't Help Falling In Love

Disc Three – The Rehearsal

1. I Got A Woman
2. I Can't Stop Loving You
3. Twenty Days And Twenty Nights
4. The Next Step Is Love
5. You Don't Have To Say You Love Me
6. Stranger In The Crowd
7. Make The World Go Away
8. Don't Cry Daddy
9. In The Ghetto
10. Peter Gunn Theme (Instrumental)
11. That's All Right
12. Cottonfields
13. Yesterday
14. I Can't Stop Loving You
15. Such A Night
16. It's Now Or Never
17. A Fool Such As I
18. Little Sister/Get Back
19. I Washed My Hands In Muddy Water
20. Johnny B. Goode
21. Mary In The Morning
22. The Wonder Of You
23. Santa Claus Is Back In Town
24. Farther Along
25. Oh Happy Day

Recording Information:

Disc One : Tracks 1 – 12 see previous page. Tracks 13 – 19 are previously released masters.
Disc Two: Recorded live at the International hotel, Las Vegas, Nevada, August 12, 1970, Midnight Show.
Disc Three: Tracks 2, 4, & 5 recorded August 10, 1970. Track 1 recorded August 11, 1970. Track 3 recorded August 12, 1970.
Tracks 6, 7, 8, & 9 recorded August 13, 1970. Tracks 1 – 9 recorded live at the International Hotel, Las Vegas.
Tracks 7 – 14 recorded July 15, 1970. Tracks 15 – 18 recorded July 29, 1970. Tracks 7 – 18 recorded during rehearsals at MGM Stage 1, Culver City, California.
Tracks 19 – 22 recorded July 24, 1970 during rehearsals at RCA Studios, Hollywood.
Tracks 23 & 24 recorded August 4, 1970 during rehearsals at the Convention Centre of the International Hotel, Las Vegas.
Track 25 recorded August 7, 1970 during stage rehearsals at the International Hotel, Las Vegas.

Above: left to right: discs one, two, and three.
Left: the Special Edition boxed set.
Below: the set also included a colour booklet with photographs and recording information.

I'M 10.000 YEARS OLD – ELVIS COUNTRY (1971)

Original Version:

1. Snowbird
2. Tomorrow Never Comes
3. Little Cabin On The Hill
4. Whole Lotta Shakin' Goin' On
5. Funny How Time Slips Away
6. I Really Don't Want To Know
7. There Goes My Everything
8. It's Your Baby You Rock It
9. The Fool
10. Faded Love
11. I Washed My Hands In Muddy Water
12. Make The World Go Away

CD Re-issue Extra Tracks:

13. It Ain't No Big Thing But It's Growing
14. A Hundred Years From Now
15. If I Were You
16. Got My Mojo Working
17. Where Did They Go Lord
18. I Was Born About 10,000 Years Ago*

Recording Information:

Tracks 3 & 9 recorded June 4, 1970.
Track 8 recorded June 5, 1970.
Tracks 2, 5, 6, 10, 11, & 12 recorded June 7, 1970.
Track 7 recorded June 8, 1970.
Tracks 1 & 4 recorded September 22, 1970.
Tracks 13 – 18 are previously released masters.
All selections recorded at RCA Studio B, Nashville.
* The song "I Was Born About 10,000 Years Ago" can be heard at the end of each track on the album. This does not feature on the extra tracks on the CD
CD re-issue. The song was first released in it's entirety on the "Elvis Now" album in 1972.
The original version of this album was also issued on CD.

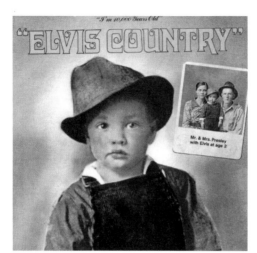

The back cover
artwork was changed on the CD
re-issue, but the original artwork
was included in the CD booklet.

LOVE LETTERS FROM ELVIS (1971)

1. Love Letters
2. When I'm Over You
3. If I Were You
4. Got My Mojo Working
5. Heart Of Rome
6. Only Believe
7. This Is Our Dance
8. Cindy Cindy
9. I'll Never Know
10. It Ain't No Big Thing But Its Growing
11. Life

Recording Information:

Track 8 recorded June 4, 1970.
Tracks 4 & 9 recorded June 5, 1970.
Tracks 5, 7, 10, & 11 recorded June 6, 1970.
Tracks 1 & 2 recorded June 7, 1970.
Tracks 3 & 6 recorded June 8, 1970.
All selections recorded at RCA Studio B, Nashville.

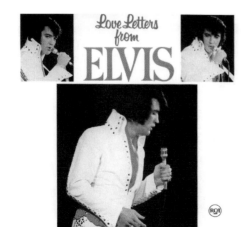

ELVIS SINGS THE WONDERFUL WORLD OF CHRISTMAS (1971)

1. O Come All Ye Faithful
2. The First Noel
3. On A Snowy Christmas Night
4. Winter Wonderland
5. The Wonderful World Of Christmas
6. It Won't Seem Like Christmas Without You
7. I'll Be Home on Christmas Day
8. If I Get Home On Christmas Day
9. Holly Leaves And Christmas Trees
10. Merry Christmas Baby
11. Silver Bells
12. If Every Day Was Like Christmas*
13. I'll Be Home On Christmas Day (country rhythm version)*

Recording Information:

Tracks 6, 8, 9, 10, & 11 recorded May, 15, 1971.
Tracks 1, 2, 3, 4, 5, & 7 recorded May 16, 1971.
All tracks recorded at RCA Studio B, Nashville.
* The CD issue added the 1966 single "If Every Day Was Like Christmas"
and an alternative version of "I'll Be Home On Christmas Day".

ELVIS NOW (1972)

1. Help Me Make It Through The Night
2. Miracle Of The Rosary
3. Hey Jude
4. Put Your Hand In The Hand
5. Until It's Time For You To Go
6. We Can Make The Morning
7. Early Morning Rain
8. Sylvia
9. Fools Rush In
10. I Was Born About 10,000 Years Ago

Recording Information:

Track 3 recorded January 21, 1969.
Track 10 recorded June 4, 1970.
Track 8 recorded June 8, 1970.
Track 7 recorded March 15, 1971.
Track 2 recorded May 15, 1971.
Tracks 1 & 5 recorded May 17, 1971.
Track 9 recorded May 18, 1971.
Track 6 recorded May 20, 1971.
Track 4 recorded June 8, 1971.

All selections recorded at RCA Studio B, Nashville, except: "Hey Jude" which was recorded at American Sound Studios, Memphis.

HE TOUCHED ME (1972)

1. He Touched Me
2. I've Got Confidence
3. Amazing Grace
4. Seeing Is Believing
5. He Is My Everything
6. Bosom Of Abraham
7. An Evening Prayer
8. Lead Me, Guide Me
9. There Is No God But God
10. A Thing Called Love
11. I, John
12. Reach Out To Jesus

Recording Information:

Track 3 recorded March 15, 1971.
Track 8 recorded May 17, 1971.
Tracks 1, 2, & 7 recorded May 18, 1971.
Tracks 4 & 10 recorded May 19, 1971.
Track 12 recorded June 8, 1971.
Tracks 5, 6, 9, & 11 recorded June 9, 1971.

All selections recorded at RCA Studio B, Nashville.

ELVIS AS RECORDED AT MADISON SQUARE GARDEN (1972)

1. Also Sprach Zarathustra
2. That's All Right
3. Proud Mary
4. Never Been To Spain
5. You Don't Have To Say You Love Me
6. You've Lost That Lovin' Feelin'
7. Polk Salad Annie
8. Love Me
9. All Shook Up
10. Heartbreak Hotel
11. Medley: Teddy Bear/Don't Be Cruel
12. Love Me Tender
13. The Impossible Dream
14. Introductions By Elvis
15. Hound Dog
16. Suspicious Minds
17. For The Good Times
18. An American Trilogy
19. Funny How Time Slips Away
20. I Can't Stop Loving You
21. Can't Help Falling In Love
22. End Theme

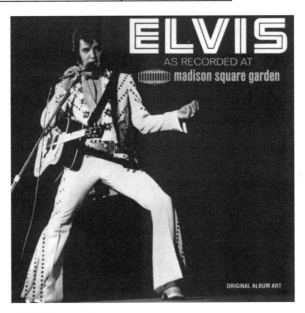

Recorded live at Madison Square Garden, New York, June 10, 1972, Evening Show.

ALOHA FROM HAWAII VIA SATELLITE (1973)

Original Version:

1. Introduction: Also Sprach Zarathustra
2. See See Rider
3. Burning Love
4. Something
5. You Gave Me A Mountain
6. Steamroller Blues
7. My Way
8. Love Me
9. Johnny B. Goode
10. It's Over
11. Blue Suede Shoes
12. I'm So Lonesome I Could Cry
13. I Can't Stop Loving You
14. Hound Dog
15. What Now My Love
16. Fever
17. Welcome To My World
18. Suspicious Minds
19. Introductions By Elvis
20. I'll Remember You
21. Medley: Long Tall Sally/
Whole Lotta Shakin' Goin' On
22. American Trilogy
23. A Big Hunk O' Love
24. Can't Help Falling In Love

CD Re-issue Extra Tracks

25. Blue Hawaii
26. KU-U-I-PO
27. No More
28. Hawaiian Wedding Song
29. Early Morning Rain.

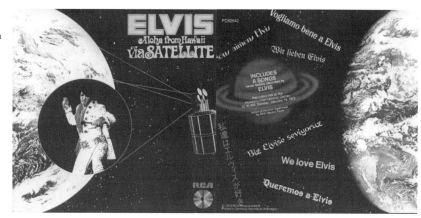

Above: original album artwork.
Below: the new CD re-issue version.

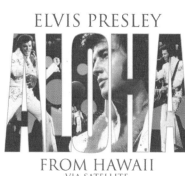

Recording Information:

Tracks 1 – 24 recorded at the Honolulu International Centre, Honolulu, Hawaii, January 14, 1973 for the live satellite broadcast "Elvis - Aloha From Hawaii Via Satellite".
Tracks 25 – 29 (CD re-issue version) were recorded after the rehearsal show at the International Centre, January 12, 1973.
The original version of this album was also issued on CD.

ELVIS – Including "Fool" (1973)

1. Fool
2. Where Do I Go From Here
3. Love Me, Love The Life I Lead
4. It's Still Here
5. It's Impossible
6. (That's What You Get) For Lovin' Me
7. Padre
8. I'll Take You Home Again Kathleen
9. I Will Be True
10. Don't Think Twice It's All Right

Recording Information:

Track 6 recorded March 15, 1971.
Track 7 recorded May 15, 1971.
Track 10 recorded May 16, 1971.
Tracks 4, 8, & 9 recorded May 19, 1971.
Track 3 recorded May 21, 1971.
Tracks 3, 4, 6, 7, 8, 9, & 10 recorded at RCA Studio B, Nashville.
Track 5 recorded live at the Hilton Hotel, Las Vegas, February 16, 1972.
Track 2 recorded March 27, 1972.
Track 1 recorded March 28, 1972.
Tracks 1 & 2 recorded at RCA Studio C, Hollywood.

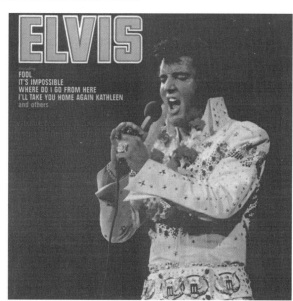

RAISED ON ROCK/FOR OL' TIMES SAKE (1973)

1. Raised On Rock
2. Are You Sincere
3. Find Out What's Happening
4. I Miss You
5. Girl Of Mine
6. For Ol' Times Sake
7. If You Don't Come Back
8. Just A Little Bit
9. Sweet Angeline
10. Three Corn Patches

Recording Information:

Tracks 7 & 10 recorded July 21, 1973.
Tracks 3 & 8 recorded July 22, 1973.
Tracks 1 & 6 recorded July 23, 1973.
Track 5 recorded July 24, 1973.
Track 9 (backing track only) recorded July 25, 1973.
Tracks 1, 3, 5, 6, 7, 8, 9 (track only), & 10 recorded at Stax Studios, Memphis.
Tracks 9 (vocal track) recorded September 22, 1973.
Tracks 2 & 4 recorded September 23, 1973.
Tracks 2, 4, & 9 (vocal) recorded at Elvis' Palm Springs Home.

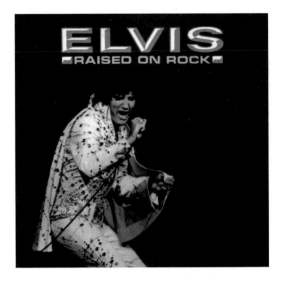

ELVIS A LEGENDARY PERFORMER VOLUME 1 (1974)

Original Version:

1. That's All Right
2. I Love You Because
3. Heartbreak Hotel
4. Don't Be Cruel
5. Interview Excerpt
6. Love Me
7. Trying To Get To You
8. Love Me Tender
9. Peace In The Valley
10. Elvis' Farewell to His Fans
11. A Fool Such As I
12. Tonight's All Right For Love
13. Are You Lonesome Tonight?
14. Can't Help Falling In Love

Recording Information:

Track two alternate take recorded July 6, 1954 at Sun Studios, Memphis. Previously unreleased.
Track 12 recorded April 27, 1960 at RCA studios, Hollywood.
Previously unreleased in the USA and English speaking countries.
Tracks 6, 7, & 13 recorded live during the 8 p.m. "Sit Down" show, June 27 1968 at Burbank Studios, California for the NBC TV Special, "Elvis". Previously unreleased.
Interview excerpts first released on the EP Album "Elvis Sails", recorded September 22, 1958.

All other performances are previously released masters.
The original version of this album has not been issued on CD.

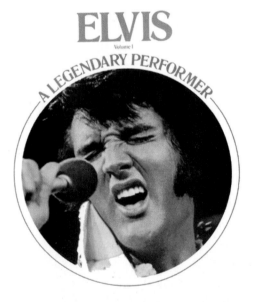

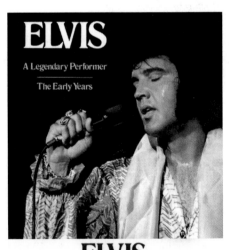

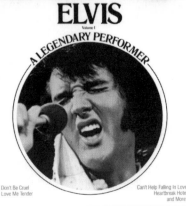

A 10 track CD version of this album was issued in Canada. (bottom right)
On this edition the live version of "Trying To Get To You" was replaced by the studio master, and the only previously unreleased performance included from the vinyl version was "Tonight's All Right For Love"

The original album also included an illustrated booklet. (top right)

GOOD TIMES (1974)

1. Take Good Care Of Her
2. Loving Arms
3. I Got A Feeling In My Body
4. If That Isn't Love
5. She Wears My Ring
6. I've Got A Thing About You Baby
7. My Boy
8. Spanish Eyes
9. Talk About The Good Times
10. Good Time Charlie's Got The Blues

Recording Information:

Track 1 recorded July 21, 1973.
Track 6 recorded July 22, 1973.
Track 3 recorded December 10, 1973.
Tracks 2, 7, & 10 recorded December 13, 1973.
Track 10 recorded December 14, 1973.
Tracks 4, 5, & 8 recorded December 16, 1973.
All selections recorded at Stax Studios, Memphis.

ELVIS RECORDED LIVE ON STAGE IN MEMPHIS (1974)

1. See See Rider
2. I Got A Woman
3. Love Me
4. Trying To Get To You
5. Medley: Long Tall Sally/
Whole Lotta Shakin' Goin' On/
Mama Don't Dance/Flip, Flop & Fly/
Jailhouse Rock/Hound Dog
6. Why Me Lord
7. How Great Thou Art
8. Medley: Blueberry Hill/
I Can't Stop Loving You
9. Help Me
10. An American Trilogy
11. Let Me Be There
12. My Baby Left Me
13. Lawdy Miss Clawdy
14. Can't Help Falling In Love
15. Closing Vamp

Recorded live at the Mid-South Coliseum, Memphis, March 20, 1974.

Below: original back cover art

Below: A 13th anniversary CD edition from Brazil featuring slightly different artwork.

PROMISED LAND (1975)

Original Version:

1. Promised Land
2. There's A Honky Tonk Angel
3. Help Me
4. Mr Songman
5. Love Song Of The Year
6. It's Midnight
7. Your Love's Been A Long Time Coming
8. If You Talk In Your Sleep
9. Thinking About You
10. You Asked Me To

CD Re-issue Extra Tracks:

11. Loving Arms
12. I Got A Feeling In My Body
13. If That Isn't Love
14. She Wears My Ring
15. My Boy
16. Spanish Eyes
17. Talk About The Good Times
18. Good Time Charlie's Got The Blues

Recording Information:

Track 6 recorded December 10, 1973.
Tracks 8 & 10 recorded December 11, 1973.
Tracks 3, 4, 5, & 9 recorded December 12, 1973.
Tracks 1, 2, & 7 recorded December 15, 1973.
All selections recorded at Stax Studios, Memphis.

The original version was also issued on CD.
All CD re-issue extra tracks were originally released on the "Good Times" album.

Above right : original back cover artwork.

Right: new back cover artwork as featured on the CD re-issue.

TODAY (1975)

1. T-R-O-U-B-L-E
2. And I Love You So
3. Susan When She Tried
4. Woman Without Love
5. Shake A Hand
6. Pieces Of My Life
7. Fairytale
8. I Can Help
9. Bringing It Back
10. Green Green Grass Of Home

Below: original back cover art.

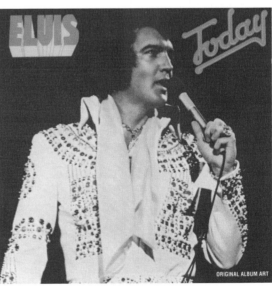

ORIGINAL ALBUM ART

Recording Information:

Track 7 recorded March 10, 1975.
Tracks 2, 3, 8, & 10 recorded March 11, 1975.
Tracks 1, 4 5, 6, & 9 recorded March 12, 1975.
All selections recorded at RCA Studio C, Hollywood.

ELVIS A LEGENDARY PERFORMER VOLUME 2 (1976)

Original Version:

1. Harbour Lights
2. Interview
3. I Want You, I Need You, I Love You
4. Blue Suede Shoes
5. Blue Christmas
6. Jailhouse Rock
7. It's Now Or Never
8. A Cane & High Starched Collar
9. Presentation Of Awards To Elvis
10. Blue Hawaii
11. Such A Night
12. Baby What You Want Me To Do
13. How Great Thou Art
14. If I Can Dream

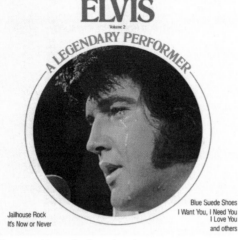

A 10 track CD version of this album was issued in Canada (left)

Although some of the previously unreleased recordings from the original album were included, four of the original tracks were omitted.

These were:

Interview, Wichita Falls, Texas, 1956
Blue Christmas (master)
A Cane & A High Starched Collar
Presentation Of Awards To Elvis

Recording Information:

Track 1 recorded July 5– 6, 1954, Sun Studios, Memphis. Previously unreleased.
Track 2 recorded Wichita Falls, Texas, early 1956. Previously unreleased.
Track 3 recorded at RCA Studio B, Nashville, April 14, 1956. Previously unreleased alternate take 14.
Track 8 recorded August 8, 1960 at Radio Recorders, Hollywood for the 20th Century Fox Motion Picture "Flaming Star". Previously unreleased.
Track 9 recorded Honolulu, Hawaii, March 25, 1961. Previously unreleased.
Track 12 recorded during the 6 p.m. "Sit Down" show, June 27, 1968 at Burbank Studios, California for the NBC TV Special "Elvis".
Track 4 recorded during the 8 p.m. "Sit Down" show, June 27, 1968 at Burbank Studios, California for the NBC TV Special "Elvis".
Tracks 4 & 12 are previously unreleased versions.
Track 10 recorded at the International Centre, Honolulu, Hawaii, January 12, 1973 for the satellite broadcast "Elvis Aloha From Hawaii Via Satellite".
Previously unreleased.
All other performances are previously released masters. The master take of "Such A Night" also included a false start.
The original album has not been issued on CD.

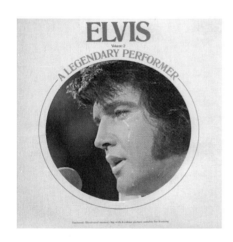

Left:

Original album art.

Right:

The original album also Included an illustrated booklet .

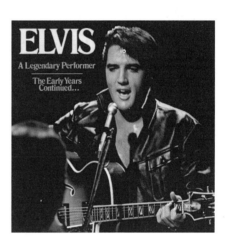

FROM ELVIS PRESLEY BOULEVARD, MEMPHIS, TENNESSEE (1976)

1. Hurt
2. Never Again
3. Blue Eyes Crying In The Rain
4. Danny Boy
5. The Last Farewell
6. For The Heart
7. Bitter They Are, Harder They Fall
8. Solitaire
9. Love Coming Down
10. I'll Never Fall In Love Again

Recording Information:

Tracks 5 & 7 recorded February 2, 1976.
Track 8 recorded February 3, 1976.
Track 10 recorded February 4, 1976.
Tracks 1, 4, & 6 recorded February 5, 1976.
Tracks 2 & 9 recorded February 6, 1976.
Track 3 recorded February 7. 1976.
All selections recorded in the "Jungle Room" of Elvis' Graceland mansion, Memphis.

WELCOME TO MY WORLD (1977)

1. Welcome To My World
2. Help Me Make It Through The Night
3. Release Me
4. I Really Don't Want To Know
5. For The Good Times
6. Make The World Go Away
7. Gentle On My Mind
8. I'm So Lonesome I Could Cry
8. Your Cheating Heart*
10. I Can't Stop Loving You

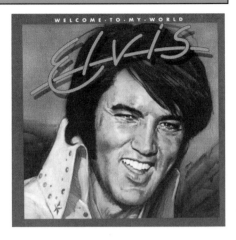

Recording Information:

All performances previously released except "I Can't Stop Loving You" recorded live at Madison Square Garden, New York, June 10, 1972, Afternoon Show.

* On the US CD issue of this album the master take of "You're Cheating Heart" was replaced by alternate take 9.

MOODY BLUE (1977)

Original Version:

1. Unchained Melody
2. If You Love Me Let Me Know
3. Little Darlin'
4. He'll Have To Go
5. Let Me Be There
6. Way Down
7. Pledging My Love
8. Moody Blue
9. She Thinks I Still Care
10. It's Easy For You

CD Re-issue Version:

1. Unchained Melody
2. If You Love Me Let Me Know
3. Little Darlin'
4. He'll Have To Go
5. Way Down
6. Pledging My Love
7. Moody Blue
8. She Thinks I Still Care
9. It's Easy For You
10. Hurt
11. Never Again
12. Blue Eyes Crying In The Rain
13. Danny Boy
14. The Last Farewell
15. For The Heart
16. Bitter They Are, Harder They Fall
17. Solitaire
18. Love Coming Down
19. I'll Never Fall In Love Again

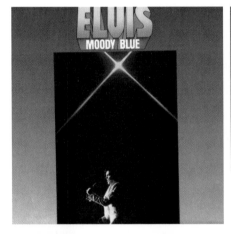

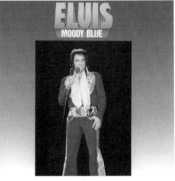

Above left : the original album art.

Above right: the new CD re-issue version.

Left: original back cover art.

Below: the CD re-issue featured new back cover art.

Recording Information:

Track 5 was previously released on the album "Elvis Recorded Live On Stage In Memphis" in 1974.
Track 9 recorded February 2, 1976.
Track 8 recorded February 4, 1976.
Tracks 6, 7, & 10 recorded October 29, 1976.
Track 4 recorded October 30, 1976.
Tracks 4, 6, 7, 8, 9, & 10 recorded in the "Jungle Room" of Elvis' Graceland Mansion, Memphis.
Tracks 1, & 3 recorded live in Ann Arbor, Michigan, April 24, 1977.
Track 2 recorded live in Saginaw, Michigan, April 25, 1977.
The CD re-issue version omitted the previously released "Let Me Be There", and added 10 tracks first released on the album "From Elvis Presley Boulevard, Memphis, Tennessee" in 1976.
Original copies of the album were pressed in blue vinyl.
The original version of the album was also released on CD.

ELVIS IN CONCERT (1977)

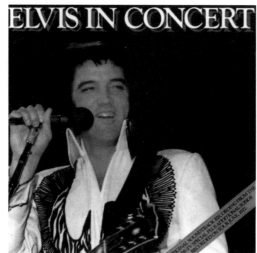

1. Elvis Fans' Comments/Opening Riff
2. Also Sprach Zarathustra
3. See See Rider
4. That's All Right
5. Are You Lonesome Tonight
6. Teddy Bear/Don't Be Cruel
7. Elvis Fans' Comments
8. You Gave Me A Mountain
9. Jailhouse Rock
10. Elvis Fans' Comments
11. How Great Thou Art
12. Elvis' Fans Comments
13. I Really Don't Want To Know
14. Elvis Introduces His Father
15. Hurt
16. Hound Dog
17. My Way
18. Can't Help Falling In Love
19. Closing Riff/Special Message
   From Elvis' Father
20. I Got A Woman/Amen
21. Elvis Talks
22. Love Me
23. If You Love Me Let Me Know
24. O Sole Mio/It's Now Or Never
25. Trying To Get To You
26. Hawaiian Wedding Song
27. Fairytale
28. Little Sister
29. Early Morning Rain
30. What'd I Say
31. Johnny B. Goode
32. And I Love You So

Recording Information:

Tracks 1 – 19 taken from the CBS TV Special "Elvis In Concert".
Tracks 1, 2, 3, 4, 5, 8, 9, 13, 14, 15, 16, 17, 20, 21, 22, 23, 24, 25, 26, 29, 30, & 31 recorded live in Rapid City, South Dakota June 21, 1977.
Tracks 6, 11, 18, 19, 27, 28, & 32 recorded live in Omaha, Nebraska, June 19, 1977.
Elvis Fans' Comments were recorded before various shows during Elvis' final tour in June 1977.

The album was first released as a two record set, and is now available as a single CD.

HE WALKS BESIDE ME (1978)

1. He Is My Everything
2. Miracle Of The Rosary
3. Where Did They Go Lord?
4. Somebody Bigger Than You And I
5. An Evening Prayer
6. The Impossible Dream
7. If I Can Dream
8. Padre
9. Known Only To Him
10. Who Am I?
11. How Great Thou Art

Recording Information:

Track 7 recorded June 23, 1968 at Western Recorders, Los Angeles for the NBC TV Special "Elvis". Previously unreleased alternate take.
Track 6 recorded live February 16, 1972 at the Hilton Hotel, Las Vegas. Previously unreleased alternate take.
All other performances are previously released masters.
This album was released on CD in Canada.

ELVIS SING S FOR CHILDREN AND GROWNUPS TOO (1978)

1. Teddy Bear
2. Wooden Heart
3. Five Sleepy Heads
4. Puppet On A String
5. Angel - 1st stereo issue
6. Old Macdonald
7. How Would You Like To Be
8. Old Shep
9. Big Boots
10. Have a Happy

Recording Information:

Track 9 recorded April 28, 1960 at RCA Studios, Hollywood for the Paramount Motion Picture "GI Blues". Previously unreleased alternate take.
All other performances are Previously released masters.
This album was released on CD in Canada.

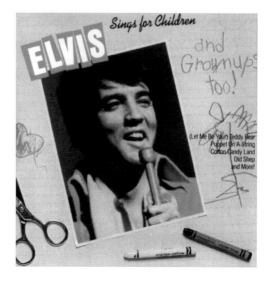

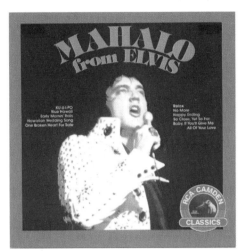

MAHALO FROM ELVIS (1978)

1. Blue Hawaii
2. Early Morning Rain
3. Hawaiian Wedding Song
4. KU-U-I-PO
5. No More
6. Relax
7. Baby If You'll Give Me All Of Your Love
8. One Broken Heart For Sale
9. So Close, Yet So Far
10. Happy Ending

Recording Information:

Tracks 1 – 5 recorded January 12, 1973 at the Honolulu International Centre, Honolulu, Hawaii for the satellite broadcast "Elvis – Aloha from Hawaii Via Satellite".
These tracks were recorded after the rehearsal performance for inclusion in the US television version of the show.
Whilst this album was released on the budget label Pickwick, this was the first official release of these performances.
All other performances are previously released masters.
This album was released on CD in Canada. (The CD version is pictured)

A CANADIAN TRIBUTE (1978)

Original Version:

1. Introduction By Red Robinson & Jailhouse Rock
2. Introduction & Teddy Bear
3. Loving You
4. Until It's Time For You To Go
5. Early Morning Rain
6. Vancouver Press Conference
7. I'm Movin' On
8. Snowbird
9. (That's What You Get) For Lovin' Me
10. Put Your Hand In The Hand
11. Little Darlin'
12. My Way

CD Version:

1. Intro by Red Robinson & Jailhouse Rock
2. Intro & Teddy Bear
3. Loving You
4. Until It's Time For You To Go
5. Early Morning Rain
6. Vancouver Press Conference
7. I'm Movin' On
8. Snowbird
9. (That's What You Get) For Lovin' Me
10. Put Your Hand In The Hand
11. Little Darlin'
12. Beyond The Reef
13. My Heart Cries For You
14. Tumblin' Tumbleweeds
15. My Way
16. Vancouver Press Conference
17. CBC Ottawa Interview With Mac Lipson
18. CBC Toronto Interview With Fans & Heartbreak Hotel (Live Excerpt From Maple Leaf Gardens, Toronto)

Collectors Notes:

The original 12 track album was pressed on gold vinyl and featured previously released Elvis performances written by Canadian songwriters.
By the time the album was re-issued on CD by RCA Canada in 1999 a number of additional performances by Canadian writers had been released on other albums, and these were added to the CD release, along with interview material from Elvis' Canadian visit in 1957.

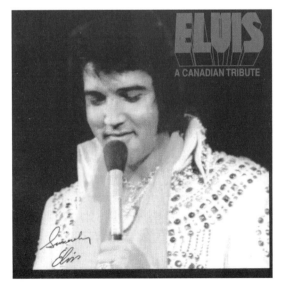

Above: the CD issue featured new back cover art.

ELVIS A LEGENDARY PERFORMER VOLUME 3 (1978)

1. Hound Dog
2. Excerpts From An Interview With Elvis And The Colonel
3. Danny
4. Fame And Fortune
5. Frankfort Special
6. Britches
7. Crying In The Chapel
8. Surrender
9. Guadalajara
10. It Hurts Me
11. Let Yourself Go
12. In The Ghetto
13. Let It Be Me

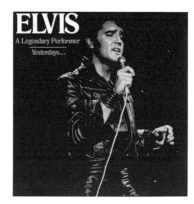

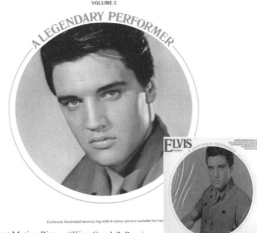

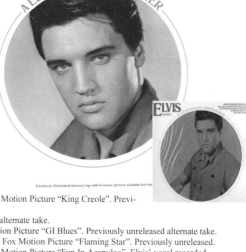

Right: the album also included an illustrated booklet.

Recording Information:

Track 2 recorded in Lakeland, Florida, August 1956.
Track 3 recorded January 28, 1958 at Radio Recorders, Hollywood for the Paramount Motion Picture "King Creole". Previously unreleased.
Track 4 recorded March 21, 1960 at RCA Studio B, Nashville. Previously unreleased alternate take.
Track 5 recorded May 6, 1960 at Radio Recorders, Hollywood for the Paramount Motion Picture "GI Blues". Previously unreleased alternate take.
Track 6 recorded August 8, 1969 at Radio Recorders, Hollywood for the 20th Century Fox Motion Picture "Flaming Star". Previously unreleased.
Track 9 recorded January 23, 1963 at Radio Recorders, Hollywood for the Paramount Motion Picture "Fun In Acapulco". Elvis' vocal recorded February 27, 1963. Previously unreleased alternate take.
Tracks 10 & 11 recorded June 20, 1968 at Western Recorders, Los Angeles for the NBC TV Special "Elvis". Previously unreleased.
Track 13 recorded live February 15, 1970 at the International Hotel, Las Vegas. Previously unreleased alternate take.
All other performances are previously released masters.
A picture disc version of this album was also released.
This album has not been released on CD.

OUR MEMORIES OF ELVIS VOLUMES 1 & 2 (1979)

Volume 1:

1. Are You Sincere
2. It's Midnight
3. My Boy
4. Girl Of Mine
5. Take Good Care Of Her
6. I'll Never Fall Again
7. Your Love's Been A Long Time Coming
8. Spanish Eyes
9. Never Again
10. She Thinks I Still Care
11. Solitaire

Volume 2:

1. I Got A Feelin' In My Body
2. Green Green Grass Of Home
3. For The Heart
4. She Wears My Ring
5. I Can Help
6. Way Down
7. Honky Tonk Angel
8. Find Out What's Happening
9. Thinking About You
10. Don't Think Twice It's All Right

Above: the Dutch Fan Club CD which included both albums.

Top Right: the original "Our Memories Of Elvis Volume 1" LP.

Bottom Right: the original "Our Memories Of Elvis Volume 2" LP.

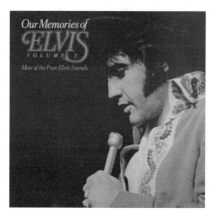

Recording Information:

Volume 1: Track 1 recorded September 23, 1973 at Elvis' Palm Springs Home, California. Previously unreleased alternate take.

Volume 2: An edited version of track 10 was first released on the album "Elvis" in 1973.
The unedited jam session was released on this album for the first time.
All other performances are previously released masters but were included on this collection without overdubs for the first time.
Both albums were issued on a single CD by the Dutch Elvis Fan Club "It's Elvis Time".
They were originally issued as two single albums.

ELVIS ARON PRESLEY (1980)

CD Disc One/Record One:
An Early Live Performance:
The Venus Room Of The New Frontier Hotel, Las Vegas, Nevada, May 6, 1956:
1. Heartbreak Hotel
2. Long Tall Sally
3. Blue Suede Shoes
4. Money Honey
All tracks previously unreleased.
An Elvis Monologue:
5. Monologue (Elvis talks to Lloyd Shearer, 1962)
Previously unreleased

Record Two:
An Early Benefit Performance:
USS Arizona Memorial Benefit Concert, Honolulu, Hawaii, March 25, 1961:
6. Introduction
7. Heartbreak Hotel
8. All Shook Up
9. A Fool Such As I
10. I Got A Woman
11. Love Me
12. Introductions
13. Such A Night
14. Reconsider Baby
15. I Need Your Love Tonight
16. That's All Right
17. Don't Be Cruel
18. One Night
19. Are You Lonesome Tonight
20. It's Now Or Never
21. Swing Down Sweet Chariot
22. Hound Dog
All tracks previously unreleased.

CD Disc Two/Record Three:
Collectors Gold From The Movie Years:
1. They Remind Me Too Much Of You (Recorded September 22, 1962)
2. Tonight's All Right For Love (Recorded May 6, 1960)
3. Follow That Dream (Recorded July 2, 1961)
4. Wild In The Country (Recorded November 7, 1960)
5. Datin' (Recorded July 26, 1965)
6. Shoppin' Around (Recorded April 27, 1960)
7. Can't Help Falling In Love (Recorded March 23, 1961)
8. A Dog's Life (Recorded July 27, 1965)
9. I'm Falling In Love Tonight (Recorded September 22, 1962)
10. Thanks To The Rolling Sea (Recorded March 26, 1962)

Tracks 1, 2, 4, 5, 7, 8, 9, & 10 recorded at Radio Recorders, Hollywood.
Track 3 recorded at RCA Studio B, Nashville.
Track 6 Recorded at RCA Studios, Hollywood.
All tracks previously unreleased.

Record Four:
The TV Specials:
11. Jailhouse Rock
12. Suspicious Minds
13. Lawdy Miss Clawdy/Baby What You Want Me To Do
14. Blue Christmas
15. You Gave Me A Mountain
16. Welcome To My World
17. Trying To Get To You
18. I'll Remember You
19. My Way

Tracks 11, 13, & 14 from the 1968 NBC TV Special "Elvis".
Tracks 12, 15, 16, & 18 from the 1973 satellite broadcast "Elvis – Aloha From Hawaii Via Satellite".
Track 19 From the 1977 CBS TV Special, "Elvis In Concert".
Track 17 was recorded for "Elvis In Concert" but not included in the TV Special.
All tracks are previously released masters

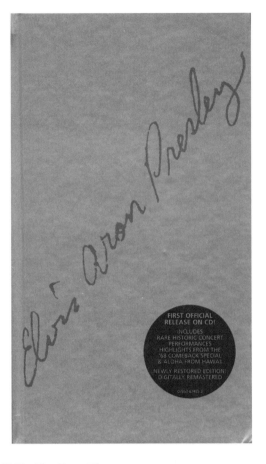

CD Disc Three/Record Five:
The Las Vegas Years:
1. Polk Salad Annie (Recorded August 13, 1970, Midnight Show)
2. You've Lost That Lovin' Feelin' (Recorded August 7, 1970)
3. Sweet Caroline (Recorded August 6, 1970)
4. Kentucky Rain (Recorded February 18, 1970)
5. Are You Lonesome Tonight – "Laughing Version" (Recorded August 21, 1969)
6. My Babe (Recorded August 26, 1969)
7. In The Ghetto (Recorded August 26, 1969)
8. An American Trilogy (Recorded February, 1972)
9. Little Sister/Get Back (Recorded August 13, 1970, Midnight Show)
10. Yesterday (Recorded August 24, 1969)

Tracks 1 – 7, 9 & 10 recorded live at the International Hotel, Las Vegas.
Track 8 recorded live at the Hilton Hotel, Las Vegas.
Tracks 2 & 3 were recorded during stage rehearsals at the International Hotel.
All tracks previously unreleased.

Record Six:
The Lost Singles:
11. I'm Leavin' (Recorded May 20, 1971)
12. The First Time Ever I Saw Your Face (Recorded March 15, 1971)
13. Hi Heel Sneakers (Recorded September 11, 1967)
14. Softly As I Leave You (Recorded December 13, 1975)
15. Unchained Melody (Recorded June 21, 1977)
16. Fool (Recorded March 28, 1972)
17. Rags To Riches (Recorded September 22, 1970)
18. It's Only Love (Recorded May 20, 1971)
19. America The Beautiful (Recorded December 13, 1975)

Tracks 11, 12, 13, 17, & 18 recorded at RCA Studio B, Nashville.
Tracks 14 & 19 live recorded at the Hilton Hotel, Las Vegas.
Track 16 recorded at RCA Studio C, Hollywood.
Track 15 recorded on tour in Rapid City, South Dakota.
All tracks are previously released masters.

ELVIS ARON PRESLEY (1980) - Continued

Record Seven:
Elvis At The Piano:
20. It's Still Here (Recorded May 19, 1971)
21. I'll Take You Home Again Kathleen (Recorded May 19, 1971)
22. Beyond The Reef (Recorded May 27, 1966)
23. I Will Be True (Recorded May 19, 1971)

All selections recorded at RCA Studio B, Nashville
Tracks 20, 21, & 23 released without overdubs for the first time.
Track 22 is previously unreleased.

CD Disc Four:
The Concert Years Part One:
Elvis In Concert, 1975:
1. Also Sprach Zarathustra
2. See See Rider
3. Medley: I Got A Woman/Amen
4. Love Me
5. If You Love Me (Let Me Know)
6. Love Me Tender
7. All Shook Up
8. Medley: Teddy Bear/Don't Be Cruel

Record Eight:
The Concert Years Concluded:
Elvis In Concert, 1975:
9. Hound Dog
10. The Wonder Of You
11. Burning Love
12. Introductions
13. Johnny B. Goode
14. Introductions/Long Live Rock 'n' Roll
15. T.R.O.U.B.L.E.
16. Why Me Lord?
17. How Great Thou Art
18. Let Me Be There
19. An American Trilogy
20. Funny How Time Slips Away
22. Medley: Mystery Train/Tiger Man
23. Can't Help Falling In Love
24. Closing Vamp

Tracks 2 & 3 recorded May 6, 1975 at the Murphy Athletic Centre, Murfreesboro, Tennessee.
Track 15 recorded June 5, 1975 at the Hofheinz Pavilion, Houston, Texas.
Tracks 4 – 14 & 17 – 24 recorded June 6, 1975 at the Memorial Auditorium, Dallas, Texas.
Track 16 recorded June 9, 1975 at the Mississippi Coliseum, Jackson, Mississippi.
Track 1 recorded June 10, 1975 at the Mid South Coliseum, Memphis, Tennessee.
All tracks previously unreleased.

This collection was originally released as an eight album box set with an illustrated booklet.
It has now been released as a four CD set in the long box format.

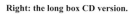

Above left: the cover of the booklet included with the original eight record set.

Above right: a page of photographs from the original booklet.

Right: the long box CD version.

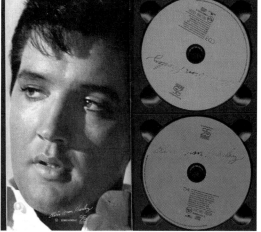

GUITAR MAN (1981)

1. Guitar Man
2. After Loving You
3. Too Much Monkey Business
4. Just Call Me Lonesome
5. Lovin' Arms
6. You Asked Me To
7. Clean Up Your Own Backyard
8. She Thinks I Still Care
9. Faded Love
10. I'm Movin On

Recording Information:

Tracks 3, 4, 6, 10 remade on October 14, 1980.
Tracks 8 & 9 remade on October 15, 1980.
Track 1 remade on October 16, 1980.
Tracks 2 & 7 remade on October 17, 1980.
Track 6 remade on November 11, 1980.
Re-recordings produced by Felton Jarvis at Young 'un Sound, Nashville.
This album featured previously released Elvis songs with new overdubs.
The master of "Guitar Man" is longer and features a few lines of "What'd I Say".
Alternate vocals were used on tracks 2, 4, 8, & 10.
This album was released on CD in Australia.

THIS IS ELVIS (1981)

1. (Marie's The Name) His Latest Flame
2. Moody Blue
3. That's All Right
4. Shake, Rattle & Roll/ Flip, Flop & Fly
5. Heartbreak Hotel
6. Hound Dog
7. Excerpt From The Hy Gardner Interview
8. My Baby Left Me
9. Merry Christmas Baby
10. Mean Woman Blues
11. Don't Be Cruel
12. (Let Me Be Your) Teddy Bear
13. Jailhouse Rock
14. Army Swearing In
15. GI Blues
16. Excerpt From The Departure
From Germany Press Conference

17. Excerpt From The Home
From Germany Press Conference
18. Too Much Monkey Business
19. Love Me Tender
20. I Got A Thing About You Baby
21. I Need Your Love Tonight
22. Blue Suede Shoes
23. Viva Las Vegas
24. Suspicious Minds/Excerpt From
Elvis' JC's Award Acceptance Speech
25. Promised Land
26. Excerpt From The Madison Square
Garden Press Conference
27. Always On My Mind
28. Are You Lonesome Tonight
29. My Way
30. An American Trilogy
31. Memories

Recording Information:

Track 4 recorded January 28, 1956 on The Dorsey Brothers Stage Show.
Track 5 recorded February 11, 1956 on The Dorsey Brothers Stage Show.
Track 6 recorded June 5, 1956 on The Milton Berle Show.
Track 7 recorded July 1, 1956.
Track 10 recorded January 14 – 18, 1957 at the Paramount Scoring Stage, Hollywood for the Paramount Motion Picture, "Loving You".
Track 11 recorded January 6, 1957 on The Ed Sullivan Show.
Track 14 recorded March 24, 1958.
Track 16 recorded September 1958.
Track 17 recorded March 8, 1960.
Track 22 recorded June 27, 1968 and June 29, 1968 at Burbank Studios, California for the NBC TV Special "Elvis".
Track 24 (JC's Speech) recorded January 9, 1971.
Track 26 recorded June 8, 1972.
Track 30 recorded April 9, 1972 during the Evening Show at the Coliseum, Hampton Roads, Virginia.
All other performances are previously released masters.
"Are You Lonesome Tonight" is the 1977 live version originally released on "Elvis In Concert" with additional dialogue included before the start of the song.
"Moody Blue", "Merry Christmas Baby" and "Always On My Mind" featured added strings.
"Too Much Monkey Business", "I Got A Thing About You Baby" and "Promised Land" were edited versions.
"Suspicious Minds" is actually an edited version from the 1973 album "Aloha From Hawaii," although the sleeve notes state that this is a previously unreleased version from 1970.
All tracks taken from the original soundtrack of the Warner Brothers Motion Picture "This Is Elvis", 1981.
Originally released as a double album.
This album has not been released officially on CD.

ELVIS GREATEST HITS VOLUME 1 (1981)

1. The Wonder Of You
2. A Big Hunk O' Love
3. There Goes My Everything
4. Suspicious Minds
5. What'd I Say
6. Don't Cry Daddy
7. Steamroller Blues
8. The Sound Of Your Cry
9. Burning Love
10. You'll Never Walk Alone

GREATEST HITS   VOLUME ONE

UK version: "The Sound Of Your Cry"

1. It's Only Love (extended version)
2. Suspicious Minds
3. Angel
4. What'd I Say
5. The Sound Of Your Cry
6. A Big Hunk O' Love
7. Are You Lonesome Tonight
8. Steamroller Blues
9. Don't Cry Daddy
10. Burning Love
11. You'll Never Walk Alone
12. Kentucky Rain.

Right:
"Greatest Hits Volume 1".

**The same artwork was used
for the UK album
"The Sound Of Your Cry".**

Below: "It's Only Love" 12 inch single.

Recording Information:

Track 5 recorded live August 23, 1969 at the International Hotel, Las Vegas. (This version was edited)
Track 6 recorded live February 17, 1970 at the International Hotel, Las Vegas.
Track 2 recorded live February 1972 at the Hilton Hotel, Las Vegas.
Track 7 recorded live January 12, 1973 at the Honolulu International Centre, Honolulu, Hawaii.
Tracks 2, 5, 6, & 7 are previously unreleased performances.
"The Sound Of Your Cry" is an unedited version of the previously released master.
"Suspicious "Minds" and "You'll Never Walk Alone" were released in stereo for the first time.
All other performances are previously released masters.
"Greatest Hits Volume 1" was released on CD in Australia.
In the UK this album was known as "The Sound Of Your Cry", and omitted the tracks "The Wonder Of You" and "There Goes My Everything".
The stereo version of "Angel" was added to the album along with the extended version of "It's Only Love" which was first released as a single in 1980.
The live "laughing version" of "Are You Lonesome Tonight" and a live version of "Kentucky Rain" which were first issued on the album "Elvis Aron Presley" in 1980 were also included.
"The Sound Of Your Cry" has not been issued on CD.

MEMORIES OF CHRISTMAS (1982)

1. O Come All Ye Faithful (alternate take)
2. Silver Bells
3. I'll Be home On Christmas Day (remake)
4. Blue Christmas
5. Santa Claus Is Back In Town
6. Merry Christmas Baby (complete studio performance)
7. If Every Day Was Like Christmas (alternate take)
8. Christmas Message From Elvis/Silent Night

UK version: "It Won't Seem Like Christmas Without You"

1. It Won't Seem Like Christmas Without You
2. On A Snowy Christmas Night
3. If Every Day Was Like Christmas (alternate take)
4. Where No One Stands Alone
5. I'll Be Home On Christmas Day (remake)
6. If We Never Meet Again
7. The Wonderful World Of Christmas
8. He Touched Me
9. Merry Christmas Baby (complete studio performance)
10. Reach Out To Jesus
11. If I Get Home On Christmas Day
12. His Hand In Mine
13. O Come All Ye Faithful (alternate take)
14. Holly Leaves And Christmas Trees
15. Christmas Message From Elvis/Silent Night

Recording information:

Track 7 recorded June 10 – 12, 1966.
Tracks 1 recorded May 16, 1971. Track 3 recorded June 10, 1971.
Tracks 1, 3, & 7 recorded at RCA Studio B, Nashville.
An edited version of "Merry Christmas Baby" was first released on the album "Elvis Sings The Wonderful World of Christmas" in 1971.
The complete studio performance is included on this album for the first time.
Tracks 1, 3, 6 & 7 are previously unreleased performances.
All other performances are previously released masters.
"Memories Of Christmas" was released on CD in the USA.

In the UK this album was known as "It Won't Seem Like Christmas Without You"
The four previously unreleased performances and the track "Christmas Message From Elvis/Silent Night" from the "Memories Of Christmas album" were included on this release, along with 10 previously released masters.
"It Won't Seem Like Christmas Without You" has not been issued on CD.

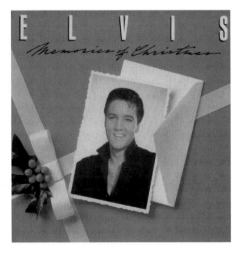

Right: the "Memories Of Christmas" album.

**The same artwork was used for the UK release
"It Wont Seem Like Christmas Without You".**

THE ELVIS MEDLEY (1982)

1. The Elvis Medley: Jailhouse Rock/Teddy Bear/Hound Dog/Don't Be Cruel/
Burning Love/Suspicious Minds
2. Jailhouse Rock
3. Teddy Beat
4. Hound Dog
5. Don't Be Cruel
6. Burning Love
7. Suspicious Minds
8. Always On My Mind
9. Heartbreak Hotel
10. Hard Headed Woman

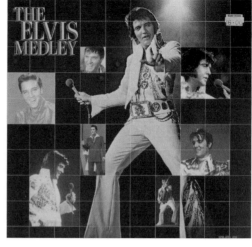

Recording Information:

"The Elvis Medley" was produced
by David Briggs.
All other performances are previously released masters.

Above right: "The Elvis Medley" album.
Above left: The Elvis Medley was also released as a picture disc single .

I WAS THE ONE (1983)

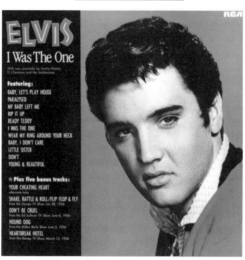

US Version:

1. My Baby Left Me
2. Baby I Don't Care
3. Little Sister
4. Don't
5. Wear My Ring Around Your Neck
6. Paralysed
7. Baby Let's Play House
8. I Was The One
9. Rip It Up
10. Young And Beautiful
11. Ready Teddy

UK Version:

1. My Baby Left Me
2. Baby Let's Play House
3. Shake, Rattle & Roll/Flip, Flop & Fly
4. Don't
5. Paralysed
6. Your Cheating Heart
7. Baby I Don't Care
8. Don't Be Cruel
9. Wear My Ring Around Your Neck
10. My Baby Left Me
11. Little Sister
12. Heartbreak Hotel
13. Ready Teddy
14. Young And Beautiful
15. Rip It Up
16. Hound Dog

Recording Information:

The 11 tracks on the original US album were given new overdubs produced by David Briggs, and Tony Brown from Elvis' 1970's TCB touring band.
Elvis' original guitarist Scotty Moore and drummer DJ Fontana replayed their original parts in an attempt to improve on the original '50's recording techniques. The Jordanaires also re-recorded their backing vocals.
When the album was issued in the UK it featured five additional tracks. Four of these tracks "Shake Rattle & Roll/Flip Flop & Fly", "Don't Be Cruel", "Heartbreak Hotel", and "Hound Dog" are live recordings from Elvis' '50's TV appearances which were first released on the 1981 album "This Is Elvis".
The version of "Your Cheating Heart" released on this album is alternate take 9 and was originally released in the UK on a vinyl re-issue of the EP "A Touch Of Gold Volume 2 " which was included in "The EP Collection Volume 2" in 1982.
The track was released for the first time in the US in error on a Readers Digest box set titled "Elvis Presley's Greatest Hits".
Neither the US or the UK version of this album has been issued on CD.

The UK version of this album (pictured above) had a different cover than the US version which featured a caricature of Elvis in '50's.

This was used on the back cover of the UK album (right)

ELVIS A LEGENDARY PERFORMER VOLUME FOUR (1983)

1. When It Rains It Really Pours
2. Interview
3. One Night
4. I'm Beginning To Forget You
5. Mona Lisa
6. Wooden Heart
7. Plantation Rock
8. The Lady Loves Me
9. Swing Down Sweet Chariot
10. That's All Right
11. Are You Lonesome Tonight
12. Reconsider Baby
13. I'll Remember You

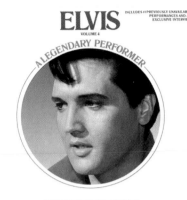

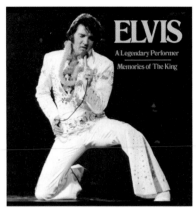

Above: the original album also included an illustrated booklet.

Recording Information:

Track 1 recorded August, 1955 at Sun Studios, Memphis. Previously unreleased version.
Track 2 recorded in Tampa, Florida, 1956. Previously unreleased.
Track 3 recorded January 14 – 18, 1957 at the Paramount Scoring Stage, Hollywood. Previously unreleased.
Tracks 4 & 5 are home recordings from 1959 made during Elvis' army service in Bad Nauheim, Germany. Previously unreleased.
Track 6 recorded April 28, 1960 at RCA Studios, Hollywood for the Paramount Motion Picture "GI Blues". Previously unreleased alternate take.
Track 7 recorded March 28, 1962 at Radio Recorders, Hollywood for the Paramount Motion Picture "Girls! Girls! Girls!" Previously unreleased.
Track 8 recorded July 11, 1963 at Radio Recorders, Hollywood for the MGM Motion Picture "Viva Las Vegas".
Previously unreleased duet with Ann Margaret.
Track 9 recorded August 23, 1968 at United Recorders, Hollywood for the MGM Motion Picture "The Trouble With Girls (And How To Get Into It)".
Previously unreleased version.
Track 10 recorded June 27, 1968 during the 8 p.m. "Sit Down" show at Burbank Studios, California for the NBC TV Special "Elvis".
Previously unreleased version.
Track 11 recorded live in August 1969 and first released on the box set "Elvis Aron Presley" in 1980. The famous laughing version.
Tracks 12 & 13 recorded June 10, 1972, during the Afternoon Show at Madison Square Garden, New York. Previously unreleased versions.
This album has not been released on CD.

ELVIS GOLD RECORDS VOLUME 5 (1984)

Original Version:

1. Suspicious Minds
2. Kentucky Rain
3. In The Ghetto
4. Clean Up Your Own Backyard
5. If I Can Dream
6. Burning Love
7. If You Talk in Your Sleep
8. For The Heart
9. Moody Blue
10. Way Down

CD Re-issue Version:

1. Suspicious Minds
2. Kentucky Rain
3. In The Ghetto
4. Clean Up Your Own Backyard
5. Burning Love
6. If You Talk in Your Sleep
7. For The Heart
8. Moody Blue
9. Way Down
10. Big Boss Man
11. Guitar Man
12. US Male
13. You Don't Have To Say You Love Me
14. Edge Of Reality
15. Memories
16. If I Can Dream

Recording Information:

Track 4 recorded August 23, 1968 at United Recorders, Hollywood for the MGM Motion Picture "The Trouble With Girls (And How To Get Into It)".
Track 5 recorded June 23, 1968 at Western Recorders, Los Angeles for the NBC TV Special "Elvis".
Track 3 recorded January 20, 1969. Track 1 recorded January 22, 1969. Track 2 recorded February 19, 1969.
Tracks 1, 2, & 3 recorded at American Sound Studios, Memphis.
Track 6 recorded March 28, 1972 at RCA Studio C, Hollywood.
Track 7 recorded December 11, 1973 at Stax Studios, Memphis.
Track 9 recorded February 4, 1976. Track 10 recorded October 29, 1976.
Tracks 9 & 10 recorded in the "Jungle Room" of Elvis' Graceland Mansion, Memphis.
The CD re-issue version featured an additional six previously released masters.
The original version has also been released on CD.

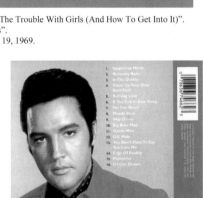

Right: the CD re-issue version featured new back cover art.

A GOLDEN CELEBRATION (1985)

Disc One:

The Sun Sessions – Out Takes – Memphis, Tennessee - 1954 and 1955:
1. Harbour Lights
2. That's All Right (alternate take)
3. Blue Moon Of Kentucky (alternate take)
4. I Don't Care If The Sun Don't Shine (alternate take)
5. I'm Left, You're Right, She's Gone (slow version)
6. I'll Never Let You Go (Little Darling) (alternate take)
7. When It Rains It Really Pours (alternate takes)

The Dorsey Brothers Stage Show, New York, New York, January 28, 1956:
8. Shake Rattle and Roll/Flip Flop and Fly
9. I Got A Woman

The Dorsey Brothers Stage Show, New York, New York, February 4, 1956:
10. Baby Lets Play House
11. Tutti Frutti

The Dorsey Brothers Stage Show, New York, New York, February 11, 1956:
12. Blue Suede Shoes
13. Heartbreak Hotel

The Dorsey Brothers Stage Show, New York, New York, February 18, 1956:
14. Tutti Frutti
15. I Was The One

The Dorsey Brothers Stage Show, New York, New York, March 17, 1956:
16. Blue Suede Shoes
17. Heartbreak Hotel

The Dorsey Brothers Stage Show, New York, New York, March 24, 1956:
18. Money Honey
19. Heartbreak Hotel

Disc Two:

The Milton Berle Show, San Diego, California. April 3, 1956:
1. Introductions
2. Heartbreak Hotel
3. Blue Suede Shoes
4. Dialogue
5. Blue Suede Shoes

The Milton Berle Show, Hollywood, California, June 5, 1956:
6. Hound Dog
7. Dialogue With Milton Berle
8. Dialogue
9. I Want You, I Need You, I Love You

The Steve Allen Show, New York, New York, July 1, 1956:
10. Dialogue With Steve Allen
11. I Want You, I Need You, I Love You
12. Dialogue With Steve Allen
13. Hound Dog

The Mississippi – Alabama Fair And Dairy Show, Tupelo Mississippi, September 24, 1956, Afternoon Performance:

14. Heartbreak Hotel
15. Long Tall Sally
16. Introductions And Presentations
17. I Was The One
18. I Want You, I Need You, I Love You
19. Elvis Talks
20. I Got A Woman
21. Don't Be Cruel
22. Ready Teddy
23. Love Me Tender
24. Hound Dog
25. Vernon And Gladys Presley
26. Nick Adams
27. A Fan
28. Elvis

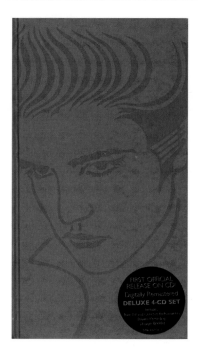

This collection was originally released as a six LP set in 1985 to Commemorate what would have been Elvis' 50th birthday.

It has now been re-issued as a four CD set with an illustrated booklet in the long box digi-pack format. The CD version and booklet are pictured.

A GOLDEN CELEBRATION (1985) - Continued

Disc Three:

The Mississippi – Alabama Fair And Dairy Show, Tupelo, Mississippi, September 24, 1956, Evening Performance:

1. Love Me Tender
2. I Was The One
3. I Got A Woman
4. Announcement
5. Don't Be Cruel
6. Blue Suede Shows
7. Announcement
8. Baby Let's Play House
9. Hound Dog
10. Announcement

The Ed Sullivan Show, California, And New York, September 9, 1956:
11. Don't Be Cruel
12. Elvis Talks
13. Love Me Tender
14. Ready Teddy
15. Hound Dog

The Ed Sullivan Show, California, And New York, October 28, 1956:
16. Don't Be Cruel
17. Ed Sullivan
18. Love Me Tender
19. Ed Sullivan Introduces Elvis
20. Love Me
21. Hound Dog
22. Elvis' Closing Remarks

The Ed Sullivan Show, New York, January 6, 1957:
23. Introduction
24. Hound Dog
25. Love Me Tender
26. Heartbreak Hotel
27. Don't Be Cruel
28. Too Much
29. Elvis Talks
30. When My Blue Moon Turns to Gold Again
31. Ed Sullivan Speaks
32. There'll Be Peace In The Valley (For Me)
34. Ed Sullivan Speaks

Disc Four:

Elvis At Home – Germany 1958 – 60:
1. Danny Boy
2. Soldier Boy
3. The Fool
4. Earth Angel
5. I Asked The Lord (He's Only A Prayer Away)

Collectors Treasures Discovered At Graceland – Date Unknown:
6. Excerpt From An Interview For TV Guide
7. My Heart Cries For You
8. Dark Moon
9. Write To Me From Naples
10. Suppose

Burbank, California, June 27, 1968:
11. Blue Suede Shoes
12. Tiger Man
13. That's All Right
14. Lawdy Miss Clawdy
15. Baby What You Want Me To Do
16. Love Me
17. Are You Lonesome Tonight
18. Baby What You Want Me To Do
19. Blue Christmas
20. One Night
21. Trying To Get To You

RECONSIDER BABY (1985)

Recording

1. Reconsider Baby
2. Tomorrow Night
3. So Glad Your Mine
4. One Night
5. When It Rains It Really Pours
6. My Baby Left Me
7. Ain't That loving You Baby
8. I Feel So Bad
9. Down In The Alley
10. High Heel Sneakers
11. Stranger In My Own Home Town
12. Merry Christmas Baby

Information:

Track 2 was overdubbed for it's first release on "Elvis For Everyone" in 1965.
The version included on this collection is the original Sun master without the overdubs.
Track 4 is the version first released on "A Legendary Performer Volume 4" known as "One Night Of Sin".
On this album some studio chat was also included before the start of the song.
Track 10 recorded June 10, 1958 at RCA Studio B, Nashville. Previously unreleased alternate take.
Track 11 was remixed by Chips Moman. This mix is shorter than the original but features a longer fade out.
Track 12 is an alternate edit of the master take.
All other performances are previously released masters.

ALWAYS ON MY MIND (1985)

1. Separate Ways
2. Don't Cry Daddy
3. My Boy
4. Solitaire
5. Bitter They Are, Harder They Fall
6. Hurt
7. Pieces Of My Life
8. I Miss You
9. It's Midnight
10. I've Lost You
11. You Gave Me A Mountain
12. Unchained Melody
13. Always On My Mind

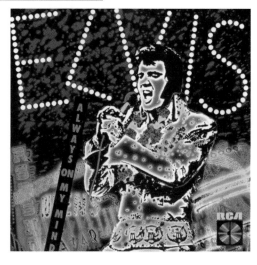

Recording Information:

"Always On My Mind" was re-mixed for this release.
"I've Lost You" is the live version first released on the album "Elvis – That's The Way It Is" in 1970.
"You Gave Me A Mountain" is the live version first released on the album "Aloha From Hawaii Via Satellite" in 1973.
"Unchained Melody" is the live version first released on the album "Moody Blue" in 1977.
All material previously released.

THE MEMPHIS RECORD (1987)

1. Stranger In My Own Home Town
2. Power Of My Love
3. Only The Strong Survive
4. Any Day Now
5. Suspicious Minds
6. Long Black Limousine
7. Wearin' That Loved On Look
8. I'll Hold You In My Heart
9. After Loving You
10. Rubberneckin'
11. I'm Movin' On
12. Gentle On My Mind
13. True Love Travels On A Gravel Road
14. It Keeps Right On A Hurtin'
15. You'll Think Of Me
16. Mama Liked The Roses
17. Don't Cry Daddy
18. In The Ghetto
19. The Fair Is Moving On
20. Inherit The Wind
21. Kentucky Rain
22. Without love
23. Who Am I

Recording Information:

Whilst all these performances are previously released masters,
all tracks were re-mixed for this compilation except "Rubberneckin'".
Originally released as a double album and now available as a
single CD.

THE COMPLETE SUN SESSIONS (1987)

1. That's All Right Mama
2. Blue Moon Of Kentucky
3. I Don't Care If The Sun Don't Shine
4. Good Rockin' Tonight
5. Milk Cow Blues Boogie
6. You're A Heartbreaker
7. Baby Let's Play House
8. I'm Left, You're Right, She's Gone
9. Mystery Train
10. I Forgot To Remember To Forget
11. I Love You Because
12. Blue Moon
13. Tomorrow Night
14. I'll Never Let You Go Little Darlin'
15. Just Because
16. Tryin' To Get To You
17. Harbour Lights
18. I Love You Because (takes 1 & 2)
19. That's All Right Mama
20. Blue Moon Of Kentucky
21. I Don't Care If The Sun Don't Shine
22. I'm Left, You're Right, She's Gone (take 9)
23. I'll Never Let You Go Little Darlin'
24. When It Rains It Really Pours
25. I Love You Because (take 3)
26. I Love You Because (take 4) *
27. I Love You Because (take 5)
28. I'm Left, You're Right, She's Gone (take 7)
29. I'm Left, You're Right, She's Gone (take 8)*
30. I'm Left, You're Right, She's Gone (take 10)*
31. I'm Left, You're Right, She's Gone (take 11)*
32. I'm Left, You're Right, She's Gone (take 13)*
33. I'm Left, You're, Right, She's Gone (take 12)

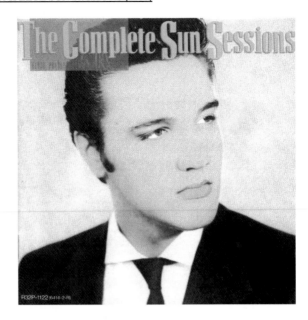

Top right: the original "Complete Sun Sessions" album.

**Bottom right: "The Sun Collection" an album originally
released in 1976 in the UK and the US.
(The UK issue is pictured)**

"The Sun Collection" included the 15 original Sun masters plus
the out take version of "I Love You Because" first released
on "Elvis A Legendary Performer Volume 1" in 1974.
This album was released as a 17 track CD which also included
"Harbour Lights" which was first released on
"Elvis A Legendary Performer Volume 2" in 1976.

The rest of the out takes on "The Complete Sun Sessions"
were first released in 1984 on "A Golden Celebration".
The alternate takes are previously unreleased.

Recording Information:

Tracks 1, 2, 11, 17, 18, 19, 20, 25, 26, & 27 recorded July 5 – 6, 1954.
Track 12 recorded August 19, 1954.
Tracks 13, 14, & 23 recorded September 10, 1954.
Tracks 3, 4, 15, & 21 recorded September 1954.
Tracks 5 & 6 recorded December 1954.
Track 7 recorded February 5, 1955.
Tracks 8, 22, 28, 29, 30, 31, 32, & 33 recorded March 5 1955.
Tracks 9, 10, & 16 recorded July 11, 1955.
Track 24 recorded August, 1955.
All selections recorded at Sun Studios, Memphis.
Exact recording dates are not known for every track..
Out take and alternate recordings of "I'm Left, You're Right, She's Gone" are slower than the master and also known as "My Baby Is Gone".
Tracks 1 – 16 are master takes. Tracks 17 – 24 are out takes. Tracks 25 – 33 are alternate takes.
Originally released as a double album. This album has also been issued on a single 28 track single CD.
* Tracks 26, 29, 30, 31, & 32 were not included on the CD version.

1. Love Me Tender
2. Let Me
3. Poor Boy
4. We're Gonna Move
5. Loving You (slow version, take 10)
6. Party (alternate take)
7. Hot Dog
8. Teddy Bear
9. Loving You (fast version, takes 20 - 21)
10. Mean Woman Blues (movie version)
11. Got A Lot O' Livin' To Do (alternate version)
12. Loving You (fast version, take 1)
13. Party
14. Lonesome Cowboy
15. Jailhouse Rock (vocal overdub, take 6)
16. Treat Me Nice (alternate take 10)
17. Young And Beautiful (alternate take 12)
18. Don't Leave Me Now
19. I Want To Be Free
20. Baby I Don't Care
21. Jailhouse Rock (alternate take 5)
22. Got A Lot O' Livin' To Do
23. Loving You (slow version, take 1)
24. Mean Woman Blues
25. Loving You (fast version, take 8)
26. Treat Me Nice
27. Love Me Tender (end title version)

ESSENTIAL ELVIS – THE FIRST MOVIES (1988)

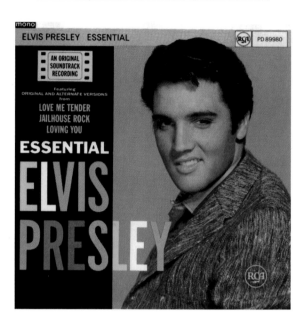

Recording Information:

Tracks 1, 3, & 4 recorded August 24, 1956. Track 2 recorded September 4 – 5, 1956. Track 27 recorded October 1, 1956.
Tracks 1, 2, 3, 4, & 27 recorded at 20th Century Fox Stage 1, Hollywood for the 20th Century Fox Motion Picture, "Love Me Tender".
Track 22 recorded January 12, 1957. Track 24 recorded January 13, 1957.
Tracks 22 & 24 recorded at Radio Recorders, Hollywood.
Track 11 recorded January 21, 1957. Tracks 5, 9, 12, 23, & 25 recorded February 14, 1957.
Tracks 5, 9, 11, 12, 23, & 25 recorded at Radio Recorders, Hollywood for the Paramount Motion Picture "Loving You".
Tracks 6, 7, 8, 10, 13, & 14 recorded at the Paramount Scoring Stage, Hollywood for the Paramount Motion Picture "Loving You"
Tracks 15, 17, & 21 recorded April 30, 1957. Tracks 16, 19, 20 (rhythm track), & 26 recorded May 3, 1957.
Tracks 15, 16, 17, 19, 21, & 26 recorded at Radio Recorders, Hollywood for the MGM Motion Picture "Jailhouse Rock".
Track 20 vocal overdub recorded May 8, 1957. Track 18 recorded May 9, 1957.
Tracks 18 & 20 recorded at MGM Studios, Hollywood for the MGM Motion Picture "Jailhouse Rock".
Tracks 1, 2, 3, 4, 7, 8, 13, 14, 18, 19, 20, 22, 24, & 26 are previously released masters. All other performances are previously unreleased.
Track 15 is the movie version. This is the master take with added vocal overdubs.

1. Also Sprach Zarathustra
2. See See Rider
3. Burning Love
4. Something
5. You Gave Me A Mountain
6. Steamroller Blues
7. My Way
8. Love Me
9. It's Over
10. Blue Suede Shoes
11. I'm So Lonesome I Could Cry
12. Hound Dog
13. What Now My Love
14. Fever
15. Welcome To My World
16. Suspicious Minds
17. Introductions By Elvis
18. I'll Remember You
19. An American Trilogy
20. A Big Hunk O' Love
21. Can't Help Falling In Love
22. Blue Hawaii
23. Hawaiian Wedding Song
24. KU-U-I-PO

THE ALTERNATE ALOHA (1988)

Recorded live at the Honolulu International Centre, Honolulu, Hawaii.
This was the rehearsal performance for the satellite broadcast "Aloha From Hawaii Via Satellite".
Tracks 22, 23, & 24 were recorded after the live performance. These performances were first issued on "Mahalo From Elvis" in 1978 but on this release dialogue and false starts were also included.

ELVIS IN NASHVILLE (1988)

1. I Got A Woman
2. A Big Hunk O' Love
3. Working On The Building
4. Judy
5. Anything That's Part Of You
6. Night Rider
7. Where No One Stands Alone
8. Just Call Me Lonesome
9. Guitar Man
10. Little Cabin On The Hill
11. It's Your Baby, You Rock It
12. Early Morning Rain
13. It's Still Here
14. I, John

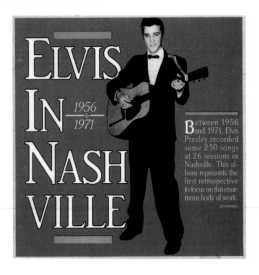

A compilation of previously released masters recorded at RCA Studio B, Nashville between 1956 and 1971.

ESSENTIAL ELVIS VOLUME 2 – STEREO '57 (1988)

1. I Beg Of You (take 1)
2. Is It So Strange (take 1)
3. Have I Told You Lately That I Love You (take 2)
4. It Is No Secret What God Can Do (takes 1, 2, & 3)
5. Blueberry Hill (take 2)
6. Mean Woman Blues (take 14)
7. Peace In The Valley (takes 2 & 3)
8. Have I Told You Lately That I Love You (take 6)
9. Blueberry Hill (take 7)
10. That's When Your Heartaches Begin (takes 4, 5, & 6)
11. Is It So Strange (takes 7 &11)
12. I Beg Of You (takes 6 & 8)
13. Peace In The Valley (take 7)
14. Have I Told You Lately That I Love You (takes 12 & 13)
15. I Beg Of You (take 12)
16. I Believe*
17. Tell Me Why*
18. Got A Lot O' Livin' To Do*
19. All Shook Up*
20. Take My Hand, Precious Lord*

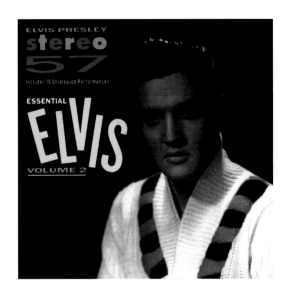

Recording Information:

Tracks 16, 17, 18, & 19 recorded January 12, 1957.
Tracks 1, 6, 7, 10, 12, 13, 15, & 20 recorded January 13, 1957.
Tracks 2, 3, 4, 5, 8, 9, 11, & 14 recorded January 19, 1957.
All tracks recorded at Radio Recorders, Hollywood.
Tracks 1 – 15 are previously unreleased alternate takes recorded in binaural two track stereo.
* Tracks 16 – 20 are original mono masters. These were added to the CD version of the album.

THE MILLION DOLLAR QUARTET (1990)

1. You Belong To My Heart
2. When God Dips His Love In My Heart
3. Just A Little Talk With Jesus
4. Jesus Walked That Lonesome Valley
5. I Shall Not Be Moved
6. Peace In The Valley
7. Down By The Riverside
8 I'm With The Crowd But Oh So Alone
9. Farther Along
10. Blessed Jesus (Hold My Hand)
11. As We Travel Along On The Jericho Road
12. I Just Can't Make It By Myself
13. Little Cabin On The Hill
14. Summertime Is Past And Gone
15. I Hear A Sweet Voice Calling
16. Sweetheart You Done Me Wrong
17. Keeper Of The Key
18. Crazy Arms
19. Don't Forbid Me
20. Too Much Monkey Business

21. Brown Eyed Handsome Man
22. Out Of Sight, Out Of Mind
23. Brown Eyed Handsome Man
24. Don't Be Cruel
25. Don't Be Cruel
26. Paralyzed
27. Don't Be Cruel
28. There's No Place Like Home
29. When The Saints Go Marching In
30. Softly And Tenderly
31. Is It So Strange
32. That's When Your Heartaches Begin
33. Brown Eyed Handsome Man
34. Rip It Up
35. I'm Gonna Bid My Blues Goodbye
36. Crazy Arms
37. That's My Desire
38. End Of The Road
39. Black Bottom Stomp
40. You're The Only Star In My Blue Heaven
41. Elvis (dialogue)

ELVIS PRESLEY

The Million Dollar Quartet

Recording Information:

All tracks recorded December 4, 1956 at Sun Studios, Memphis.

These are informal recordings made when Elvis visited the Sun Studios during a Jerry Lee Lewis session which also featured Carl Perkins and the Carl Perkins band.

These recordings became known as the "Million Dollar Quartet" sessions as Johnny Cash was also in the studio at the time, and posed for photographs with Elvis, Carl and Jerry Lee.

Unfortunately Johnny Cash doesn't feature on these recordings, although it's rumoured that there may be another tape in existence which does feature Johnny Cash.

"Reconsider Baby" was also performed at these sessions, and was released on "Elvis – The King Of Rock N Roll – The Complete '50's Masters" in 1992.

ESSENTIAL ELVIS VOLUME 3 – HITS LIKE NEVER BEFORE (1990)

1. King Creole (track E – take 18)
2. I Got Stung (alternate take 1)
3. A Fool Such As I (alternate take 3)
4. Wear My Ring Around Your Neck (take 22 – undubbed master)
5. Your Cheatin' Heart (take 9)
6. Ain't That Loving You Baby (mid tempo, take 1)
7. Doncha' Think It's Time (album master)
8. I Need Your Love Tonight (takes 2 & 10)
9. Lover Doll ((track H – take 7 – undubbed master)
10. As Long As I Have You (track N – take 8)
11. Danny
12. King Creole (track E – take 3)
13. Crawfish (track F – take 7)
14. A Big Hunk O' Love (take 1)
15. Ain't That Loving You Baby (fast version, takes 5 & 11)
16. I Got Stung (takes 13 & 14)
17. Your Cheating Heart (master)
18. Wear My Ring Around Your Neck (single master)
19. Steadfast, Loyal And True (track M – take 6)
20. I Need Your Love Tonight (take 5)
21. Doncha' Think It's Time (single master)
22. I Got Stung (take 12)
23. King Creole (track R – take 8, main title instrumental version)
24. As Long As I Have You (track N – take 4)

ESSENTIAL **ELVIS** HITS LIKE NEVER BEFORE
Including 16 Unreleased Performances
KING CREOLE
I NEED YOUR LOVE TONIGHT
A FOOL SUCH AS I
YOUR CHEATING HEART
A BIG HONK O'LOVE
I GOT STUNG
VOL.3

Recording Information:

Tracks 1, 12, & 13 recorded January 15, 1958. Tracks 9, 10, 19, & 24 recorded January 15, 1958.

Track 23 recorded January 23, 1958. Track 11 recorded January 28, 1958.

Tracks 1, 9, 10, 12, 13, 19, 23, & 24 recorded at Radio Recorders, Hollywood for the Paramount Motion Picture "King Creole".

Track 11 recorded at the Paramount Scoring Stage, Hollywood for the Paramount Motion Picture "King Creole".

Tracks 4, 5, 7, 17, 18, & 21 recorded February 1, 1958 at Radio Recorders, Hollywood.

Tracks 3, 6, 8, 14, 15 & 20 recorded June 10, 1958. Tracks 2, 16, & 22 recorded June 11, 1958.

Tracks 2, 3, 6, 8, 14, 15, 16, 20, & 22 recorded at RCA Studio B, Nashville.

"Your Cheating Heart" was first released on "Elvis For Everyone" in 1965.

Alternate take 9 was first released on album in the UK on "I Was The One" in 1983.

An alternate version of "Doncha' Think It's Time" was included on "Elvis' Gold Records Volume 2" in 1959.

Both this version and the original single version are included on this release.

"Danny" was first released on "Elvis A Legendary Performer Volume 3" in 1978.

The single version of "Wear My Ring Around Your Neck" included on this release featured Elvis' "piano and guitar slapping" overdubs.

All other performances are previously unreleased versions.

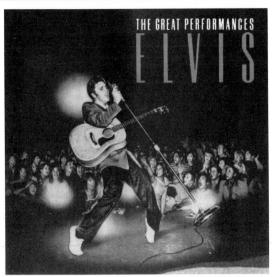

THE GREAT PERFORMANCES (1990)

1. My Happiness
2. That's All Right
3. Shake, Rattle & Roll/Flip, Flop & Fly (live)
4. Heartbreak Hotel
5. Blue Suede Shoes
6. Ready Teddy (live)
7. Don't Be Cruel
8. Teddy Bear
9. Got A Lot O' Livin' To Do
10. Jailhouse Rock
11. Treat Me Nice
12. King Creole
13. Trouble
14. Fame And Fortune
15. Return To Sender
16. Always On My Mind
17. An American Trilogy (live)
18. If I Can Dream
19. Unchained Melody (live)
20. Memories

Recording Information/Notes:

Track 1 recorded in 1953 at Sun Studios, Memphis. Exact date unknown.
All other performances are previously released masters.
"Treat Me Nice" & "Memories" are stereo versions.
"Shake, Rattle & Roll/Flip, Flop & Fly" recorded live January 28, 1956 on The Dorsey Brothers Stage Show.
"Ready Teddy" recorded live September 9, 1956 on The Ed Sullivan Show.
"An American Trilogy" recorded live January 14, 1973 for the satellite broadcast "Aloha From Hawaii".
"Unchained Melody" recorded live June 21, 1977 in Rapid City, South Dakota – undubbed version.
This recording was originally overdubbed for single release in 1978, and was then included on the box set "Elvis Aron Presley" in 1980.

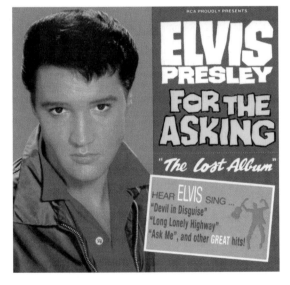

THE LOST ALBUM /FOR THE ASKING (1991)

1. Long, Lonely Highway
2. Western Union
3. Witchcraft
4. Love Me Tonight
5. What now, What Next, Where To
6. Please Don't Drag That String Around
7. Blue River
8. Never Ending
9. Devil In Disguise
10. Finders Keepers, Losers Weepers
11. Echoes Of Love
12. Slowly But Surely
13. It Hurts Me
14. Memphis, Tennessee
15. Ask Me

Recording Information/Notes:

This album features previously released masters recorded at RCA Studio B, Nashville between 1963 and 1964.
"Witchcraft", "Please Don't Drag That String Around", "Blue River", "Never Ending", "Devil In Disguise", "It Hurts Me" and "Ask Me" were released as singles. An alternate version of "Long , Lonely Highway" was also issued as a single.
"Long, Lonely Highway", "Love Me Tonight," "Blue River", "Never Ending", Echoes Of Love" and "Slowly But Surely" were used as bonus tracks on Elvis' movie soundtrack albums.
"Finders Keepers, Losers Weepers" and "Memphis Tennessee" were first released on "Elvis For Everyone" in 1965.
The album was known as "The Lost Album" in the US and "For The Asking" in Europe. The European release is pictured.

COLLECTORS GOLD (1991)

Disc One: Hollywood:

1. GI Blues
2. Pocketful Of Rainbows
3. Big Boots
4. Black Star
5. Summer Kisses, Winter Tears
6. I Slipped, I Stumbled, I Fell
7. Lonely Man
8. What A Wonderful Life
9. A Whistling Tune
10. Beyond The Bend
11. One Broken Heart For Sale
12. You're The Boss
13. Roustabout
14. Girl Happy
15. So Close, Yet So Far
16. Stop, Look And Listen
17. Am I Ready
18. How Can You Lose What You Never Had

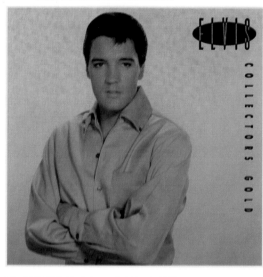

Left: the 3 CD box set
also included an
illustrated booklet .
The same photograph was
used for the cover of
the box set, the booklet
and the individual discs.

A vinyl version was also
Released.

Recording Information:

Track 1 recorded April 27, 1960. Track 3 recorded April 28, 1960. Track 2 recorded May 6, 1960
Tracks 1 & 3 recorded at RCA Studios, Hollywood. Track 2 recorded at Radio Recorders, Hollywood.
Tracks 1, 2, & 3 recorded for the Paramount Motion Picture "GI Blues".
Tracks 4 & 5 recorded August 8, 1960 at Radio Recorders, Hollywood for the 20th Century Fox Motion Picture "Flaming Star".
Track 7 recorded November 7, 1960. Track 6 recorded November 8, 1960.
Tracks 6 & 7 recorded at Radio Recorders, Hollywood for the 20th Century Fox Motion Picture "Wild In The Country".
Tracks 8 & 9 recorded July 2, 1961 at RCA Studio B Nashville for the Mirisch United Artists Motion Picture "Follow That Dream".
Tracks 10 & 11 recorded September 22, 1962 at Radio Recorders, Hollywood for the MGM Motion Picture "It Happened At The World's Fair".
Track 12 recorded July 11, 1963 at Radio Recorders, Hollywood for the MGM Motion Picture "Viva Las Vegas".
Track 13 recorded April 29, 1964 at Radio Recorders, Hollywood for the Paramount Motion Picture "Roustabout".
Track 14 recorded June 11, 1964 at Radio Recorders, Hollywood for the MGM Motion Picture "Girl Happy".
Track 15 recorded February 25, 1965 at RCA Studio B, Nashville for the MGM Motion Picture "Harum Scarum".
Track 16 recorded February 16, 1966. Track 17 recorded February 17, 1966.
Tracks 16 & 17 recorded at Radio Recorders, Hollywood for the MGM Motion Picture "Spinout".
Track 18 recorded February 21, 1967 at RCA Studio B, Nashville for the United Artists Motion Picture "Clambake".
"You're The Boss" is a duet with Ann Margaret.
All selections previously unreleased.

Disc Two: Nashville:

1. Like A Baby
2. There's Always Me
3. I Want You With Me
4. Gently
5. Give Me The Right
6. I Met Her Today
7. Night Rider
8. Just Tell Her Jim Said Hello
9. Ask Me
10. Memphis, Tennessee
11. Love Me Tonight
12. Witchcraft
13. Come What May
14. Love Letters
15. Going Home

Recording Information:

Track 1 recorded April 3, 1960.
Tracks 2, 3, 4, & 5 recorded March 12, 1961.
Tracks 6 & 7 recorded October 15, 1961.
Track 8 recorded March 19, 1962.
Tracks 10, 11, & 12 recorded May 27, 1963.
Track 9 recorded May 28, 1963.
Track 14 recorded May 26, 1966.
Track 13 recorded May 28, 1966.
Track 15 recorded January 15, 1968 for the
MGM Motion Picture "Stay Away Joe".
All selections recorded at RCA Studio B, Nashville.
All selections previously unreleased.

Disc Three: Live In Las Vegas:

1. Blue Suede Shoes
2. I Got A Woman
3. Heartbreak Hotel
4. Love Me Tender
5. Baby What You Want Me To Do
6. Runaway
7. Surrender/Are You Lonesome Tonight – "Laughing Version"
8. Rubberneckin'
9. Memories
10. Introductions By Elvis
11. Jailhouse Rock/Don't Be Cruel
12. Inherit The Wind
13. This Is The Story
14. Mystery Train/Tiger Man
15. Funny How Time Slips Away
16. Loving You/Reconsider Baby
17. What'd I Say

Recording Information:

Tracks 7 & 10 recorded August 21, 1969, Midnight Show.
Tracks 4, 11, & 14 recorded August 22, 1969, Midnight Show.
Tracks 16 & 17 recorded August 23, 1969, Midnight Show.
Track 3 recorded August 24, 1969, Dinner Show.
Tracks 1, 2, 9, & 15 recorded August 25, 1969, Dinner Show.
Tracks 5, 6, ,8, 12, & 13 recorded August 26, 1969, Midnight Show.
All selections recorded at the International Hotel, Las Vegas.
All selections except "Are You Lonesome Tonight" are previously unreleased.

1. Hound Dog
2. Love Me
3. Loving You
4. Hot Dog
5. I Want To Be Free
6. Jailhouse Rock
7. Treat Me Nice
8. Baby I Don't Care
9. Trouble
10. King Creole
11. Steadfast, Loyal And True
12. Santa Claus Is Back In Town
13. Don't
14. Dirty, Dirty Feeling
15. Just Tell Her Jim Said Hello
16. Girls! Girls! Girls!
17. Bossa Nova Baby
18. You're The Boss
19. Little Egypt
20. Fools Fall In Love
21. Saved

All selections are previously released masters.
"You're The Boss" was added to the CD release of this album.

ELVIS SINGS LEIBER AND STOLLER (1991)

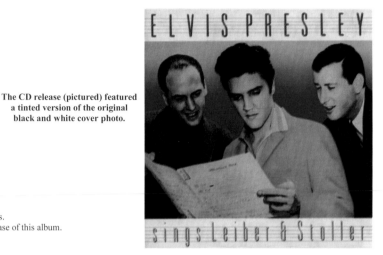

The CD release (pictured) featured a tinted version of the original black and white cover photo.

ELVIS – THE KING OF ROCK N ROLL – THE COMPLETE '50'S MASTERS (1992)

Disc One:

1. My Happiness
2. That's All Right
3. I Love You Because
4. Harbour Lights
5. Blue Moon Of Kentucky
6. Blue Moon
7. Tomorrow Night
8. I'll Never Let You Go (Little Darlin')
9. I Don't Care If The Sun Don't Shine
10. Just Because
11. Good Rockin' Tonight
12. Milkcow Blues Boogie
13. You're A Heartbreaker
14. Baby Lets Play House
15. I'm Left, Your Right, She's Gone
16. Mystery Train
17. I Forgot To Remember To Forget
18. Trying To Get To You
19. When It Rains It Really Pours
20. I Got A Woman
21. Heartbreak Hotel
22. Money Honey
23. I'm Counting On You
24. I Was The One
25. Blue Suede Shoes
26. My Baby Left Me
27. One Sided Love Affair
28. So Glad Your Mine
29. I'm Gonna Sit Right Down And Cry (Over You)
30. Tutti Frutti

Recording Information:

Track 1 recorded 1953. Exact date unknown.
Tracks 2, 3, 4, & 5, recorded July 5 – 6, 1954.
Track 6 recorded August 19, 1954.
Tracks 7 & 8 recorded September 10, 1954.
Tracks 9, 10, & 11 recorded September 1954.
Tracks 12 & 13 recorded December 1954.
Track 14 recorded February 5, 1955.
Track 15 recorded March 5, 1955.
Tracks 16, 17, & 18 recorded July, 1955.
Track 19 recorded August, 1955.
Tracks 1 – 19 recorded at Sun Studios, Memphis.
Tracks 20, 21, & 22 recorded January 10, 1956.
Tracks 23 & 24 recorded January 11, 1956.
Tracks 20 – 24 recorded at RCA Studios, Nashville.
Tracks 25, 26, 27, & 28 recorded January 30, 1956.
Tracks 29 & 30 recorded January 31, 1956.
Tracks 25 – 30 recorded at RCA Studios, New York.

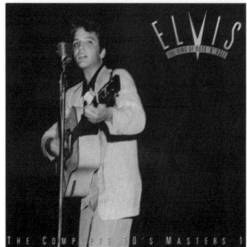

ELVIS – THE KING OF ROCK N ROLL – THE COMPLETE '50'S MASTERS (1992) Continued

Disc Two:

1. Lawdy Miss Clawdy
2. Shake, Rattle And Roll
3. I Want You, I Need You, I Love You
4. Hound Dog
5. Don't Be Cruel
6. Any Way You Want Me (That's How I Will Be)
7. Were Gonna Move
8. Love Me Tender
9. Poor Boy
10. Let Me
11. Playing For Keeps
12. Love Me
13. Paralyzed
14. How Do You Think I Feel
15. How's The World Treating You
16. When My Blue Moon Turns To Gold Again
17. Long Tall Sally
18. Old Shep
19. Too Much
20. Anyplace Is Paradise
21. Ready Teddy
22. First In Line
23. Rip It Up
24. I Believe
25. Tell Me Why
26. Got A Lot O' Livin' To Do
27. All Shook Up
28. Mean Woman Blues
29. (There'll Be) Peace In the Valley (For Me)

Recording Information:

Tracks 1 & 2 recorded February 3, 1956 at RCA Studios New York.
Track 3 recorded April 4, 1956 at RCA Studio B, Nashville.
Tracks 4, 5, & 6 recorded July 2, 1956 at RCA Studios, New York.
Tracks 7, 8, & 9 recorded August 24, 1956.
Track 10 recorded September 4 - 5, 1956.
Tracks 7, 8, 9, & 10 recorded at 20 Century Fox Stage 1, Hollywood
for the 20th Century Fox Motion Picture "Love Me Tender".
Tracks 11, 12, 14, & 15 recorded September 1, 1956.
Tracks 13, 16, 17, 18, 19, & 20 recorded September 2, 1956.
Tracks 21, 22, & 23 recorded September 3, 1956.
Tracks 11 – 23 recorded at Radio Recorders, Hollywood.
Tracks 24, 25, 26, & 27 recorded January 12, 1957.
Tracks 28 & 29 recorded January 13, 1957.
Tracks 24 – 29 recorded at Radio Recorders, Hollywood.
Tracks 26 & 28 from the Paramount Motion Picture "Loving You".

Disc Three:

1. That's When Your Heartaches Begin
2. Take My Hand, Precious Lord
3. It Is No Secret (What God Can Do)
4. Blueberry Hill
5. Have I Told You Lately That I Love You
6. Is It So Strange
7. Party
8. Lonesome Cowboy
9. Hot Dog
10. One Night Of Sin
11. (Let Me Be Your) Teddy Bear
12. Don't Leave Me Now
13. I Beg Of You
14. One Night
15. True Love
16. I Need You So
17. Loving You
18. When It Rains It Really Pours
19. Jailhouse Rock
20. Young And Beautiful
21. I Want To Be Free
22. (You're So Square) Baby I Don't Care
23. Don't Leave Me Know
24. Blue Christmas
25. White Christmas
26. Here Comes Santa (Right Down Santa Claus Lane)
27. Silent Night
28. O Little Town Of Bethlehem
29. Santa Bring My Baby Back (To Me)
30. Santa Claus Is Back In Town
31. I'll Be Home For Christmas

Recording Information:

Tracks 1 & 2 recorded January 13, 1957.
Tracks 3, 4, 5, & 6 recorded January 19, 1957.
Tracks 1 – 6 recorded at Radio Recorders, Hollywood.
Tracks 7, 8, 9, 10, & 11 recorded January 14 – 18, 1957
Tracks 7 – 11 recorded at the Paramount Scoring Stage, Hollywood.
Tracks 12, 13, , 14, 15, & 16 recorded February 23, 1957.
Tracks 17 & 18 recorded February 24, 1957.
Tracks 7, 8, 9, 11, & 17 from the Paramount Motion Picture "Loving You".
Tracks 19 & 20 recorded April 30, 1957.
Tracks 21 & 22 (rhythm track) recorded May 3, 1957.
Tracks 19 – 22 recorded at Radio Recorders, Hollywood
Track 22 (vocal overdub) recorded May 8, 1957.
Track 23 recorded May 9, 1957.
Tracks 22 (vocal overdub) & 23 recorded at MGM Studios, Hollywood.
Tracks 19 – 23 from the MGM Motion Picture "Jailhouse Rock".
Track 24 recorded September 25 1957.
Tracks 25, 26, & 27 recorded September 6, 1957.
Tracks 28, 29, 30, & 31 recorded September 7, 1957.
Tracks 24 – 31 recorded at Radio Recorders, Hollywood.

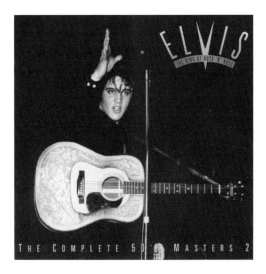

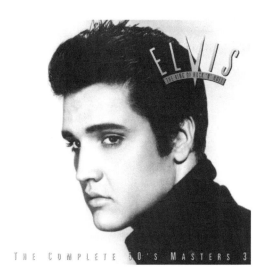

ELVIS – THE KING OF ROCK N ROLL – THE COMPLETE '50'S MASTERS (1992) Continued

Disc Four:

1. Treat Me Nice
2. My Wish Came True
3. Don't
4. Danny
5. Hard Headed Woman
6. Trouble
7. New Orleans
8. Crawfish
9. Dixieland Rock
10. Lover Doll
11. Don't Ask Me Why
13. As Long As I Have You
14. Young Dreams
15. Steadfast, Loyal And True
16. Doncha' Think It's Time
17. Your Cheating Heart
18. Wear My Ring Around Your Neck
19. I Need Your Love Tonight
20. A Big Hunk O' Love
21. Ain't That Loving You Baby
22. (Now And Then There's) A Fool Such As I
23. I Got Stung
24. Interview With Elvis

Recording Information:

Track 1 recorded September 5, 1957.
Tracks 2 & 3 recorded September 6, 1957.
Tracks 1 – 3 recorded at Radio Recorders, Hollywood.
Track 1 from the MGM Motion Picture "Jailhouse Rock".
Track 4 recorded January 28, 1958 at the Paramount Scoring Stage,
Hollywood for the Paramount Motion Picture "King Creole".
Tracks 5, 6, 7, & 8 recorded January 15, 1958.
Tracks 9, 10, 11, & 12 recorded January 16, 1958.
Tracks 13, 14, & 15 recorded January 23, 1958.
Tracks 5 – 15 recorded at Radio Recorders, Hollywood for
the Paramount Motion Picture "King Creole".
Tracks 16, 17, 18 recorded February 1, 1958 at Radio Recorders,
Hollywood.
Tracks 19, 20, 21, & 22 recorded June 10, 1958.
Track 23 recorded June 11, 1958.
Tracks 19 – 23 recorded at RCA Studio B, Nashville.
Track 24 recorded September 22, 1958 – the "Elvis Sails"
press interviews.

Disc Five: Rare & Rockin': (*indicates a previously unreleased performance)

1. That's When Your Heartaches Begin*
2. Fool, Fool, Fool (demo)*
3. Tweedle Dee
4. Maybelline
5. Shake, Rattle And Roll (demo)*
6. Blue Moon Of Kentucky (early take)*
7. Blue Moon (alternate take 1)
8. I'm Left, Your Right, She's Gone (alternate 11)
9. Reconsider Baby*
10. Lawdy, Miss Clawdy (alternate 3)*
11. Shake, Rattle And Roll (alternate take 8)*
12. I Want You, I Need You, I Love You (alternate take 16)
13. Heartbreak Hotel
14. Long Tall Sally
15. Blue Suede Shoes
16. Money Honey
17. We're Gonna Move (alternate take 4)*
18. Old Shep (alternate master – take 5)*
19. I Beg Of You (alternate master – take 12)
20. Loving You (slow version - master take 12)*
21. Loving You (uptempo version – alternate take 13)*
22. Young And Beautiful (alternate master - take 3)*
23. I Want To Be Free (alternate master - take 10)*
24. King Creole (alternate master – take 3)*
25. As Long As I Have You (alternate master – take 8)
26. Aint That Loving You Baby (fast version– alternate take 10)

Recording Information:

Track 1 recorded 1953 (exact date unknown) at Sun Studios, Memphis.
Tracks 2 & 5 recorded early 1955 in Lubbock, Texas.
Track 3 recorded 1995. Exact date unknown.
Track 4 recorded September 24, 1955.
Tracks 3 & 4 recorded at the Louisiana, Hayride, Shreveport, Louisiana.
Track 6 recorded July 5 - 6, 1954. Track 7 recorded August 19, 1954.
Track 8 recorded March 5, 1955.
Track 9 recorded December 4, 1956. From the "Million Dollar Quartet" sessions.
Tracks 6, 7, 8, & 9 recorded at Sun Studios, Memphis.
Tracks 10 & 11 recorded February 3, 1956 at RCA Studios, New York.
Track 12 recorded April 14, 1956 at RCA Studio B, Nashville.
Tracks 13 - 16 recorded May 6, 1956 at the New Frontier Hotel, Las Vegas.
Track 17 recorded August 24, 1956 at 20th Century Fox Stage 1, Hollywood
for the 20th Century Fox Motion Picture "Love Me Tender".
Track 18 recorded September 2, 1956 at Radio Recorders, Hollywood.
Track 19 recorded January 13, 1957 at Radio Recorders, Hollywood.
Tracks 20 & 21 recorded February 14, 1957 at Radio Recorders, Hollywood
for the Paramount Motion Picture "Loving You".
Track 22 recorded April 30, 1957. Track 23 recorded May 3, 1957.
Tracks 22 & 23 recorded at Radio Recorders, Hollywood for the MGM
Motion Picture "Jailhouse Rock".
Track 24 recorded January 15, 1958.
Track 25 recorded January 16, 1958
Tracks 24 & 25 recorded at Radio Recorders, Hollywood for the Paramount
Motion Picture "King Creole".
Track 26 recorded June 10, 1958 at RCA Studio B, Nashville.

**Released as a 5 CD box set with an illustrated colour booklet
and sheet of stamps of Elvis' original 50's record covers.
A vinyl edition was also produced.**

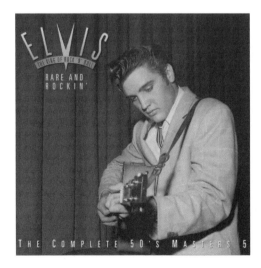

DOUBLE FEATURES: HAREM HOLIDAY & GIRL HAPPY (1993)

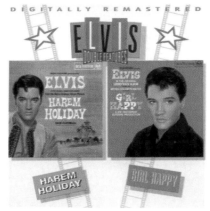

Harem Holiday:

1. Harem Holiday
2. My Desert Serenade
3. Go East Young Man
4. Mirage
5. Kismet
6. Shake That Tambourine
7. Hey Little Girl
8. Golden Coins
9. So Close, Yet So Far (From Paradise)
10. Animal Instinct
11. Wisdom Of The Ages

Girl Happy:

12. Girl Happy
13. Spring Fever
14. Fort Lauderdale Chamber Of Commerce
15. Startin' Tonight
16. Wolf Call
17. Do Not Disturb
18. Cross My Heart And Hope To Die
19. The Meanest Girl In Town
20. Do The Clam
21. Puppet On A String
22. I've Got To Find My Baby

Artwork shown is the European CD version which featured original album cover art.

The American version featured a photograph from each movie in place of the album covers.

Recording Information:

Tracks 1 – 11 first released on the album "Harem Holiday" a.k.a."Harum Scarum" in 1965.
Tracks 12 – 22 first released on the album "Girl Happy" in 1965.
All material previously released.

DOUBLE FEATURES: LOVE IN LAS VEGAS & ROUSTABOUT (1993)

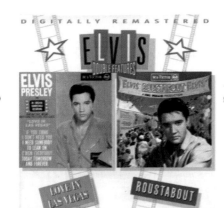

Love In Las Vegas:

1. Viva Las Vegas
2. If You Think I Don't Need You
3. I Need Somebody To Lean On
4. You're The Boss (with Ann Margret)
5. What'd I Say
6. Do The Vega
7. C'mon Everybody
8. The Lady Loves Me (with Ann Margret)
9. Night Life
10. Today, Tomorrow, And Forever)
11. The Yellow Rose Of Texas/
The Eyes Of Texas (medley)
12. Santa Lucia

Roustabout:

13. Roustabout
14. Little Egypt
15. Poison Ivy League
16. Hard Knocks
17. It's a Wonderful Life
18. Big Love, Big Heartache
19. One Track Heart
20. It's Carnival Time
21. Carny Town
22. There's A Brand New Day On The Horizon
23. Wheels On My Heels

Artwork shown is the European CD version which featured original album cover art.

The American version featured a photograph from each movie in place of the album covers.

**Right: the title of the movie was changed from "Viva Las Vegas" to "Love In Las Vegas" for its European release.
The UK "Love In Las Vegas" EP is pictured.**

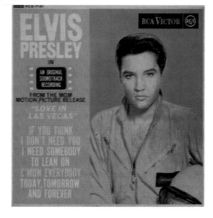

Recording Information:

Tracks 1, 2, 7, & 9 recorded July 9, 1963.
Tracks 3. 6, 11, & 12 recorded July 10, 1963.
Tracks 4, 8, & 10 recorded July 11, 1963.
Track 5 recorded August 30, 1963.
Tracks 1 – 12 recorded at Radio Recorders, Hollywood for the MGM Motion Picture "Viva Las Vegas".
Tracks 2, 3, 7, & 10 first released on the EP "Viva Las Vegas" in 1964.
Tracks 1 & 5 first released as a single in 1964.
Track 12 first released on the album "Elvis For Everyone" in 1965.
Tracks 6, 9, & 11 first released on the album "Elvis Sings Flaming Star" in 1969.
Track 8 first released on the album "Elvis A Legendary Performer Volume 4" in 1983.
A version of track 4 was first released on the album "Collectors Gold" in 1991. An alternate version features on this CD.
Tracks 13 – 23 first released on the album "Roustabout" in 1964
Track 21 is a longer version of the original master and features Elvis singing, "we gotta end" as the song fades out.

DOUBLE FEATURES: KID GALAHAD & GIRLS! GIRLS! GIRLS! (1993)

Kid Galahad:

1. King Of The Whole Wide World
2. This Is Living
3. Riding The Rainbow
4. Home Is Where The Heart Is
5. I Got Lucky
6. A Whistling Tune

Girls! Girls! Girls!

7. Girls! Girls! Girls!
8. I Don't Wanna Be Tied
9. Where Do You Come From?
10. I Don't Want To
11. We'll be Together
12. A Boy Like Me, A Girl Like You
13. Earth Boy
14. Return To Sender
15. Because Of Love
16. Thanks To The Rolling Sea
17. Song Of The Shrimp
18. The Walls Have Ears
19. We're Coming In Loaded
20. Mama
21. Plantation Rock
22. Dainty Little Moonbeams
23. Girls! Girls! Girls! (end title version)

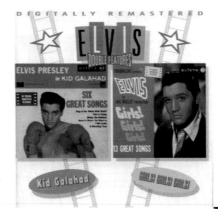

Artwork shown is the European CD version which featured original album cover art.

The American version featured a photograph from each movie in place of the album covers.

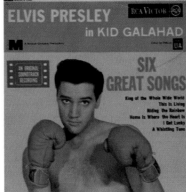

Right: the original "Kid Galahad" EP

Recording Information:

Tracks 4, 5, & 6 recorded October 26, 1961.
Tracks 1, 2, & 3 recorded October 27, 1961
Tracks 1 – 6 recorded at Radio Recorders, Hollywood for the Mirisch United Artists Motion Picture "Kid Galahad".
Tracks 1 – 6 were first released on the EP "Kid Galahad" in 1962. The original masters were edited on the EP release.
The unedited stereo masters were released for the first time on this CD.
Tracks 7 – 20 first released on the album "Girls! Girls! Girls!" in 1962.
Track 20 first released on the album "Let's Be Friends" in 1970.
A version of track 21 was first released on "Elvis A Legendary Performer Volume 4" in 1983. An alternate version features on this CD.
Tracks 22 and 23 recorded March 28, 1962 at Radio Recorders, Hollywood for the Paramount Motion Picture "Girls! Girls! Girls!".
Tracks 22 & 23 are previously unreleased recordings.

DOUBLE FEATURES: IT HAPPENED AT THE WORLD'S FAIR & FUN IN ACAPULCO (1993)

It Happened At The World's Fair:

1. Beyond The Bend
2. Relax
3. Take Me To The Fair
4. They Remind Too Much Of You
5. One Broken Heart For Sale
(film version)
6. I'm Falling In Tonight
7. Cotton Candy Land
8. A World Of Own
9. How Would You Like To Be
10. Happy Ending
11. One Broken Heart For Sale

Fun In Acapulco:

12. Fun In Acapulco
13. Vino, Dinero, Y Amor
14. Mexico
15. El Toro
16. Marguerita
17. The Bullfighter Was A Lady
18. (There's) No Room To Rhumba In A Sports Car
19. I Think I'm Gonna Like It Here
20. Bossa Nova Baby
21. You Can't Say No In Acapulco
22. Guadalajara

Artwork shown is the European CD version which featured original album cover art.

The American version featured a photograph from each movie in place of the album covers.

Recording Information:

Tracks 1 – 4 and tracks 6 – 11 first released on the album "It Happened At The World's Fair" in 1963.
Track 5 first released on the album "Collectors Gold" in 1991.
Tracks 12 – 22 first released on the album "Fun In Acapulco" in 1963.
All material previously released.

FROM NASHVILLE TO MEMPHIS – THE ESSENTIAL 60's MASTERS VOLUME 1 (1993)

Disc One:

1. Make Me Know It
2. Soldier Boy
3. Stuck On You
4. Fame And Fortune
5. A Mess Of Blues
6. It Feels So Right
7. Fever
8. Like A Baby
9. It's Now Or Never
10. The Girl Of My Best Friend
11. Dirty, Dirty Feeling
12. Thrill Of Your Love
13. I Gotta Know
14. Such A Night
15. Are You Lonesome Tonight
16. The Girl Next Door Went A Walkin'
17. I Will Be Home Again
18. Reconsider Baby
19. Surrender
20. I'm Coming Home
21. Gently
22. In Your Arms
23. Give Me The Right
24. I Feel So Bad
25. It's A Sin
26. I Want You With Me
27. There's Always Me

Recording Information:

Tracks 1 & 2 recorded March 20, 1960.
Tracks 4 – 6 recorded March 21, 1960.
Tracks 7 – 9 recorded April 3, 1960.
Tracks 10 – 18 recorded April 4, 1960.
Track 19 recorded October 30, 1960.
Tracks 20 – 27 recorded March 12, 1961.
All tracks recorded at RCA Studio B, Nashville.

Disc Two:

1. Starting Today
2. Sentimental Me
3. Judy
4. Put The Blame On Me
5. Kiss Me Quick
6. That's Someone You Never Forget
7. I'm Yours
8. His Latest Flame
9. Little Sister
10. For The Millionth And The Last Time
11. Good Luck Charm
12. Anything That's Part Of You
13. I Met Her Day
14. Night Rider
15. Something Blue
16. Gonna Get Back Home Somehow
17. (Such An) Easy Question
18. Fountain Of Love
19. Just For Old Times Sake
20. You'll Be Gone
21. I Feel That I've Known You Forever
22. Just Tell Her Jim Said Hello
23. Suspicion
24. She's Not You
25. Echoes Of Love
26. Please Don't Drag That String Around
27. (You're The) Devil In Disguise
28. Never Ending
29. What Now, What Next, Where To
30. Witchcraft
31. Finders Keepers, Loser Weepers
32. Love Me Tonight

Recording Information:

Tracks 1 – 4 recorded March 13, 1961.
Tracks 5 & 6 recorded June 25, 1961.
Tracks 7 – 9 recorded June 26, 1961.
Tracks 10 – 12 recorded October 15, 1961.
Tracks 13 & 14 recorded October 16, 1961.
Tracks 15 – 20 recorded March 18, 1962.
Tracks 21 – 24 recorded March 19, 1962.
Tracks 25 – 28 recorded May 26, 1963.
Tracks 29 – 32 recorded May 27, 1963.
All tracks recorded at RCA Studio B, Nashville.

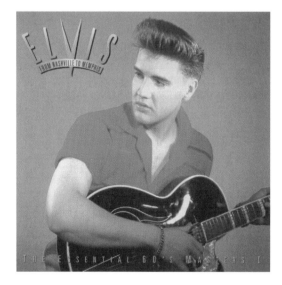

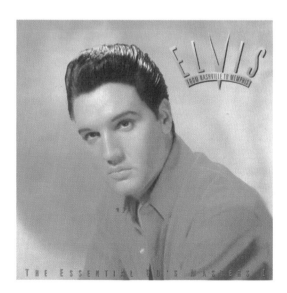

FROM NASHVILLE TO MEMPHIS – THE ESSENTIAL 60's MASTERS VOLUME 1 (1993) - Continued

Disc Three: (*indicates a previously unreleased performance)

1. (It's A) Long Lonely Highway
2. Western Union
3. Slowly But Surely
4. Blue River
5. Memphis Tennessee
6. Ask Me
7. It Hurts Me
8. Down In The Alley
9. Tomorrow Is A Long Time
10. Love Letters
11. Beyond The Reef (original undubbed master)*
12. Come What May (alternate take 7)*
13. Fools Fall In Love
14. Indescribably Blue
15. I'll Remember You (original unedited master)*
16. If Everyday Was Like Christmas
17. Suppose (master)*
18. Guitar Man/What'd I Say (original unedited master)*
19. Big Boss Man
20. Mine
21. Just Call Me Lonesome
22. Hi-Heel Sneakers (original unedited master)*
23. You Don't Know Me
24. Singing Tree
25. Too Much Monkey Business
26. US Male

Recording Information:

Tracks 1 & 2 recorded May 27, 1963.
Tracks 3 – 5 recorded May 28, 1963.
Tracks 5 – 7 recorded January 12, 1964.
Tracks 8 – 10 recorded May 26, 1966.
Track 11 recorded May 27, 1966.
Tracks 12 & 13 recorded May 28, 1966.
Tracks 14 – 16 recorded June 10 – 12, 1966.
Track 17 recorded March 20, 1967.
Tracks 18 & 19 recorded September 10, 1967.
Tracks 20 – 24 recorded September 11, 1967.
Track 25 recorded January 15, 1968.
Track 26 recorded January 17, 1968.
All tracks recorded at RCA Studio B, Nashville.
An alternate take of "Come What May" was used as the master was lost at the time of this release. The master has now been located and was issued on the album "Long Lonely Highway" through the Follow That Dream collectors label in 2000.

Disc Four:

1. Long Back Limousine
2. This Is The Story
3. Wearin' That Loved On Look
4. You'll Think Of Me
5. A Little Bit Of Green
6. Gentle On My Mind
7. I'm Movin' On
8. Don't Cry Daddy
9. Inherit The Wind
10. Mama Liked The Roses
11. My Little Friend
12. In The Ghetto
13. Rubberneckin'
14. From A Jack To A King
15. Hey Jude
16. Without Love (There Is Nothing)
17. I'll Hold You In My Heart (Till I Can Hold You In My Arms)
18. I'll Be There
19. Suspicious Minds
20. True Love Travels On A Gravel Road
21. Stranger In My Own Home Town
22. And The Grass Won't Pay No Mind
23. Power Of My Love

Recording Information:

Tracks 1– 3 recorded January 13, 1969.
Tracks 4 – 7 recorded January 14, 1969.
Tracks 8 – 10 recorded January 15, 1969.
Track 11 recorded January 16, 1969.
Tracks 12 & 13 recorded January 20, 1969.
Tracks 14 & 15 recorded January 21, 1969.
Tracks 16 – 19 recorded January 22, 1969.
Tracks 20 – 22 recorded February 17, 1969.
Track 23 recorded February 18, 1969.
All tracks recorded at American Sound Studios, Memphis.

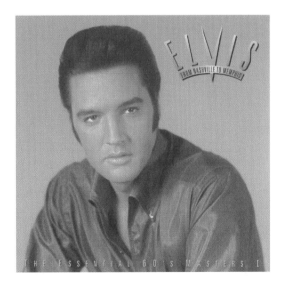

FROM NASHVILLE TO MEMPHIS – THE ESSENTIAL 60's MASTERS VOLUME 1 (1993) - Continued

Disc Five: (*indicates a previously unreleased performance)

1. After Loving You
2. Do You Know Who I Am
3. Kentucky Rain
4. Only The Strong Survive
5. It A Keeps Right On A Hurtin'
6. Any Day Now
7. If I'm A Fool (For Loving You)
8. The Fair Is Moving On
9. Who Am I
10. This Time/I Can't Stop Loving You (informal recording)*
11. In The Ghetto (take 4)*
12. Suspicious Minds (alternate take 6)*
13. Kentucky Rain (alternate take 9)*
14. Big Boss Man (alternate take 2)*
15. Down In The Alley (alternate take 1)*
16. Memphis Tennessee (1963 version – alternate take 1)*
17. I'm Yours (undubbed version – alternate take 1)*
18. His Latest Flame (alternate take 4)*
19. That's Someone You Never Forger (alternate take 1)*
20. Surrender (alternate take 1)*
21. It's Now Or Never (original undubbed master)*
22. Love Me Tender/Witchcraft (from "The Frank Sinatra Timex Special")*

Recording Information:

Track 11 recorded January 20, 1969
Track 12 recorded January 22, 1969.
Track 10 recorded February 17, 1969.
Tracks 1 & 2 recorded February 18, 1969.
Tracks 3, 4, & 13 recorded February 19, 1969.
Tracks 5 – 7 recorded February 20, 1969.
Track 8 recorded February 21, 1969.
Track 9 recorded February 22, 1969.
Tracks 1 – 13 recorded at American Sound Studios, Memphis.
Track 22 recorded March 26, 1960 at the Fountainbleau Hotel, Miami for "The Frank Sinatra Timex Show".
Track 21 recorded April 3, 1960.
Track 20 recorded October 30, 1960.
Track 19 recorded June 25, 1961.
Tracks 17 & 18 recorded June 26, 1961.
Track 16 recorded May 27, 1963.
Track 15 May 26, 1966.
Track 14 recorded September 10, 1967.
Tracks 14 – 21 recorded at RCA Studio B, Nashville.

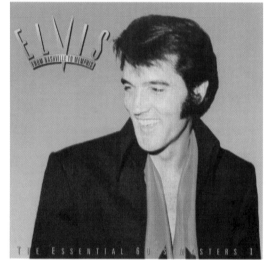
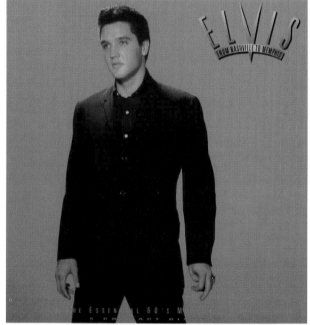

Released as a 5 CD box set with an illustrated colour booklet, sheet of stamps of Elvis' original 60's record covers, and an original 29 cent Elvis stamp and first day of issue envelope (right)
A vinyl edition was also produced.

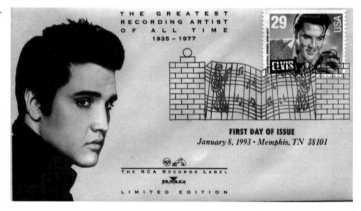

DOUBLE FEATURES: FRANKIE AND JOHNNY & PARADISE HAWAIIAN STYLE (1994)

Frankie And Johnny:

1. Frankie And Johnny
2. Come Along
3. Petunia, The Gardener's Daughter
4. Chesay
5. What Every Woman Lives For
6. Look Out Broadway
7. Beginner's Luck
8. Down By The Riverside And When The Saints Go Marching In
9. Shout It Out
10. Hard Luck
11. Please Don't Stop Loving Me
12. Everbody Come Aboard

Paradise Hawaiian Style:

13. Paradise Hawaiian Style
14. Quennie Wahine's Papaya
15. Scratch My Back
16. Drums Of The Islands
17. Datin'
18. A Dog's Life
19. House Of Sand
20. Stop Where You Are
21. This Is My Heaven
22. Sand Castles

Recording Information:

Tracks 1– 12 first released on the album "Frankie And Johnny" in 1966.
Tracks 13 – 22 first released on the album "Paradise Hawaiian Style" in 1966.
All material previously released.

DOUBLE FEATURES: SPINOUT & DOUBLE TROUBLE (1994)

Spinout:

1. Stop, Look And Listen
2. Adam And Evil
3. All That I Am
4. Never Say Yes
5. Am I Ready
6. Beach Shack
7. Spinout
8. Smorgasbord
9. I'll Be Back

Double Trouble:

10. Double Trouble
11. Baby If You'll Give Me All Of Your Love
12. Could I Fall In Love
13. Long Legged Girl With The Short Dress On
14. City By Night
15. Old MacDonald
16. I Love Only One Girl
17. There Is So Much World To See
18. It Won't Be Long

Recording Information:

Tracks 1 – 9 first released on the album "Spinout" a.k.a "California Holiday" in 1966.
Tracks 10 – 18 first released on the album "Double Trouble" in 1967.
All material previously released.

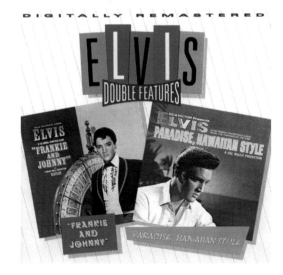

DOUBLE FEATURES: KISSIN' COUSINS & CLAMBAKE & STAY AWAY JOE (1994)

Kissin' Cousins:

1. Kissin' Cousins (number 2)
2. Smokey Mountain Boy
3. There's Gold In The Mountains
4. One Boy, Two Little Girls
5. Catchin' On Fast
6. Tender Feeling
7. Anyone (Could Fall In Love With You)
8. Barefoot Ballad
9. Once Is Enough
10. Kissin' Cousins

Recording Information:

Tracks 1 – 10 first released on the album
"Kissin' Cousins" in 1964.
Tracks 11 – 15, 17, & 18 first released on the
album "Clambake" in 1967.
Track 16 recorded February 21, 1967. Track 19 recorded February 23, 1967.
Tracks 16 & 19 recorded at RCA Studio B, Nashville for the United Artists Motion Picture "Clambake".
Tracks 20, 21, & 22 recorded October 1, 1967. Track 23 recorded January 16, 1968. Track 24 recorded January 17, 1968.
Tracks 20 – 24 recorded at RCA Studio B, Nashville for the MGM Motion Picture "Stay Away Joe".
Track 23 first released on the album "Speedway" in 1968.
Track 22 first released on the album "Flaming Star" in 1969.
Track 20 first released on the album "Let's Be Friends" in 1970.
Track 24 first released as 1968 single and included on the album "Almost In Love" in 1970.
Tracks 16, 19, & 21 are previously unreleased performances.

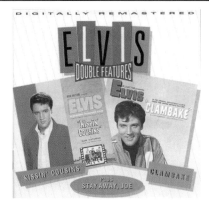

Clambake:

11. Clambake
12. Who Needs Money
13. A House That Has Everything
14. Confidence
15. Hey, Hey, Hey
16. You Don't Know Me (original film version)
17. The Girl I Never Loved
18. How Can You Lose What You Never Had
19. Clambake (reprise)

Stay Away Joe:

20. Stay Away Joe
21. Dominic
22. All I Needed Was The Rain
23. Going Home
24. Stay Away

AMAZING GRACE – HIS GREATEST SACRED PERFORMANCES (1994)

Disc One:

1. I Believe
2. Peace In The Valley
3. Take My Hand Precious Lord
4. It Is No Secret
5. Milky White Way
6. His Hand In Mine
7. I Believe In The Man In The Sky
8. He Knows Just What I Need
9. Mansion Over The Hilltop
10. In My Father's House
11. Joshua Fit The Battle
12. Swing Down Sweet Chariot
13. I'm Gonna Walk Dem Golden Stairs
14. If We Never Meet Again
15. Known Only To Him
16. Working On The Building
17. Crying In The Chapel
18. Run On
19. How Great Thou Art
20. Stand By Me
21. Where No One Stands Alone
22. So High
23. Farther Along
24. By And By
25. In The Garden
26. Somebody Bigger Than You And I
27. Without Him
28. If The Lord Wasn't Walking By My Side
29. Where Could I Go But To The Lord

Disc Two:

1. We Call On Him
2. You'll Never Walk Alone
3. Only Believe
4. Amazing Grace
5. Miracle of The Rosary
6. Lead Me, Guide Me
7. He Touched Me
8. I've Got Confidence
9. An Evening Prayer
10. Seeing Is Believing
11. A Thing Called Love
12. Put Your Hand In The Hand
13. Reach Out To Jesus
14. He Is My Everthing
15. There Is No God But God
16. I, John
17. Bosom Of Abraham
18. Help Me
19. If That Isn't Love
20. Why Me Lord (live)
21. How Great Thou Art (live)
22. I John
23. Bosom Of Abraham
24. You Better Run
25. Lead Me, Guide Me
26. Turn Your Eyes Upon Jesus/
Nearer My God To Thee

Recording Information:

Disc One:

Tracks 1 – 4 first released on the EP "Peace in The Valley" in 1957
and also included on "Elvis' Christmas Album" in 1957.
Tracks 5 – 16 first released on the album "His Hand In Mine" in
1960.
Track 17 first released as a 1965 single and also included on the
album "How Great Thou Art" in 1967.
Tracks 18 – 29 first released on the album "How Great Thou Art"
in 1967.

Disc Two:

Tracks 1 & 2 first released as a 1968 single and also included on
The album "You'll Never Walk Alone" in 1971.
Track 3 first released as a single and also included on the album
"Love Letters" in 1971.
Tracks 4 –11 & 13 – 17 first released on the album "He Touched
Me" in 1972.
Track 12 first released on the album "Elvis Now" in 1972.
Track 19 first released on the album "Good Times" in 1974.
Tracks 20 & 21 first released on the album "Elvis Recorded Live
On Stage In Memphis" in 1974.
Track 18 first released as a 1974 single and also included on the
album "Promised Land" in 1975.
Tracks 22 – 26 recorded March 31, 1972 during rehearsals at RCA
Studio A, Hollywood.
Tracks 22 – 26 are previously unreleased performances.

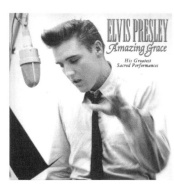

Left:

**An illustrated booklet was
included with this collection.**

IF EVERYDAY WAS LIKE CHRISTMAS (1994)

1. If Every Day Was Like Christmas
2. Blue Christmas
3. Here Comes Santa Claus
4. White Christmas
5. Santa Bring My Baby Back To Me
6. I'll Be Home For Christmas
7. O Little Town of Bethlehem
8. Santa Claus Is Back In Town
9. It Wont Seem Like Christmas Without You
10. If I Get Home On Christmas Day
11. Holly Leaves And Christmas Trees
12. Merry Christmas Baby
13. Silver Bells
14. I'll Be Home On Christmas Day (remake)
15. On A Snowy Christmas Night
16. Winter Wonderland
17. The Wonderful World Of Christmas
18. O Come All Ye Faithful
19. The First Noel
20. It Wont Seem Like Christmas Without You (alternate take 6)
21. Silver Bells (alternate take 1)
22. Holly Leaves And Christmas Trees (alternate take 8)
23. I'll Be Home On Christmas Day
24. Christmas Message From Elvis/Silent Night

Recording Information:

Track 1 first released as a 1966 single and also included on the 1970 budget issue of "Elvis' Christmas Album".
Tracks 2 – 8 & 24 ("Silent Night" only) first released on "Elvis' Christmas Album" in 1957.
Tracks 9 – 13, 15 – 18, & 23 first released on "Elvis Sings The Wonderful World Of Christmas" in 1971.
Track 14 first released on the album "Memories Of Christmas" in 1982 in the US, and "It Won't Seem Like Christmas Without You" in the UK.
Track 21 first released as a cassette single in 1992.
Tracks 20, 21, & 22 recorded May 15, 1971. Track 14 recorded June 10, 1971.
Tracks 14, 20, 21, & 22 recorded at RCA Studio B, Nashville.
Tracks 20 & 22 are previously unreleased versions.

HEART AND SOUL (1995)

1. Love Me Tender (stereo version)
2. Young And Beautiful
3. Love Me
4. I Want You, I Need You, I Love You
5. Don't
6. As Long As I Have You
7. Loving You
8. Fame And Fortune
9. The Girl Of My Best Friend
10. Are You Lonesome Tonight
11. Can't Help Falling In Love
12. She's Not You
13. Anything That's Part Of You
14. Love Letters
15. It's Now Or Never
16. It Hurts Me
17. I Just Can't Help Believin'
18. Always On My Mind
19. Suspicious Minds
20. I've Lost You
21. You Don't Have To Say You Love Me
22. Bridge Over Troubled Water.

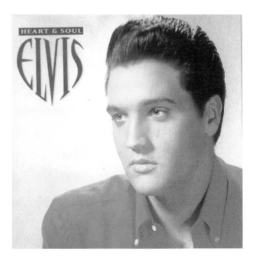

Recording Information:

"Love Me Tender" and "I've Lost You" were released in stereo for the first time.
"I've Lost You" is the studio version which was recorded June 4, 1970 at RCA Studio B, Nashville, and originally released as a single in 1970.
The version included on this album has a longer fade out than the single version.
The studio version of "Bridge Over Troubled Water" was first issued on the "That's The Way It Is" album in 1970 with overdubbed applause added at the end of the song. It is included on this release without the overdubbed applause for the first time.
All other performances are previously released masters.

DOUBLE FEATURES: FLAMING STAR & FOLLOW THAT DREAM & WILD IN THE COUNTRY (1995)

Flaming Star:

1. Flaming Star
2. Summer Kisses, Winter Tears
3. Britches
4. A Cane And A High Starched Collar
5. Black Star
6. Summer Kisses, Winter Tears (movie version)
7. Flaming Star (end title version)

Wild In The Country:

8. Wild In the Country
9. I Slipped, I Stumbled, I Fell
10. Lonely Man
11. In My Way
12. Forget Me Never
13. Lonely Man (solo)
14. I Slipped, I Stumbled, I Fell (alternate master)

Follow That Dream:

15. Follow That Dream
16. Angel
17. What A Wonderful Life
18. I'm Not The Marrying Kind
19. A Whistling Tune
20. Sound Advice

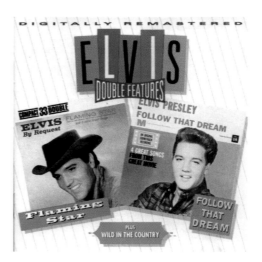

Recording Information:

Tracks 2– 6 recorded August 8. 1960. Tracks 1 & 7 recorded October 7, 1960.
Tracks 1– 7 recorded at Radio Recorders, Hollywood for the 20th Century Fox Motion Picture "Flaming Star".
Tracks 1 & 2 first released on the EP "Elvis By Request" in 1961.
Track 4 first released on the album "Elvis A Legendary Performer Volume 2" in 1976.
Track 3 first released on the album "Elvis A Legendary Performer Volume 3" in 1978.
Track 5 first released on the album "Collectors Gold" in 1991.
Tracks 6 &7 are previously unreleased versions.
Tracks 8 & 10 – 13 recorded November 7, 1960. Tracks 9 & 14 recorded November 8, 1960.
Tracks 8 – 14 recorded at Radio Recorders, Hollywood for the 20th Century Fox Motion Picture "Wild In The Country".
Tracks 8 & 10 first released as singles in 1961.
Track 9 first released on the album "Something For Everybody" in 1961.
Tracks 11 & 12 first released on the album "Elvis For Everyone" in 1965.
Track 13 was first released on the album "Collectors Gold" in 1991.
Track 14 is a previously unreleased version.
Tracks 15 – 20 recorded July 2, 1961 at RCA Studio B, Nashville for the Mirisch United Artists Motion Picture "Follow That Dream".
Tracks 15 – 18 first released on the EP "Follow That Dream" in 1962.
Track 20 first released on the album "Elvis For Everyone" in 1965.
Track 19 was first released on the album "Collectors Gold" in 1991.
The stereo masters for tracks 15, 17 18, & 20 have been lost. Mono masters were used on this release.

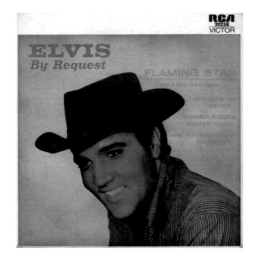

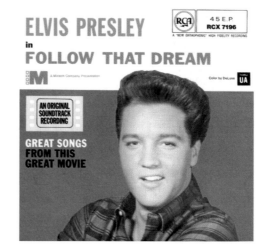

Above left: the 1961 EP Elvis By Request which included "Flaming Star" and "Summer Kisses, Winter Tears".

Above right: the "Follow That Dream" EP.

DOUBLE FEATURES: EASY COME, EASY GO & SPEEDWAY (1995)

Easy Come, Easy Go:

1. Easy Come, Easy Go
2. The Love Machine
3. Yoga Is As Yoga Does
4. You Gotta Stop
5. Sing You Children
6. I'll Take Love
7. She's A Machine
8. The Love Machine (alternate take 7)
9. Sing You Children (alternate take 1)
10. She's A Machine (alternate take 13)

Speedway:

11. Suppose
12. Speedway
13. There Ain't Nothing Like A Song (with Nancy Sinatra)
14. Your Time Hasn't Come Yet Baby
15. Who Are You (Who Am I?)
16. He's Your Uncle, Not Your Dad
17. Let Yourself Go
18. Five Sleepy Heads
19. Suppose
20. Your Groovy Self (Nancy Sinatra)

Recording Information:

Tracks 1, 5, 6, & 9 recorded September 28, 1966. Tracks 2, 3, 4, 7, 8, & 10 recorded September 29, 1966.
Tracks 1 – 10 recorded at Paramount Studios, Hollywood for the Paramount Motion Picture "Easy Come, Easy Go".
Tracks 1 – 6 first released on the EP "Easy Come, Easy Go" in 1967.
Track 7 first released on the album "Elvis Sings Flaming Star" in 1969.
Tracks 8, 9, & 10 are previously unreleased versions.
Track 11 recorded June 20, 1967 at MGM Studios, Hollywood for the MGM Motion Picture "Speedway".
Tracks 12 – 20 first released on the album "Speedway" in 1968.

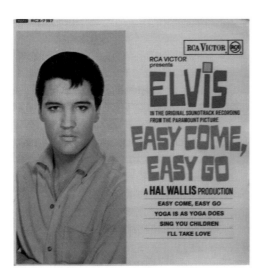

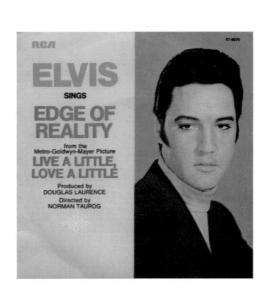

Above left: the original "Easy Come, Easy Go" EP.

Above right: the single "Edge Of Reality" from "Live A Little, Love A Little" featured on the album:
"Double Features: Live A Little, Love A Little & The Trouble With Girls & Charro & Change Of Habit". (1995)

Further details are on the next page.

DOUBLE FEATURES: LIVE A LITTLE, LOVE A LITTLE & THE TROUBLE WITH GIRLS & CHARRO & CHANGE OF HABIT (1995)

Live A Little, Love A Little:

1. Almost In Love
2. A Little Less Conversation
3. Wonderful World
4. Edge Of Reality
5. A Little Less Conversation (album version)

Charro:

6. Charro
7. Let's Forget About The Stars

The Trouble With Girls:

8. Clean Up Your Own Backyard
9. Swing Down Sweet Chariot
10. Signs Of The Zodiac
11. Almost
12. The Whiffenpoof Song
13. Violet
14. Clean Up Your Own Backyard (undubbed version)
15. Almost (undubbed version)

Change Of Habit

16. Have A Happy
17. Let's Be Friends
18. Change Of Habit
19. Let Us Pray
20. Rubberkneckin'

Recording Information:

Tracks 1– 5 recorded March 7, 1968 at Western Recorders, Los Angeles for the MGM Motion Picture "Live A Little, Love A Little".
Tracks 1, 2, & 4 were first released as singles in 1968.
Tracks 1 & 4 were also included on the album "Almost In Love" in 1970.
Track 3 was first released on the album "Elvis Sings Flaming Star" in 1969.
Track 5 was first released on the album "Almost In Love" in 1970.
Tracks 6 & 7 recorded October 15, 1968 at Samuel Goldwyn Studios, Hollywood for the National General Motion Picture "Charro".
Track 6 first released as a 1969 single and also included on the album "Almost In Love" in 1970.
Track 7 first released on the album "Let's Be Friends" in 1970.
Tracks 8 -15 recorded August 23, 1968 at United Recorders, Hollywood for the MGM Motion Picture "The Trouble With Girls And How To Get Into It".
Track 8 first released as 1969 single and also included on the album "Almost In Love" in 1970.
Track 11 first released on the album "Let's Be Friends" in 1970.
Track 9 first released on the album "Elvis A Legendary Performer Volume 4" in 1983.
Tracks 10 & 12 – 15 are previously unreleased.
Track 20 recorded January 20, 1969 at American Sound Studios, Memphis.
Tracks 17 & 18 recorded March 5, 1969. Tracks 16 & 19 recorded March 6, 1969.
Tracks 16 – 19 recorded at Decca Universal Studios, Hollywood for the Universal Motion Picture "Change Of Habit".
Although not recorded at a soundtrack session "Rubberneckin'" was also included in the soundtrack of the Universal Motion Picture "Change Of Habit".
Track 20 was first released as a 1969 single and also included on the album "Almost In Love" in 1970.
Tracks 16, 17, & 18 first released on the album "Let's Be Friends" in 1970.
Track 19 first released on the album "You'll Never Walk Alone" in 1971.

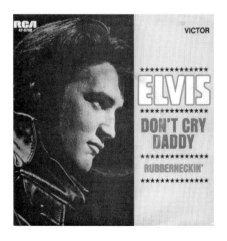

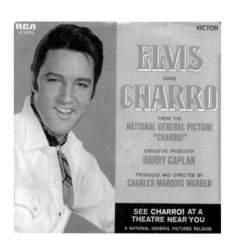

Above left: the single "Rubberneckin'" from "Change Of Habit".

Above right: the single "Charro".

COMMAND PERFORMANCES - THE ESSENTIAL '60's MASTERS VOLUME 2 (1995)

Disc One:

1. GI Blues
2. Wooden Heart
3. Shoppin' Around
4. Doin' The Best I Can
5. Flaming Star
6. Wild In The Country
7. Lonely Man
8. Blue Hawaii
9. Rock A Hula Baby
10. Can't Help Falling In Love
11. Beach Boy Blues
12. Hawaiian Wedding Song
13. Follow That Dream (alternate take 2)
14. Angel
15. King Of The Whole Wide World
16. I Got Lucky
17. Girls! Girls! Girls!
18. Because Of Love
19. Return To Sender
20. One Broken Heart For Sale
21. I'm Falling In Love Tonight
22. They Remind Me Too Much Of You
23. Fun In Acapulco
24. Bossa Nova Baby
25. Marguerita
26. Mexico
27. Kissin' Cousins
28. One Boy, Two Little Girls
29. Once Is Enough
30. Viva Las Vegas
31. What'd I Say

Disc Two:

1. Roustabout
2. Poison Ivy League
3. Little Egypt
4. There's A Brand New Day On The Horizon
5. Girl Happy
6. Puppet On A String
7. Do The Clam
8. Harem Holiday
9. So Close, Yet So Far
10. Frankie And Johnny
11. Please Don't Stop Loving Me
12. Paradise Hawaiian Style
13. This Is My Heaven
14. Spinout
15. All That I Am
16. I'll Be Back
17. Easy Come, Easy Go
18. Double Trouble
19. Long Legged Girl (With The Short Dress On)
20. Clambake
21. You Don't Know Me
22. Stay Away Joe
23. Speedway
24. Your Time Hasn't Come Yet Baby
25. Let Yourself Go
26. Almost In Love
27. A Little Less Conversation
28. Edge Of Reality
29. Charro
30. Clean Up Your Own Back Yard
31. Change Of Habit

Recording Information:

Disc One:

Tracks 1– 4 from the Paramount Motion Picture "GI Blues".
Track 5 from the 20th Century Fox Motion Picture "Flaming Star".
Tracks 6 & 7 from the 20th Century Fox Motion Picture "Wild In The Country".
Tracks 8 – 12 from the Paramount Motion Picture "Blue Hawaii".
Tracks 13 & 14 from the Mirisch United Artists Motion Picture "Follow That Dream".
Tracks 15 & 16 from the Mirisch United Artists Motion Picture "Kid Galahad".
Tracks 17 – 19 from the Paramount Motion Picture "Girls! Girls! Girls!"
Tracks 20 – 22 from the MGM Motion Picture "It Happened At The Worlds Fair".
Tracks 23 –26 from the Paramount Motion Picture "Fun In Acapulco".
Tracks 27 – 29 from the MGM Motion Picture "Kissin' Cousins".
Tracks 30 & 31 from the MGM Motion Picture "Love In Las Vegas" a.k.a "Viva Las Vegas".

Disc Two:

Tracks 1– 4 from the Paramount Motion Picture "Roustabout".
Tracks 5 – 7 from the MGM Motion Picture "Girl Happy".
Tracks 8 & 9 from the MGM Motion Picture "Harem Holiday" a.k.a "Harum Scarum".
Tracks 10 & 11 from the United Artists Motion Picture "Frankie And Johnny".
Tracks 12 & 13 from the Paramount Motion Picture "Paradise Hawaiian Style".
Tracks 13 – 16 from the MGM Motion Picture "California Holiday" a.k.a "Spinout".
Track 17 from the Paramount Motion Picture "Easy Come, Easy Go".
Tracks 18 & 19 from the MGM Motion Picture "Double Trouble".
Tracks 20 & 21 from the United Artists Motion Picture "Clambake".
Track 22 from the MGM Motion Picture "Stay Away Joe".
Tracks 23 – 25 from the MGM Motion Picture "Speedway".
Tracks 26 – 28 from the MGM Motion Picture "Live A Little, Love A Little".
Track 29 from the National General Motion Picture "Charro".
Track 30 from the MGM Motion Picture "The Trouble With Girls And How To Get Into It".
Track 31 from the Universal Motion Picture "Change Of Habit".
All tracks are previously released.
As the stereo master take of "Follow That Dream" has been lost, alternate take 2 was used on this release.
This version was first released on the album "Elvis Aron Presley" in 1980.

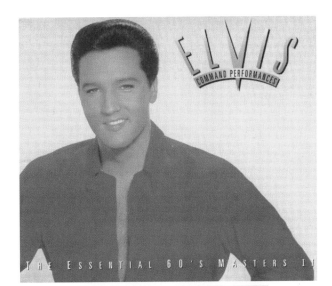

Right:

**an illustrated booklet was
included with this collection.**

WALK A MILE IN MY SHOES - THE ESSENTIAL '70's MASTERS (1995)

Disc One: The Singles

1. The Wonder Of You
2. I've Lost You
3. The Next Step Is Love
4. You Don't Have To Say You Love Me
5. Patch It Up
6. I Really Don't Want To Know
7. There Goes My Everything
8. Rags To Riches
9. Where Did They Go Lord
10. Life
11. I'm Leavin'
12. Heart Of Rome
13. It's Only Love
14. The Sound Of Your Cry
15. I Just Can't Help Believin'
16. How The Web Was Woven
17. Until It's Time For You To Go
18. We Can Make The Morning
19. An American Trilogy
20. The First Time Ever I Saw Your Face
21. Burning Love
22. It's A Matter Of Time
23. Separate Ways

Disc Two: The Singles

1. Always On My Mind
2. Fool
3. Steamroller Blues
4. Raised On Rock
5. For Ol' Times Sake
6. I've Got A Thing About You Baby
7. Take Good Care Of Her
8. If You Talk In Your Sleep
9. Promised Land
10. It's Midnight
11. My Boy
12. Loving Arms
13. T.R.O.U.B.L.E
14. Mr Songman
15. Bringing It Back
16. Pieces Of My Life
17. Green Grass Of Home
18. Thinking About You
19. Hurt
20. For The Heart
21. Moody Blue
22. She Thinks I Still Care
23. Way Down
24. Pledging My Love

Recording Information:

Track 1 recorded live February 18, 1970 at the International Hotel Las Vegas.
Tracks 2 & 14 recorded June 4, 1970.
Track 16 recorded June 5, 1970.
Tracks 4, 10, & 12 recorded June 6, 1970.
Tracks 3 & 6 recorded June 7, 1970.
Tracks 5 & 7 recorded June 8, 1970.
Tracks 8 & 9 recorded September 22, 1970.
Track 20 recorded March 15, 1971.
Track 17 recorded May 17, 1971.
Tracks 11, 13, & 18 recorded May 20, 1971.
Tracks 2 – 14, 16 – 18, & 20 recorded at RCA Studio B, Nashville.
Track 15 recorded live August 11, 1970, Dinner Show at the International, Hotel, Las Vegas.
Track 19 recorded live February 16, 1972 at the Hilton Hotel, Las Vegas.
Track 23 recorded March 27, 1972.
Track 21 recorded March 28, 1972.
Track 22 recorded March 29, 1972.
Tracks 21– 23 recorded at RCA Studio C, Hollywood.

Recording Information:

Track 2 recorded March 28, 1972.
Track 1 recorded March 29, 1972.
Tracks 1 & 2 recorded at RCA Studio C, Hollywood.
Track 3 recorded live January 14, 1973 at the Honolulu, International Centre, Honolulu, Hawaii.
Track 7 recorded July 21, 1973.
Track 6 recorded July 22, 1973.
Tracks 4 & 5 recorded July 23, 1973.
Track 10 recorded December 10, 1973.
Track 8 recorded December 11, 1973.
Tracks 14 & 18 recorded December 12, 1973.
Track 9 recorded December 15, 1973.
Tracks 11& 12 recorded December 13, 1973.
Tracks 4 – 12, 14, & 18 recorded at Stax Studios, Memphis.
Track 17 recorded March 11, 1975.
Tracks 13, 15, & 16 recorded March 12, 1975.
Tracks 13, 15, 16, & 17 recorded at RCA Studio C, Hollywood.
Track 22 recorded February 2, 1976.
Track 21 recorded February 4, 1976.
Tracks 19 & 20 recorded February 5, 1976.
Tracks 23 & 24 recorded October 29, 1976.
Tracks 19 – 24 recorded in the "Jungle Room" of Elvis' Graceland, Mansion, Memphis.

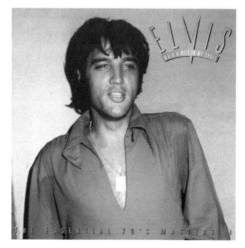

WALK A MILE IN MY SHOES - THE ESSENTIAL '70's MASTERS (1995) Continued

Disc Three: Studio Highlights 1970 – 71:

1. Twenty Days And Twenty Nights
2. I Was Born About Ten Thousand Years Ago
3. The Fool
4. A Hundred Years From Now (informal recording)
5. Little Cabin On The Hill
6. Cindy, Cindy
7. Bridge Over Troubled Water
8. Got My Mojo Working/Keep Your Hands Off Of It
9. It's Your Baby, You Rock It
10. Stranger In The Crowd
11. Mary In The Morning
12. It Ain't No Big Thing (But It's Growing)
13. Just Pretend
14. Faded Love (original unedited version)
15. Tomorrow Never Comes (including false start)
16. Make The World Go Away
17. Funny How Time Slips Away
18. I Washed My Hands In Muddy Water (long version)
19. Snowbird
20. Whole Lotta Shakin' Goin' On
21. Amazing Grace (alternate take 2)
22. (That's What You Get) For Lovin' Me
23. Lady Madonna (informal recording)

Recording Information:

Tracks 1 – 6 recorded June 4, 1970.
Tracks 7 – 11 recorded June 5, 1970.
Tracks 12 & 13 recorded June 6, 1970.
Tracks 14 – 18 recorded June 7, 1970.
Tracks 19 & 20 recorded September 22, 1970.
Tracks 21 & 22 recorded March 15, 1971.
Tracks 23 recorded May 1971.
All tracks recorded at RCA Studio B, Nashville.

Notes on the unreleased tracks:

Disc One:
Edited versions of tracks 14 & 18 were first released on the "Elvis Country" album in 1971. The unedited masters are included on this release for the first time.
Track 15 was also first released on the "Elvis Country" album, and only the false start, which features Elvis singing one line of Roy Orbison's "Running Scared" is previously unreleased.
Tracks 4, 21, & 23 are previously unreleased recordings.

Disc Two:
Track 3 was recorded during a jam session and was edited for it's inclusion on the "Elvis" album in 1973.
A longer edit was included on this release.
The complete master can be found on the 1979 album "Our Memories Of Elvis Volume 2".
Tracks 2, 7, 8, 10, 16, & 20 are previously unreleased recordings.

Disc Four: Studio Highlights 1971 – 76:

1. Merry Christmas Baby
2. I Shall Be Released (informal recording)
3. Don't Think Twice It's All Right (jam edit)
4. It's Still Here (original undubbed version)
5. I'll Take You Home Again Kathleen (original undubbed version)
6. I Will Be True
7. My Way (master)
8. For The Good Times (master)
9. Just A Little Bit
10. It's Diff'rent Now (rehearsal)
11. Are You Sincere
12. I Got A Feelin' In My Body
13. You Asked Me To
14. Good Time Charlie's Got The Blues
15. Talk About The Good Times
16. Tiger Man (jam)
17. I Can Help
18. Susan When She Tried
19. Shake A Hand
20. She Thinks I Still Care (alternate take 2B)
21. Danny Boy
22. Love Coming Down
23. He'll Have To Go

Recording Information:

Track 1 recorded May 15, 1971.
Track 2 recorded May 1971.
Track 3 recorded May 16, 1971.
Tracks 4, 5, & 6 recorded May, 1971.
Track 7 recorded June 10, 1971.
Tracks 1 – 7 recorded at RCA Studio B, Nashville.
Track 8 recorded March 27, 1972 at RCA Studio C, Hollywood.
Track 9 recorded July 22, 1973.
Track 10 recorded July 1973. Exact date unknown.
Tracks 9 & 10 recorded at Stax Studios, Memphis.
Track 11 recorded September 23, 1973 at Elvis' Palm Springs Home, California.
Track 12 recorded December 10, 1973.
Track 13 recorded December 11, 1973.
Track 14 recorded December 13, 1973.
Track 15 recorded December 14, 1973.
Tracks 12 – 15 recorded at Stax Studios, Memphis.
Track 17 & 18 recorded March 11, 1975.
Track 16 & 19 recorded March 12, 1975.
Tracks 16 – 19 recorded at RCA Studio C, Hollywood.
Track 20 recorded February 2, 1976.
Track 21 recorded February 5, 1976.
Track 22 recorded February 6, 1976.
Track 23 recorded October 30, 1976.
Tracks 20 – 23 recorded in the "Jungle Room" of Elvis' Graceland mansion, Memphis.

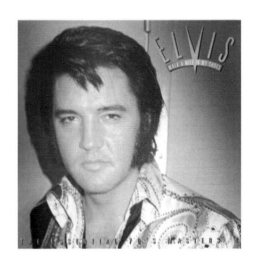

WALK A MILE IN MY SHOES - THE ESSENTIAL '70's MASTERS (1995) Continued

Disc Five: The Elvis Presley Show:

1. See See Rider
2. Men With Broken Hearts (short poem)
3. Walk A Mile in My Shoes
4. Polk Salad Annie
5. Let It Be Me
6. Proud Mary
7. Something (master)
8. You've Lost That Lovin' Feelin'
9. Heartbreak Hotel
10. I Was The One
11. One Night
12. Never Been To Spain (master)
13. You Gave Me A Mountain (master)
14. It's Impossible
15. A Big Hunk O' Love (master)
16. It's Over (master)
17. The Impossible Dream
18. Reconsider Baby
19. I'll Remember You
20. I'm So Lonesome I Could Cry
21. Suspicious Minds
22. Unchained Melody
23. The Twelfth Of Never (rehearsal)
24. Softly As I Leave You (rehearsal)
25. Alla' En El "Rancho Grande" (informal rehearsal)
26. Froggy Went A Courtin' (informal rehearsal)
27. Stranger In My Own Home Town (informal rehearsal)

Recording Information:

Track 6 recorded live February 16, 1970.
Track 5 recorded live February 17, 1970.
Tracks 1 & 4 recorded live February 18, 1970.
Track 3 recorded live February 19, 1970.
Tracks 2, 7, 9, & 11 recorded live August 11, 1970, Midnight Show.
Tracks 8 & 10 recorded live August 13, 1970, Midnight Show.
Tracks 1 – 11 recorded a the International Hotel, Las Vegas.
Tracks 12 – 15 & 17 recorded live February 16, 1972.
Track 16 recorded live February 17, 1972.
Tracks 12 – 17 recorded at the Hilton Hotel, Las Vegas.
Tracks 18 & 19 recorded live June 10, 1972 during the Afternoon Show at Madison Square Garden, New York.
Tracks 20 & 21 recorded live January 14, 1973 at the Honolulu International Centre, Honolulu, Hawaii.
Track 22 recorded live April 24, 1977 at the Crisler Arena, Ann Arbor, Michigan.
Track 25 recorded July 15, 1970.
Track 26 recorded July 29, 1970.
Tracks 25 & 26 recorded during rehearsals at MGM Stage 1, Culver City, California.
Track 27 recorded July 24, 1970.
Tracks 23 & 24 recorded August 16, 1974.
Tracks 23, 24, & 27 recorded during rehearsals at RCA Studios, Hollywood.
Tracks 2, 7, 9, 10, 11, 12, 13, 15, 16, 23, 24, 25, 26, & 27 are previously unreleased recordings.

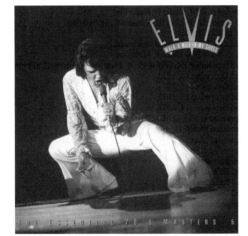

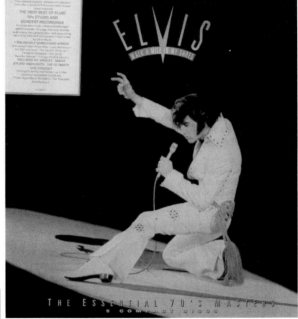

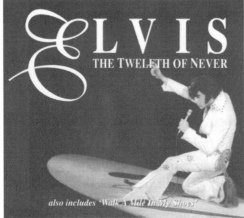

Released as a 5 CD box set with an illustrated colour booklet featuring liner notes by Dave Marsh.

Left: a Dutch promotional CD single featuring "The Twelfth Of Never" and "Walk A Mile In My Shoes".

ELVIS '56 (1996)

1. Heartbreak Hotel
2. My Baby Left Me
3. Blue Suede Shoes
4. So Glad Your Mine
5. Tutti Frutti
6. One Sided Love Affair
7. Love Me
8. Any Place Is Paradise
9. Paralyzed
10. Ready Teddy
11. Too Much
12. Hound Dog
13. Any Way You Want Me
14. Don't Be Cruel
15. Lawdy Miss Clawdy
16. Shake Rattle And Roll (alternate take 8)
17. I Want You, I Need You, I Love You
18. Rip It Up
19. Heartbreak Hotel (alternate take 5)
20. I Got A Woman
21. I Was The One
22. Money Honey

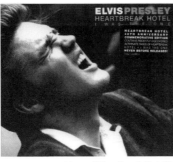

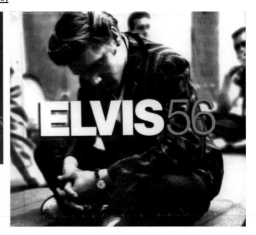

Above: "Heartbreak Hotel"
CD Single

Right "Elvis '56"

Recording Information:

All material previously released except "Heartbreak Hotel" (alternate take 5) - recorded January 10, 1956 at RCA Studios, Nashville.
Alternate take 5 of "Heartbreak Hotel" was also included on a 4 track CD single issued to promote the album.
The single also included the previously unreleased "I Was The One" (alternate take 2) which was not included on the album.
"I Was The One " (alternate take 2) recorded January 11, 1956 at RCA Studios, Nashville.

ESSENTIAL ELVIS VOLUME 4 - A HUNDRED YEARS FROM NOW (1996)

1. I Didn't Make It On Playing Guitar (informal jam)
2. I Washed My Hands In Muddy Water
(undubbed/unedited master)
3. Little Cabin On The Hill (alternate take 1)
4. A Hundred Years From Now (alternate take 2)
5. I've Lost You (alternate take 6)
6. Got My Mojo Working/Keep Your Hands Off It
(undubbed/unedited master)
7. You Don't Have To Say You Love Me (alternate take 2)
8. It Ain't No Big Thing (But It's Growing) (alternate take 2)
9. Cindy, Cindy (alternate take 1)
10. Faded Love (country version)
11. The Fool (alternate take 1)
12. Rags To Riches (alternate take 3)
13. Just Pretend (alternate take 2)
14. If I Were You (alternate take 5)
15. Faded Love (alternate take 3)
16. Where Did They Go Lord (alternate take 1)
17. It's Only Love (alternate take 9)
18. Until It's Time For You To Go
(alternate master – take 10)
19. Patch It Up (alternate take 9)
20. Whole Lotta Shakin' Goin' On
(undubbed/unedited master)
21. Bridge Of Troubled Water (alternate take 5)
22. The Lord's Prayer (informal Performance)

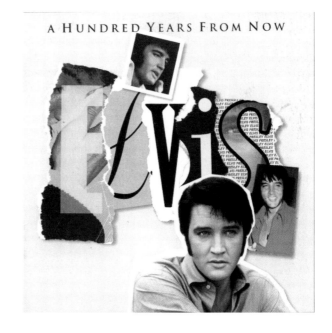

A HUNDRED YEARS FROM NOW

Recording Information:

Tracks 3, 4, 5, 9, 10, & 11 recorded June 4, 1970.
Track 6 & 21 recorded June 5, 1970.
Track 1, 7, 8, & 13 recorded June 6, 1970.
Track 2 & 15 recorded June 7, 1970.
Track 14 & 19 recorded June 8, 1970.
Track 12, 16, & 20 recorded September 22, 1970.
Track 22 recorded May 16, 1971.
Track 17 recorded May 20, 1971.
Track 18 recorded June 8, 1971.
All tracks recorded at RCA Studio B, Nashville.
Tracks 2, 6, & 20 are previously released masters.
The complete performances of tracks 6 & 20 are included on this release for the first time.
All other tracks are previously unreleased performances.

GREAT COUNTRY SONGS (1996)

1. I Forgot To Remember To Forget
2. Blue Moon Of Kentucky
3. When My Blue Moon Turns To Gold Again
4. Old Shep
5. Your Cheatin' Heart (alternate take 9)
6. (Now And Then) There's A Fool Such As I
7. Just Call Me Lonesome (alternate take 6)
8. There Goes My everything (alternate take 1)
9. Kentucky Rain
10. From A Jack To A King
11. I'll You In My Heart (Till I Can't Hold You In My Arms)
12. I Really Don't Want To Know
13. It Keeps Right On A Hurtin'
14. Green, Green Grass Of Home (alternate take 1)
15. Fairytale (alternate take 2)
16. Gentle On My Mind
17. Make The World Go Away
18. You Asked Me To
19. Funny How Time Slips Away
20. Help Me Make It Through The Night (alternate take 3)
21. Susan When She Tried
22. He'll Have To Go
23. Always On My Mind
24. Guitar Man (remake)

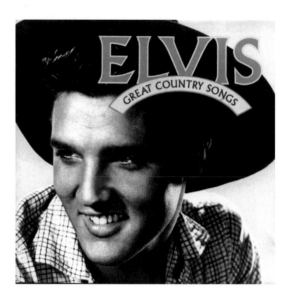

Recording Information:

Track 7 recorded September 11, 1967.
Track 8 recorded June 8, 1970.
Track 20 recorded May 17, 1971.
Tracks 7, 8, & 20 recorded at RCA Studio B, Nashville.
Track 15 recorded March 10, 1975.
Track 14 recorded March 11, 1975.
Tracks 14 & 15 recorded at RCA Studio C, Hollywood.
Tracks 7, 8, 14, 15, & 20 are previously unreleased alternate takes.
All other tracks are previously released performances.

AN AFTERNOON IN THE GARDEN (1997)

1. Introduction: Also Sprach Zarathustra
2. That's All Right
3. Proud Mary
4. Never Been To Spain
5. You Don't Have To Say You Love Me
6. Until It's Time For You To Go
7. You've Lost That Lovin' Feelin'
8. Polk Salad Annie
9. Love Me
10. All Shook Up
11. Heartbreak Hotel
12. Teddy Bear/Don't Be Cruel
13. Love Me Tender
14. Blue Suede Shoes
15. Reconsider Baby
16. Hound Dog
17. I'll Remember You
18. Suspicious Minds
19. Introductions By Elvis
20. For The Good Times
21. An American Trilogy
22. Funny How Time Slips Away
23. I Cant Stop Loving You
24. Can't Help Falling In Love

Recording Information:

All tracks recorded live June 10, 1972 during the afternoon show at Madison Square Garden, New York.
"I Can't Stop Loving You" was first released on the album "Welcome To My World" in 1977.
"Reconsider Baby" and "I'll Remember You" were first released on the album "Elvis A Legendary Performer Volume 4" in 1983, and were also included on the '70's box set "Walk A Mile In My Shoes" in 1995.
All other performances are previously unreleased.

PLATINUM – A LIFE IN MUSIC (1997)

Disc One:

1. I'll Never Stand In Your Way (demo)
2. That's All Right (alternate take)
3. Blue Moon (alternate take)
4. Good Rockin' Tonight (master)
5. Mystery Train (master)
6. I Got A Woman (alternate take)
7. Heartbreak Hotel (alternate take)
8. I'm Counting On You (alternate take)
9. Shake Rattle & Roll/Flip, Flop & Fly (live)
10. Lawdy Miss Clawdy (alternate take)
11. I Want You, I Need You, I Love You (alternate take)
12. Hound Dog (master)
13. Don't Be Cruel (master)
14. Rip It Up (alternate take)
15. Love Me Tender (master)
16. When The Saints Go Marching In (home recording)
17. All Shook Up (master)
18. Peace In The Valley (alternate take)
19. Blueberry Hill (demo)
20. Teddy Bear (master)
21. Jailhouse Rock (master)
22. New Orleans (master)
23. I Need Your Love Tonight (alternate take)
24. A Big Hunk O' Love (alternate take)
25. Bad Nauheim Medley:
a) I'll Take You Home Again Kathleen
b) I Will Be True
c) It's Been So Long Darling
d) Apron Strings
e) There's No Tomorrow

Recording Information:

Track 1 recorded 1953 at Sun Studios, Memphis.
Track 3 recorded August 19, 1954 at Sun Studios, Memphis.
Tracks 6 & 7 recorded January 10, 1956.
Track 8 recorded January 11, 1956.
Tracks 6 – 8 recorded at RCA Studios, Nashville.
Track 10 recorded February 3, 1956 at RCA Studios, New York.
Track 11 recorded April 14, 1956 at RCA Studio B, Nashville.
Track 14 recorded September 3, 1956 at Radio Recorders, Hollywood.
Track 16 recorded December, 1956.
Track 18 recorded January 13, 1957 at Radio Recorders, Hollywood.
Track 19 recorded January 14 – 18, 1957 at the Paramount Scoring Stage, Hollywood.
Tracks 23 & 24 recorded June 10, 1958 at RCA Studio B, Nashville.
Track 25 recorded 1959 during Elvis' army service in Bad Nauheim, Germany.
All other tracks are previously released recordings.

Disc Two:

1. Stuck On You (live)
2. Fame And Fortune (live)
3. It's Now Or Never (master)
4. It Feels So Right (alternate take)
5. A Mess Of Blues (alternate take)
6. Are You Lonesome Tonight (master)
7. Reconsider Baby (master)
8. Tonight Is So Right For Love (alternate take)
9. His Hand In Mine (alternate take)
10. Milky White Way (alternate take)
11. I'm Comin' Home (alternate take)
12. I Feel So Bad (alternate take)
13. Can't Help Falling In Love (master)
14. Something Blue (alternate take)
15. Return To Sender (master)
16. Bossa Nova Baby (alternate take)
17. How Great Thou Art (alternate take)
18. Guitar Man (alternate take)
19. You'll Never Walk Alone (alternate take)
20. Oh How I Love Jesus (home recording)
21. Tennessee Waltz (home recording)
22. Blowin' In The Wind (home recording)
23. I Cant Help it (If I'm Still In Love With You) (home recording)
24. I'm Beginning To Forget You (home recording)
25. After Loving You (home recording)

Recording Information:

Tracks 1 & 2 recorded March 26, 1960 at the Fountainbleau Hotel, Miami for "The Frank Sinatra Timex Show".
Tracks 4 & 5 recorded March 21, 1960 at RCA Studio B, Nashville.
Track 8 recorded April 27, 1960 at RCA Studios, Hollywood for the Paramount Motion Picture "GI Blues".
Tracks 9 & 10 recorded October 30, 1960.
Tracks 11 & 12 recorded March 12, 1961.
Track 14 recorded March 18, 1962.
Tracks 9 – 12, & 14 recorded at RCA Studio B, Nashville.
Track 16 recorded January 22, 1963 at Radio Recorders, Hollywood for the Paramount Motion Picture "Fun In Acapulco".
Track 17 recorded May 25, 1966.
Track 18 recorded September 10, 1967.
Track 19 recorded September 11, 1967.
Tracks 17 – 19 recorded at RCA Studio B, Nashville.
Tracks 20 – 22 recorded 1966 at Rocca Place, Hollywood.
Tracks 23 & 24 recorded 1961.
Track 25 recorded 1966 at Rocca Place, Hollywood.
All other tracks are previously released masters.

Released as a 4 CD set in the long box digi-pack format with an illustrated booklet.

PLATINUM – A LIFE IN MUSIC (1997) - Continued

Disc Three:

1. I Got A Woman (dressing room rehearsal)
2. Tiger Man (dressing room rehearsal)
3. When My Blue Moon Turns To Gold Again (live)
4. Trying To Get To You (live)
5. If I Can Dream (alternate take)
6. In The Ghetto (alternate take)
7. Suspicious Minds (alternate take)
8. Power Of My Love (alternate take)
9. Baby What You Want Me To Do (live)
10. Words (live)
11. Johnny B. Goode (live)
12. Release Me (stage rehearsal)
13. See See Rider (stage rehearsal)
14. The Wonder Of You (stage rehearsal)
15. The Sound Of Your Cry (alternate take)
16. You Don't Have To Say You Love Me (master)
17. Funny How Time Slips Away (master)
18. I Washed My Hands In Muddy Water (rehearsal)
19. I Was The One (rehearsal)
20. Cattle Call (rehearsal)
21. Baby Let's Play House (rehearsal)
22. Don't (rehearsal)
23. Money Honey (rehearsal)
24. What'd I Say (rehearsal)
25. Bridge Over Troubled Water (live)

Recording Information:

Track 1 recorded June 24, 1968.
Track 2 recorded June 25, 1968.
Tracks 1 & 2 recorded during Elvis' dressing room rehearsals at Burbank Studios, California.
Tracks 3 & 4 recorded June 27, 1968 during the 6 p.m. show at Burbank Studios, California.
Track 5 recorded June 23, 1968 at Western Recorders, Los Angeles.
Tracks 1 – 5 recorded for the NBC TV Special, "Elvis".
Track 6 recorded January 20, 1969.
Track 7 recorded January 22, 1969.
Track 8 recorded February 18, 1969.
Tracks 6 – 8 recorded at American Sound Studios, Memphis.
Tracks 9 – 11 recorded live August 24, 1969 during the Midnight Show at the International Hotel, Las Vegas.
Tracks 12 – 14 recorded February 18, 1970 during stage rehearsals at the International Hotel, Las Vegas.
Track 15 recorded June 4, 1970 at RCA Studio B, Nashville.
Tracks 18 – 24 recorded July 29, 1970 during rehearsals at MGM Stage 1, Culver City, California.
Track 25 recorded live August 11, 1970, during the Midnight Show at the International Hotel, Las Vegas.
All other tracks are previously released masters.

Disc Four:

1. Miracle Of The Rosary (alternate take)
2. He Touched Me (alternate take)
3. Bosom Of Abraham (alternate take)
4. I'll Be Home On Christmas Day (alternate take)
5. For The Good Times (alternate take)
6. Burning Love (alternate take)
7. Separate Ways (alternate take)
8. Always On My Mind (alternate take)
9. An American Trilogy (live – remix)
10. Take Good Care Of Her (alternate take)
11. I've Got A Thing About You Baby (master)
12. Are You Sincere (alternate take)
13. It's Midnight (alternate take)
14. Promised Land (alternate take)
15. Steamroller Blues (live – remix)
16. And I Love You So (alternate take)
17. T.R.O.U.B.L.E. (master)
18. Danny Boy (alternate take)
19. Moody Blue (master)
20. Hurt (alternate take)
21. For The Heart (alternate take)
22. Pledging My Love (alternate take)
23. Way Down (alternate take)
24. My Way (live)
25. Excerpt From The Jaycees Speech

Recording Information:

Track 1 recorded May 15, 1971.
Track 2 recorded May 18, 1971.
Track 3 recorded June 9, 1971.
Track 4 recorded May 16, 1971.
Tracks 1 – 4 recorded at RCA Studio B, Nashville.
Tracks 5 & 7 recorded March 27, 1972.
Track 6 recorded March 28, 1972.
Track 8 recorded March 29, 1972.
Tracks 5 – 8 recorded at RCA Studio C, Hollywood.
Track 9 is a re-mixed version of the performance originally released on the album "The Alternate Aloha" in 1988.
Track 10 recorded July 21, 1973 at Stax Studios, Memphis.
Track 12 recorded September 23, 1973 at Elvis' Palm Springs Home.
Track 13 recorded December 10, 1973.
Track 14 recorded December 15, 1973.
Track 15 is a re-mixed version of a performance first released on the album "Elvis Recorded Live On Stage In Memphis" in 1974.
Track 16 recorded March 11, 1975 at RCA Studio C, Hollywood.
Tracks 18, 20, & 21 recorded February 5, 1976.
Tracks 22 & 23 recorded October 29, 1976.
Tracks 18 & 20 – 23 recorded in the "Jungle Room" of Elvis' Graceland mansion, Memphis.
Track 24 recorded live April 25, 1977 at the Saginaw Civic Centre, Saginaw, Michigan.
Track 25 recorded January 16, 1971 at the Ellis Auditorium, Memphis.
All other tracks are previously released masters.

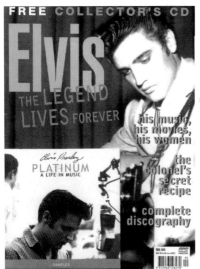

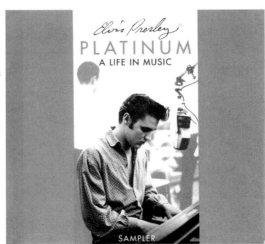

Left: a six track sampler CD was given free with this Australian magazine.

Right: a 12 track sampler was also issued in Europe.

TIGER MAN (1998)

1. Heartbreak Hotel
2. Baby What You Want Me To Do
3. Introductions 8 p.m.
4. That's All Right
5. Are You Lonesome Tonight
6. Baby What You Want Me To Do
7. Blue Suede Shoes
8. One Night
9. Love Me
10. Trying To Get To You
11. Lawdy Miss Clawdy
12. Santa Claus Is back In Town
13. Blue Christmas
14. Tiger Man
15. When My Blue Moon Turns To Gold Again
16. Memories

Recording Information:

All tracks recorded June 27, 1968 during the 8 p.m. "Sit Down" show at Burbank Studios, California for the NBC TV Special "Elvis".
Although some of these tracks had been previously released on other albums, this was the first official release of the complete show.
Tracks 1, 2, 6, 8, 12, 15, & 16 are previously unreleased recordings.

MEMORIES – THE '68 COMEBACK SPECIAL (1998)

Disc One:

1. Trouble/Guitar Man
2. Heartbreak Hotel
3. Hound Dog
4. All Shook Up
5. Can't Help Falling In Love
6. Jailhouse Rock
7. Don't Be Cruel
8. Blue Suede Shoes
9. Love Me Tender
10. Baby What You Want Me To Do
11. Trouble/Guitar Man
12. Gospel Medley:
Sometimes I Feel Like A Motherless Child/
Where Could I Go But To The Lord/
Up Above My Head/Saved
13. Memories
14. A Little Less Conversation
15. Road Medley:
Nothingville/Big Boss Man/
Let Yourself Go/It Hurts Me/
Guitar Man/Little Egypt/Trouble
18. If I Can Dream

Disc Two:

1. When It Rains It Really Pours
2. Lawdy Miss Clawdy
3. Baby What You Want Me To Do
4. That's All Right
5. Heartbreak Hotel
6. Love Me
7. Baby What You Want Me To Do
8. Blue Suede Shoes
9. Baby What You Want Me To Do
10. Lawdy Miss Clawdy
11. Are You Lonesome Tonight
12. When My Blue Moon Turns To Gold Again
13. Blue Christmas
14. Trying To Get To You
15. One Night
16. Baby What You Want Me To Do
17. One Night
18. Memories
19. If I Can Dream

Recording Information:

Disc One:

Track 15 recorded June 20 – 21, 1968.
Track 12 recorded June 21– 22, 1968.
Track 1 recorded June 22, 1968.
Tracks 13, 14, & 16 recorded June 23, 1968.
Tracks 1 & 12 – 16 recorded at Western Recorders, Los Angeles.
Tracks 2, 3, 4, 5, 6, 7, 9, & 10 recorded June 29, 1968 during the 6 p.m. "Stand Up" show.
Tracks 8 & 11 recorded June 29, 1968 during the 8 p.m. "Stand Up" show.
Tracks 2 – 11 recorded at Burbank Studios, California.
Lead vocal on "Sometimes I Feel Like A Motherless Child" by Darlene Love.
Tracks 6 –11, & 14 are previously unreleased performances.

Disc Two:

Track 19 recorded June 23, 1968 at Western Recorders, Los Angeles.
Track 1 recorded June 24, 1968.
Tracks 2 & 3 recorded June 25, 1968.
Tracks 1 – 3 recorded during Elvis' dressing room rehearsals at Burbank Studios, California.
Track 4 – 18 recorded June 27, 1968 during the 6 p.m. "Sit Down" show at Burbank Studios, California.
Tracks 1 – 7, 10 – 15, 18, & 19 are previously unreleased performances.

All tracks recorded for the NBC TV Special "Elvis".

ESSENTIAL ELVIS VOLUME 5 – RHYTHM AND COUNTRY (1998)

1. I Got A Feeling In My Body (alternate take 1)
2. Loving Arms (alternate take 2)
3. I've Got A Thing About You Baby (alternate take 14)
4. She Wears My Ring (alternate take 8)
5. You Asked Me To (alternate take 2)
6. There's A Honky Tonk Angel (alternate take 1)
7. Good Time Charlie's Got The Blues (alternate take 8)
8. Find Out What's Happening (alternate take 6)
9. For Ol' Times Sake (alternate take 3)
10. If You Don't Come Back (alternate take 3)
11. Promised Land (alternate 4)
12. Thinking About You (alternate 4)
13. Three Corn Patches (alternate take 14)
14. Girl Of Mine (alternate take 9)
15. Your Love's Been A Long Time Coming (alternate take 4)
16. Spanish Eyes (alternate take 2)
17. Talk About the Good Times (alternate take 3)
18. If That Isn't Love (alternate take 1)

Recording Information:

Tracks 10 & 13 recorded July 21, 1973.
Tracks 3 & 8 recorded July 22, 1973.
Track 9 recorded July 23, 1973.
Track 14 recorded July 24, 1973.
Track 1 recorded December 10, 1973.
Track 12 recorded December 12, 1973.
Track 5 recorded December 11, 1973.
Tracks 2 & 7 recorded December 13, 1973.
Track 17 recorded December 14, 1973.
Tracks 6, 11, & 15 recorded December 15, 1973.
Tracks 4, 16, & 18 recorded December 16, 1973.
All tracks recorded at Stax Studios, Memphis,
All tracks are previously unreleased performances.

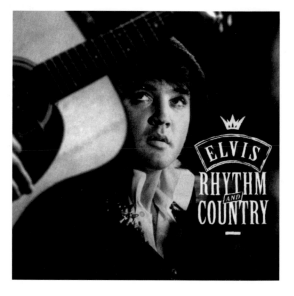

ELVIS THE CONCERT 1999 WORLD TOUR (1988)

Disc One:

1. Introduction: Also Sprach Zarathustra
2. See See Rider
3. Burning Love
4. Steamroller Blues
5. I Can't Stop Loving You
6. Johnny B. Goode
7. You Gave Me A Mountain
8. Polk Salad Annie
9. You've Lost That Loving Feeling
10. Proud Mary
11. Never Been To Spain
12. Just Pretend
13. Make The World Go Away
14. In The Ghetto
15. How Great Thou Art
16. Bridge Over Troubled Water

Disc Two:

1. Trouble/Guitar Man
2. Hound Dog
3. Teddy Bear/Don't Be Cruel
4. All Shook Up
5. Heartbreak Hotel
6. One Night
7. Love Me Tender
8. The Wonder Of You
9. Lawdy Miss Clawdy
10. Funny How Time Slips Away
11. Suspicious Minds
12. I'll Remember You
13. A Big Hunk O' Love
14. My Way
15. An American Trilogy
16. Can't Help Falling In Love
17. Closing Vamp

Recording Information/Notes:

"Elvis The Concert" featured live performance footage of Elvis with the original backing tracks removed leaving only Elvis' original vocal.
Elvis' original TCB band and vocal groups perform live on stage with the recorded Elvis vocals in order to create a virtual Elvis concert.
This CD featured mainly previously released live recordings of songs that were featured in the show, and is not a recording of one of the virtual concerts.
All material is previously released except "In The Ghetto" and "Suspicious Minds" which were recorded live in Las Vegas in February 1970.
These two performances were also added to the CD re-issue version of the album "Elvis On Stage".
It is also worth noting that the versions of "Just Pretend" & "Make The World Go Away" included on this release are the studio masters with added applause.

Above left: the original CD release came in a cardboard slip case and was a numbered limited edition of 25,000.

Above right: the CD was re-issued for the 2nd world tour in 2000 without the cardboard slip case.

SUNRISE (1999)

Disc One:

1. That's All Right Mama
2. Blue Moon Of Kentucky
3. I Don't Care If The Sun Don't Shine
4. Good Rockin' Tonight
5. Milk Cow Blues Boogie
6. You're A Heartbreaker
7. Baby Let's Play House
8. I'm Left, You're Right, She's Gone
9. I Forgot To Remember To Forget
10. Mystery Train
11. I Love You Because
12. Harbour Lights
13. Blue Moon
14. Tomorrow Night
15. I'll Never Let You Go Little Darlin'
16. Just Because
17. I'm Left, You're Right, She's Gone (slow version)
18. Tryin' To Get To You
19. When It Rains It Really Pours

Disc Two;

1. My Happiness
2. That's When Your Heartaches Begin
3. I'll Never Stand In Your Way
4. It Wouldn't Be The Same Without You
5. I Love You Because (alternate take)
6. That's All Right (alternate take)
7. Blue Moon Of Kentucky (alternate take)
8. Blue Moon (alternate take)
9. I'll Never Let You Go Little Darlin' (alternate take)
10. I Don't Care If The Sun Don't Shine (alternate take)
11. I'm Left, You're Right, She's Gone
(slow version – alternate take)
12. Fool, Fool, Fool (demo)
13. Shake, Rattle, & Roll (demo)
14. I'm Left, You're Right, She's Gone (live)
15. That's All Right Mama (live)
16. Money Honey (live)
17. Tweedle Dee (live)
18. I Don't Care If The Sun Don't Shine (live)
19. Hearts Of Stone (live)

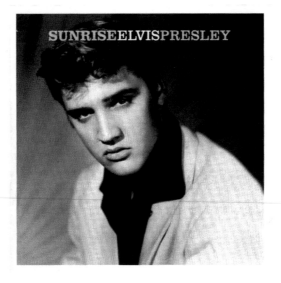

Recording Information:

Disc One:

All material previously released.

Disc Two:

Track 4 recorded 1953.
Track 8 recorded August 19, 1954.
Tracks 4 & 8 recorded at Sun Studios, Memphis.
Tracks 14 – 19 recorded live early 1955 at the Louisiana Hayride, Shreveport, Louisiana.
All other performances are previously released recordings.

THE HOME RECORDINGS (1999)

1. When The Saints Go Marching In
2. I Understand Just How You Feel
3. I Asked The Lord (alternate take)
4. I'm Beginning To Forget You
5. Mona Lisa
6. Hands Off
7. Make Believe
8. If I Loved You
9. What Now My Love
10. Tumblin' Tunbleweeds
11. San Antonio Rose
12. Tennessee Waltz
13. Show Me Thy Ways, O Lord
14. After Loving You
15. I've Been Blue
16. Mary Lou Brown
17. It's No Fun Being Lonely
18. Suppose
19. Indescribably Blue
20. Write To Me From Naples
21. My Heart Cries For You
22. Dark Moon

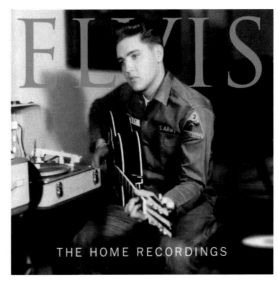

Recording Information:

Track 1 recorded December 1956.
Track 2 recorded Summer 1958 at the home of Eddie Fadal, Killeen, Texas.
Tracks 3 – 5 recorded 1959 during Elvis' Army service in Bad Nauheim, Germany.
Tracks 6 & 7 recorded Autumn 1960 at Monovale Drive, Hollywood.
Tracks 8 – 22 recorded 1966 – 1967 at Rocca Place, Hollywood.

SUSPICIOUS MINDS – THE MEMPHIS 1969 ANTHOLOGY (1999)

Disc One:

1. Wearin' That Loved On Look
2. Only The Strong Survive
3. I'll Hold You In My Heart
4. Long Black Limousine
5. It Keeps Right On A Hurtin'
6. I'm Movin' On
7. Power Of My Love
8. Gentle On My Mind
9. After Loving You
10. True Love Travels On A Gravel Road
11. Any Day Now
12. In The Ghetto
13. Mama Liked The Roses
14. Suspicious Minds
15. You'll Think Of Me
16. Don't Cry Daddy
17. The Fair Is Moving On
18. Kentucky Rain
19. Stranger In My Own Home Town
20. Without Love (There Is Nothing)

Disc Two:

1. This Time/I Can't Stop Loving You (informal recording)
2. After Loving You (alternate take)
3. Without Love (There Is Nothing) (alternate take)
4. I'm Movin' On (alternate mix & vocal)
5. From A Jack To A King
6. It Keeps Right On A Hurtin' (alternate take)
7. True Love Travels On A Gravel Road (alternate take)
8. Power Of My Love (alternate take)
9. You'll Think of Me (alternate take)
10. If I'm A Fool For Loving You
11. Do You Know Who I Am
12. A Little Bit Of Green
13. And The Grass Won't Pay No Mind
14. This Is The Story
15. I'll Be There
16. Hey Jude
17. Rubberneckin'
18. Poor Man's Gold (incomplete)
19. Inherit The Wind
20. My Little Friend
21. Who Am I
22. Kentucky Rain (alternate take)
23. Suspicious Minds (alternate take)
24. In the Ghetto (alternate take)

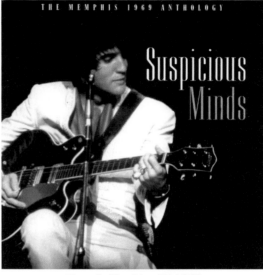

Above: the "Suspicious Minds" CD

Below: the original UK release of the "Suspicious Minds" single.

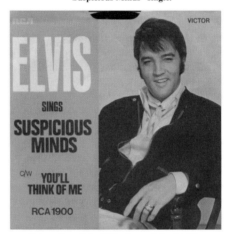

Below: the original US release of the "In The Ghetto" single.

Recording Information:

Disc One:

All material previously released

Disc Two:

Tracks 4 & 9 recorded January 14, 1969.
Track 18 recorded January 15, 1969.
Track 3 recorded January 22, 1969.
Track 7 recorded February 17, 1969.
Tracks 2 & 8 recorded February 18, 1969.
Track 22 recorded February 19, 1969.
Track 6 recorded February 20, 1969.
All tracks recorded at American Sound Studios, Memphis.
Tracks 1, 23, & 24 were first released on the '60's box set "From Nashville   To Memphis –
The Essential '60's Masters Volume 1" in 1993.
All other tracks are previously unreleased performances.
This collection features the complete masters from the 1969 Memphis sessions.

ARTIST OF THE CENTURY (1999)

Disc One:
1. That's All Right
2. Good Rockin' Tonight
3. Baby Lets Play House
4. Mystery Train
5. Trying To Get To You
6. Heartbreak Hotel
7. Blue Suede Shoes
8. My Baby Left Me
9. Lawdy Miss Clawdy
10. Hound Dog
11. Any Way You Want Me (That's How I Will Be)
12. Don't Be Cruel
13. Love Me Tender
14. Love Me
15. Anyplace Is Paradise
16. All Shook Up
17. Got A Lot O' Livin' To Do!
18. (Let Me Be Your) Teddy Bear
19. One Night
20. Jailhouse Rock
21. (You're So Square) Baby I Don't Care
22. Treat Me Nice
23. Don't
24. Santa Claus Is Back In Town
25. Trouble
26. Hard Headed Woman
27. Wear My Ring Around Your Neck
28. A Big Hunk O' Love
29. (Now And Then) There's A Fool Such As I

Disc Two:
1. Stuck On You
2. It's Now Or Never
3. Are You Lonesome Tonight
4. A Mess Of Blues
5. Like A Baby
6. The Girl Of My Best Friend
7. Such A Night
8. Reconsider Baby
9. Surrender
10. Can't Help Falling In Love
11. That's Someone You Never Forget
12. Little Sister
13. (Marie's The Name) His Latest Flame
14. Anything That's Part Of You
15. Good Luck Charm
16. She's Not You
17. Return To Sender
18. (You're The) Devil In Disguise
19. Memphis Tennessee
20. It Hurts Me
21. Down In The Alley
22. Run On
23. Tomorrow Is A Long Time
24. Big Boss Man
25. Guitar Man
26. Tiger Man

Disc Three:
1. If I Can Dream
2. In The Ghetto
3. Suspicious Minds
4. Don't Cry Daddy
5. I'll Hold You In My Heart
6. Stranger In My Own Home Town
7. After Loving You
8. Only The Strong Survive
9. The Wonder Of You
10. Polk Salad Annie
11. I've Lost You
12. You Don't Have To Say You Love Me
13. I Just Can't Help Believin'
14. Merry Christmas Baby
15. I'm Leavin'
16. An American Trilogy
17. Burning Love
18. Always On My Mind
19. Promised Land
20. For The Heart

Recording Information:
All material previously released
The Australian release of this album included the following 5 extra tracks:

Judy
Raised On Rock
Kentucky Rain
Edge Of Reality
Way Down

A vinyl edition was also produced.

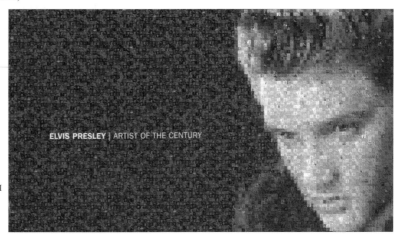

Above: the CD was released in the long box digi-pack format.
Below: a booklet was included with each individual disc featuring quotes about Elvis from other artists, liner notes, and cover art from around the world.

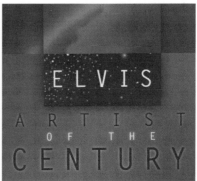

Above: a 7 track "Artist Of The Century" promo CD issued in 1998 which also included tracks from "Sunrise", "Tiger Man", "Memories", "Suspicious Minds", "Rhythm And Country", and "The Home Recordings"

TOMORROW IS A LONG TIME (1999)

1. Too Much Monkey Business
2. Guitar Man
3. Tomorrow Is A Long Time
4. US Male
5. Big Boss Man
6. Love Letters
7. Indescribably Blue
8. Fools Fall I Love
9. Hi – Heel Sneakers
10. Down In The Alley
11. Come What May
12. Mine
13. Just Call Me Lonesome
14. You Don't Know Me
15. Stay Away
16. Singing Tree
17. Going Home
18. I'll Remember You

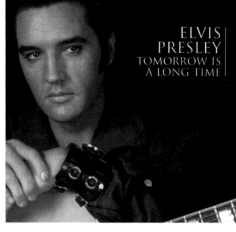

Recording Information/Notes:

This album features previously released masters recorded at RCA Studio B, Nashville between 1966 – 1968.

" Too Much Monkey Business", Guitar Man", "US Male", Big Boss Man", "Love Letters", Indescribably Blue", "Fools Fall In Love",

"Hi – Heel Sneakers", "Come What May", "You Don't Know Me ", and "Stay Away" were originally issued as singles.

"Guitar Man", "Tomorrow Is A Long Time", "Big Boss Man", "Down In The Alley", "Mine", "Just Call Me Lonesome", "Singing Tree", "Going Home" and "I'll Remember You" were issued as bonus tracks on Elvis' movie soundtrack albums.

Alternate take 7 of "Come What May" was used as the master was lost at the time of this release.

BURNING LOVE (1999)

1. Burning Love
2. Never Been To Spain (live)
3. You Gave Me A Mountain (live)
4. I'm Leavin'
5. It's Only Love
6. Always On my Mind
7. It's Impossible (live)
8. It's Over (live)
9. Separate Ways
10. Fool
11. Hound Dog (live)
12. Little Sister/Get Back (live)
13. A Big Hunk O' Love (live)
14. Where Do I Go From Here
15. For The Good Times
16. It's A Matter Of Time
17. An American Trilogy (live)
18. The Impossible Dream (live)

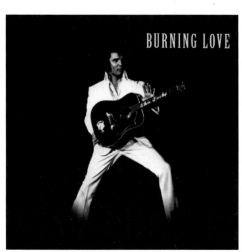

Recording Information/Notes:

In 1972 RCA were planning an album titled "Standing Room Only" which was to include material recorded live in Las Vegas in February 1972, and

additional recordings from RCA Studio C, Hollywood in March of the same year. However, after the decision was taken to record Elvis in concert at Madison Square Garden in June 1972 the "Standing Room Only" album was cancelled.

This release uses a similar concept to the cancelled "Standing Room Only" project, and also included two non album singles from 1971:

"I'm Leavin'" and "It's Only Love".

Of the rest of the material included here "Burning Love", "Always On My Mind", "Separate Ways", "Fool", and "It's A Matter Of Time" were first released as singles, whilst "Where Do I Go From Here" and "It's Impossible" were first released on the album "Elvis" in 1973.

"Hound Dog" & "Little Sister/Get Back" are previously unreleased live performances recorded February 14, 1972 at the Hilton Hotel, Las Vegas.

"The Impossible Dream" was first released on the album "He Walks Beside Me" in 1978.

"An American Trilogy" is not the single version. The version included on this release was first issued on the box set "Elvis Aron Presley" in 1980.

The remainder of the live material: "Never Been To Spain", "You Gave Me A Mountain", "It's Over", & " A Big Hunk O' Love" remained officially unreleased until they were included on the '70's box set "Walk A Mile In My Shoes – The Essential '70's Masters" in 1995.

The studio master of "For The Good Times" was also first released on the '70's box.

Left to right: original US single releases:

"Its Only Love" /"The Sound of Your Cry"

"Always On My Mind"/"Separate Ways"

"Burning Love"/ "It's A Matter Of Time".

ESSENTIAL ELVIS VOLUME 6 – SUCH A NIGHT (2000)

1. Such A Night (master with false start)
2. Make Me Know It (alternate take 3)
3. Stuck On You (alternate take 2)
4. Fever (alternate take 1)
5. The Girl Of My Best Friend (alternate take 6)
6. Soldier Boy (alternate take 1)
7. Surrender (alternate take 9)
8. I Believe In The Man Sky (alternate take 1)
9. Give Me The Right (alternate take 2)
10. I'm Coming Home (alternate take 2)
11. There's Always Me (alternate take 9)
12. Little Sister (alternate take 9)
13. I Met Her Today (alternate take 4)
14. Gonna Get Back Hone Somehow (alternate take 5)
15. Night Rider (alternate take 5)
16. (Such An) Easy Question (alternate take 1)
17. Suspicion (alternate take 2)
18. Please Don't Drag That String Around (alternate take 1)
19. Memphis, Tennessee (alternate take 5)
20. It Hurts Me (alternate take 1)

Recording Information:

Tracks 2 & 6 recorded March 20, 1960.
Track 3 recorded March 21, 1960.
Track 4 recorded April 3, 1960.
Tracks 1 & 5 recorded April 4, 1960.
Tracks 7 & 8 recorded October 30, 1960.
Tracks 9, 10, & 11 recorded March 12, 1961.
Track 12 recorded June 26, 1961.
Track 13 recorded October 16, 1961.
Tracks 14, 15, & 16 recorded March 18, 1962.
Track 17 recorded March 19, 1962.
Track 18 recorded May 26, 1963.
Tracks 19 & 20 recorded January 12, 1964.
All tracks recorded at RCA Studio B, Nashville.
Tracks 2 – 20 are previously unreleased performances.

PEACE IN THE VALLEY – THE COMPLETE GOSPEL RECORDINGS (2000)

Disc One:

1. His Hand In Mine
2. I'm Gonna Walk Dem Golden Stairs
3. In My Father's House
4. Milky White Way
5. Known Only To Him
6. I Believe In The Man In The Sky
7. Joshua Fit The Battle
8. He Knows Just What I Need
9. Swing Down Sweet Chariot
10. Mansion Over The Hilltop
11. If We Never Meet Again
12. Working On The Building
13. Crying In the Chapel
14. How Great Thou Art
15. In The Garden
16. Somebody Bigger Than You Or I
17. Farther Along
18. Stand By Me
19. Without Him
20. So High
21. Where Could I Go But To The Lord
22. If The Lord Wasn't Walking By Side
24. Run On
25. Where No One Stands Alone
26. We Call On Him
27. You'll Never Walk Alone
28. Who Am I
29. Life

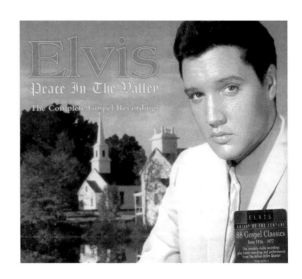

PEACE IN THE VALLEY – THE COMPLETE GOSPEL RECORDINGS (2000) - Continued

Disc Two:

1. Only Believe
2. He Touched Me
3. I've Got Confidence
4. Amazing Grace
5. Seeing Is Believing
6. He Is My Everything
7. Bosom Of Abraham
8. An Evening Prayer
9. Lead Me, Guide Me
10. There Is No God But God
11. A Thing Called Love
12. I, John
13. Reach Out To Jesus
14. Miracle Of The Rosary
15. Put Your Hand In The Hand
16. I Got A Feelin' In My Body
17. Help Me
18. If That Isn't Love
19. Help Me
20. Why Me Lord
21. How Great Thou Art
22. Farther Along
23. Oh Happy Day
24. I John
25. Bosom Of Abraham
26. You Better Run
27. Lead Me, Guide Me
28. Turn Your Eyes Upon Jesus/Nearer My God To Thee

Disc Three:

1. When The Saints Go Marchin' In
2. Just A Little Talk With Jesus
3. Jesus Walked That Lonesome Valley
4. I Shall Not Be Moved
5. (There'll Be) Peace In The Valley (For Me)
6. Down By The Riverside
7. Farther Along
8. Blessed Jesus (Hold My Hand)
9. On The Jericho Road
10. I Just Can't Make It By Myself
11. I Hear A Sweet Voice Calling
12. When The Saints Go Marchin' In
13. Softly And Tenderly
14. (There'll Be) Peace In The Valley For Me
15. It Is No Secret (What God Can Do)
16. I Believe
17. Take My Hand Precious Lord
18. I Asked The Lord
19. He
20. Oh How I Love Jesus
21. Show Me Thy Ways O Lord
22. Hide Thou Me
23. Down By The Riverside/When The Saints Go Marchin' In
24. Sing You Children
25. Swing Down Sweet Chariot
26. Let Us Pray
27. Gospel Medley: Sometimes I Feel Like A Motherless Child/
Where Could I Go But To The Lord/Up Above My Head/Saved
28. The Lord's Prayer
29. How Great Thou Art
30. (There'll Be) Peace In The Valley (For Me)

Recording Information:

Since the release of "Amazing Grace" in 1994 several new gospel recordings have been issued on other albums. This collection featured all the newly discovered recordings, and also included informal recordings, home recordings, and songs from movie soundtracks and TV specials which were not included on "Amazing Grace".

Disc One:

All tracks are studio masters.

Disc Two:

Tracks 1– 18 are studio masters.
Tracks 19 – 21 are live recordings from March, 1974.
Tracks 22 & 23 are rehearsals from August, 1970.
Tracks 24 – 28 are rehearsals from March, 1972.

Disc Three:

Track 1 is a home recording.
Tracks 2 – 13 are from the "Million Dollar Quartet" sessions.
Tracks 14 – 17 are studio masters.
Tracks 18 – 22 are home recordings
Track 23 from the United Artists Motion Picture "Frankie And Johnny".
Track 24 from the Paramount Motion Picture "Easy Come, Easy Go".
Track 25 from the MGM Motion Picture "The Trouble With Girls And How To Get Into It".
Track 26 from the Universal Motion Picture "Change Of Habit".
Track 27 is from the 1968 NBC TV Special "Elvis".
Track 28 is an informal recording from 1971.
Track 29 recorded live June 1977 for the CBS TV Special "Elvis In Concert".
Track 30 recorded live on the Ed Sullivan show in 1957.

All material previously released.

Above right: an original US Gold Standard single release "Milky White Way"/ "Swing Down Sweet Chariot".

Right: an original US Gold Standard single release "Joshua Fit The Battle"/ "Known Only To Him".

LIVE IN LAS VEGAS (2001)

Disc One:

1. Blue Suede Shoes
2. I Got A Woman
3. All Shook Up
4. Elvis Welcomes The Audience
5. Love Me Tender
6. Jailhouse Rock/Don't Be Cruel
7. Heartbreak Hotel
8. Hound Dog
9. I Can't Stop Loving You
10. Johnny B. Goode
11. Baby What You Want Me To Do
12. Runaway
13. Are You Lonesome Tonight
14. Yesterday/Hey Jude
15. Introductions
16. In The Ghetto
17. Suspicious Minds
18. What'd I Say
19. Can't Help Falling In Love
20. Elvis Talks About His Career

Disc Two:

1. That's All Right
2. I Got A Woman
3. Hound Dog
4. Love Me Tender
5. There Goes My Everything
6. Just Pretend
7. I Just Can't Help Believin'
8. Something
9. Men With Broken Hearts
10. Walk A Mile In My Shoes
11. You've Lost That Loving Feeling
12. Polk Salad Annie
13. One Night
14. Don't Be Cruel
15. Love Me
16. Instrumental Vamp
17. Heartbreak Hotel
18. Introductions
19. Bridge Over Troubled Water
20. Suspicious Minds
21. Can't Help Falling In Love
22. When The Snow Is On The Roses

Disc Three:

1. See See Rider
2. Release Me
3. Sweet Caroline
4. The Wonder Of You
5. Polk Salad Annie
6. Proud Mary
7. Walk A Mile In My Shoes
8. In The Ghetto
9. Let It Be Me
10. Don't Cry Daddy
11. Kentucky Rain
12. Long Tall Sally
13. I Can't Stop Loving You
14. Suspicious Minds
15. Never Been To Spain
16. You Gave Me A Mountain
17. It's Impossible
18. It's Over
19. Hound Dog
20. Little Sister/Get Back
21. A Big Hunk O' Love
22. The Impossible Dream
23. An American Trilogy

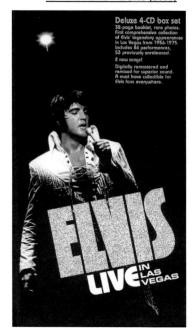

Disc Four:

1. Heartbreak Hotel
2. Long Tall Sally
3. Blue Suede Shoes
4. Money Honey
5. Promised Land
6. It's Midnight
7. If You Talk In Your Sleep
8. I'm Leavin'
9. Why Me Lord
10. Help Me
11. Softly As I Leave You
12. My Baby Left Me
13. It's Now Or Never
14. Hawaiian Wedding Song
15. Trying To Get To You
16. Green, Green Grass Of Home
17. You're The reason I'm Living
18. Big Boss Man
19. Burning Love
20. My Boy
21. And I Love You So
22. Just Pretend
23. How Great Thou Art
24. America The Beautiful

Recording Information:

Disc One:

Recorded live August 24, 1969 during the Dinner Show at the International Hotel, Las Vegas.
"Elvis Talks About His Career" was moved to the end of the disc for this release.
The monologue was actually spoken before the performance of "Baby What You Want Me To Do".
"Heartbreak Hotel" was first released on the box set "Collectors Gold" in 1991.
All other tracks are previously unreleased performances.

Disc Two:

Tracks 1 – 21 recorded live August 11, 1970 during the Midnight Show at the International Hotel, Las Vegas.
Tracks 8, 9, 13, & 17 were first released on the box set "Walk A Mile In My Shoes – The Essential '70's Masters" in 1995.
All other tracks are previously unreleased performances.
Track 22 recorded live August 24, 1970 during the Midnight Show at the International Hotel, Las Vegas.
Track 22 is a previously unreleased audience recording.

Disc Three:

Tracks 1– 14 were released on the CD up-grade version of the album "Elvis On Stage, February 1970".
Tracks 15 – 23 were released on the CD "Burning Love" in 1999.
All material previously released.

Disc Four:

Tracks 1 – 4 recorded live May 6, 1956 at the Venus Room of the New Frontier Hotel, Las Vegas .
Tracks 1 – 4 first released on the box set "Elvis Aron Presley" in 1980.
Tracks 5 & 12 recorded August 19, 1974.
Track 15 recorded August 20, 1974.
Tracks 6 – 9, 11, & 14 recorded August 21, 1974.
Track 10 recorded August 22, 1974.
Track 13 recorded August 27, 1974.
Tracks 16 & 17 recorded March 22, 1975, Midnight Show.
Tracks 18 – 20 recorded March 30, 1975.
Tracks 21 – 24 recorded December 6, 1975.
Tracks 5 – 24 are previously unreleased performances.

**Released as a Four CD set in the long box
digi-pack format with an illustrated booklet.**

The first compilations of Elvis' Greatest Hits were the "Elvis' Golden Records" series, which were covered in detail in the first section of the book. Since the release of these albums there have many been many additional collections released world wide on both vinyl and CD. Over the next few pages

Above: Worldwide 50 Gold Award Hits – originally released as a four album set with bonus Elvis Photo Book.

Below: Worldwide 50 Gold Award Hits Vol. 2 – originally released as a four album set with a piece of material from Elvis' wardrobe and pull out Elvis Portrait.

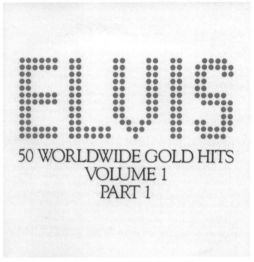

Above: Worldwide 50 Gold Award Hits CD version.

Below: Worldwide 50 Gold Award Hits Vol. 2 CD version: A two CD box set including photo booklet and Elvis Stamp with first day of issue envelope.

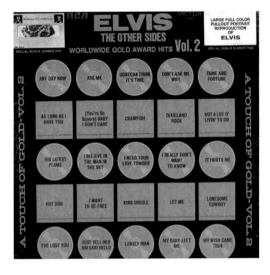

Above: the bonus material from the original box set was pictured on the back of the booklet of the CD set.

Below: Worldwide 50 Gold Award Hits Vol. 2 – disc one.

Below: Worldwide 50 Gold Award Hits Vol. 2 – disc two.

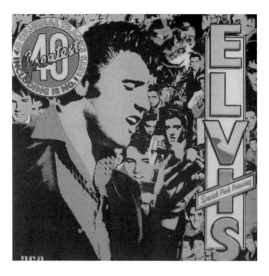

Above: Elvis' 40 Greatest. (UK double album – Arcade label)

Above: Elvis' 40 Greatest (UK double album – RCA label)
Originally pressed in pink vinyl.

Below: Les 40 Plus Grands Succes
(France double album – K-Tel label)

Below: Elvis At His Best (UK double album – RCA label)

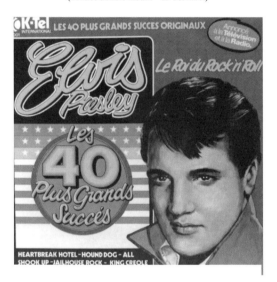

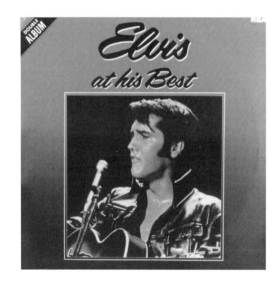

Below: 20 Fantastic Hits (Holland LP – RCA label)

Below: Rock 'N' On (Australia double album – RCA label)

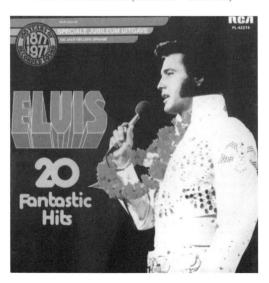

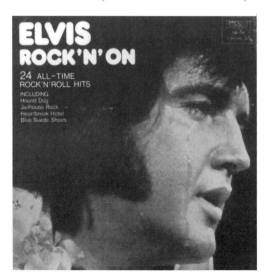

Above: Country Club – The Hits Of Elvis Presley (USA LP – RCA label)

Above: Elvis (USA double album – RCA label)

Below: Elvis Forever (Canada LP – RCA label)

Below: Elvis Forever (Germany double album – RCA label)

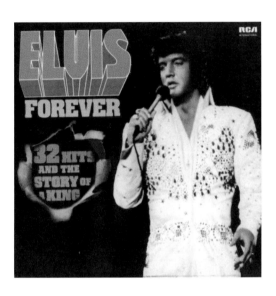

Below: Elvis Forever Volume 2 (Germany double album – RCA label)

Below: Elvis Forever Volume 3 (Germany double album – RCA label)

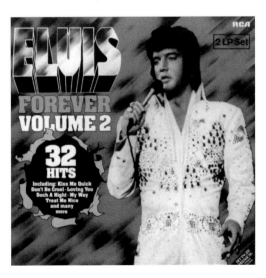

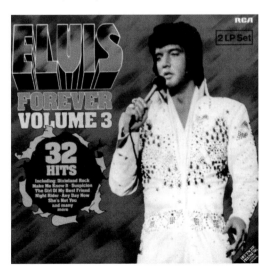

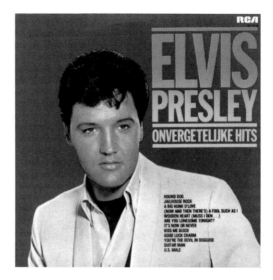

**Above: Elvis Rocks – 14 Golden Hits
(UK LP – Readers Digest label)**

**Below: Presley – The All Time Greatest Hits
(Europe Double CD – RCA label)**

Above: Onvergetelijke Hits (Germany LP – RCA label)

Below: The Top Ten Hits (USA double CD – RCA Label)

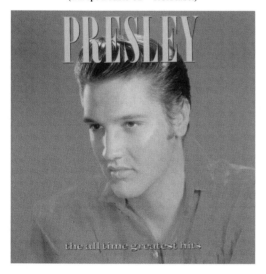

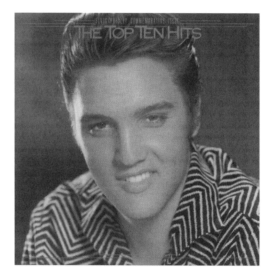

Below Left: Elvis – The Legend Lives On (UK 5 CD set – Readers Digest label)

Below right: The Readers Digest set also included programme notes

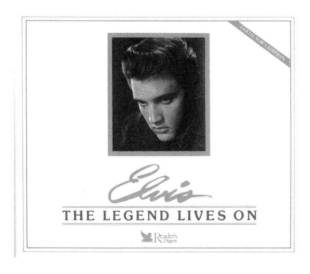

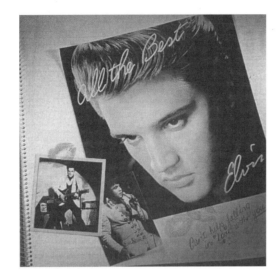

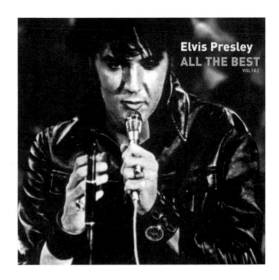

Above: All The Best (Australia double CD – RCA label)

Below: Elvis Svenska Hits (Sweden CD – RCA label)

Above: All The Best – alternate artwork
(Australia double CD – RCA label)

Below: The Essential Collection (Europe CD – RCA label)

Below Left: The Essential Collection (Australia digi-pack CD – RCA label)

Below right: The Australian version of The Essential Collection also included an Ameri Vox Elvis Presley phone card.

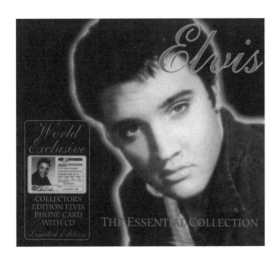

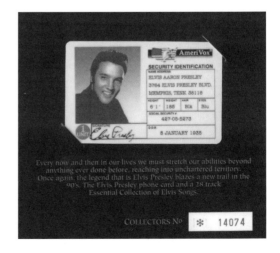

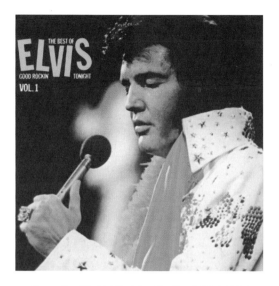

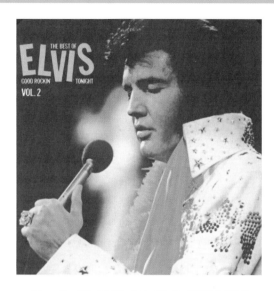

Above: Good Rockin' Tonight – The Best Of Elvis Vol. 1
(Brazil CD – RCA label)
Below: Good Rockin' Tonight – The Best Of Elvis Vol. 3
(Brazil CD – RCA label)

Above: Good Rockin' Tonight – The Best Of Elvis Vol. 2
(Brazil CD – RCA label)
Below: Good Rockin' Tonight – The Best Of Elvis Vol. 4
(Brazil CD – RCA label)

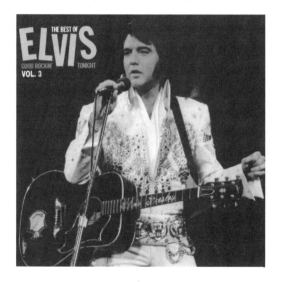

Below: Danske Single Hits (Denmark CD – RCA label)

Below: Always Elvis – The Dutch Album
(Holland CD – RCA label)

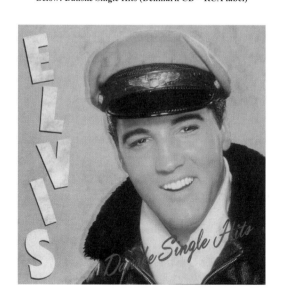

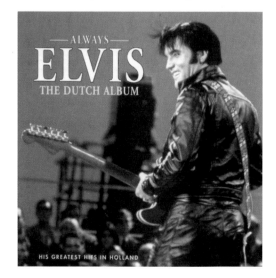

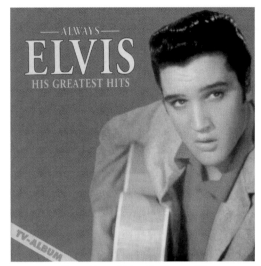

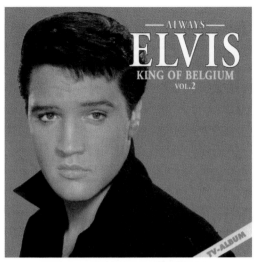

Above: Always Elvis – His Greatest Hits
(Belgium CD – RCA label)

Below: Can't Help Falling In Love – The Hollywood Hits
(Europe CD – RCA label)

Above: Always Elvis Vol. 2 – King Of Belgium
(Belgium CD – RCA label)

Below: Elvis 2000 – The Best Of The King
(Germany double CD – RCA label)

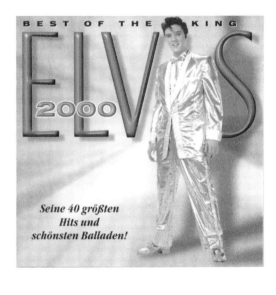

Below: The 50 Greatest Hits
(Europe double CD – RCA label)

Below: The Live Greatest Hits
(Europe CD – RCA label)

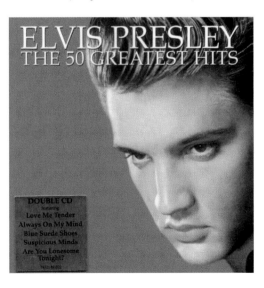

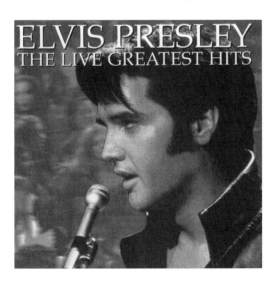

Between 1969 and 1973 ten budget albums were released by RCA on the International/Camden label. The material featured on these albums consisted mainly of tracks from previously released EP's and LP's. However, in some cases the budget albums did provide the collector with previously unreleased recordings.

Songs from Elvis' later movies, and even out takes from the legendary 1969 Memphis Sessions were first released on budget albums, and a number of tracks only previously released as singles appeared on budget albums for the first time.

With the exception of the 1978 album "Mahalo From Elvis", (see first section) the many budget albums released world wide after 1973 contained only previously released material.

ELVIS SINGS FLAMING STAR (1969)

1. Flaming Star
2. Wonderful World
3. Night Life
4. All I Needed Was The Rain
5. Too Much Monkey Business
6. Yellow Rose Of Texas/
The Eyes Of Texas
7. She's A Machine
8. Do The Vega
9. Tiger Man

Left: the original cover art.

Right: a later UK re-issue on the Camden label.

Recording Information:

Track 1 recorded October 7, 1960, at Radio Recorders, Hollywood for the 20th Century Fox Motion Picture "Flaming Star".
Track 3 recorded July 9, 1963 Tracks 6 & 8 recorded July 10, 1963.
Tracks 3, 6 &, 8 recorded at Radio Recorders Hollywood for the MGM Motion Picture "Viva Las Vegas".
Track 7 recorded September 29, 1966 at Paramount Studios, Hollywood for the Paramount Motion Picture, "Easy Come, Easy Go".
Track 4 recorded October 1, 1967 at RCA Studio B, Nashville for the MGM Motion Picture "Stay Away Joe".
Track 5 recorded January 5, 1968 at RCA Studio B, Nashville.
Track 2 recorded March 7, 1968 at Western Recorders, Los Angeles for the MGM Motion Picture "Live A Little, Love A Little".
Track 9 recorded June 27, 1968 during the 8 p.m. "Sit Down" show at Burbank Studios, California for the NBC TV Special "Elvis".
This album was first released in 1968 by the Singer Sewing Company as "Singer Presents Elvis Singing Flaming Star And Others".
The album was re-issued in 1969 and became Elvis' first budget album.
This album has not been issued on CD.

LET'S BE FRIENDS (1970)

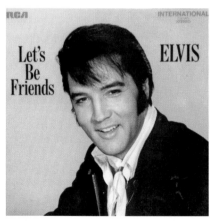

1. Stay Away Joe
2. If I'm A Fool For Loving You
3. Let's Be Friends
4. Let's Forget About The Stars
5. Mama
6. I'll Be There
7. Almost
8. Change Of Habit
9. Have A Happy

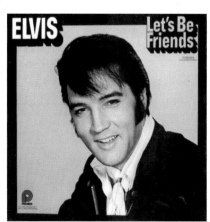

Left: original cover art.

Right: a later US re-issue on the Pickwick label.

Recording Information:

Track 5 recorded March 28, 1962 at Radio Recorders, Hollywood for the Paramount Motion Picture "Girls!, Girls!, Girls!".
Track 1 recorded October 1, 1967 at RCA Studio B, Nashville for the MGM Motion Picture "Stay Away Joe".
Track 7 recorded August 23, 1968 at United Recorders, Hollywood for the MGM Motion Picture "The Trouble With Girls And How To Get Into It".
Track 4 recorded October 15, 1968 at Samuel Goldwyn Studios, Hollywood for the Nation General Motion Picture "Charro".
Track 6 recorded January 22, 1969. Track 2 February 20, 1969. Tracks 2 & 6 recorded at American Sound Studios, Memphis.
Tracks 3 & 8 recorded March 5, 1969. Track 9 recorded March 6, 1969.
Tracks 3, 8, & 9 recorded at Decca Universal Studios, Hollywood for the Universal Motion Picture "Change Of Habit".
This album has not been issued on CD.

ALMOST IN LOVE (1970)

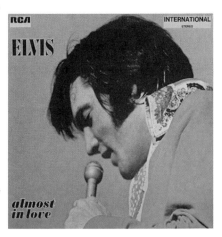

1. Almost In Love
2. Long Legged Girl
3. Edge Of Reality
4. My Little Friend
5. A Little Less Conversation
6. Rubberneckin'
7. Clean Up Your Own Backyard
8. U.S. Male
9. Charro
10. Stay Away Joe*

Left: the original UK cover art.

Right: the original US cover art.

Recording Information:

Track 3 recorded June 28, 1966 at MGM Studios, Hollywood for the MGM Motion Picture "Double Trouble".
Track 10 recorded October 1, 1967 at RCA Studio B, Nashville for the MGM Motion Picture "Stay Away Joe".
Track 8 recorded January 17, 1968 at RCA Studio B, Nashville.
Tracks 1, 3, & 5 recorded March 7, 1968 at Western Recorders, Los Angeles for the MGM Motion Picture "Live A Little, Love A Little".
Track 7 recorded August 23, 1968 at United Recorders, Hollywood for the MGM Motion Picture "The Trouble With Girls And How To Get Into It".
Track 9 recorded October 15, 1968 at Samuel Goldwyn Studios, Hollywood for the National General Motion Picture "Charro".
Track 4 recorded January 16, 1969. Track 6 recorded January 20, 1969. Tracks 4 & 6 recorded at American Sound Studios, Memphis.
* An alternate take of "Stay Away Joe" was originally issued on this album by mistake. On later issues of the album it was replaced by the song "Stay Away" from the same movie, which was recorded on January 17, 1968 at RCA Studio B, Nashville.
Although not recorded at a soundtrack session "Rubberneckin'" was also included in the soundtrack of the Universal Motion Picture "Change Of Habit".
The album is not widely available on CD, but a Canadian CD version has been issued.

ELVIS CHRISTMAS ALBUM (1970)

1. Blue Christmas
2. Silent Night
3. White Christmas
4. Santa Claus Is Back In Town
5. I'll Be Home For Christmas
6. If Everyday Was Like Christmas
7. Here Comes Santa Claus
8. O Little Town Of Bethlehem
9. Santa Bring My Baby Back To Me
10. Mama Liked The Roses*

Recording Information:

Tracks 1-5 & 7-9 first released on "Elvis' Christmas Album" in 1957.
Track 6 recorded June 10 – 12, 1966 at RCA Studio B, Nashville.
Track 10 recorded January 15, 1969 at American Sound Studios, Memphis.
This album has not been released on CD.

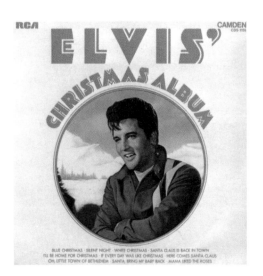

Above: the original cover art.

Left: A later UK re-issue on the Camden label.

RCA International: The Budget Albums

YOU'LL NEVER WALK ALONE (1971)

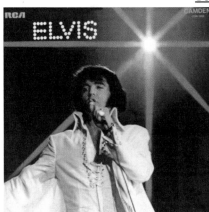

1. You'll Never Walk Alone
2. Who Am I?
3. Let Us Pray
4. Peace In The Valley
5. We Call On Him
6. I Believe
7. It Is No Secret
8. Sing You Children
9. Take My Hand Precious Lord

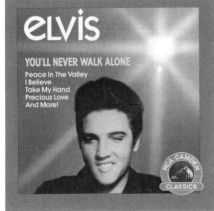

Left: the original cover art.

Right: a CD version from Canada.

Recording Information:

Tracks 6 recorded January 12, 1957. Tracks 4 & 9 recorded January 13, 1957. Track 7 recorded January 19, 1957.
Tracks 4, 6, 7, & 9 recorded at Radio Recorders, Hollywood.
Track 8 recorded September 28, 1966 at Paramount Studios, Hollywood for the Paramount Motion Picture "Easy Come, Easy Go".
Tracks 1 & 5 recorded September 11, 1967 at RCA Studio B, Nashville.
Track 3 recorded March 6, 1968 at Decca Universal Studios, Hollywood for the Universal Motion Picture "Change Of Habit".
Track 2 recorded February 22, 1969 at American Sound Studios, Memphis.
The UK vinyl version featured 10 tracks, and also included the song "Swing Down Sweet Chariot" from the 1960 album "His Hand In Mine".
The album is not widely available on CD, but a Canadian CD version has been issued.

C'MON EVERYBODY (1971)

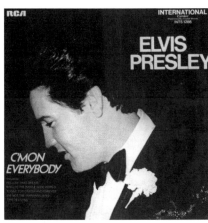

1. C'mon Everybody
2. Angel
3. Easy Come, Easy Go
4. A Whistling Tune
5. Follow That Dream
6. King Of The Whole Wide World
7. I'll Take Love
8. Today, Tomorrow And Forever
9. I'm Not The Marrying Kind
10. This Is Living

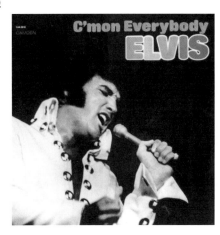

Left: original UK cover art.

Right: original US cover art.

Recording Information:

Track 2, 5, & 9 recorded July 2, 1961 at Radio Recorders, Hollywood for the Mirisch United Artists Motion Picture "Follow That Dream".
Track 4 recorded October 26, 1961. Tracks 6 & 10 recorded October 27, 1961.
Tracks 4, 6, & 10 recorded at Radio Recorders, Hollywood for the Mirisch United Artists Motion Picture "Kid Galahad".
Track 1 recorded July 9, 1963. Track 8 recorded July 11, 1963.
Tracks 1 & 8 recorded at Radio Recorders, Hollywood for the MGM Motion Picture "Viva Las Vegas".
Tracks 3 & 7 recorded September 28, 1966 at Paramount Studios, Hollywood for the Paramount Motion Picture "Easy Come Easy Go".
The album has not been issued on CD.

RCA International: The Budget Albums

I GOT LUCKY (1971)

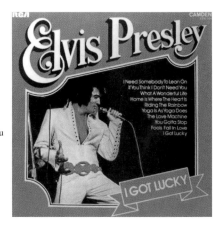

1. I Got Lucky
2. What A Wonderful Life
3. I Need Somebody To Lean On
4. Yoga Is As Yoga Does
5. Riding The Rainbow
6. Fools Fall In Love
7. The Love Machine
8. Home Is Where The Heart Is
9. You Gotta Stop
10. If You Think I Don't Need You

Left: original album art.

Right : a later UK re-issue on the Camden label.

Recording Information:

Track 2 recorded July 2, 1961 at Radio Recorders, Hollywood for the Mirisch United Artists Motion Picture "Follow That Dream".
Tracks 5 & 8 recorded October 26, 1961. Track 1 recorded October 27, 1961.
Tracks 1, 5, & 8 recorded at Radio Recorders, Hollywood for the Mirisch United Artists Motion Picture "Kid Galahad.
Track 10 recorded July 9, 1963. Track 3 recorded July 10, 1963.
Tracks 3 & 10 recorded at Radio Recorders, Hollywood for the MGM Motion Picture "Viva Las Vegas".
Track 6 recorded May 28, 1966 at RCA Studio B, Nashville.
Tracks 4, 7, & 9 recorded September 29, 1966 at Paramount Studios, Hollywood for the Paramount Motion Picture "Easy Come, Easy Go".
This album has not been released on CD.

ELVIS SINGS HITS FROM HIS MOVIES – PLUS TWO RECENT HITS (1972)

1. Down By The Riverside And When The Saints Go Marching In
2. They Remind Me Too Much Of You
3. Confidence
4. Frankie And Johnny
5. Guitar Man
6. Long Legged Girl
7. You Don't Know Me
8. How Would You Like To Be
9. Big Boss Man
10. Old Macdonald

Recording Information:

Tracks 2 & 7 recorded September 22, 1962 at Radio Recorders, Hollywood for the MGM Motion Picture "It Happened At The Worlds Fair".
Track 4 recorded May 13, 1965. Track 1 recorded May 14 – 15, 1965.
Tracks 1 & 4 recorded at Radio Recorders, Hollywood for the United Artists Motion Picture "Frankie And Johnny".
Track 6 recorded June 28, 1966. Track 10 recorded June 29, 1966.
Tracks 6 & 10 recorded at MGM Studios, Hollywood for the MGM Motion Picture "Double Trouble".
Track 3 recorded February 22, 1967 at RCA Studio B, Nashville for the United Artists Motion Picture "Clambake"
Tracks 5 & 9 recorded September 10, 1967. Track 7 recorded September 11, 1967.
Tracks 5, 7, & 9 recorded at RCA Studio B, Nashville.
This album has not been released on CD.

RCA International: The Budget Albums

BURNING LOVE AND HITS FROM HIS MOVIES VOLUME 2 (1972)

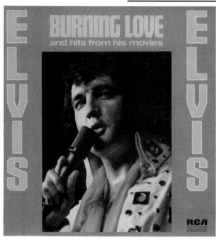

1. Burning Love
2. Tender Feeling
3. Am I Ready
4. Tonight Is So Right For Love
5. Guadalajara
6. It's A Matter Of Time
7. No More
8. Santa Lucia
9. We'll Be Together
10. I Love Only One Girl

Left: the original album.

Right: a Canadian CD version.

Recording Information:

Track 4 recorded April 27, 1960 at RCA Studios, Hollywood for the Paramount Motion Picture "GI Blues".
Track 7 recorded March 21, 1961 at Radio Recorders, Hollywood for the Paramount Motion Picture "Blue Hawaii".
Track 9 recorded March 29, 1962 at Radio Recorders, Hollywood for the Paramount Motion Picture "Girls! Girls! Girls!"
Track 5 recorded January 23, 1963 at Radio Recorders, Hollywood for the Paramount Motion Picture "Fun In Acapulco".
(Elvis' vocal overdub recorded February 27, 1963)
Track 8 recorded July 10, 1963 at Radio Recorders, Hollywood for the MGM Motion Picture "Viva Las Vegas".
Track 2 recorded September 30, 1963 at RCA Studio B, Nashville for the MGM Motion Picture "Kissin' Cousins".
Track 3 recorded February 16, 1966 at Radio Recorders, Hollywood for the MGM Motion Picture "Spinout".
Track 10 recorded July 29, 1966 at MGM Studios, Hollywood for the MGM Motion Picture "Double Trouble".
Track 1 recorded March 28, 1972. Track 6 recorded March 29, 1972.
Tracks 1 & 6 recorded at RCA Studio C, Hollywood.
The album is not widely available on CD, but a Canadian CD version has been issued.

SEPARATE WAYS (1973)

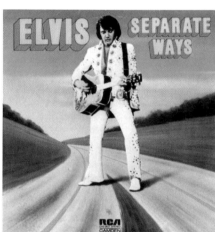

1. Separate Ways
2. Sentimental Me
3. In My Way
4. I Met Her Today
5. What Now, What Next, Were To
6. Always On My Mind
7. I Slipped, I Stumbled, I Fell
8. Is It So Strange
9. Forget Me Never
10. Old Shep

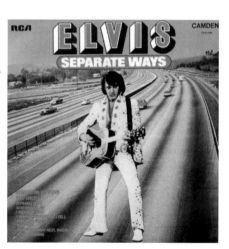

Left: the original US version.

**Right: the UK release featured
different cover art.**

Recording In formation:

Track 10 recorded September 2, 1956 at Radio Recorders, Hollywood.
Track 8 recorded January 19, 1957 at Radio Recorders, Hollywood.
Tracks 3 & 9 recorded November 7, 1960. Track 7 recorded November 8, 1960.
Tracks 3, 7, & 9 recorded at Radio Recorders, Hollywood for the 20th Century
Fox Motion Picture "Wild In The Country".
Track 2 recorded March 13, 1961 at RCA Studio B, Nashville.
Track 4 recorded October 16, 1961 at RCA Studio B, Nashville.
Track 5 recorded May 27, 1963 at RCA Studio B Nashville.
Track 1 recorded March 27, 1972. Track 6 recorded March 29, 1972.
Tracks 1 & 6 recorded at RCA Studio C, Hollywood.
The album is not widely available on CD, but a Canadian CD version has been issued (bottom right)

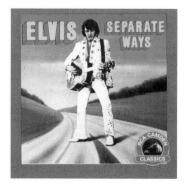

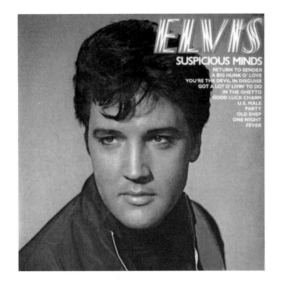

Above: Suspicious Minds (UK LP)

Below: King Of Rock N Roll (Australian LP)

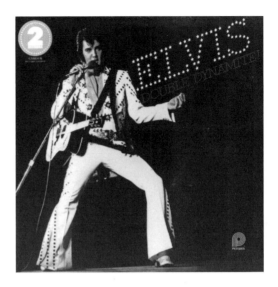

Above: Double Dynamite (US LP)

Below: The Legend (UK LP)

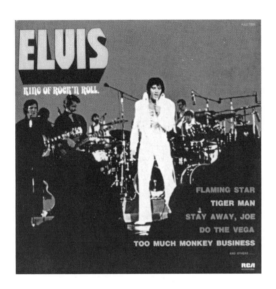

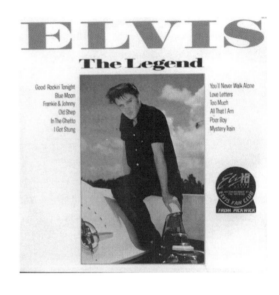

Below: Solid Rocks (France LP)

Below: US.Male (UK LP)

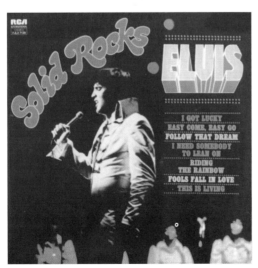

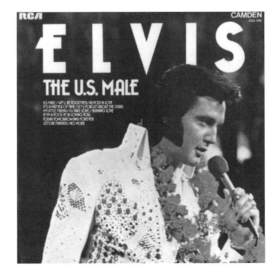

Follow That Dream: The RCA/BMG Collectors Label

Elvis bootleg albums have been common place amongst collectors since the early seventies, but over the last ten years as more previously unreleased material became available on CD, the standard of bootleg releases in terms of both packaging and sound quality has improved significantly.

Much of the material that has been bootlegged has remained officially unreleased, as whilst it would be of interest to the collector to own this material, it is often not suited for a commercial release.

By 1999 the amount of unofficial product available had reached a level that was unacceptable to both Elvis' record company RCA/BMG, and the Elvis Presley Estate, and as a result of this the decision was taken to launch a collectors label, and make previously unreleased recordings legally available to the Elvis collector.

The collectors label was named "Follow That Dream", and it was originally planned that there would be four releases per year. However, due to the popularity of these albums amongst collectors there have already been some additional releases, and it is quite possible that this policy will continue.

So far along with the standard "Follow That Dream" releases RCA/BMG have released "Too Much Monkey Business" which featured the long deleted recordings from the 1981 album "Guitar Man", a gospel "Easter Special" and a CD & book package "The Way It Was" featuring previously unseen photographs and out takes from the recently released "Elvis – That's The Way It Is – Special Edition".

These CD's are only available through fan clubs, Elvis magazines and specialist retailers.

BURBANK '68 – THE NBC TV COMEBACK SPECIAL (FTD – 1999)

1. Danny Boy (Instrumental)*
2. Baby What You Want Me To Do (instrumental)*
3. Love Me*
4. Tiger Man
5. Dialogue
6. Lawdy Miss Clawdy
7. One Night*
8. Blue Christmas*
9. Baby What You Want Me To Do
10. When My Blue Moon Turns To Gold Again*
11. Blue Moon Of Kentucky*
12. Dialogue
13. Heartbreak Hotel*
14. Hound Dog*
15. All Shook Up*
16. Can't Help Falling In Love*
17. Jailhouse Rock
18. Don't Be Cruel
19. Love Me Tender
20. Blue Suede Shoes
21. Trouble/Guitar Man (alternate take 4)*
22. If I Can Dream (alternate vocal take 4)*
23. Let Yourself Go (instrumental)*

Recording Information:

Tracks 22 & 23 recorded June 23, 1968 at Western Recorders, Los Angeles.
Tracks 1 – 12 recorded June 25, 1968 during Elvis' dressing room rehearsals at Burbank Studios, California.
Tracks 20 & 21 recorded June 29, 1968 during the 6 p.m. "Stand Up" show at Burbank Studios, California.
Tracks 13 – 19 recorded June 29, 1968 during the 8 p.m. "Stand Up" show at Burbank Studios, California.
* Previously unreleased performances.
All tracks recorded for the 1968 NBC TV Special "Elvis".

OUT IN HOLLYWOOD (FTD 1999)

1. Mexico (alternate take 7)
2. Cross My Heart And Hope To Die (alternate take 6)
3. Wild In The Country (alternate take 11)
4. Adam And Evil (alternate take 16)
5. Lonely Man (alternate take 4)
6. Thanks To The Rolling Sea (alternate take 3)
7. Where Do You Come From (alternate take 13)
8. King Of The Whole Wide World (alternate take 3)
9. Little Egypt (alternate take 21)
10. Wonderful World (alternate take 7)
11. This Is My Heaven (vocal overdub – take 4)
12. Spinout (alternate take 2)
13. All That I Am (alternate take 2)
14. We'll Be Together (alternate take 10)
15. Frankie And Johnny (alternate take 1)
16. I Need Somebody To Lean On (alternate take 8)
17. The Meanest Girl In Town (alternate take 9)
18. Night Life (alternate take 3)
19. Puppet On A String (alternate take 7)
20. Hey Little Girl (alternate takes 1 & 2)
21. Edge Of Reality (alternate take 6)
22. (You're So Square) Baby I Don't Care (vocal overdub take 6)

Recording Information:

Track 22 recorded May 8, 1957 for the MGM Motion Picture "Jailhouse Rock".
Tracks 3 & 5 recorded November 7, 1960 for the 20th Century Fox Motion Picture "Wild In The Country".
Track 8 recorded October 27, 1961 for the Mirisch United Artists Motion Picture "Kid Galahad".
Track 6 recorded March 26, 1962. Track 7 recorded March 27, 1962. Track 14 recorded March 29, 1962.
Tracks 6, 7, & 14 recorded for the Paramount Motion Picture "Girls! Girls! Girls!"
Track 1 recorded January 22, 1963 for the Paramount Motion Picture "Fun In Acapulco".
Track 18 recorded July 9, 1963. Track 16 recorded July 10, 1963.
Tracks 16 & 18 recorded for the MGM Motion Picture "Viva Las Vegas".
Track 9 recorded March 2, 1964 for the Paramount Motion Picture "Roustabout".
Tracks 17 & 19 recorded June 10, 1964. Track 2 recorded June 11, 1964.
Tracks 2, 17, & 19 recorded for the MGM Motion Picture "Girl Happy".
Track 20 recorded February 25, 1965 for the MGM Motion Picture "Harum Scarum".
Track 15 recorded May 14, 1965 for the United Artists Motion Picture "Frankie And Johnny".
Track 11 recorded August 2, 1965 for the Paramount Motion Picture "Paradise Hawaiian Style".
Tracks 4, 12, & 13 recorded February 17, 1966 for the MGM Motion Picture "Spinout".
Tracks 10 & 21 recorded March 7, 1968 for the MGM Motion Picture "Live A Little, Love A Little".
Tracks 1 – 9 , 11 – 19, & 22 recorded at Radio Recorders, Hollywood. Tracks 10 & 21 recorded at Western Recorders, Los Angeles.
Track 20 recorded at RCA Studio B, Nashville.
All tracks previously unreleased except "Little Egypt" which was first released on the Time Life compilation "Movie Magic" in the US.

IN A PRIVATE MOMENT (FTD 2000)

1. Loving You
2. Danny Boy
3. I'm Beginning To Forget You
4. Beyond The Reef
5. Sweet Leilani
6. If I Loved You
7. Lawdy Miss Clawdy
8. I Wonder, I Wonder, I Wonder
9. He
10. When The Swallows Come Back To Capistrano
11. She Wears My Ring
12. Sweet Leilani (alternate take)
13. Moonlight Sonata
14. Blue Hawaii
15. Hide Thou Me
16. Oh How I Love Jesus
17. Fools Rush In
18. It's A Sin To Tell A Lie
19. What Now My Love
20. Blowin' In The Wind
21. 500 Miles
22. I, John
23. I'll Take You Home Again Kathleen (fast version)
24. I Will Be true
25. Apron Strings
26. It's Been So Long Darling
27. I'll Take You Home Again Kathleen (slow version)
28. There's No Tomorrow
29. Number Eight

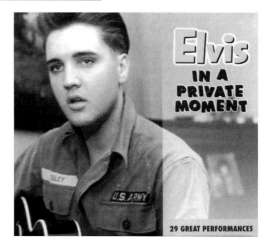

Recording Information:

Tracks 1 – 3 & 23 – 29 recorded 1959 during Elvis' army service in Bad Nauheim, Germany.
Tracks 4 – 12 recorded 1960 at Monovale Drive, Hollywood.
Tracks 13 – 22 recorded 1966 at Rocca Place, Hollywood..

THE JUNGLE ROOM SESSIONS (FTD 2000)

1. Bitter They Are, Harder They Fall (alternate takes 2 – 5)
2. She Thinks I Still Care (alternate take 2A)
3. The Last Farewell (alternate take 2)
4. Solitaire (alternate take 3)
5. I'll Never Fall In Love Again (alternate take 5)
6. Moody Blue (alternate take 3)
7. For The Heart (alternate takes 2 & 3)
8. Hurt (alternate take 3, 5/2/76)
9. Danny Boy (alternate take 8)
10. Never Again (alternate take 11)
11. Love Coming Down (alternate take 2)
12. Blue Eyes Crying In The Rain (alternate take 2)
13. It's Easy For You (alternate take 1)
14. Way Down (alternate take 2)
15. Pledging My Love (unedited master)
16. He'll have To Go (rough mix master)
17. Fire Down Below (instrumental)

Recording Information:

Tracks 1, 2, & 3 recorded February 2, 1976.
Track 4 recorded February 3, 1976.
Tracks 5 & 6 recorded February 4, 1976.
Tracks 7, 8, & 9 recorded February 5, 1976.
Tracks 10 & 11 recorded February 6, 1976.
Track 12 recorded February 7, 1976.
Tracks 13, 14, & 15 recorded October 29, 1976.
Tracks 16 & 17 recorded October 30, 1976.
Elvis attempted a studio recording of "America The Beautiful" on February 3, 1976 but the results were unsatisfactory and most of the tape was erased. A excerpt from this recording is featured at the end of this disc. It is likely that this excerpt is all that remains in the vaults from this recording.
All tracks recorded in the "Jungle Room" of Elvis' Graceland mansion, Memphis.
"Way Down" (alternate take 2) was first released on the album "Platinum – A Life In Music" in 1997.
All other performances are previously unreleased versions.

LONG LONELY HIGHWAY – NASHVILLE 1960 – 1968 (FTD 2000)

1. It's Now Or Never (alternate take 1)
2. A Mess Of Blues (alternate take 1)
3. It Feels So Right (alternate take 2)
4. I'm Yours (alternate take 2)
5. Anything That's Part Of You (alternate take 2)
6. Just For Old Times Sake (alternate take 1)
7. You'll Be Gone (alternate take 4)
8. I Feel That I've Known You Forever (alternate take 3)
9. Just Tell Her Jim Said Hello (alternate take 5)
10. She's Not You (alternate take 2 & work part take 4)
11. (You're The) Devil In Disguise (alternate takes 2 & 3)
12. Never Ending (alternate take 1)
13. Finders Keepers, Losers Weepers (alternate take 1)
14. (It's A) Long Lonely Highway (alternate take 1, single master)
15. Slowly But Surely (alternate take 1)
16. By And By (alternate take 4)
17. Fools Fall In Love (alternate take 4)
18. Come What May (take 8, stereo master)
19. Guitar Man (alternate take 10)
20. Singing Tree (take 13, unused master)
21. Too Much Monkey Business (alternate take 9)
22. Stay Away (slow version)

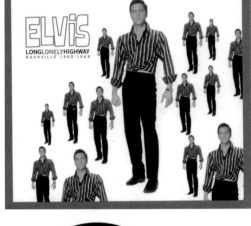

Recording Information:

Tracks 2 & 3 recorded March 21, 1960.
Track 1 recorded April 3, 1960.
Track 4 recorded June 26, 1961.
Track 5 recorded October 15, 1961.
Tracks 6 & 7 recorded March 18, 1962.
Tracks 8, 9, & 10 recorded March 19, 1962.
Tracks 11 & 12 recorded May 26, 1963.
Tracks 13 & 14 recorded May 27, 1963.
Track 15 recorded May 28, 1963.
Track 16 recorded May 27, 1966.
Tracks 17 & 18 recorded May 28, 1966.
Tracks 19 recorded September 10, 1967.
Track 20 recorded September 11, 1967.
Track 21 recorded January 15, 1968.
Track 22 recorded January 17, 1968.
All tracks recorded at RCA Studio B, Nashville .

Left: a later issue of the "Come What May" single on the Gold Standard label.

The version of "Long, Lonely Highway" included here is the single master. It is included on this collection in stereo for the first time.
The stereo master of "Come What May" was also located and given it's first CD release on this collection.
"Stay Away" (slow version) was first released in Argentina on the CD "Elvis Latino" in 1996.
Alternate take 1 of "A Mess Of Blues" and alternate take 3 of "It Feels So Right" were issued on the album "Platinum – A Life In Music" in 1997.
When this collection was issued it was said that both tracks would be included in improved sound quality, and whilst a better source tape has been used, the version of "It Feels So Right" included here is actually the previously unreleased alternate take 2.
All other performances are also previously unreleased versions.

TUCSON '76 (FTD 2000)

1. See See Rider
2. I Got A Woman/Amen
3. Love Me
4. If You Love Me Let Me Know
5. You Gave Me A Mountain
6. All Shook Up
7. Teddy Bear/Don't Be Cruel
8. And I Love You So
9. Jailhouse Rock
10. Help Me
11. Fever
12. Polk Salad Annie
13. Introductions:
Early Morning Rain
What'd I Say
Love Letters
Long Live Rock 'n' Roll
14. Hurt
15. Burning Love
16. Help Me Make It Through The Night
17. Danny Boy
18. Hound Dog
19. Funny How Time Slips Away
20. Can't Help Falling In Love

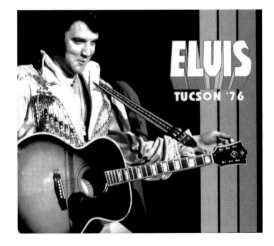

All Songs Recorded June 1, 1976 At The Community Centre Arena, Tucson, Arizona except:
Track 1 recorded May 30, 1976 during the Afternoon Show at the Ector County Coliseum, Odessa, Texas.
"Love Letters" from the Introductions recorded May 30, 1976 during the Evening Show at the Ector County Coliseum, Odessa Texas.
All material previously unreleased.

TOO MUCH MONKEY BUSINESS (FTD 2000)

1. Burning Love
2. I'll Be There
3. Guitar Man
4. After loving You
5. Too Much Monkey Business
6. Just Call Me Lonesome
7. Lovin' Arms
8. You Asked Me To
9. Clean Up Your Own Backyard
10. She Thinks I Still Care
11. Faded Love
12. I'm Movin' On
13. I'll Hold You In My Heart
14. In The Ghetto
15. Long Black Limousine
16. Only The Strong Survive
17. Hey Jude
18. Kentucky Rain
19. If You Talk In Your Sleep
20. Blue Suede Shoes

Recording Information:

Tracks 3 – 12 were first released on the "Guitar Man" album in 1981
Track 18 was first released in error on the promo CD "Golden Country Oldies".
1, 2, 13 – 17, 19, & 20 are previously unreleased recordings from the "Guitar Man" re-recording sessions produced by Felton Jarvis at Young 'un Sound, Nashville in 1980
Tracks 14 & 16 remade January 24, 1980.
Track 17 remade January 28, 1980.
Track 20 remade February 5, 1980. (This is an overdubbed version of the 1969 live recording and features Carl Perkins on electric guitar.)
Track 13 remade October 14, 1980.
Tracks 1 & 2 remade October 15, 1980.
Tracks 18 & 19 remade October 16, 1980.
Track 15 remade November 10, 1980.

ONE NIGHT IN VEGAS (FTD 2000)

1. Opening Riff
2. That's All Right
3. Mystery Train/Tiger Man
4. Talk
5. I Can't Stop Loving You
6. Love Me Tender
7. The Next Step Is Love
8. Words
9. I Just Can't Help Believin'
10. Something
11. Sweet Caroline
12. You've Lost That Lovin' Feelin'
13. You Don't Have To Say You Love Me
14. Polk Salad Annie
15. I've Lost You
16. Bridge Over Troubled Water
17. Patch It Up
18. Can't Help Falling In Love
19. Words
20. Cattle Call/Yodel
21. Twenty Days And Twenty Nights
22. You Don't Have To Say You Love Me
23. Bridge Over Troubled Water

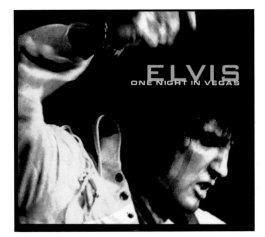

Recording Information:

Tracks 1– 18 recorded live August 10, 1970 during the Midnight Show at the International Hotel, Las Vegas.
Tracks 19 – 23 recorded August 4, 1970 during rehearsals in the Convention Centre at the International Hotel, Las Vegas.
"I Can't Stop Loving You", "The Next Step Is Love", and "You Don't Have To Say You Love Me" were first released on the album "Elvis – That's The Way It Is – Special Edition" in 2000.
All other tracks are previously unreleased performances.

6363 SUNSET (FTD 2001)

1. Always On My Mind (take 3)
2. Burning Love (take 2)
3. For The Good Times (take 3)
4. Where Do I Go From Here (take 6)
5. Fool (take 1)
6. It's A Matter Of Time (alternate take)
7. See See Rider (take 2)
8. Until It's Time For You To Go
9. A Big Hunk O' Love (take 2)
10. All Shook Up
11. Heartbreak Hotel
12. Teddy Bear/Don't Be Cruel
13. Can't Help Falling In Love
14. Green, Green Grass Of Home (takes 2 & 3)
15. Susan When She Tried (takes 1 & 2)
16. And I Love You So (take 1)
17. Bringing It Back (takes 2 & 3)
18. T.R.O.U.B.L.E. (take 1)
19. Shake A Hand (take 2)

Recording Information:

Tracks 3 & 4 recorded March 27, 1972.
Tracks 2 & 5 recorded March 28, 1972.
Tracks 1 & 6 recorded March 29, 1972.
Tracks 1 – 6 recorded at RCA Studio C, Hollywood.
Tracks 7 – 13 recorded March 31, 1972.
Tracks 7 – 13 recorded during rehearsals at RCA Studio A, Hollywood.
Tracks 14, 15, & 16 recorded March 11, 1975.
Tracks 17, 18, & 19 recorded March 12, 1975.
Tracks 14 – 19 recorded at RCA Studio C, Hollywood.
All material previously unreleased.

EASTER SPECIAL (FTD 2001)

1. March Of Dimes
2. It Is No Secret (take 12)
3. He Knows Just What I Need (take 1)
4. Mansion Over The Hilltop (take 1)
5. Joshua Fit The Battle (take 1)
6. I'm Gonna Walk Dem Golden Stairs (takes 2 & 3)
7. Known Only To Him (takes 1 & 2)
8. Run On (take 2)
9. Stand By Me (take 2)
10. So High (take 2)
11. Somebody Bigger Than You Or I (take 12)
12. We Call On Him (takes 4 & 5)
13. Saved (take 1)
14. An Evening Prayer (take 2)
15. Seeing Is Believing (take 4)
16. There Is No God But God (takes 1 & 2)
17. He Is My Everything (take 1)
18. Bosom Of Abraham (take 7)
19. I Got A Feeling In My Body (takes 6 & 7)
20. If That Isn't Love (takes 2, 6, & 7)

Recording Information:

Track 1 is a radio spot from 1957.
Track 2 recorded January 19, 1957 at Radio Recorders, Hollywood.
Tracks 3 & 4 recorded October 30, 1960.
Tracks 5, 6, & 7 recorded October 31, 1960.
Track 8 recorded May 25, 1966.
Track 9 recorded May 26, 1966.
Tracks 10 & 11 recorded May 27, 1966.
Track 12 recorded September 11, 1967.
Tracks 3 – 12 recorded at RCA Studio B, Nashville.
Track 13 recorded June 22, 1968 at Western Recorders, Los Angeles.
Track 14 recorded May 18, 1971.
Track 15 recorded May 19, 1971.
Tracks 16, 17, 18 recorded June 9, 1971.
Tracks 14 – 18 recorded at RCA Studio B, Nashville.
Tracks 19 recorded December 10, 1973.
Track 20 recorded December 16, 1973.
Tracks 19 & 20 recorded at Stax Studios, Memphis.
All material previously unreleased.

DIXIELAND ROCKS (FTD 2001)

1. Also Sprach Zarathustra
2. See See Rider
3. I Got A Woman/Amen
4. Love Me
5. If You Love Me Let Me Know
6. You Don't Have To Say Love Me
7. All Shook up
8. Teddy Bear/Don't Be Cruel
9. The Wonder Of You
10. Polk Salad Annie
11. Introductions/Johnny B. Goode/Long Live Rock 'n' Roll
12. My Boy
13. T.R.O.U.B.L.E.
14. I'll Remember You
15. Why Me Lord
16. Let Me Be There
17. An American Trilogy
18. Fairytale
19. Little Darlin'
20. Funny How Time Slips Away
21. Can't Help Falling In Love
22. Closing Vamp
23. Bridge Over Troubled Water
24. Love Me Tender

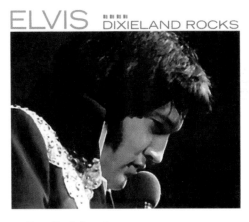

Recording Information:

Tracks 1 – 18 recorded live at the Murphy Athletic Centre, Middle Tennessee State University, Murfreesboro, May 6, 1975.
Tracks 19 – 24 recorded live at the Murphy Athletic Centre, Middle Tennessee State University, Murfreesboro, May 7, 1975.
The ending of the May 6 performance was not recorded.
"See See Rider" & "I Got A Woman/Amen" were first released on the album "Elvis Aron Presley" in 1980.
All other performances are previously unreleased.

ELVIS THE WAY IT WAS – AN AUDIO VISUAL DOCUMENTARY (FTD 2001)

MGM Rehearsal, July 14, 1970:
1. Words
2. The Next Step Is Love
MGM Rehearsal, July 15, 1970:
3. Ghost Riders In The Sky
4. Love Me
RCA Rehearsal, July 24, 1970:
5. That's All Right
6. I Got A Woman
7. I've Lost You
8. I Can't Stop Loving You
9. Just Pretend
MGM Rehearsal, July 29, 1970:
10. Words
11. I Just Can't Help Believin'
Las Vegas Rehearsal, August 4, 1970:
12. Something
Las Vegas Rehearsal, August 7, 1970:
13. Polk Salad Annie
14. Mary In The Morning
Las Vegas Stage Rehearsal, August 10, 1970:
15. You've Lost That Loving Feeling
Show 1: Las Vegas, August 10, 1970, Midnight Show:
16. Sweet Caroline
Show 2: Las Vegas, August 11, 1970, Dinner Show:
17. Hound Dog
18. Heartbreak Hotel
Show 3: Las Vegas, August 11, 1970, Midnight Show:
19. Don't Be Cruel
Show 4: Las Vegas, August 12, 1970, Dinner Show:
20. Blue Suede Shoes
21. You Don't Have To Say You Love Me.
Show 5: Las Vegas, August 12, 1970, Midnight Show:
22. Mystery Train/Tiger Man
Show 6: Las Vegas, August 13, 1970, Dinner Show:
23. The Wonder Of You
24. One Night
25. All Shook Up

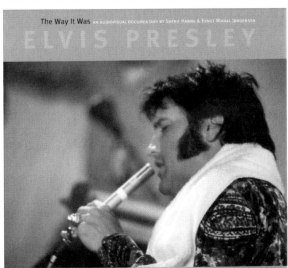

Following the release of the "That's The Way It Is – Special Edition" in 2001, there was a demand amongst Elvis fans for further previously unreleased material from this productive period of Elvis' career. The FTD release "One Night In Vegas" featured a concert recorded for the movie, and this was followed by the CD and book "The Way It Was" (by Sherif Hanna & Ernst Mikael Jorgenson) which featured previously unseen photographs, and a further disc of out takes from the movie

Recording Information:

"You've Lost That Loving Feeling" was first released on the album "Elvis Aron Presley" in 1980.
"Sweet Caroline" was first released on the FTD release "One Night In Vegas" in 2001.
"Don't Be Cruel" was first released on the album "Live In Las Vegas" in 2001.
"Mystery Train/Tiger Man" was first released on the album "Elvis – That's The Way It Is – Special Edition" in 2000.
All other tracks are previously unreleased performances.

MEMPHIS SESSIONS (FTD 2001)

1. After loving You (take 3)
2. Stranger In My Own Home Town (undubbed master)
3. In The Ghetto (take 11)
4. Suspicious Minds (rehearsal & take 6)
5. Any Day Now (take 2)
6. Only The Strong Survive (take 22)
7. Wearin' That Loved On Look (takes 3 & 10)
8. Do You Know Who I Am (take 1)
9. And The Grass Won't Pay No Mind
(undubbed master – alternate vocal)
10. You'll Think Of Me (take 14)
11. Power Of My Love (take 6)
12. This Is The Story (takes 1 & 2)
13. True Love Travels On A Gravel Road (takes 6 & 7)
14. Long Black Limousine (take 6)
15. Kentucky Rain (take 9)
16. Without Love (takes 3 & 4)
17. Hey Jude (spliced from takes 5 & 1)
18 If I'm A Fool For Loving You (take 3)
19. From A Jack To A King (takes 1, 2, & 3
20. I'm Movin' On (undubbed master – takes 1 & 2)

Recording Information:
Tracks 7, 12, & 14 recorded January 13, 1969.
Tracks 10 & 20 recorded January 14, 1969.
Track 3 recorded January 20, 1969.
Tracks 17 & 19 recorded January 21, 1969.
Tracks 4 & 16 recorded January 22, 1969.
Tracks 2, 9, & 13 recorded February 17, 1969.
Tracks 1, 8, & 11 recorded February 18, 1969.
Tracks 6 & 15 recorded February 19, 1969.
Tracks 5 & 18 recorded February 20, 1969.
All tracks recorded at American Sound Studios, Memphis.
Different mixes and overdubbed versions of tracks 2, 9, 12, & 20 have been previously released
Alternate take 6 of "Suspicious Minds" was first released on the album "From Nashville To Memphis – The Essential '60's Masters Volume 1" in 1993.
The rehearsal version of Suspicious Minds" is previously unreleased.
All other performances are previously unreleased.

Over the next few pages we take a look at some of the many compilation albums released over the years on both vinyl and CD.

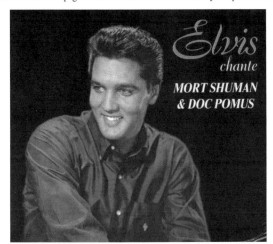 

Above left : Elvis Chante Mort Shuman & Doc Pomus (France double CD digi-pack – RCA label)
Above right: An illustrated booklet was also included with this CD

Below left : Elvis Chante Sid Tepper & Roy C. Bennett (France double CD digi-pack – RCA label)
Below right: An illustrated booklet was also included with this CD

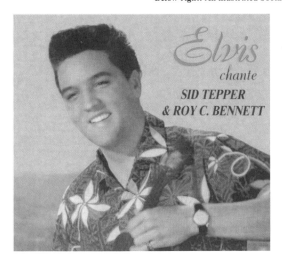 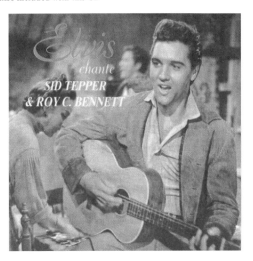

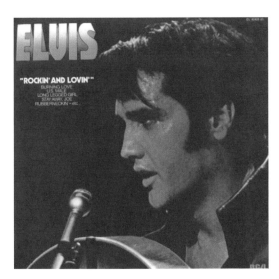 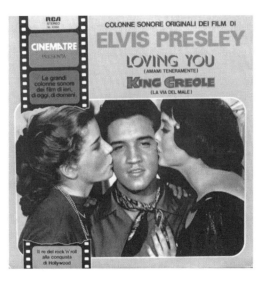

Above: Rockin' And Lovin' (Canada double LP – RCA label)   Above: Loving You & King Creole (Italy LP – RCA label)

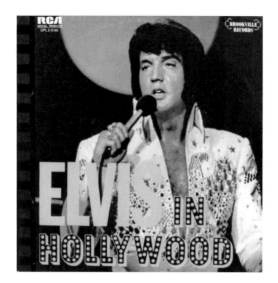

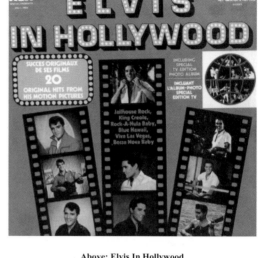

Above: Elvis In Hollywood
(USA double album – Brookville/ RCA label)

Below: Elvis In Hollywood (UK LP – Everest label)

Above: Elvis In Hollywood
(Canada LP with Photo Book – RCA label)

Below: Pictures Of Elvis (UK LP – RCA/Starcall label)

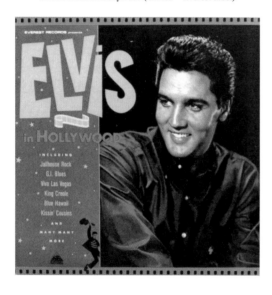

Below: Pictures Of Elvis
(Germany LP RCA/Take Off! Label)

Below: Elvis Sings World Hits
(Germany LP – RCA label)

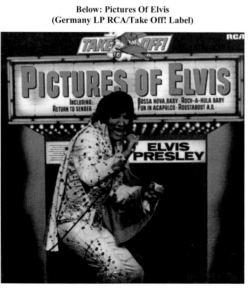

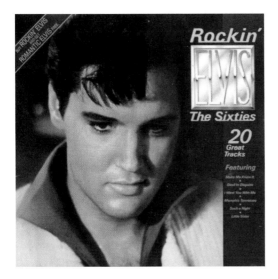

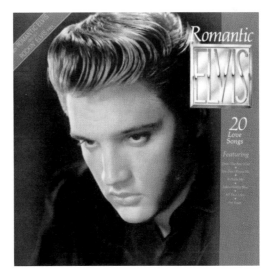

Above: Rockin' Elvis – The Sixties (UK LP – RCA label)

Below: Elvis The Romantic (Australia CD – RCA label)

Above: Romantic Elvis – 20 Love Songs (UK LP – RCA label)

Below: More Romantics (Australia CD – RCA label)

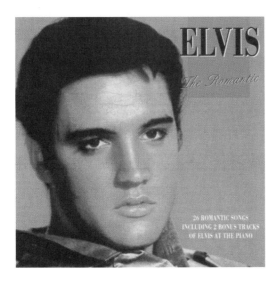

Below: Rendez–Vous Avec Elvis – 20 Love Songs
(France LP – K-Tel label)

Below : Love Songs (UK LP – K-Tel label)

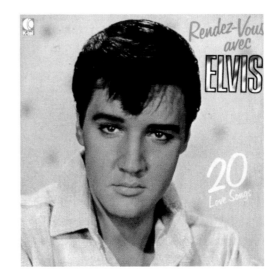

Above: The Rockin' Days (Italy LP – RCA label)

Below: Images (UK double album – Cambra label)

Above: Rock 'N' Roll Album
(Japan double album – RCA label)

Below: Golden Boy Elvis (Germany LP – Horzu label)

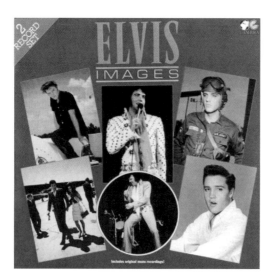

Below : Elvis La Pelvis (Argentina CD – RCA label)

Below: Elvis – A Celebration (Australia CD – RCA label)

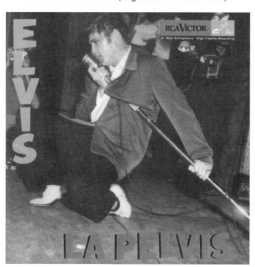

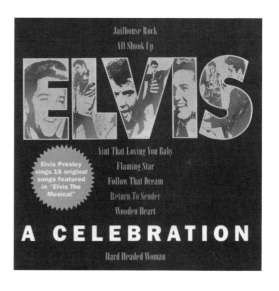

Above: The '56 Sessions Volume 1 (UK LP – RCA label)

Below: Elvis In The '70's
(Australia double album – RCA label)

Above: The '56 Sessions Volume 2 (UK LP – RCA label)

Below: Hits Of The '70's (UK LP – RCA label)

Below : Inspirations (UK LP – K-Tel label)

Below: Gospel Favourites (Australia CD – RCA label)

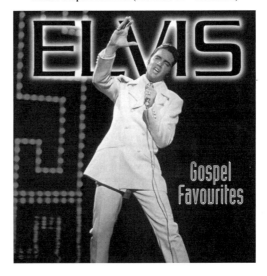

Above: Elvis In Demand (UK LP – RCA label)

Below: Elvis In Germany
(Germany LP – RCA/Take Off! label)

Above: Elvis By Request (Japan CD – RCA label)

Below: Elvis Latino (Argentina CD – RCA label)

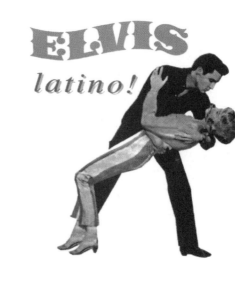

Below: The Country Side Of Elvis
(Australia CD – RCA label)

Below: Rarities (Holland LP – RCA label)

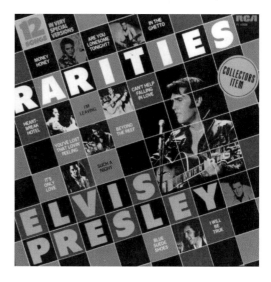

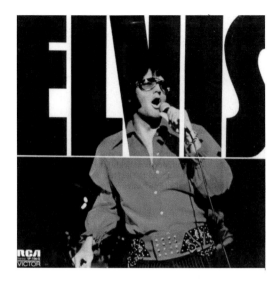

Above: Elvis (Australia LP – RCA label)

Above: Flaming Star & Summer Kisses (UK LP – RCA label)

Below : A Mi Manera (My Way) (Argentina CD – RCA label)

Below: A Portrait In Music (Germany LP – RCA label)

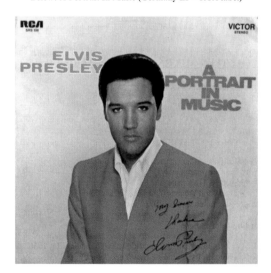

Below: Always On My Mind (Europe CD – RCA label)

Below: Historia De La Musica Rock (Spain LP – RCA label)

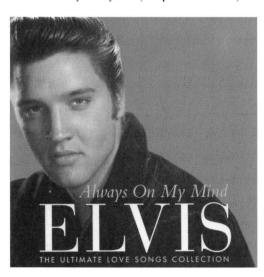

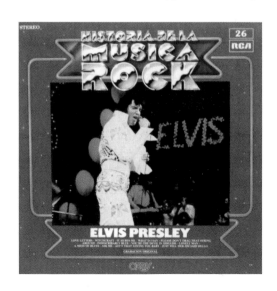

LAWDY MISS CLAWDY (MEMORY RECORDS)

Studio recordings 1956

1. I Got A Woman (alternate take)
2. Heartbreak Hotel (take 5)
3. Heartbreak Hotel (take 6)
4. Money Honey (master)
5. I'm Counting On You (take 13)
6. I Was The One (takes 1-3)
7. Blue Suede Shoes (master)
8. My Baby Left Me (master)
9. One Sided Love Affair (chat/master)
10. So Glad You're Mine (master)
11. I'm Gonna Sit Right Down
And Cry Over You (master)
12. Tutti Frutti (master)

13. Lawdy Miss Clawdy (takes 1 & 3)
14. Lawdy Miss Clawdy (take 6)
15. Lawdy Miss Clawdy (takes 7, 8, & 9)
16. Lawdy Miss Clawdy (take 12)
17. Shake Rattle And Roll (takes 1, 2, 3, & 5)
18. Shake Rattle And Roll (take 7)
19. Shake Rattle And Roll (take 8)
20. I Want You, I Need You, I Love You (take 3)
21. I Want You, I Need You, I Love You (take 4)
22. Send Me Some Lovin' (home recording)
23. Elvis Presents The New RCA Record Player
24. Perfect For Parties (edited version)

Recording Information:

Tracks 1 – 4 recorded January 10, 1956. Tracks 5 & 6 recorded January 11, 1956.
Tracks 1 – 6 recorded at RCA Studios, Nashville.
Tracks 7 – 10 recorded January 30, 1956. Tracks 11 & 12 recorded January 31, 1956.
Tracks 13 – 19 recorded February 3, 1956.
Tracks 7 – 19 recorded at RCA Studios, New York.
Tracks 20 & 21 recorded April 14, 1956 at RCA Studio B, Nashville.
Track 22 recorded 1959 during Elvis' army service in Bad Nauheim, Germany.
Track 23 from a 1956 promotional radio spot.
Track 24 is an edited version of the 1956 EP "Perfect For Parties" which featured Elvis introducing tracks by other RCA artists.

THE TEEN-AGE RAGE (HIS MASTER'S VOICE)

Studio recordings 1956 – 1958

1. Lawdy Miss Clawdy (alternate take 6)
2. First In Line (master take 27)
3. I Need Your Love Tonight (alternate take 13)
4. I'm Counting On You (master take 17)
5. A Big Hunk O' Love (alternate take 4)
6. One Sided Love Affair (master take 8 with unreleased countdown)
7. I Was The One (master take 7)
8. A Fool Such As I (alternate take 8)
9. How's The World Treating You (master take 7)
10. I Got Stung (alternate take 10)

Recording Information:

Tracks 4 & 7 recorded at RCA Studios, Nashville, January 11, 1956.
Track 6 recorded at RCA Studios, New York, January 30, 1956.
Track 1 recorded at RCA Studios, New York, February 3, 1956.
Track 9 recorded at Radio Recorders, Hollywood, September 1, 1956.
Track 2 recorded at Radio Recorders, Hollywood, September 3, 1956.
Tracks 3, 5 & 8 recorded at RCA Studio B, Nashville, June 10, 1958.
Track 10 recorded at RCA Studio B, Nashville, June 11, 1958.

PERFECT FOR PARTIES (SPECIAL PRODUCTS)

CD copy of a 1956 EP featuring Elvis Introducing tracks by other RCA recording artists

1. Love Me – Elvis Presley
2. Anchors Aweigh – Tony Cabot
3. That's A Puente - Tito Puente
4. Rock Me But Don't Roll Me – Tony Scott
5. Happy Face Baby – The Three Suns
6. Prom To Prom – Dave Bell

Each track featured a spoken introduction by Elvis. Elvis' version of "Love Me" is the RCA master from the 1956 album "Elvis".

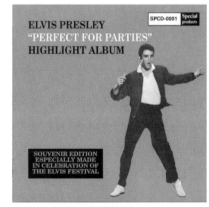

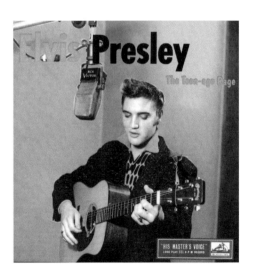

The CD EP was released
with new cover artwork
(above)
and also with the original
artwork (left)

WHEN ALL WAS KOOL (MYSTERY TRAIN)

1950's out takes, live recordings and radio broadcasts.

1. I Want You, I Need You, I Love You (alternate take 3)
2. I Want You, I Need You, I Love You (alternate take 4)
3 Elvis in Canada (radio broadcast April 4, 1957)
4 Live In Toronto/Heartbreak Hotel – part one (April 2, 1957)
5. Toronto Teenagers Talk About Elvis
6. Heartbreak Hotel – part two
7. Elvis Talks To Mac Lipson In Ottawa (April 3, 1957)
8. I'm Left, You're Right, She's Gone
9. Trying To Get To You
10. That's Al Right
11. Blue Moon Of Kentucky
12. I Don't Care If The Sun Don't Shine
13. Good Rockin' Tonight
14. Baby Let's Play House
15. Mystery Train
16. How Do You Think I Feel?
17. Radio Promo for the June 3, 1956 Concert In Oakland, California
18. Elvis Live On The Milton Berle Show:
Shake, Rattle And Roll
Heartbreak Hotel
Blue Suede Shoes
Comedy Skit
19. Elvis Talks To "Happy" On NBC (late 1956)

Recording Information:

Tracks 1 & 2 recorded at RCA Studio B, Nashville, April 11, 1956.
Tracks 8 – 15 are original Sun master recordings from first generation master tapes:
Track 8 recorded March 5, 1955, Sun Studios, Memphis.
Tracks 9 & 15 recorded July 11, 1955, Sun Studios, Memphis.
Tracks 10 & 11 recorded July 5 – 6, 1954, Sun Studios, Memphis.
Tracks 12 & 13 recorded September 1954, Sun Studios, Memphis.
Track 14 recorded February 5, 1955, Sun Studios, Memphis.
Track 16 Sun Studio rehearsal featuring Scotty Moore, Johnny Bernero, & Elvis – exact date unknown.
Track 18 recorded during a TV broadcast from San Diego, California, April 3, 1956.

I BEG OF YOU (DESPERADO RECORDS)

Studio out takes 1956 – 1957.

1. I Beg Of You (take 1)
2. I Beg Of You (takes 2, 3, & 4)
3. I Beg Of You (take 5)
4. I Beg Of You (take 5)
5. I Beg Of You (take 6)
6. I Beg Of You (takes 7, 8, & 9)
7. I Beg Of You (take 11)
8. I Beg Of You (take 12)
9. That's When Your Heartaches Begin (take 1)
10. That's When Your Heartaches Begin (take 2)
11. That's When Your Heartaches Begin (takes 3-5)
12. That's When Your Heartaches Begin (take 6)
13. That's When Your Heartaches Begin (take 7-13)
14. Shake Rattle And Roll (take 1)
15. Shake rattle And Roll (take 2)
16. Shake Rattle And Roll (takes 3, 5, & 6)
17. Shake Rattle And Roll (take 7)
18. Shake Rattle And Roll (take 8)
19. Shake Rattle And Roll (takes 9-11)
20. Shake Rattle And Roll (take 12)*
21. Shake Rattle And Roll (take 12)*
22. Lawdy Miss Clawdy (takes 7-8)
23. Lawdy Miss Clawdy (take 9)
24. Lawdy Miss Clawdy (takes 10-11)
25. Lawdy Miss Clawdy (take 12)
26. I Want You. I Need You, I Love You (take 3)
27. I Want You, I Need You, I Love You (take 4)
28. I Want You, I Need You, I Love You (take 5)
29. I Want You, I Need You, I Love You (take 11)

Recording Information:

Tracks 14 – 25 recorded February 3, 1956 at RCA Studios, New York.
Tracks 26 – 29 recorded April 4, 1956 at RCA Studio B, Nashville.
Tracks 1 – 13 recorded January 13, 1957 at Radio Recorders, Hollywood.
* Take 12 of "Shake Rattle & Roll" (track 20) is an incomplete performance.
The engineer also called "take 12" for the following take which was completed and used as the master.

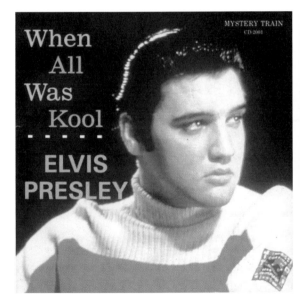

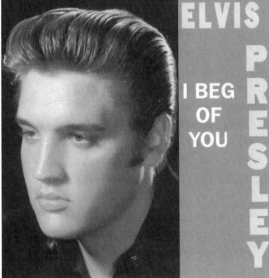

THE BEST OF THE LOST BINUARAL TAKES (BILKO)

1. Peace In The Valley (take 1)
2. I Beg Of You (take 5)
3. That's When Your Heartaches Begin (take 1)
4. It Is No Secret (take 12)
5. Blueberry Hill (take 80)
6. Have I Told You Lately That I Love You (take 1)
7. Have I Told You Lately That I Love You (take 7)
8. Is It So Strange (take 8)
9. Is It So Strange (take 9)
10. I Beg Of You (take 10)
11. I Beg Of You (take 11)

Recording Information:

Tracks 1, 2, 3, 10, & 11 recorded January 13, 1957 at Radio Recorders, Hollywood.
Tracks 4 – 9 recorded January 19, 1957 at Radio Recorders, Hollywood.

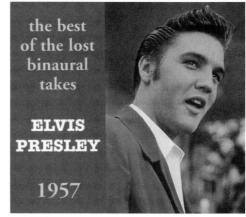

I GOT STUNG (NO LABEL NAME)

Studio out takes 1957 – 58

1. I Got Stung (take 1)
2. I Got Stung (takes 2-7)
3. I Got Stung (take 8)
4. Got Stung (take 9)
5. I Got Stung (take 11)
6. I Got Stung (take 12)
7. I Got Stung (take 13)
8. I Got Stung (take 14)
9. I Got Stung (take 15)
10. I Got Stung (take 16)
11. I Got Stung (takes 17-18)
12. I Got Stung (take 20)
13. I Got Stung (take 21)
14. I Got Stung (take 22)
15. Peace In The Valley (take 1)
16. Peace In The Valley (take 2)
17. Peace In The Valley (take 3)

18. Peace In The Valley (take 4)
19. Peace In The Valley (takes 5-6)
20. Peace In The Valley (take 7)
21. Peace In The Valley (take 8)
22. Peace In The Valley (Take 9)
23. Ain't That Loving You Baby (take 1)
24. Aint That Loving You Baby (takes 2-3)
25. Ain't That Loving You Baby (take 4)
26. Ain't That Loving You Baby (takes 5-11)
27. A Fool Such As I (takes 1-2)
28. A Fool Such As I (take 3)
29. A Fool Such As I (take 4)
30. A Fool Such As I (take 5)
31. A Fool Such As I (takes 6-7)
32. A Fool Such As I (take 8)
33. Interview

Recording Information:

Tracks 15 – 22 recorded January 13, 1957 at Radio Recorders, Hollywood.
Tracks 23 – 32 recorded June 10, 1958. Tracks 1 – 13 recorded June 11, 1958.
Tracks 1– 13 & 23 – 32 recorded at RCA Studio B, Nashville.

TOTALLY STUNG (MADISON)

Studio out takes 1956 – 1958.

1. I Got Stung (take 8/take 20 pre-song banter)
2. A Fool Such As I (takes 4-5)
3. Ain't That Loving You Baby (medium tempo – takes 2-4)
4. A Big Hunk O' Love (take 2)
5. A Fool Such As I (takes 6-8)
6. I Need Your Love Tonight (take 1)
7. I Got Stung (takes 15-16)
8. Lawdy Miss Clawdy (take 4)
9. I Was The One (takes 1-3)
10. One Sided Love Affair (master take 8 with count in)
11. Ain't That Loving You Baby (fast tempo – take 8)
12. I Need Your Love Tonight (takes 11-13)
13. A Big Hunk O' Love (take 3)
14. I Got Stung (takes 21-22)
15. Lawdy Miss Clawdy (take 5)
16. I Want You, I Need You, I Love You (take 14 with take 5 count in added)
17. I Need Your Love Tonight (take 4)
18. Ain't That Loving You Baby (fast tempo – takes 9-10)
19. I Got Stung (take 11)
20. I Need Your Love Tonight (take 15)
21. Lawdy Miss Clawdy (take 6)
22. I Want You, I Need You, I Love You (take 16)
23. Ain't That Loving You Baby (fast tempo – take 11)
24. I Got Stung (takes 17-18)
25. I Need Your Love Tonight (takes 16-17 & 8-9)
26. Lawdy Miss Clawdy (take 1)
27. A Big Hunk O' Love (take 4)

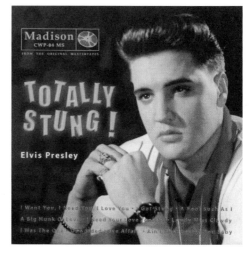

Recording information:

Tracks 1, 7, 14, 19, & 24 recorded June 11, 1958.
Tracks 2, 3, 4, 5, 6, 11, 12, 13, 17, 18, 20, 23, 25, & 27 recorded June 10, 1958.
Tracks 1 – 7, 11 – 14, 17 – 20, 23 – 25, & 27 recorded at RCA Studio B, Nashville.
Track 10 recorded January 30, 1956.
Tracks 8, 15, 21, & 26 recorded February 3, 1956.
Tracks 8, 10, 15, 21, & 26 recorded at RCA Studios, New York.
Track 9 recorded January 11, 1956 at RCA Studios, Nashville.
Tracks 16 & 22 recorded April 14, 1956 at RCA Studio B, Nashville.

ABSENT WITHOUT LEAVE (DOUBLE G)

Elvis' last pre-army recording session.

Disc One:

I Need Your Love Tonight:

1. Take 1
2. Takes 2-3
3. Take 4
4. Take 5
5. Take 6
6. Take 7
7. Take 8
8. Take 9
9. Take 10
10. Take 10b
11. Takes 11-12
13. Take 14
14. Take 15
15. Take 18 (master)

A Big Hunk O' Love:

16. Take 1
17. Take 2
18. Take 3
19. Take 4
20. Spliced Master (splice of takes 3 & 4)

Ain't That Loving You Baby:

21. Take 1 – medium tempo
22. Takes 2-3
23. Take 4
24. Takes 5-11 – fast tempo

A Fool Such As I:

25. Takes 1 –2
26. Take 3
27. Take 4
28. Take 5
29. Takes 6-7
30. Take 8
31. Take 9 (master)

Disc Two:

I Got Stung:

1. Take 1
2. Takes 2-7
3. Take 8
4. Take 9
5. Take 10
6. Take 10
7. Take 11
8. Takes 12-13
9. Take 14
10. Take 15
11. Take 16
12. Takes 17-18
13. Take 20
14. Take 20
15. Take 22
16. Take 24 (master)

Press Interviews:

17. Brooklyn Army Terminal, September 22, 1958
18. Brooklyn Army Terminal, September 22, 1958
19. Army Newsreel Interview
20. With Pat Heron In The Library Of The USS Randall
21. John Paris Interview In Germany
22. Elvis Arrives In Bremerhaven

Recording Information:

Disc One recorded June 10, 1958. Disc Two (music) recorded June 11, 1958.
All musical performances recorded at RCA Studio B, Nashville.

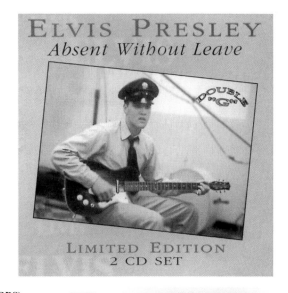

SOLDIER BOY IS BACK (MEMORY RECORDS)

1. Make Me Know It (take 3)
2. Soldier Boy (take 1)
3. Soldier Boy (takes 2-7)
4. Stuck On you (alt take)
5. Fame And Fortune (take 1)
6. Fame And Fortune (take 3)
7. Fame And Fortune (takes 4-7)
8. Fame And Fortune (take 9)
9. Fame And Fortune (take 10)
10. Fame And Fortune (take 11)
11. Fame And Fortune (take 12)
12. A Mess Of Blues (take 1)
13. It Feels So Right (take 3)
14. Fever (takes 2-3)
15. Like A Baby (takes 1-2)
16. Like A Baby (takes 3-4)
17. It's Now Or Never (undubbed master)
18. The Girl Of My Best Friend (take 6)
19. Dirty Dirty Feeling (alt take)
20. Thrill of Your Love (alt take)
21. I Gotta Know (alt mix)
22. Such A Night (alt take)
23. Such A Night (alt mix)
24. Are You Lonesome Tonight (alt mix)
25. The Girl Next Door Went A Walking (take 6)
26. I Will Be Home Again (master)
27. Reconsider Baby (master)

Studio out takes from the "Elvis Is Back"
Sessions.

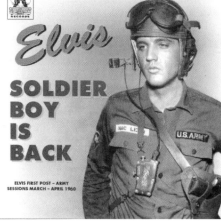

Recording Information:

Tracks 1– 3 recorded March 20, 1960.
Tracks 4 – 13 recorded March 21, 1960.
Tracks 14 – 17 recorded April 3, 1960.
Tracks 18 – 27 recorded April 4, 1960.
All tracks recorded at RCA Studio B, Nashville.

SURRENDER BY ELVIS
(THE FAMOUS GROOVE RECORDS)

Studio out takes from the "His Hand In Mine" sessions.

 1. Milky White Way (takes 1-3)
 2. Milky White Way (takes 4-6)
 3. Milky White Way (take 7)
 4. His Hand In Mine (take 1)
 5. His Hand In Mine (takes 2-3)
 6. His Hand In Mine (take 4)
 7. His Hand In Mine (take 5)
 8. I Believe In The Man In The Sky (take 1)
 9. I Believe In The Man In The Sky (takes 2-3)
10. I Believe In The Man In The Sky (take 4)
11. He Knows Just What I Need (take 1)
12. He Knows Just What I Need (takes 2-3)
13. He Knows Just What I Need (take 4)
14. He Knows Just What I Need (takes 5-6)
15. He Knows Just What I Need (take 7)
16. He Knows Just What I Need (take 8)
17. He Knows Just What I Need (take 9)
18. He Knows Just What I Need (take 10)
19. Surrender (take 1)
20. Surrender (take 2)
21. Surrender (take 3)
22. Surrender (take 4)
23. Surrender (takes 5-6)
24. Surrender (take 7)
25. Mansion Over The Hilltop (false start & take 2)
26. In My Fathers House (take 8)
27. In My Fathers House (work part – take 1)

Recording Information:

Tracks 1 – 25 recorded October 30, 1960.
Tracks 26 & 27 recorded October 31, 1960.
All tracks recorded at RCA Studio B, Nashville.

THE NASHVILLE SESSIONS 1960-61
(DESPERADO RECORDS)

1. Fame And Fortune
2. A Mess Of Blues
3. It Feels So Right
4. Soldier Boy (takes 2-6)
5. Soldier Boy (take 7)
6. Fever (take 1)
7. Fever (take 2)
8. Fever (take 3)
9. Like A Baby (take 1)
10. Like A Baby (take 2)
11. Like A Baby (take 3)
12. Like A Baby (take 4)
13. Like A Baby (take 5)
14. Dirty Dirty Feeling
15. Thrill Of Your Love (take 1)
16. Thrill Of Your Love (take 2)
17. Such A Night
18. Are You Lonesome Tonight
19. The Girl Next Door Went A Walking
20. My Jesus Knows Just What I Need
21. Surrender
22. Working On The Building
23. I'm Coming Home (take 5)
24. I'm Coming Home (take 6)
25. I'm Coming Home (take 7)
26. Gently
27. In Your Arms
28. I Feel So Bad
29. It's A Sin (take 1)
30. It's A Sin (take 2)
31. It's A Sin (take 3)
32. I Want You With Me (take 1)
33. I Want You With Me (take 2)

Recording Information:

Tracks 1, 4, & 5 recorded March 20, 1960.
Tracks 2 & 3 recorded March 21, 1960.
Tracks 6 – 13 recorded April 3, 1960.
Tracks 14 – 19 recorded April 4, 1960.
Tracks 20 & 21 recorded October 30, 1960.
Track 22 recorded October 31, 1960.
Tracks 23 – 33 recorded March 12, 1961.
All tracks recorded at RCA Studio B, Nashville.

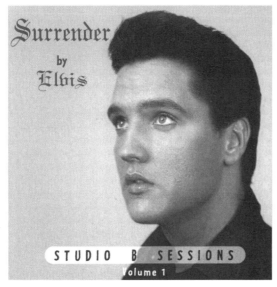

ANYTHING THAT'S PART OF YOU
(MEMORY RECORDS)

Disc One:

1. For The Millionth And The Last Time (takes 1-2)
2. For The Millionth And The Last Time (takes 3-6)
3. For The Millionth And The Last Time (takes 7-11)
4. Good Luck Charm (takes 1-3)
5. Anything That's Part Of You (takes 1-2)
6. Anything That's Part Of You (takes 3-5)
7. Anything That's Part Of You (takes 6-9)
8. I Met Her Today (takes 1-3)
9. I Met Her Today (takes 4-6)
10. I Met Her Today (takes 7-13)
11. I Met Her Today (takes 14-16)
12. I Met Her Today (takes 17-20)
13. (Such An) Easy Question (false start & take 3)
14. Just For Old Times Sake (take 1)

Disc Two:

1. Just For Old Times Sake (takes 2-4)
2. Something Blue (takes (1- 2)
3. Something Blue (take 3)
4. Something Blue (takes 5-6)
5. Gonna Get Back Home Somehow (takes 1-2)
6. Gonna Get Back Home Somehow (takes 3-4)
7. Gonna Get Back Home Somehow (takes 5-6)
8. Fountain Of Love (takes 1-4)
9. Fountain Of Love (takes 5-6)
10. Fountain Of Love (takes 7-9)
11. Night Rider (takes 1-3)
12. Night Rider (takes 4-5)
13. I Feel That I've Known You Forever (takes 1-2)
14. I Feel That I've know You Forever (takes 3-4)
15. Just Tell Her Jim Said Hello (takes 1-3)
16. Just Tell Her Jim Said Hello (takes 4-5)
17. Suspicion (takes 1-2)
18. Suspicion (takes 3-4)
19. She's Not You (takes 1-2)
20. She's Not You (work parts 1-4)

Recording Information:

Disc One:
Tracks 1 – 7 recorded October 15, 1961.
Tracks 8 – 12 recorded October 16, 1961.
Tracks 13 & 14 recorded March 18, 1962.

Disc Two:
Tracks 1– 12 recorded March 18, 1962.
Tracks 13 – 20 recorded March 19, 1962.
All tracks recorded at RCA Studio B, Nashville.

THE NASHVILLE SESSIONS 1961 – 63
(DESPERADO RECORDS)

1. There's Always Me (take 1)
2. There's Always Me (take 2)
3. There's Always Me (take 3)
4. There's Always Me (take 4)
5. There's Always Me (takes 5, 6, 7, & 8)
6. There's Always Me (take 9)
7. Starting Today (take 1)
8. Starting Today (take 2)
9. Sentimental Me
10. Judy (take 1)
11. Judy (takes 2 & 3)
12. Judy (take 4)
13. Judy (takes 5 & 6)
14. Judy (take 7)
15. Put The Blame On Me (take 1)
16. Put The Blame On Me (take 2)
17. Put The Blame On Me (takes 3 & 4)
18. For The Millionth And The Last Time
19. Night Rider
20. Something Blue
21. Gonna Get Back Home Somehow
22. (Such An) Easy Question
23. Fountain Of Love
24. Just For Old Times Sake
25. Just Tell Her Jim Said Hello
26. Suspicion
27. Devil In Disguise (takes 1 & 2)
28. Devil In Disguise (takes 3)
29. Devil In Disguise (takes 4 & 5)
30. Never Ending (take 1)
31. Never Ending (take 2)
32. Witchcraft
33. Finders Keepers, Losers Weepers

Recording Information:

Tracks 1 – 6 recorded March 12, 1961.
Tracks 7 – 17 recorded March 13, 1961.
Track 18 recorded October 15, 1961.
Track 19 recorded October 16, 1961.
Tracks 20 – 24 recorded March 18, 1962.
Tracks 25 & 26 recorded March 19, 1962.
Tracks 27 – 31 recorded May 26, 1963.
Tracks 32 & 33 recorded May 27, 1963.
All tracks recorded at RCA Studio B, Nashville.

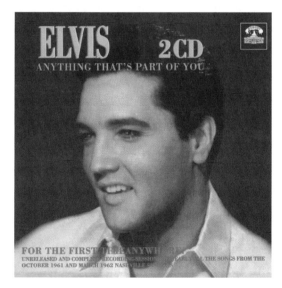

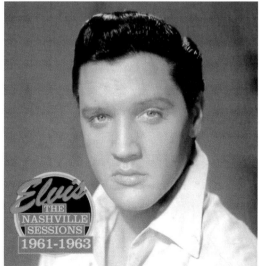

STAND BY ME – THE GOSPEL ACCORDING TO ELVIS (1) (2001)

1. Peace In The Valley – take 4
2. It Is No Secret – take 5
3. Milky White Way – take 3
4. His Hand In Mine – take 1
5. I Believe In The Man In The Sky – take 1
6. He Knows Just What I Need
7. Known Only To Him – take 2
8. Working On The Building – take 2
9. Run On – take 6
10. How Great Thou Art – take 2
11. Stand By Me – take 2
12. So High – take 3
13. By And By – take 9
14. Somebody Bigger Than You I – take 12
15. Without Him – take 8
16. If the Lord Was Walking By My Side – take 1
17. We Call On Him – take 3
18. You'll Never Walk Alone – take 2
(with extra verse)

Recording Information:

Track 1 recorded at Radio Recorders, Hollywood, January 13, 1957.
Track 2 recorded at Radio Recorders, Hollywood, January 19, 1957.
Tracks 3 – 6 recorded at RCA Studio B, Nashville, October 30, 1960.
Tracks 7 & 8 recorded at RCA Studio B, Nashville, October 31, 1960.
Tracks 9 & 10 recorded at RCA Studio B, Nashville, May 25, 1966.
Track 11 recorded at RCA Studio B, Nashville, May 26, 1966.
Tracks 12 – 15 recorded at RCA Studio B, Nashville, May 27, 1966.
Track 16 recorded at RCA Studio B, Nashville, May 28, 1966.
Tracks 17 & 18 recorded at RCA Studio B, Nashville, September 11, 1967.

STAND BY ME – THE GOSPEL ACCORDING TO ELVIS VOLUME 2 (2001)

1. He Knows Just What I Need – take 1
2. Milky White Way – takes 1, 2, 4 & 5
3. He Knows Just What I Need – takes 3 & 7
4. Crying In The Chapel – Takes 1, 2 & 3
5. Working On The Building – take 1
6. He Knows Just What I Need – take 9
7. Somebody Bigger Than You And I – takes 2, 4 & 11
8. Stand By Me – takes 3, 4 & 2
9. Run On – takes 1 & 2
10. If The Lord Wasn't Walking By Side – take 4
11. Where No Stands Alone – take 3
12. Without Him – take 1
13. Stand By Me – takes 9 & 10
14. So High – take 1
15. Farther Along – takes 1 & 2
16. By And By – takes 3 & 4
17. Somebody Bigger Than You I - takes 8 & 15
18. Without Him – takes 6, 10 & 14
19. If The Lord Wasn't Walking By My Side – take 6
20. We Call On Him - take 2

Recording Information:

Tracks 1, 2, 3, & 6 recorded at RCA Studio B, Nashville, October 30, 1960.
Tracks 4 & 5 recorded at RCA Studio B, Nashville, October 31, 1960.
Track 9 recorded at RCA Studio B, Nashville May 25, 1966.
Tracks 8, 11, & 13 recorded at RCA Studio B, Nashville, May 26, 1966.
Tracks 7, 12, 14, 15, 16, 17, & 18 recorded at RCA Studio B, Nashville, May 27, 1966.
Tracks 10 & 19 recorded at RCA Studio B, Nashville, May 28, 1966.
Track 20 recorded at RCA Studio B, Nashville, September 11, 1967.

SOMETHING FOR EVERBODY & POT LUCK WITH ELVIS – BEST OF THE ALTERNATES (MEMORY RECORDS)

1. There's Always Me (take 2)
2. Give Me The Right (take 2)
3. It's A Sin (take 2)
4. Sentimental Me (take 1)
5. Starting Today (take 1)
6. Gently (take 2)
7. I'm Coming Home (take 4)
8. In Your Arms (take 1)
9. Put The Blame On Me (take 2)
10. Judy (take 1)
11. I Want You With Me (take 1)
12. I Slipped, I Stumbled, I Fell (take 10)
13. Kiss Me Quick (take 1)
14. Just For Old Times Sake (take 3)
15. Gonna Get Back Home Somehow (take 2)
16. (Such An) Easy Question (take 3)
17. Steppin' Out Of Line (movie version)
18. I'm Yours (splice from take 1 & the overdubbed master take)
19. Something Blue (take 1)
20. Suspicion (take 1)
21. I Feel That I've Known You Forever (take 1)
22. Night Rider (take 2)
23. Fountain Of Love (take 6)
24. That's Someone You Never Forget (take 5)

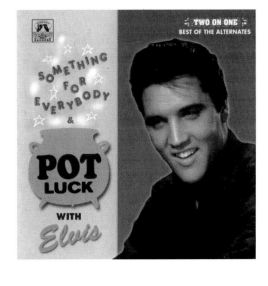

Recording Information:

Track 12 recorded November 8,1960 at Radio Recorders, Hollywood for the 20th Century Fox Motion Picture "Wild In The Country".
Track 17 recorded March 22, 1961 at Radio Recorders, Hollywood for the Paramount Motion Picture "Blue Hawaii".
Tracks 1 2, 3, 6, 7, 8, & 11 recorded March 12, 1961.
Tracks 4, 5, 9 & 10 recorded March 13, 1961.
Tracks 13 & 24 recorded June 25, 1961.
Track 18 recorded June 26, 1961.
Tracks 14, 15, 16, 19, 22, & 23 recorded March 18, 1962.
Tracks 20 & 21 recorded March 19, 1962.
All tracks (except 12 & 17) recorded at RCA Studio B, Nashville.

ALTERNATE GOLDEN HITS VOLUME 3 – THE LITTLE SISTER SESSIONS (ORIGINAL MASTER SERIES)

1. 2. & 3. Little Sister Sessions (part one)
4. It's Now Or Never
5. Stuck On You
6. Fame And Fortune
7. & 8. Gonna Get Back Home Somehow
9. Surrender
10. I Feel So Bad
11. Are You Lonesome Tonight
12. & 13. (Marie's The Name Of) His Latest Flame
14. & 15. Good Luck Charm
16. Anything That's Part Of You
17. & 18. She's Not You
19. 20. 21. & 22. Can't Help Falling In Love
23. 24. & 25. Little Sister Sessions (part two)
26. Little Sister/Get Back
27. It's Now Or Never
28. Little Sister

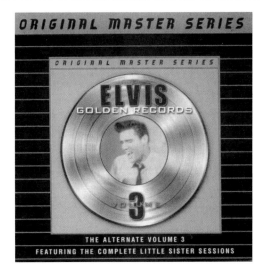

Recording Information:

Tracks 5 & 6 recorded March 21, 1960.
Tracks 4 & 11 recorded April 3, 1960.
Track 9 recorded October 30, 1960.
Track 10 recorded March 12, 1961.
Tracks 14, 15, & 16 recorded October 15, 1961.
Tracks 1, 2, 3, 12, 13, 23, 24, & 25 recorded June 26, 1961.
Tracks 7 & 8 recorded March 18, 1962.
Tracks 17 & 18 recorded March 19, 1962.
Tracks 1 – 18 & 23 – 25 recorded at RCA Studio B, Nashville.
Tracks 19 – 22 recorded March 23, 1961 at Radio Recorders, Hollywood for the Paramount Motion Picture "Blue Hawaii".
Track 26 & 27 recorded July 29, 1970 during rehearsals at MGM Studios, Culver City, California.
Track 28 recorded live April 23, 1977, Toledo, Ohio.

AMERICAN REJECTS (NO LABEL NAME)

1. In The Ghetto (alternate take)
2. Hey Jude (alternate take)
3. Without Love (undubbed version)
4. This Is The Story (undubbed version)
5. A Little Bit Of Green (alternate take)
6. Mama Like The Roses (undubbed version)
7. Inherit The Wind (alternate take)

Recording Information:

Track 4 recorded January 13, 1969.
Track 5 recorded January 14, 1969.
Tracks 6 & 7 recorded January 15, 1969.
Track 1 recorded January 20, 1969.
Track 2 recorded January 21, 1969.
Track 3 recorded January 22, 1969.
All tracks recorded at American Sound Studios, Memphis.

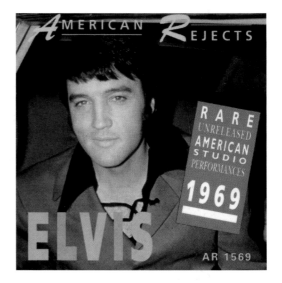

AMERICAN CROWN JEWELS (BILKO)

1. Long Black Limousine (take 6)
2. Wearin' That Loved On Look (alternate take)
3. You'll Think Of Me (take 7)
4. A Little Bit Of Green (take 1)
5. In The Ghetto (take 3)
6. Rubberneckin' (take 1)
7. From A Jack To A King (take 2)
8. Without Love (take 3)
9. Suspicious Minds (take 7)
10. True Love Travels On A Gravel Road (take 1)
11. Power Of My Love (take 1)
12. After Loving You (take 3)
13. And The Grass Won't Pay No Mind (take 6)
14. Do You Know Who I Am? (take 1)
15. Kentucky Rain (take 8)
16. It Keeps Right On A Hurtin' (take 2)
17. Only The Strong Survive (alternate take)
18. Any Day Now (take 2)
19. If I'm A Fool (For Loving You) (take 3)

Recording Information:

Tracks 1 & 2 recorded January 13, 1969.
Tracks 3 & 4 recorded January 14, 1969.
Tracks 5 & 6 recorded January 20, 1969.
Track 7 recorded January 21, 1969.
Tracks 8 & 9 recorded January 22, 1969.
Tracks 10 & 13 recorded February 17, 1969.
Tracks 11, 12, & 14 recorded February 18, 1969.
Tracks 15 & 17 recorded February 19, 1969.
Tracks 16, 18, & 19 recorded February 20, 1969.
All tracks recorded at American Sound Studios, Memphis.

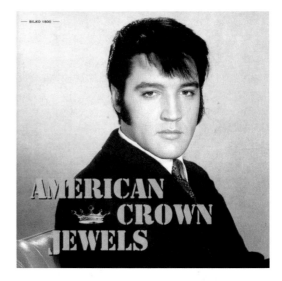

FINDING THE WAY HOME (SOUTHERN STYLE)

Disc One:

1. Wearin' That Loved On Look (7 false starts & 1 alternate take)
2. Only The Strong Survive (4 false starts)
3. Long Black Limousine (takes 1, 2, 4, 7, 8, & 6)
4. Only The Strong Survive (2 false starts)
5. You'll Think Of Me (takes 1, 2, 3, & 6)
6. From A Jack To A King (takes 1 & 2)
7. Only The Strong Survive (1 false start)
8. Without Love (takes 1 & 2)
9. Only The Strong Survive (1 alternate take)
10. If I'm A Fool (For Loving You) (takes 1, 2, & 3)
11. Suspicious Minds (takes 1, 2, 3, & 7)
12. Only The Strong Survive (take 1, 3 false starts & 1 alternate take)
13. In The Ghetto (takes 2 & 1)

Disc Two:

1. Kentucky Rain (take 1, 4 false starts & 1 alternate take)
2. Suspicious Minds (takes 4, 5, & 6)
3 & 4. In The Ghetto (takes 7, 8, 9, 10, & 11)
5. You'll Think Of Me (takes 4, 5, & 8)
6. From A Jack to A King (2 false starts & 1 alternate take)
7. Without Love (take 4)
8. Wearin' That Loved On Look (3 false starts & 1 alternate take)
9. If I'm A Fool (For Loving You) (takes 6, 7, & 5)
10. Only The Strong Survive (3 false starts & 1 alternate take)
11. A Little Bit Of Green (takes 2 & 1)
12. Kentucky Rain (2 false starts & takes 7 & 10)

Recording Information:

Disc One:

Tracks 1 & 3 recorded January 13, 1969.
Track 5 recorded January 14, 1969.
Track 13 recorded January 20, 1969.
Track 6 recorded January 21, 1969.
Tracks 8 & 11 recorded January 22, 1969.
Track 2, 4, 7, 9, & 12 recorded February 19, 1969.
Track 10 recorded February 20, 1969.
All tracks recorded at American Sound Studios, Memphis.

Disc Two:

Track 8 recorded January 13, 1969.
Tracks 5 & 11 recorded January 14, 1969.
Tracks 3 & 4 recorded January 20, 1969.
Track 6 recorded January 21, 1969.
Tracks 2 & 7 recorded January 22, 1969.
Track 1, 10, & 12 recorded February 19, 1969.
Track 9 recorded February 20, 1969.
All tracks recorded at American Sound Studios, Memphis.

Left:

**Back cover artwork showing
Elvis at American Studios.**

THERE'S A WHOLE LOTTA SHAKIN GOIN' ON (CIRCLE G)

1. Warming Up (instrumental)
2. Little Cabin On The Hill (alternate version)
3. A Hundred Years From Now (unreleased)
4. Faded Love (country version)
5. The Fool (alternate version)
6. There Goes My Everything (alternate version)
7. It Ain't No Big Thing (But It's Growing) (alternate version)
8. Got My Mojo Working/Keep Your Hands Off Her (unedited version)
9. Yellow Rose Of Texas (one line)
10. If I Were You (undubbed version)
11. Snowbird (alternate version)
12. Cindy, Cindy (unedited alternate version)
13. Where Did They Go Lord? (alternate version)
14. Patch It Up (alternate version)
15. Running Scared (one line)
16. Tomorrow Never Comes (alternate version)
17. Faded love (alternate version)
18. I Washed My Hands In Muddy Water (unedited version)
19. Whole Lotta Shakin' Goin' On (unedited version with horn dub)
20. Bridge Over Troubled Water (alternate version)

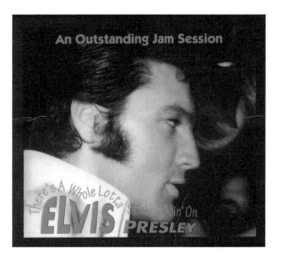

Recording Information:

Tracks 2, 3, 4, 5, & 12 recorded June 4, 1970.
Tracks 8 & 20 recorded June 5, 1970.
Tracks 1 & 7 recorded June 6, 1970.
Tracks 15, 16, 17, & 18 recorded June 7, 1970.
Tracks 6, 10, & 14 recorded June 8, 1970.
Track 9 recorded June 4 – 8, 1970.
Tracks 11, 13, & 19 recorded September 22, 1970.
All tracks recorded at RCA Studio B, Nashville.
Track one was titled "I Didn't Make It On Playing Guitar" for it's official release on "Essential Elvis Volume 4".

MAKE THE WORLD GO AWAY (CAPTAIN MARVEL JR. RECORDS)

Live and studio out takes 1970.

1. Arlene Calling Elvis
2. Make The World Go Away (take 3)
3. The Next Step Is Love (take 11)
4. Walk A Mile In My Shoes (live)
5. The Wonder Of You (live)
6. Funny How Time Slips Away (take 1)
7. I Washed My Hands In Muddy Water (take 1)
8. Love Letters (take 5)
9. Don't Cry Daddy/In The Ghetto (live)
10. Just Pretend (live)
11. When I'm Over You (take 1)
12. I Really Don't Want To Know (take 4)
13. Faded Love (take 2)
14. There Goes My Everything (live)
15. Make The World Go Away (live)
16. Twenty Days And Twenty Nights (live)
17. Faded Love (take 1)
18. Tomorrow Never Comes (take 13)
19. Tomorrow Never Comes (work part ending – take 1)

Recording Information:

Track 1 recorded early 1970. Telephone conversation.
Tracks 2, 3, 6, 7, 8, 11, 12, 13, 17, 18, & 19 recorded June 7, 1970 at RCA Studio B, Nashville.
Tracks 4, 10, & 14 recorded August 11, 1970, Midnight Show.
Track 16 recorded August 12, 1970, Midnight Show.
Track 5, 9, & 15 recorded August 13, 1970, Dinner Show.
Tracks 4, 5, 9, 10, 14, 15, & 16 recorded live at the International Hotel, Las Vegas.
The live recordings are taken from the Warner Brothers home video "Elvis – The Lost Performances".

FOR THE GOOD TIMES (ROCK LEGENDS)

Acetate recordings 1969 – 1972.

1. Miracle Of The Rosary
2. Fools Rush In
3. He Touched Me
4. I've Got Confidence
5. An Evening Prayer
6. For The Good Times
7. Where Do I Go From Here
8. I'll Take You Home Again Kathleen
9. Fool
10. Always On My Mind
11. It's A Matter Of Time
12. Separate Ways
13. My Little Friend
14. The Sound Of Your Cry
15. I Washed My Hands In Muddy Water
16. Patch It Up
17. It Ain't No Big Thing But It's Growing
18. Bridge Over Troubled Water
19. Got My Mojo Working/Keep Your Hands Off Her
20. Cindy, Cindy
21. When I'm Over You
22. Make The World Go Away
23. Rags To Riches

Recording Information:

Track 13 recorded at American Sound Studios, Memphis, January 16, 1969.
Tracks 14 & 20 recorded June 4, 1970.
Tracks 18 & 19 recorded June 5, 1970.
Track 17 recorded June 6, 1970.
Track 15, 21 & 22 recorded June 7, 1970.
Track 16 recorded June 8, 1970.
Track 23 recorded September 22, 1970.
Track 1 recorded May 15, 1971.
Tracks 2, 3, 4, & 5 recorded May 16, 1971.
Track 8 recorded May 19, 1971.
Tracks 1– 5, 8, & 14 – 23 recorded at RCA Studio B, Nashville.
Tracks 6 , 7, & 12 recorded March 27, 1972.
Track 9 recorded March 28, 1972.
Tracks 10 & 11 recorded March 29, 1972.
Tracks 6, 7, 9, 10, 11, & 12 recorded at RCA Studio C, Hollywood.

ROUGH CUT DIAMONDS (ROCK LEGENDS)

Acetate recordings 1968 – 1971.

1. Funny How Time Slips Away
2. Snowbird
3. Where Did They Go Lord?
4. Until It's Time For You To Go
5. It's Only Love
6. This Our Dance
7. We Can Make The Morning
8. Heart Of Rome
9. It's Your Baby, You Rock It
10. The First Time Ever I Saw Your Face.
11. If I Were You
12. Only Believe
13. I'll Never Know
14. Just Pretend
15. Life
16. Stranger In The Crowd
17. Help Me Make It Through The Night
18. Almost In Love
19. You'll Think Of Me
20. Mary In The Morning
21. You Don't Have To Say You Love Me
22. Britches (bonus track)

Recording Information:

Track 22 recorded at Radio Recorders, Hollywood, August 8, 1960
for the 20th Century Fox Motion Picture "Flaming Star"
Track 18 recorded at Western Recorders, Los Angeles, March 7, 1968
for the MGM Motion Picture "Live A Little, Love A Little".
Track 19 recorded at American Sound Studios, Memphis, January 14, 1969.
Tracks 9, 13, 16, & 20 recorded June 5, 1970.
Tracks 6, 8, 14, 15, & 21 recorded June 6, 1970.
Track 1 recorded June 7, 1970.
Tracks 11 & 12 recorded June 8, 1970.
Tracks 2 & 3 recorded September 22, 1970.
Track 10 recorded March 15, 1971.
Tracks 4 & 17 recorded May 17, 1971.
Tracks 5 & 7 recorded May 20, 1971.
Tracks 1 – 17, 20, & 21 recorded at RCA Studio B, Nashville.

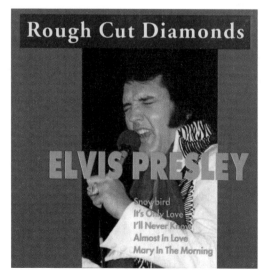

PURE DIAMONDS VOLUME 3 – GOSPEL GREATS AND STAX (FLASHBACK)

Acetate recordings 1971 – 1973.

1. Put Your Hand In The Hand
2. Reach Out To Jesus
3. He Is My Everything
4. There Is No God But God
5. I John
6. Bosom Of Abraham
7. Put Your Hand In The Hand
8. Raised On Rock
9. Just A Little Bit
10. If You Don't Come Back
11. Three Corn Patches
12. Take Good Care Of Her
13. Find Out What's Happening
14. I've Got A Thing About You Baby
15. Just A Little Bit
16. For Ol' Times Sake
17. Raised On Rock

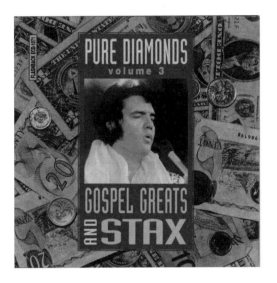

Recording Information:

Tracks 1, 2, & 7 recorded June 8, 1971.
Tracks 3, 4, 5, & 6 recorded June 9, 1971.
Tracks 1 – 7 recorded at RCA Studio B, Nashville.
Tracks 10, 11, & 12 recorded July 21, 1973.
Tracks 9, 13, 14, & 15 recorded July 22, 1973.
Tracks 8, 16, & 17 recorded July 23, 1973.
Tracks 8 – 17 recorded at Stax Studios, Memphis.

PURE DIAMONDS VOLUME 4 – FROM NASHVILLE TO HOLLYWOOD (FLASHBACK)

Acetate recordings 1970 –1972.

1. Twenty Days And Twenty Nights
2. I've Lost You
3. I Was Born About 10,00o Years Ago
4. The Sound Of Your Cry
5. The Fool
6. Little Cabin On The Hill
7. Cindy, Cindy
8. Bridge Over Troubled Water
9. Got My Mojo Working
10. How The Web Was Woven
11. The First Time Ever I Saw Your Face
12. Until It's Time For You To Go
13. Separate Ways
14. For The Good Times
15. Where Do I Go From Here?
16. Burning Love
17. Fool
18. Always On My Mind
19. It's A Matter Of Time
20. For The Good Times
21. Until It's Time For You To Go

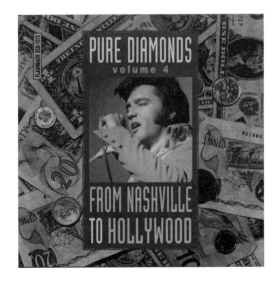

Recording Information:

Tracks 1 – 7 recorded June 4, 1970.
Tracks 8 – 10 recorded June 5, 1970.
Track 11 recorded March 15, 1971.
Tracks 12 & 21 recorded June 8, 1971.
Tracks 1 – 12 & 21 recorded at RCA Studio B, Nashville.
Tracks 13 – 15 & 20 recorded March 27, 1972.
Tracks 16 & 17 recorded March 28, 1972.
Tracks 18 & 19 recorded March 29, 1972.
Tracks 13 – 20 recorded At RCA Studio C, Hollywood.

STAX TRAX (BILKO)

1. If You Talk In Your Sleep
2. Mr. Songman
3. Promised Land
4. Love Song Of The Year
5. Help Me
6. Your Love's Been A Long Time Coming
7. Thinkin' About You
8. You Asked Me To
9. It's Midnight
10. Honky Tonk Angel

Recording Information:

Track 9 recorded December 10, 1973.
Tracks 1 & 8 recorded December 11, 1973.
Tracks 2, 4, 5, & 7 recorded December 12, 1973.
Tracks 3, 6, & 10 recorded December 15, 1973.
All tracks recorded at Stax Studios, Memphis.
All tracks are undubbed or re-mixed masters from the "Promised Land" album.

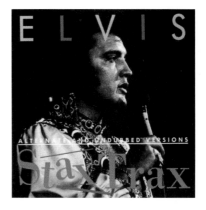

YESTERDAY/TODAY (BILKO)

1. T.R.O.U.B.L.E.
2. Fairytale
3. Shake A Hand
4. Woman Without Love
5. Pieces Of My Life
6. Bringing Back
7. Susan When She Tried
8. And I Love You So
9. I Can Help
10. Green, Green Grass Of Home

Recording Information:

Track 2 recorded March 10, 1975.
Tracks 7, 8, 9, & 10 recorded March 11, 1975.
Tracks 1, 3, 4, 5, & 6 recorded March 12, 1975.
All tracks recorded at RCA Studio C, Hollywood.
All tracks are undubbed or re-mixed masters from the "Elvis Today" album.

AMONG FRIENDS (WHITEHAVEN)

Studio and live out takes 1976.

1. Bitter They Are, Harder They Fall
2. She Thinks I Still Care
3. The Last Farewell
4. Solitaire
5. Moody Blue
6. I'll Never Fall In Love Again
7. For The Heat
8. Hurt
9. Danny Boy
10. Never Again
11. Love Coming Down
12. Blue Eyes Crying In The Rain
13. Hurt (X rated version)
14. Monologue/I Saw The Light (excerpt)
15. Rip It Up (excerpt)/My Way
16. Burning Love
17. Why Me Lord?
18. Elvis Introduces His Father Vernon
19. Early Morning Rain
20. Happy Birthday (with reprise)
21. Heartbreak Hotel
22. Ku-u-i-po (excerpt)/Hawaiian Wedding Song
23. Can't Help Falling In Love*

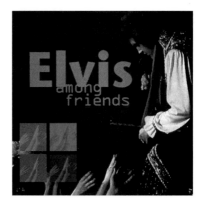

Recording Information:

Tracks 1 – 3 recorded February 2, 1976.
Track 4 recorded February 3, 1976.
Tracks 5 & 6 recorded February 4, 1976.
Tracks 7, 8, 9, & 13 recorded February 5, 1976.
Tracks 10 & 11 recorded February 6, 1976.
Track 12 recorded February 7, 1976.
Tracks 1– 13 recorded in the "Jungle Room" of Elvis' Graceland mansion, Memphis.
Tracks 14 – 23 recorded live May 1– 8, 1976 at the Sahara Tahoe Hotel, Lake Tahoe, Nevada.
(audience recordings)

PURE DIAMONDS VOLUME 2 (FLASHBACK)

Acetate recordings 1970.

1. When I'm Over You
2. Make The World Go Away
3. Funny How Time Slips Away
4. Snowbird
5. Where Did They Go Lord?
6. Rags To Riches
7. The Sound Of Your Cry
8. I Washed My Hands In Muddy Water
9. Patch It Up
10. It Ain't No Big Thing, But It's Growing
11. Bridge Over Troubled Water
12. Cindy, Cindy
13. Got My Mojo Working

Recording Information:

Track 7 & 12 recorded June 4, 1970.
Tracks 11 & 13 recorded June 5, 1970.
Track 10 recorded June 6, 1970.
Tracks 1, 2, 3, & 8 recorded June 7, 1970.
Track 9 recorded June 8, 1970.
Tracks 4, 5, & 6 recorded September 22, 1970.
All tracks recorded at RCA Studio B, Nashville.

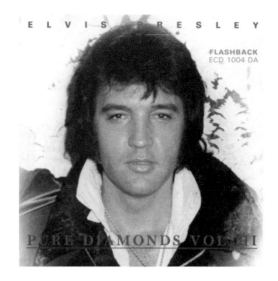

MORE PURE ELVIS – THE LOST ALBUM (BILKO)

Acetate recordings 1970 – 1976.

1. Moody Blue
2. When I'm Over You
3. It's A Matter Of Time
4. Sweet Angeline
5. Hurt
6. Shake A Hand
7. Promised Land
8. Heart Of Rome
9. If You Don't Come Back
10. Mr Songman
11. For Ol' Times Sake
12. Love Coming Down

Recording Information:

Track 8 recorded June 6, 1970.
Track 2 recorded June 7, 1970
Tracks 2 & 8 recorded at RCA Studio B, Nashville.
Track 3 recorded March 29, 1972 at RCA Studio C, Hollywood.
Track 9 recorded July 21, 1973.
Track 11 recorded July 23, 1973.
Track 10 recorded December 12, 1973
Track 7 recorded December 15, 1973.
Tracks 7, 9, 10, & 11 recorded at Stax Studios, Memphis.
Track 4 vocal recorded September 22, 1973 at Elvis' Palm Springs Home, California. (backing track recorded July 25, 1973 at Stax Studios, Memphis)
Track 6 recorded March 12, 1975 at RCA Studio C, Hollywood.
Track 1 recorded February 4, 1976.
Track 5 recorded February 5, 1976.
Track 12 recorded February 6, 1976.
Tracks 1, 5, & 12 recorded in the "Jungle Room" of Elvis' Graceland mansion, Memphis.

SEASONS GREETINGS FROM ELVIS (LCE)

1. Announcer:
How Great Thou Art
2. In The Garden
3. Announcer:
Somebody Bigger Than You Or I
4. Stand By Me
5. Announcer:
Without Him
6. Where Could I Go But To The Lord
7. Announcer:
Where No One Stands Alone
8. Announcer:
Crying In The Chapel
9. Announcer:
Here Comes Santa Claus
10. Announcer:
Blue Christmas
11. Announcer:
O Little Town Of Bethlehem
12. Announcer:
Silent Night
13. I'll Be Home For Christmas
14. Announcer:
I Believe
15. Announcer:
If Everyday Was like Christmas
16. Announcer:
How Great Thou Art
17. His Hand In Mine
18. Announcer:
Elvis' Special Message
19. I'll Be Home Christmas
20. Announcer
21. I Believe In The Man In The Sky (takes 1 – 4)

Recording Information:

Tracks 1 – 8: Elvis Presley Special Palm Sunday Radio Show, March 19, 1967.
Tracks 9 – 20: The Christmas Special, December 3, 1967.
Track 21 recorded October 30, 1960 at RCA Studio B, Nashville.
The two radio shows featured previously released RCA masters.

GREETINGS FROM GERMANY (VIK)

1. At The Hop (piano solo)
2. I'll Take You Home Again Kathleen (slow version)
3. Apron Strings
4. It's Been So Long Darling
5. Earth Angel (introduction)/I Will Be True
6. There's No Tomorrow
7. I'll Take You Home Again Kathleen (slow version)
8. Que Sera/Hound Dog
9. I Asked The Lord
10. I'll Take You Home Again Kathleen (fast version)
11. Apron Strings
12. Number Eight (On The Jukebox)
13. At The Hop (2 lines only)
14. Que Sera/Hound Dog
15. Piano Solo
16. Send Me Some Lovin'
17. Soldier Boy
18. Earth Angel
19. Danny Boy
20. The Fool
21. I'm Beginning To Forget You
22. I Asked The Lord
23. Mona Lisa
24. I'm Beginning To Forget You
25. I Can't Help It (If I'm Still In Love With You)

Recording Information:

All tracks recorded during Elvis' army service in Bad Nauheim, Germany, 1959.

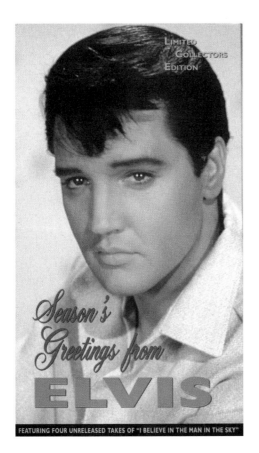

Both discs featured on this page were packaged in the
long box digi-pack format.

A PRIVATE MOMENT WITH THE KING (OUT WEST ENTERTAINMENT)

1. Spanish Eyes
2. Baby What You Want Me To Do
3. I'm So Lonesome I Could Cry
4. See See Rider
5. That's All Right
6. You're Life Has Just Begun
7. Teardrops

Recording Information:

Home recordings made at the Memphis home of Sam Thompson (brother of Elvis' girlfriend Linda Thompson). Recorded 1974.

SONGS TO SING (WHITEHAVEN)

1. I'm Beginning To Forget You
2. Mona Lisa
3. My Heart Cries For You
4. Dark Moon
5. Write To Me From Naples
6. Suppose
7. Are You Sincere
8. Sweet Angeline
9. Spanish Eyes
10. Baby What You Want Me To Do
11. I'm So Lonesome I Could Cry
12. Rocky Top (instrumental)
13. Spanish Eyes
14. That's All Right
15. See See Rider
16. Moody Blue
17. Hurt
18. Love Coming Down
19. Way Down (takes 1 & 2)

Recording Information:

Tracks 1 & 2 recorded 1959 during Elvis' army service in Bad Nauheim, Germany.
Tracks 3 – 6 recorded during 1966 at Rocca Place, Hollywood.
Track 8 recorded September 22, 1973.
Track 7 recorded September 23, 1973.
Tracks 7 & 8 recorded at Elvis' Palm Springs Home, California.
Tracks 9 – 15 recorded at the Memphis home of Sam Thompson (brother of Elvis' girlfriend Linda Thompson). Recorded 1974.
Track 16 recorded February 4, 1976.
Track 17 recorded February 5, 1976.
Track 18 recorded February 6, 1976.
Track 19 recorded October 29, 1976.
Tracks 16 – 19 recorded in the "Jungle Room" of Elvis' Graceland mansion, Memphis.
All tracks are informal home recordings except tracks 16 – 19 which were professionally recorded by RCA's mobile recording equipment.

THERE'S ALWAYS ME VOLUME ONE (BILKO)

Disc One:

1. Shake Rattle And Roll (takes 1, 2, 3, & 5)
2. Lawdy Miss Clawdy (takes 7, 8, & 9)
3. I Want You, I Need You, I Love (take 3)
4. I Need Your Love Tonight (take 7)
5. I Got Stung (takes 18 – 20)
6. Ain't That Loving You Baby (takes 9 & 10)
7. Lawdy Miss Clawdy (take 12)
8. Shake Rattle And Roll (take 7)
9. Fever (take 1)
10. Like A Baby (takes 3 & 4)
11. Stuck On You (alternate take)
12. I Feel So Bad (alternate take)
13. Dirty, Dirty Feeling (alternate take)
14. Thrill Of Your Love (alternate take)
15. Such A Night (alternate take)
16. Are You Lonesome Tonight (alternate take)
17. The Girl Next Door Went A Walking (alternate take)
18. A Mess Of Blues (alternate take)
19. It Feels So Right (alternate take)
20. Fame And Fortune (alternate take)
21. Surrender (alternate take)
22. Working On The Building (take 2)
23. I'm Coming Home (alternate take)
24. It's A Sin (takes 1 & 2)
25. I Want You With Me (take 1)

Disc Two:

1. There's Always Me (takes 2 & 6)
2. Starting Today (take 1)
3. Sentimental Me (take 1)
4. Judy (false start & take 1)
5. Put The Blame On Me (false start & take 1)
6. For The Millionth And The Last Time (takes 2, 6, & 10)
7. Good Luck Charm (takes 1, 2, & 3)
8. Anything That's Part Of You (take 2)
9. I Met Her Today (takes 1 & 7)
10. I Feel That I've Known You Forever (takes 1 & 2)
11. Just Tell Her Jim Said Hello (takes 2, 5, & 6)
12. Suspicion (takes 1 & 2)
13. She's Not You (takes 1 & 2)
14. Echoes Of Love (takes 2 & 3)
15. Please Don't Drag That String Around (takes 1, 4, & 5)
16. Devil In Disguise (takes 1, 2, & 3)
17. Never Ending (takes 1 & 2)

Recording Information:

Disc One:

Tracks 1, 2, 7, & 8 recorded February 23, 1956 at RCA Studios, New York.
Track 3 recorded April 14, 1956.
Tracks 4 & 6 recorded June 10, 1958.
Track 5 recorded June 11, 1958.
Tracks 11, 18, 19, & 20 recorded March 21, 1960.
Tracks 13, 14, 15, 16, & 17 recorded April 4, 1960.
Tracks 9 & 10 recorded April 3, 1960.
Track 21 recorded October 30, 1960.
Track 22 recorded October 31, 1960.
Track 12, 23, 24, & 25 recorded March 12, 1961.
Tracks 3 – 6 & 9 – 25 recorded at RCA Studio B, Nashville.

Disc Two:

Track 1 recorded March 12, 1961.
Tracks 2 – 5 recorded March 13, 1961.
Tracks 6 – 8 recorded October 15, 1961.
Track 9 recorded October 16, 1961.
Tracks 10 – 13 recorded March 19, 1962.
Track 14 – 17 recorded May 26, 1963.
All tracks recorded at RCA Studio B, Nashville.

Below:

This album was packaged in the long box digi-pack format, and the cover art featured photographs and memorabilia from the time.

THERE'S ALWAYS ME VOLUME TWO (BILKO)

Disc One:

1. You'll Be Gone (false start & take 4)
2. Indescribably Blue (vocal overdub – take 1)
3. I'll Remember You (vocal overdub – takes 1 & 2)
4. Suppose (take 1)
5. Witchcraft (take 2)
6. Finders Keepers (take 1)
7. Western Union (false start & takes 1 & 4)
8. Slowly But Surely (take 1)
9. Blue River (takes 1 & 2)
10. It Hurts Me (alternate take)
11. Stay Away (alternate take)
12. Singing Tree (remake – take 1)
13. Singing Tree (alternate take)
14. Summer Kisses, Winter Tears (takes 23, 25, & 26)
15. Britches (takes 1, 5, & 7)
16. We'll Be Together (two alternate takes)
17. I Don't Wanna Be Tied (false start)/
Plantation Rock (alternate take & vocal repair)
18. I'm Comng Home (takes 1 & 2)
19. Kiss Me Quick (take 1)

Disc Two:

1. US Male (take 1)/Wings Of An Angel (informal jam)
2. US Male (take 4)
3. Guitar Man (take 4)
4. After Lovin' You (takes 1 – 4)
5. Do You Know Who I Am
(the session – approximately 10 takes)
6. Any Day Now (the session – approximately 12 takes)
7. Power Of My Love (alternate take)

Recording Information:

Disc One:

Track 18 recorded March 12, 1961.
Track 19 recorded June 25, 1961.
Track 1 recorded March 18, 1962.
Tracks 5, 6, & 7 recorded May 27, 1963.
Tracks 8 & 9 recorded May 28, 1963.
Track 10 recorded January 10, 1964.
Tracks 2 & 3 recorded June 10 – 12, 1966.
Tracks 12 & 13 recorded September 11, 1967.
Tracks 1 – 3, 5 – 10, 12, 13, 18, & 19 recorded at RCA Studio B, Nashville.
Tracks 14 & 15 recorded August 8, 1960 at Radio Recorders, Hollywood for the 20th Century Fox Motion Picture "Flaming Star".
Track 17 recorded March 28, 1962. Track 16 recorded March 29, 1962.
Tracks 16 & 17 recorded at Radio Recorders, Hollywood for the Paramount Motion Picture "Girls! Girls! Girls!".
Track 4 recorded June 20, 1967 at MGM Studios, Hollywood for the MGM Motion Picture "Speedway".
Track 11 recorded January 17, 1968 at RCA Studio B, Nashville for the MGM Motion Picture "Stay Away Joe".

Disc Two:

Track 3 recorded September 10, 1967.
Tracks 1 & 2 recorded January 17, 1968.
Tracks 1 – 3 recorded at RCA Studio B, Nashville.
Tracks 4, 5, & 7 recorded February 18, 1969.
Track 6 recorded February 20, 1969.
Tracks 4 – 7 recorded at American Sound Studios, Memphis.

Below:

This album was packaged in the long box digi-pack format, and the cover art featured photographs and memorabilia from the time.

THERE'S ALWAYS ME VOLUME THREE (BILKO)

Disc One:

1. Something Blue (takes 1 & 2)
2. Fountain Of Love (takes 1 – 6)
3. Gonna Get Back Home Somehow (takes 1 & 2)
4. That's Someone You Never Forget (takes 1, 2, & 5)
5. I'm Yours (takes 1 & 4 and work part take 1)
6. Little Sister (false start & takes 3 & 9)
7. His Latest Flame (try out – takes 1 – 3)
8. (Such An) Easy Question (false start & take 3)
9. Give Me The Right (takes 2 & 3)
10. Lawdy Miss Clawdy (takes 1 & 3)

Disc Two:

1. Rubberneckin' (take 1)
2. True Love Travels On A Gravel Road (takes 1 – 7)
3. And The Grass Won't Pay No Mind (takes 1 –5)
4. Power Of My Love (takes 2 – 6)
5. Come Out, Come Out (instrumental try out)
6. It Keeps Right On A Hurtin' (take 2)
7. I Met Her Today (takes 19 & 20)
8. Love Me Tonight (takes 4 & 5)

Recording Information:

Disc One:

Track 10 recorded February 3, 1956 at RCA Studios, New York.
Track 9 recorded March 12, 1961.
Track 4 recorded June 25, 1961.
Tracks 5 – 7 recorded June 26, 1961.
Tracks 1, 2, 3 & 8 recorded March 18, 1962.
Tracks 1– 9 recorded at RCA Studio B, Nashville.

Disc Two:

Track 7 recorded October 16, 1961.
Track 8 recorded May 27, 1963.
Tracks 7 & 8 recorded at RCA Studio B, Nashville.
Track 5 recorded January 13, 1969.
Track 1 recorded January 20, 1969.
Tracks 2 & 3 recorded February 17, 1969.
Track 4 recorded February 18, 1969.
Track 6 recorded February 20, 1969.
Tracks 1 – 6 recorded at American Sound Studios, Memphis.

Below:

This album was packaged in the long box digi-pack format,
and the cover art featured photographs and memorabilia
from the time.

THERE'S ALWAYS ME VOLUME FOUR (BILKO)

Disc One:

1. Mine (false start & takes 3 & 4)
2. Fame And Fortune (take 1)
3. His Latest Flame (false start & takes 9 – 12)
4. Fame And Fortune (false start & takes 4, 6, & 7)
5. Just For Old Times Sake (false start & takes 2 & 3)
6. Night Rider (1962 remake – false start & takes 1 – 3)
7. Tomorrow Is A Long Time (false start & takes 1 & 2)
8. Beyond The Reef (breakdown version – take 1)
9. Down In The Alley (false start & takes 2, 4, & 6)
10. Love Letters (false start & takes 5 & 8)
11. Big Boss Man (false start & takes 4, 5, & 9)
12. Mine (take 9)
13. US Male (false start & takes 6, 9, & 10)
14. Stay Away (short Jam/false start & takes 3, 7, 8, 11, & 14)
15. US Male (false start & takes 6, 9, & 10)
16. Mine (instrumental)

Disc Two:

1. Don't It Make You Wanna Go home
2. Something
3. Words
4. I Just Can't Help Believin'
5. Little Sister/Get Back
6. I Washed My Hands In Muddy Water
7. I Was The One
8. Cattle Call
9. Baby Let's Play House
10. Don't
12. A Fool Such As I
13. Froggy Went A Courtin' (complete version)
14. Such A Night
15. It's Now or Never
16. What'd I Say
17. The Lord's Prayer

Recording Information:

Disc One:

Tracks 2 & 4 recorded March 21, 1960.
Track 3 recorded June 26, 1961.
Tracks 5 & 6 recorded March 18, 1962.
Tracks 7, 9, & 10 recorded May 26, 1966.
Track 8 recorded May 27, 1966.
Track 11 recorded September 10, 1967.
Tracks 1, 12, & 16 recorded September 11, 1967.
Tracks 13, 14, & 15 recorded January 17, 1968.
All tracks recorded at RCA Studio B, Nashville.
Track 14 recorded for the MGM Motion Picture "Stay Away Joe".

Disc Two:

All tracks recorded July 29, 1970 during rehearsals at MGM Studios, Stage 1, Culver City, California.
An edited version of "Froggy Went A Courtin'" was officially released on the 70's box set "Walk A Mile In My Shoes" in 1995.

Below:

This album was packaged in the long box digi-pack format, and the cover art featured photographs and memorabilia from the time.

THE COLONELS COLLECTION (MAC)

Studio and live out takes 1960 – 1977.

1. The "Soldier Boy" Recording Session
2. AFN Radio Interview
3. Are You Lonesome Tonight? (take 2)
4. Puppet On String (take 7)
5. Puppet On A String (take 10)
6. You'll Never Walk Alone (undubbed master)
7. If Everyday Was Like Christmas
8. Anything That's Part Of You
9. Moonlight Swim
10. Where No One Stands Alone
11. Spanish Eyes

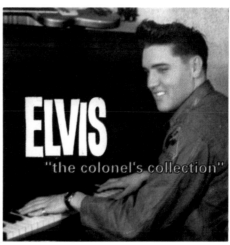

Recording Information:

Track 1 recorded at RCA Studio B, Nashville, March 20, 1960.
Track 2 interview recorded March, 1960.
Track 3 recorded at RCA Studio B, Nashville, April 4, 1960.
Track 9 recorded during 1961. Home recording
Track 8 recorded at RCA Studio B, Nashville, October 15, 1961.
Tracks 4 & 5 recorded at Radio Recorders, Hollywood, June 10, 1964 for the MGM Motion Picture "Girl Happy".
Track 7 is a demo version of a song written by Elvis friend and bodyguard Red West and features Red on vocals.
Track 6 recorded at RCA Studio B, Nashville, September 11, 1967.
Track 11 recorded at Elvis' Palm Springs Home, 1974. Track 10 recorded live in Montgomery, Alabama, February 16, 1977. (audience recording)

ESPECIALLY FOR YOU (HIS MASTERS VOICE)

Nashville out takes 1961 – 1962.

1. Follow That Dream (take 4)
2. Angel (take 2)
3. I'm Not The Marrying Kind (take 6)
4. A Whistling Tune (take 3)
5. Sound Advice (take 1)
6. Kiss Me Quick (take 10)
7. For The Millionth And The Last Time (take 10)
8. Anything That's Part Of You (take 3)
9. I Met Her Today (take 6)
10. Gonna Get Back Home Somehow (take 4)

Recording Information:

Tracks 1 – 5 recorded July 2, 1961 for the Mirisch United Artists Motion Picture "Follow That Dream".
Track 6 recorded June 26, 1961.
Tracks 7 & 8 recorded October 15, 1961.
Track 9 recorded October 16, 1961.
Track 10 recorded March 18, 1962.
All tracks recorded at RCA Studio B, Nashville.

Left: the CD version.
Below: a 10 inch vinyl version was also released.

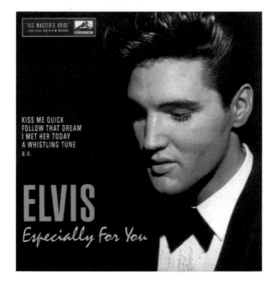

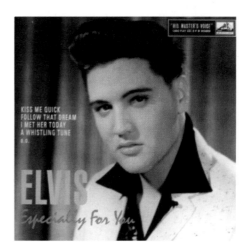

24 CARAT GOLD (2001)

Studio out takes 1960 –1968.

Disc One:

1. Fame And Fortune (take 5)
2. Gently (take 2)
3. There's Always Me (take 1)
4. Starting Today (take 2)
5. That's Someone You Never Forget (take 7)
6. I'm Yours (take 5)
7. For The Millionth And The Last Time (take 4)
8. Anything That's Part Of You (take 5)
9. I Met Her Today (take 4)
10. Something Blue (take 6)
11. Gonna Get Back Home Somehow (take 6)
12. Fountain Of Love (take 9)
13. Night Rider (take 5)
14. Just Tell Her Jim Said Hello (take 4)
15. Echoes Of Love (take 1)
16. Please Don't Drag That String Around (take 2)
17. Ask Me (take 1)
18. Western Union (take 3)
19. Love Letters (take 2)
20. The Girl I Never Loved (take 11)
21. You Don't Know Me (take 18 –movie version)
22. A House That Has Everything (take 6)
24. US Male (take 11)

Disc Two:

1. Fame And Fortune (takes 3 & 9)
2. Gently (takes 1 & 4)
3. I'm Yours (takes 3 & 2)
4. For The Millionth and The Last Time (takes 3 & 5)
5. Anything That's Part Of You (takes 4, 6, 7, & 9)
6. Fame And Fortune (takes 10, 12, & 11)
7. I Met Her Today (takes 2 & 5)
8. Something Blue (takes 3 & 4)
9. For The Millionth And The Last Time (takes 11 & 8)
10. Gonna Get Back Home Somehow (takes 3 & 5)
11. Just Tell Her Jim Said Hello (take 3)
12. Ask Me (takes 3 & 4)
13. Stay Away (takes 1, 4, & 9)
14. You Don't Know Me (takes 1, 2, & 3 – movie version)
15. A House That Has Everything (takes 2, 3, & 5)
16. You Don't Know Me (takes 12 & 13 – movie version)
17. Stay Away (takes 12 & 13)
18. Stay Away (take 15 – undubbed master)

Recording Information:

"Fame And Fortune" recorded March 21, 1960.
"Gently" & "There's Always Me" recorded March 12, 1961.
"Starting Today" recorded March 13, 1961.
"That's Someone You Never Forget" recorded June 25, 1961.
"I'm Yours" recorded June 26, 1961.
"For The Millionth And The Last Time" & "Anything That's Part Of You" recorded October 15, 1961.
"I Met Her Today" recorded October 16, 1961.
"Something Blue", "Gonna Get Back Home Somehow", "Fountain Of Love", & "Night Rider" recorded March 18, 1962.
"Just Tell Her Jim Said Hello" recorded March 19, 1962.
"Echoes Of Love" & "Please Don't Drag That String Around" recorded May 26, 1963.
"Ask Me" & "Western Union" recorded May 27, 1963.
"Love Letters" recorded May 26, 1966.
"The Girl I Never Loved", "You Don't Know Me", & "A House That Has Everything" recorded February 21, 1967 for the United Artists Motion Picture "Clambake".
"Stay Away" & "US Male" recorded January 17, 1968.
"Stay Away" recorded for the MGM Motion Picture "Stay Away Joe".
All tracks recorded at RCA Studio B, Nashville.

DATIN' WITH ELVIS (SCREEN)

Studio out takes 1960 – 1967.

1. Datin' (takes 6-8, 11, & 1)
2. Shoppin' Around (takes 1 & 2)
3. Frankfort Special
4. Vienna Woods Rock N Roll (takes 3, 4, 7, 8, & 9)
5. GI Blues
6. What's She Really Like
7. Doin' The Best I Can
8. Pocketful of Rainbows
9. His Latest Flame (takes 1 – 7)
10. Good Luck Charm (take 1)
11. Judy (takes 1 – 4)
12. Little Sister (takes 1 – 6)
13. He's Your Uncle Not Your Dad (movie version)
14. Big Boots

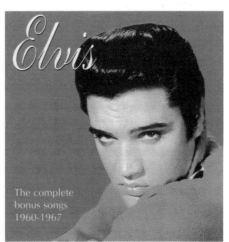

Recording Information:

Track 1 recorded at Radio Recorders, Hollywood, July 26, 1965 for the Paramount Motion Picture "Paradise Hawaiian Style".
Tracks 2, 3, 5 & 7 recorded at RCA Studios, Hollywood, April 27, 1960.
Tracks 6, 8 & 14 recorded at RCA Studios, Hollywood, April 28, 1960. Track 4 recorded at Radio Recorders, Hollywood, May 6, 1960.
Tracks 2, 3, 4, 5, 6, 7, 8, & 14 recorded for the Paramount Motion Picture "GI Blues".
Track 11 recorded at RCA Studio B, Nashville, March 13, 1961. Track 10 recorded October 15, 1961.
Tracks 9 & 12 recorded at RCA Studio B, Nashville, June 26, 1961.
Track 13 recorded at MGM Studios, Hollywood, June 21, 1967 for the MGM Motion Picture "Speedway".

THE COMPLETE BONUS SONGS (CD/DRIVE)/THE COMPLETE BONUS SONGS (PSP)

Previously released RCA masters 1960 – 1967.

1. Slipped, I Stumbled, I Fell
2. Love Me Tonight
3. Slowly But Surely
4. Echoes Of Love
5. Long Lonely Highway
6. You'll Be Gone
7. Animal Instinct
8. Wisdom Of The Ages
9. Sand Castles
10. Tomorrow Is A Long Time
11. Down In The Alley
12. I'll Remember You
13. It Won't Be Long
14. Never Ending
15. Blue River
16. What Now, What Next, Where To
17. Guitar Man
18. How Can You Lose What You Never Had
19. Big Boss Man
20. Singing Tree
21. Just Call me Lonesome
22. Five Sleepy Heads
23. Western Union
24. Mine
25. Going Home
26. Suppose

RCA released this compilation on vinyl in 1983. The CD/Drive release (top) retained the original album artwork, whilst the PSP release gave the album a new sleeve design. Both CD's contained the same material but from different sources.

CD/Drive version

Track Information:

Track 1 from the film "Wild In The Country". Included on the album "Something For Everybody".
Tracks 2 & 3 studio masters included on the "Fun In Acapulco" soundtrack album.
Tracks 4 & 5 studio masters included on the "Kissin' Cousins" soundtrack album.
Track 6 studio master included on the "Girl Happy" soundtrack album.
Tracks 7 & 8 cut from the film "Harum Scarum" and included on the soundtrack album.
Track 9 cut from the film "Paradise Hawaiian Style" and included on the soundtrack album.
Tracks 10 – 12 studio masters included on the "Spinout" soundtrack album.
Track 13 cut from the film "Double Trouble" and included on the soundtrack album.
Tracks 14 – 16 studio masters included on the "Double Trouble" soundtrack album.
Track 17 studio master included on the "Clambake" soundtrack album.
Track 18 cut from the film "Clambake" and included on the soundtrack album.
Tracks 19 – 21 studio masters included on the "Clambake" soundtrack album.
Track 22 cut from the film "Speedway" and included on the soundtrack album.
Tracks 23 & 24 studio masters included on the "Speedway" soundtrack album.
Track 25 from the film "Stay Away Joe". Included on the "Speedway" soundtrack album.
Track 26 cut from the film "Speedway" and included on the soundtrack album.

PSP version

WINGS OF AN ANGEL (ANGEL RECORDS)

Studio out takes 1958 – 68.

1. I Need Your Love Tonight (takes 1 – 15)
2. Milky White Way (takes 1 – 5)
3. His Hand In Mine (takes 1 – 5)
4. Echoes Of Love (takes 2 –7, & 9)
5. Please Don't Drag That String Around (takes 1 – 4)
6. US Male (take 1)
7. Wings Of An Angel (informal recording)
8. US Male (takes 2 – 4)

Recording Information:

Track 1 recorded June 10, 1958.
Tracks 2 & 3 recorded October 30, 1960.
Tracks 4 & 5 recorded May 26, 1963.
Tracks 6 – 8 recorded January 17, 1968.
All tracks recorded at RCA Studio B, Nashville.

EDGE OF REALITY (GROOVY RECORDS/MAC)

Studio and live out takes 1968 – 74.

1. Edge Of Reality (take 6)
2. Wonderful World (take 5)
3. A Little Less Conversation (take 10)
4. Gentle On My Mind (undubbed master)
5. Suspicious Minds (undubbed master)
6. Rubberneckin' (undubbed master)
7. You'll Think Of Me (undubbed master)
8. Wonderful World (take 17)
9. Wonderful World (take 15)
10. Edge Of Reality (take 8)
11. A Little Less Conversation (take 16)
12. Almost In Love (backing track)
13. Crying Time (live)
14. Suzie Q (live)
15. Blue Suede Shoes/Whole Lotta Shakin' Goin' On (live)

Recording Information:

Tracks 1, 2, 3, 8, 9, 10, 11, & 12 recorded March 7, 1968 at Western Recorders, Los Angeles for the MGM Motion Picture "Live A Little, Love A Little".
Tracks 4 & 7 recorded January 14, 1969.
Track 6 recorded January 20, 1969.
Track 5 recorded January 22, 1969.
Tracks 4 – 7 recorded at American Sound Studios, Memphis.
Track 15 recorded live August 19, 1970 at the International Hotel, Las Vegas. (audience recording)
Track 13 recorded live August 21, 1970 at the International Hotel, Las Vegas. (audience recording)
Track 15 recorded live on tour in 1974. (audience recording)

FROM THE BOTTOM OF MY HEART (SAVANAH RECORDS)

Various recordings 1960 – 1972.

1. Western Union (alternate take)
2. Ask Me (take 1)
3. Have A Happy (alternate take)
4. Let Us Pray (alternate take)
5. Change Of Habit (alternate take)
6. Ask Me (take 2)
7. Girl Happy (alternate take)
8. Beach Shack (alternate take)
9. I've Got To Find My Baby (alternate take)
10. There's A Brand New Day On The Horizon (alternate take)
11. Roustabout (alternate take)
12. John Paris Interview
13. Fame And Fortune (take 2)
14. Frankfort Special (take 2)
15. Wooden Heart (take 3)
16. Such A Night (takes 2, 3 & 4)
17. A Cane And A High Starched Collar (take 2)
18. Award Presentation To Elvis
19. I'm Beginning To Forget You
20. Mona Lisa
21. Guadalajara (take 2)
22. If I Can Dream (take 4)
23. Let It Be Me (live)
24. The Impossible Dream (live)
25. Reconsider Baby (live)
26. I'll Remember You (live)
27. Tony Prince Interview
28. Jaycee's Awards Speech
29. Aloha From Hawaii Press Conference

Recording Information:

Tracks 19 and 20 are home recordings from 1959 recorded during Elvis' army service in Bad Nauheim, Germany.
Track 12 recorded in Germany during Elvis' army service.
Track 13 recorded March 21, 1960.
Track 16 recorded April 4, 1960.
Track 1 recorded May 27, 1963.
Tracks 2 & 6 recorded May 28, 1963.
Tracks 1, 2, 6, 13, & 16 recorded at RCA Studio B, Nashville.
Track 14 recorded April 27, 1960.
Track 15 recorded April 28, 1960.
Tracks 14 & 15 recorded at RCA Studios, Hollywood for the Paramount Motion Picture "GI Blues".
Track 17 recorded August 8, 1960 for the 20th Century Fox Motion Picture "Flaming Star".
Track 21 recorded January 23, 1963 for the Paramount Motion Picture "Fun In Acapulco".
Tracks 10 recorded March 3, 1964 for the Paramount Motion Picture "Roustabout".
Track 11 recorded April 29, 1964 for the Paramount Motion Picture "Roustabout".
Track 7 recorded June 10, 1964 for the MGM Motion Picture "Girl Happy".
Track 9 recorded June 11, 1964 for the MGM Motion Picture "Girl Happy".
Track 8 recorded February 16, 1966 for the MGM Motion Picture "Spinout".
Tracks 7, 8, 9, 10, 11, 17, & 21 recorded at Radio Recorders, Hollywood.
Track 3 recorded March 5, 1969. Tracks 4 & 5 recorded March 6, 1969.
Tracks 3, 4, & 5 recorded at Decca Universal Studios, Hollywood the Universal Motion Picture "Change Of Habit".
Track 18 recorded March 25, 1961, Pearl Harbour, Hawaii.
Track 22 recorded June 23, 1968 at Western Recorders, Los Angeles for the NBC TV Special "Elvis".
Track 23 recorded live February 15, 1970 at The International Hotel, Las Vegas.
Track 28 recorded January 16, 1971 at the Ellis Auditorium, Memphis.
Track 24 recorded live February 16, 1972 at The Hilton Hotel, Las Vegas.
Tracks 25 & 26 recorded live June 10, 1972 during the afternoon show at Madison Square Garden, New York.
Track 29 recorded September 4, 1972 at the Hilton Hotel, Las Vegas.
Track 27 recorded 1973 in Las Vegas.

ELVIS 60TH ANNIVERSARY CELEBRATION VOLUME ONE (TOD)

Studio and live out takes 1958 – 1977.

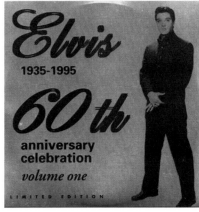

1. Ain't That Loving You Baby (medium tempo)
2. A Big Hunk O' Love
3. Ain't That Loving You Baby (fast tempo)
4. A Fool Such As I
5. I Got Stung
6. I Need Your Love Tonight
7. He Knows Just What I Need
8. Pocketful Of Rainbows
9. Doin' The Best I Can
10. Stay Away
11. Going Home
12. Hurt
13. Blueberry Hill
14. Where No One Stands Alone

Recording Information:

Tracks 1, 2, 3, 4 & 6 recorded June 10, 1958. Track 5 recorded June 11, 1958.
Track 7 recorded October 30, 1960. Tracks 1 - 7 recorded at RCA, Studio B, Nashville.
Track 9 recorded April 27 1960. Track 8 recorded April 28 1960.
Tracks 8 & 9 recorded at RCA Studios, Hollywood for the Paramount Motion Picture "GI Blues".
Track 11 recorded January 16, 1968. Track 10 recorded January 17, 1968.
Tracks 1 & 11 recorded at RCA Studio B, Nashville for the MGM Motion Picture, "Stay Away Joe".
Tracks 12 – 14 recorded live on tour in Montgomery, Alabama, February 16, 1977.

FROM THE BOTTOM OF MY HEART VOLUME 2 (SAVANAH RECORDS)

Various recordings 1954 – 1976.

1. I Love You Because (takes 1 & 2)
2. I Love You Because (takes 3 & 4)
3. I Love Because (take 5)
4. Red Robinson Calls The Colonel
5. Live In Canada, 1957.
6. My Baby's Gone (takes 7, 8, & 9)
7. My Baby's Gone (takes 10 & 11)
8. My Baby's Gone (takes 12 & 13)
9. I Was The One (take 2)
10. Elvis For The March Of Dimes, 1957.
11. Love Me Tender (stereo version)
12. Wolf Call (alternate take)
13. There's So Much World To See (take 10)
14. Just Let Me Make Believe A While
15. You Don't Have To Say You Love Me (rehearsal)
16. Any Day Now (rehearsal)
17. Medley: Polk Salad Annie/I John (live)
18. His Latest Flame (live)
19. Wooden Heart (live)
20. Tony Prince Talks With Elvis
21. Shake a Hand (live)
22. Why Me Lord (live)
23. Hurt (alternate take)

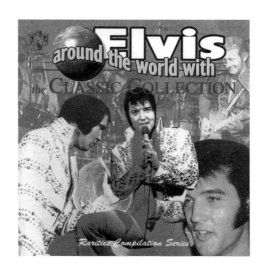

Recording Information:

Tracks 1 – 3 recorded July 5 – 6, 1954.
Tracks 6 – 8 recorded March 5, 1955.
Tracks 1– 3 & 6 – 8 recorded at Sun Studios, Memphis.
Track 4 recorded in Vancouver, Canada in the early 60's.
Track 5 recorded in Vancouver, Canada, August 31, 1957.
Track 9 recorded at RCA Studios, Nashville, January 11, 1956.
Track 10 Radio Spot recorded December, 1956.
Track 11 recorded August 24, 1956 at 20th Century Fox Stage One, Hollywood for the 20th Century Fox Motion Picture "Love Me Tender".
Track 12 recorded June 12, 1964 at Radio Recorders, Hollywood, for the MGM Motion Picture "Girl Happy".
Track 13 recorded June 28, 1966 at MGM Studios, Hollywood for the MGM Motion Picture "Double Trouble".
Track 14 is a mid 60's demonstration disc in the Elvis style.
Tracks 15 & 16 are showroom rehearsals from Las Vegas, exact dates unknown. (possibly August, 1970)
Tracks 17 – 19 recorded live at the Hilton Hotel, Las Vegas, September 3, 1971. (audience recordings)
Track 20 recorded 1973 in Las Vegas.
Track 21 recording live in Atlanta, Georgia, June 5, 1976. (audience recording)
Track 22 recorded live in Asheville, North Carolina, July 22, 1975. (audience recording)
Track 23 recorded February 5, 1976 in the "Jungle Room" of Elvis' Graceland mansion.

AROUND THE WORLD WITH ELVIS (GOLDEN AGE)

Previously released RCA masters.

1. Wonderful World
2. Memphis Tennessee
3. Viva Las Vegas
4. Medley:
The Yellow Rose Of Texas
The Eyes Of Texas
5. New Orleans
6. Hawaiian Sunset
7. Heart Of Rome
8. Write To Me From Naples
9. Santa Lucia
10. Frankfurt Special
11. Wooden Heart
12. I Love Only One Girl
13. Mexico
14. Guadalajara
15. Spanish Eyes*
16. My Desert Serenade
17. Earth Boy
18. Chesay
19. Home Is Where The Heart Is

*The version of "Spanish Eyes" included here is the previously bootlegged home recording from Elvis' Palm Springs home in 1974.
All other performances are RCA masters.

RARITIES (AJ RECORDS)

Studio out takes 1960 –1971.

1. I Slipped, I Stumbled, I Fell
2. Aloha–Oe (take 6)
3. Hawaiian Sunset (take 2)
4. No More (takes 2 & 7)
5. KU-U-I-PO (take 1)
6. Slicin' Sand (takes 15 & 17)
7. Steppin' Out Of Line (takes 4, 5 & 15)
8. Can't Help Falling In Love (takes 7, 8 & 9)
9. Rock A Hula Baby (takes 1, 2 & 3)
10. Home Is Where The Heart Is (take 4)
11. Ridin' The Rainbow (takes 3 & 4)
12. King Of The Whole Wide World (alternate take)
13. Patch It Up (undubbed acetate)
14. It's Your Baby, You Rock It (undubbed acetate)
15. Tomorrow Never Comes (undubbed acetate)
16. Funny How Time Slips Away (undubbed acetate)
17. I Washed My Hands In Muddy Water (undubbed acetate)
18. Only Believe (undubbed acetate)
19. The First Time Ever I Saw Your Face. (undubbed acetate)
20. Don't Think Twice, It's All Right (complete studio performance)

Recording Information:

Track 1 recorded November 8, 1960 at Radio Recorders, Hollywood for the 20th Century Fox Motion Picture, "Wild In The Country".
Tracks 2, 3, 4, 5 & 6 recorded March 21, 1961. Track 7 recorded March 22, 1961. Tracks 8 & 9 recorded March 23 1961.
Tracks 2 – 9 recorded at Radio Recorders, Hollywood for the Paramount Motion Picture, "Blue Hawaii".
Tracks 10, 11 & 12 recorded October 26 1961 at Radio Recorders, Hollywood for the Mirisch United Artists Motion Picture, "Kid Galahad".
Track 14 recorded June 5, 1970. Tracks 15, 16 & 17 recorded June 7, 1970. Tracks 13 & 18 recorded June 8, 1970.
Track 19 recorded March 15, 1971. Track 20 recorded May 16, 1971.
Tracks 14 – 20 recorded at RCA Studio B, Nashville.

ELVIS MEETS PRESLEY (JAR)

Studio and live out takes 1960 –1975.

1. Memphis Tennessee
2. In Your Arms
3. Forget Me Never
4. It's A Sin
5. There's Always Me
6. Put The Blame On Me
7. Long Lonely Highway
8. I'm Coming Home
9. Fever
10. In My Way
11. Gently
12. Slowly But Surely
13. You're The Reason I'm Living
14. Don't Cry Daddy
15. Green Grass Of Home
16. Medley:
When My Blue Moon Turns To Gold Again/
Blue Christmas/I Got A Woman/ Amen
17. Introduction By Priscilla
18. Don't Cry Daddy
19. Closing Announcement By Lisa Marie

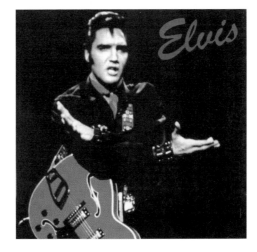

Recording Information:

Track 9 recorded April 3, 1960. Tracks 2, 4 5, 8, & 11 recorded March 12, 1961. Track 6 recorded March 13, 1961.
Tracks 1 & 7 recorded May 27, 1963. Track 12 recorded May 28, 1963.
Tracks 1, 2, 4, 5, 6, 7, 8, 9, 11, & 12 recorded at RCA Studio B, Nashville.
Tracks 3 & 10 recorded November 7, 1960 at Radio Recorders, Hollywood for the 20th Century Fox Motion Picture, "Wild In The Country".
Track 14 recorded live at the International Hotel, Las Vegas, February 16, 1970.
Track 16 recorded live in Kansas City, June 29, 1974, Evening Show.
Tracks 13 & 15 recorded live at the Hilton Hotel Las Vegas, March 22, 1975, Midnight Show.
Tracks 17, 18 & 19 recorded live at the Midsouth Coliseum, Memphis, August 16, 1997 via video technology.
Track 18 is duet between Elvis and Lisa Marie Presley.

LOOSE ENDS VOL. 1 (LUCKY RECORDS)

Rare and deleted RCA recordings.

1. I'm Beginning To Forget You (home recording)
2. Mona Lisa (home recording)
3. My Heart Cries For You (home recording)
4. Dark Moon (home recording)
5. Write To Me from Naples (home recording)
6. Suppose (home recording)
7. Fame & Fortune (alternate take)
8. Anything That's Part Of You (alternate take)
9. You'll Be Gone (single version)
10. Such An Easy Question (alternate take)
11. I Feel That I've Known You Forever (movie Version)
12. Long, Lonely Highway (single version)

13. Beyond The Reef (master)
14. Come What May (master)
15. Fools Fall in Love (master)
16. Mine (master)
17. Singing Tree (master)
18. My Little Friend (undubbed master)
19. I'll Be There (master)
20. Kentucky Rain (remake 1980)
21. If I'm A Fool For Loving You (master)
22. The Sound Of Your Cry (unedited master)
23. I'll Take You Home Again Kathleen (undubbed master)
24. Silver Bells (alternate take)

LOOSE ENDS VOL. 2 (LUCKY RECORDS)

Rare and deleted RCA recordings.

1. Tonight Is So Right For Love (alternate take)
2. Shoppin' Around (alternate take)
3. Follow That Dream (alternate take)
4. Thanks To The Rolling Sea (alternate take)
5. Mama (alternate take)
6. Earth Boy (acetate)
7. I Don't Want To Be Tied (acetate)
8. I'm Falling In Love Tonight (alternate take)
9. They Remind Me Too Much Of You (alternate take)
10. Guadalajara (alternate take)
11. Anyone (master)
12. House Of Sand (movie version)
13. Sand Castles (master)
14. A Dog's Life (alternate take)
15. It Won't Be Long (master)

16. She's A Machine (master)
17. You Don't Know Me (movie version)
18. You Don't Know Me (studio version/master)
19. Stay Away (master)
20. Stay Away Joe #1 (master)
21. Stay Away Joe #2 (alternate master)
22. Dominic (movie version)
23. All I Needed Was The Rain (master)
24. Too Much Monkey Business (master)
25. A Little Less Conversation (single version)
26. Almost In Love (single version)
27. Wonderful World (master)
28. Swing Down Sweet Chariot (1968 version/master)
29. Almost (master)
30. Let's Forget About The Stars (master)
31. Lets' Be Friends (master)

LOOSE ENDS VOL. 3 (LUCKY RECORDS)

Rare and deleted RCA recordings.

1. I Love You Because (take 1)
2. I Love You Because (take 2)
3. I love You Because (take 3)
4. I love You Because (take 4)
5. I Love You Because (take 5)
6. I'm Left, You're Right, She's Gone (take 7)
7. I'm Left, You're Right, She's Gone (take 8)
8. I'm Left, You're Right, She's Gone (take 9)
9. I'm Left, You're Right, She's Gone (take 10)
10. I'm Left, You're Right, She's Gone (take 11)
11. I'm Left, You're Right, She's Gone (take 12)
12. I'm Left, You're Right, She's Gone (take 13)
13. Promised Land (re-mixed shorter version)
14. I've Got A Thing About You Baby (re-mixed shorter version)
15. Too Much Monkey Business (re-mixed shorter version)
16. Blue Suede Shoes (live 1968 spliced version)
17. Bossa Nova Bay (12 inch remix)
18. The Elvis Medley (single version)
19. Club Mix Medley (UK disco club mix, 1988)
20. Interview (Tampa, 1956.)
20. Interview (movie set, 1962)
21. Elvis' Message To UK Fans, 1964

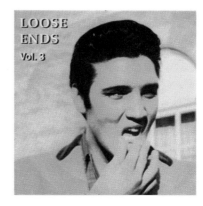

Collectors Notes:

These albums collected previously released performances which had not been officially issued on CD at the time. These consisted of alternate single masters, and master and alternate takes from deleted albums, along with alternate mixes and re-mixes.

Whilst the majority of these tracks were first issued on official RCA releases, some acetate recordings and songs lifted directly from the movie soundtracks were also included.

COME WHAT MAY (2001)

Studio and soundtrack out takes 1965 – 1967.

1. Come What May (takes 1 & 2)
2. Stay Away Joe (takes 1 & 2)
3. A House Of Sand (repairs – takes 4, 5 & 6)
 A Dog's Life (take 1)
4. How Can You Lose What You Never Had? (take 3)
5. So Close Yet So Far (take 4)
6. My Desert Serenade (take 5)
7. Wisdom Of The Ages (take 9)
8. Kismet (take 4)
9. Hey Little Girl (takes 1 & 2)
10. Golden Coins (takes 3, 4, & 6)
11. Animal Instinct (takes 1 & 2)
12. Shake That Tambourine (takes 21, 22, 23, & 19)
13. So Close Yet So Far (take 5)
14. My Desert Serenade (takes 6, 7, & 8)
15. Stay Away Joe (takes 5, 6, & 8)
16. Come What May (takes 5 & 4)
17. Just Call Me Lonesome (alternate take)
18. Stay Away Joe (take 9)

Recording Information:

Track 12 recorded February 24, 1965. Tracks 5 – 11, 13, & 14 recorded February 25, 1965.
Tracks 5 – 14 recorded at RCA Studio B, Nashville for the MGM Motion Picture "Harum Scarum".
Track 3 recorded July 27, 1965 at Radio Recorders, Hollywood for the Paramount Motion Picture, "Paradise Hawaiian Style".
Track 4 recorded February 21, 1967 at RCA Studio B, Nashville for the United Artists Motion Picture "Clambake".
Tracks 15 & 18 recorded October 1, 1967. Track 2 recorded January 17, 1968.
Tracks 2, 15, &18 recorded at RCA Studio B, Nashville for the MGM Motion Picture "Stay Away Joe".
Tracks 1 & 16 recorded May 28, 1966. Track 17 recorded September 11, 1967.
Tracks 1, 16, & 17 recorded at RCA Studio B, Nashville.

CUT ME AND I BLEED – THE OTHER SIDE OF ELVIS (DOUBLE G)

Studio, live, and rehearsal out takes.

1. Ode To A Robin (short poem)
2. Wings Of An Angel
3. US Male
4. 100 Years From Now
5. Got My Mojo Working
6. I Washed My Hands In Muddy Water
7. Only The Strong Survive
8. It's Midnight
9. Promised Land
10. Hurt
11. Cindy, Cindy
12. Goin' Home
13. Beach Shack
14. Don't Cry Daddy
15. Heart Of Rome
16. Memories
17. Stranger In My Own Home Town
18. Good Time Charlie's Got The Blues
19. You Gave Me A Mountain
20. Polk Salad Annie
21. American Trilogy
22. Monologue

Recording Information:

Track 13 recorded February 16, 1966 at Radio Recorders, Hollywood for the MGM Motion Picture "Spinout".
Track 12 recorded January 16, 1968 for the MGM Motion Picture "Stay Away Joe".
Tracks 2 & 3 recorded January 17, 1968.
Tracks 2, 3, & 12 recorded at RCA Studio B, Nashville.
Track 7 recorded February 19, 1969 at American Sound Studios, Memphis.
Tracks 4 & 11 recorded June 4, 1970. Track 5 recorded June 5, 1970. Track 6 recorded June 7,1970.
Tracks 4 – 6, & 11 recorded at RCA Studio B, Nashville.
Tracks 14 – 17 recorded July 24, 1970 during rehearsals at RCA Studios, Hollywood.
Track 20 recorded August 6, 1970 during stage rehearsals at the International Hotel, Las Vegas.
Tracks 19 recorded March 31, 1972 during rehearsals at RCA Studio C, Hollywood.
Track 1 is a home recording from 1974. Recorded at the Memphis home of Sam Thompson (brother of Elvis' girlfriend Linda Thompson)
Tracks 8 & 9 recorded August 16, 1974 during rehearsals at RCA Studios, Hollywood.
Track 18 recorded live August 19, 1974, Opening Show.
Track 21 recorded live August 30, 1974, 3 a.m. Show.
Track 22 recorded live September 2, 1974, Closing Show.
Tracks 18, 21, & 22 recorded at the Hilton Hotel, Las Vegas.
Track 10 recorded February 5, 1976 in the "Jungle Room" of Elvis' Graceland mansion, Memphis.

FROM THE VAULTS NO. 1 – IN MY DREAMS (MEMORY RECORDS)

Various out takes 1956 – 1965.

1. Judy (take 1)
2. Night Rider (take 3)
3. Fountain Of Love (take 2)
4. Shake, Rattle and Roll (take 7)
5. Good Luck Charm (take 1)
6. Please Don't Drag That String Around (take 5)
7. She's Not You (take 1)
8. Western Union (take 1)
9. Slowly But Surely (take 1)
10. Little Sister (take 3)
11. Kiss Me Quick (take 1)
12. I Got Lucky (takes MX5-1 & M5-5)
13. King Of The Whole Wide World (take M1-6)
14. Cross My Heart And Hope To Die (take 11)

15. Witchcraft (take 2)
16. In Your Arms (studio rehearsal)
17. In My Dreams
Bonus Tracks:
18. My Way
19. Don't Be Cruel
20. Are You Lonesome Tonight
21. Heartbreak Hotel
22. Love Me Tender
23. Mystery Train
24. One Night
25. It's Now Or Never
26. King Creole

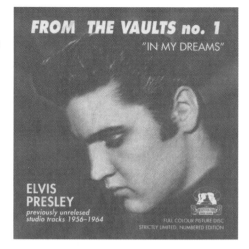

Recording Information:

Track 4 recorded February 3, 1956 at RCA Studios, New York.
Track 16 recorded March 12, 1961. Track 1 recorded March 13, 1961.
Track 10 recorded June 26, 1961. Track 11 recorded June 25, 1961.
Track 5 recorded October 15, 1961. Track 2 recorded October 16, 1961.
Track 3 recorded March 18, 1962. Track 7 recorded March 19, 1962.
Track 6 recorded May 26, 1963. Tracks 8 & 15 recorded May 27, 1963. Track 9 recorded May 28, 1963.
Tracks 1 – 3, 5 – 11, & 15 recorded at RCA Studio B, Nashville.
Tracks 12 & 13 recorded October 27, 1961 at Radio Recorders, Hollywood for The Mirisch United Artists Motion Picture "Kid Galahad".
Track 14 recorded June 11, 1964 at Radio Recorders, Hollywood for the MGM Motion Picture "Girl Happy".
Track 17 is not an Elvis performance. The sleeve notes don't claim that this is an Elvis recording but let the listener draw their own conclusions.
It likely that the recording was taken from a demo disc made in the Elvis style.
Tracks 18 – 22 performed by Vlada Lichnovsky. Tracks 23 – 26 performed by Karel Zich.

FROM THE VAULTS VOL.2 – NEVER ENDING (MEMORY RECORDS)

Various out takes 1956 – 1965.

1. For The Millionth And The Last Time (take 6)
2. (You're The) Devil In Disguise (take 1)
3. You'll Be Gone (take 4)
4. Almost Always True (alternate master)
5. A Dog's Life (take 8)
6. Ain't That Loving You Baby (take 10)
7. The Girl Next Door Went A Walking
(alternate take)
8. Never Ending (take 1)
9. His Latest Flame (take 2)
10. I Met Her Today (take 7)
11. Gonna Get Back Home Somehow (take 1)
12. I'm Yours (take 4)
13. Such A Night (alternate master)
14. Give Me The Right (take 2)

15. Riding The Rainbow (take M4-1)
16. This Is Living (take 1)
17. Can't Help Falling In Love
(movie version – early take)
18. It Hurts Me (alternate master)
19. I'm Not The Marrying Kind (take 6)
20. In My Dreams
Bonus Tracks:
21. I'm Beginning To Forget You
22. (You're So Square) Baby I Don't Care
23. Young And Beautiful
24. Love Me Tender
25. That's All Right Mama
26. Lonesome Town

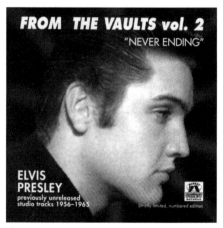

Recording Information:

Track 6 recorded June 10, 1958.
Tracks 7 & 13 recorded April 4, 1960.
Track 14 recorded March 12, 1961.
Tracks 9 & 12 recorded June 26, 1961.
Track 1 recorded October 15, 1961. Track 10 recorded October 16, 1961.
Tracks 3 & 11 recorded March 18, 1962.
Tracks 2 & 8 recorded May 26, 1963.
Track 18 recorded January 12, 1964.
Tracks 1 –3, 6– 14, & 18 recorded at RCA Studio B, Nashville.
Track 4 recorded March 22, 1961. Track 17 recorded March 23, 1961.
Tracks 4 & 17 recorded at Radio Recorders, Hollywood for the Paramount Motion Picture "Blue Hawaii".
Track 19 recorded at July 2, 1961 at RCA Studio B, Nashville for the Mirisch United Artists Motion Picture "Follow That Dream".
Track 15 recorded October 26, 1961. Track 16 recorded October 17, 1961.
Tracks 15 & 16 recorded at Radio Recorders, Hollywood for the Mirisch United Artists Motion Picture "Kid Galahad".
Track 5 recorded July 27, 1965 at Radio Recorders, Hollywood for the Paramount Motion Picture "Paradise Hawaiian Style".
Track 20 is not an Elvis performance. The sleeve notes don't claim that this is an Elvis recording but let the listener draw their own conclusions.
It likely that the recording was taken from a demo disc made in the Elvis style. (This is a different recording than the version used on Volume 1)
Tracks 21 – 26 performed by Carl Fisher and his Rockin' Makers.

LOVING YOU RECORDING SESSIONS (VIK)

Loving You (rockin' version) Takes 1 – 21
Loving You (ballad version) Takes 1 – 12

Recording Information:

All tracks recorded February 14, 1957 at Radio Recorders, Hollywood for the Paramount
Motion Picture "Loving You"

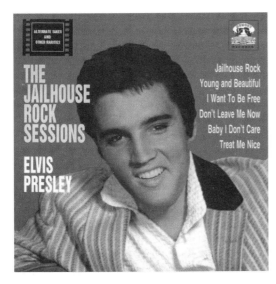

Recording Information:

Tracks 1 – 7, 17, & 18 recorded April 30, 1957 at Radio Recorders, Hollywood.
Tracks 8, 9, 15, 16, 19, & 20 recorded May 3, 1957 at Radio Recorders, Hollywood
Vocal overdubs for tracks 9 & 20 recorded May 8, 1957 at MGM Studios, Hollywood.
Tracks 10 – 14, & 21 recorded May 9, 1957 at MGM Studios, Hollywood
Track 22 recorded September 5, 1957 at Radio Recorders, Hollywood.
All tracks recorded for the MGM Motion Picture "Jailhouse Rock".
Tracks 23 – 25 first released on the RCA EP "Elvis Sails" in 1958.

THE JAILHOUSE ROCK SESSIONS (MEMORY RECORDS)

Young And Beautiful:
1. Take 3
2. Take 9
3. Take 10
4. Take 12
Jailhouse Rock:
5. Take 5
6. Take 6 – long fade
7. Take number unknown
8. I Want To Be Free (take 8)
9. (You're So Square) Baby I Don't Care (take 14)
Don't Leave Me Now:
10. Take 6
11. Take 7
12. Take 8
13. Take 9
14. Alternate master
Treat Me Nice:
15. Take 10
16. Alternate stereo version
17. Young And Beautiful (master)
18. Jailhouse Rock (master)
19. I Want To Be Free (master)
20. (You're So Square) Baby I Don't Care (master)
21. Don't Leave Me Now (master)
22. Treat Me Nice (master)
Elvis Sails:
23. Press Interview With Elvis
24. Elvis' Newsreel Interview
25 Pat Heron Interview

WELCOME IN GERMANY (ROMA)

"GI Blues" soundtrack and additional recordings.

1. Ankunft In Bremerhaven
2. Wooden Heart*
3. Tonight Is So Right For Love*
4. Frankfort Special*
5. Danny Boy
6. Shoppin' Around*
7. Doin' The Best I Can/
Blue Suede Shoes*
8. Pocketful Of Rainbows*
9. GI Blues*
10. The Fool
11. Tonight Is So Right For Love*
12. What's She Really Like*
13. Wooden Heart*
14. Frankfort Special*
15. Pocketful Of Rainbows*
16. Doin' The Best I Can*
17. Didja Ever*
18. Soldier Boy
19. Wooden Heart
20. Vienna Woods Rock And Roll*
21. What's She Really Like*
22. He's Only A Prayer Away
23. Shoppin' Around*
24. GI Blues*
25. Big Boots*
26. Blue Suede Shoes*
27. Earth Angel
28. O Sole Mio

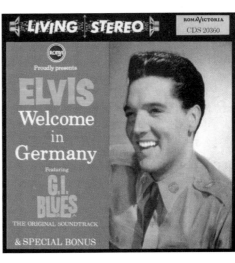

Recording Information:

Track 1 interview recorded 1 October, 1958.
Tracks 5, 10, 18, 22 & 27 recorded in 1959 during Elvis' army service in Bad Nau-
heim,Germany.
Tracks 2, 3, 4, 6, 7, 8, 9, 11, 12, 13, 14, 15, 16, 17, 21, 22, 23, 24, 25 & 26 recorded at RCA Studios, Hollywood, April 27 & 28, 1960.
Track 20 recorded at Radio Recorders, Hollywood, May 6, 1960. (correct title is "Tonight's All Right For Love")
* Recorded for the Paramount Motion Picture "GI Blues"
Tracks 19& 28 recorded live at the Hilton Hotel, Las Vegas, December 13, 1975. (audience recordings)

THE CAFÉ EUROPA SESSIONS (TULSA RECORDS)

Disc One:

1. Shoppin' Around (Instrumental – AO takes 1 – 4)
2. Shoppin' Around (BO takes 1 – 11)
3. Didja Ever (CO take 1)
4. Doin' The Best I Can (DO takes 1 – 13)
5. GI Blues (EO takes 1 – 10)
6. Tonight Is So Right For Love (FO takes 1 –6)

Disc Two:

1. Tonight Is So Right For Love (FO takes 7 – 11)
2. What's She Really Like (GO takes 1 – 22)
3. Frankfort Special (HO takes 1 – 3)
4. Tonight Is So Right For Love (Music/Chorus – KO takes 1 – 4)
5. Big Boots (Slow Tempo – MO takes 1 – 4)

Disc Three:

1. Whistling Blues (Instrumental – JO Take 1)
2. Big Boots (Fast Tempo – M10 takes 2 – 7)
3. Pocketful of Rainbows (NO takes 1 – 28)
4. Blue Suede Shoes (PO take 1)
5. Wooden Heart (QO takes 1 – 4)

Disc Four:

1. Big Boots (Medium Tempo – MIOX takes 1 & 2)
2. Shoppin' Around (BOX takes 1– 7)
3. Pocketful Of Rainbows (NOX takes 1 – 3)
4. Frankfort Special (NOX takes 1 – 10)
5. Tonight's All Right For Love (R10 takes 1 – 17)
6. Tonight's All Right For Love (Tempo – R20 takes 1& 2)
7. Big Boots (Slow Tempo – MOX takes 1 – 6)
8. Big Boots (Slow Tempo Insert - M20X takes 1 – 4)
9. Tonight's All Right For Love (Music/Chorus – RO takes 1 – 5)

Disc Five:
Highlights from discs 1 – 4

Recording Information:

Disc One:
All tracks recorded April 27, 1960.
Disc Two:
Tracks 1, 3 & 4 recorded April 27, 1960.
Tracks 2 & 5 recorded April 28, 1960.
Disc Three:
All tracks recorded April 28, 1960.
Disc Four:
All tracks recorded May 6, 1960.
Discs One, Two, & Three recorded at RCA Studios, Hollywood.
Disc Four recorded at Radio Recorders, Hollywood.
All selections recorded for the Paramount Motion Picture "GI Blues".

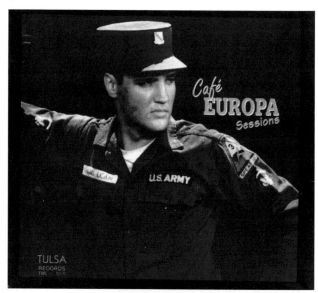

GI BLUES 35th ANNIVERSARY EDITION (BILKO)

GI BLUES 35th ANNIVERSARY EDITION - 2 (BILKO)

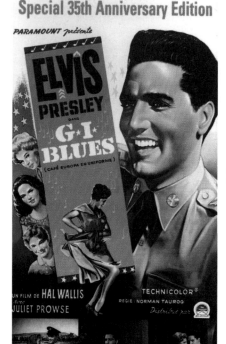

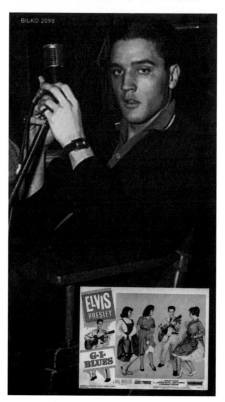

Out takes from the "GI Blues" sessions are also available on these two single CD's on the Bilko label, which were packaged in the long box digi-pack format.

FLAMING STAR (DOUBLE G)

1. Black Star (master)
2. Black Star (take 6 – end title)
3. Black Star (acetate)
4. Summer Kisses, Winter Tears (takes 1 & 14 – spliced)
5. Summer Kisses, Winter Tears (take 20)
6. Summer Kisses, Winter Tears (takes 21 – 23)
7. Summer Kisses, Winter Tears (take 24)
8. Summer Kisses, Winter Tears (take 25)
9. Summer Kisses, Winter Tears (take 26)
10. Summer Kisses, Winter Tears (movie version)
11. Summer Kisses, Winter Tears (master)
12. Britches (instrumental – take 1)
13. Britches (vocal overdub – takes 1 – 7)
14. Britches (insert – take 1)
15. Britches (master – takes 5 & 4 – spliced)
16. A Cane & A High Starched Collar (takes 2 & 3)
17. A Cane & A High Starched Collar (master)
18. Flaming Star (vocal overdub)*
19. Flaming Star (stereo version)*
20. Flaming Star (master – take 6)*
21. Flaming Star (instrumental – take 1)*
22. Flaming Star (end title version)*
23. Flaming Star (movie version)*
24. A Cane & A High Starched Collar (movie version)
25. Original Movie Theatre Trailer

Recording Information:

All tracks except "Flaming Star" recorded at Radio Recorders Hollywood, August 8, 1960 for the 20th Century Fox Motion Picture "Flaming Star".
*The movie was originally titled "Black Star", after the title change Elvis re-recorded the title track as "Flaming Star" at Radio Recorders, Hollywood on October 7, 1960.

THE COMPLETE WILD IN THE COUNTRY SESSIONS (TCB RECORDS)

"Wild In The Country" session out takes and additional soundtrack out takes.

1. Wild In The Country (movie version)
2. Lonely Man (solo – takes 1 – 4)
3. In My way (takes 1 – 8)
4. Wild In The Country (takes 1 – 13)
5. Plantation Rock (take 17)
6. Plantation Rock (instrumental)
7. Wild In The Country (takes 14 – 19)
8. Forget Me Never (take 1)
9. Husky Dusky Day (movie version)
10. I Slipped, I Stumbled, I Fell (master)
11. One Broken Heart For Sale (movie version)
12. I Slipped, I Stumbled, I Fell (takes 1 – 13)
13. I Slipped, I Stumbled, I Fell (lower key – takes 14 – 18)

Recording Information:

Tracks 1 – 4, 7 & 8 recorded November 7, 1960. Tracks 10 – 13 recorded November 8, 1960.
Track 9 was not recorded at the soundtrack sessions. The song only consisted of a few lines, and was recorded on the set of the film.
Tracks 1 – 4, 7, 8, & 10 recorded at Radio Recorders, Hollywood for the 20th Century Fox Motion Picture "Wild In The Country"
Tracks 5 & 6 recorded March 28, 1962 at Radio Recorders, Hollywood for the Paramount Motion Picture "Girls! Girls! Girls!"
Track 11 recorded September 22, 1962 at Radio Recorders, Hollywood for the MGM Motion Picture "It Happened At The World's Fair"
Note: original copies of this disc were not banded.

THE BEST OF THE BLUE HAWAII SESSIONS (MEMORY RECORDS)

1. Hawaiian Sunset (take 1)
2. Aloha-Oe (takes 2, 4, & 6)
3. KU-U-I-PO (takes 2, 4, 6, & 8)
4. No More (takes 1 – 5, & 8)
5. Slicin' Sand (takes 15 – 18)
6. Blue Hawaii (takes 1 – 7)
7. Ito Eats (takes 1 – 3, & 6 – 8)
8. Hawaiian Wedding Song (take 1)
9. Island Of Love
(takes 1 – 3, 5 – 7, 9, 11, & 12)

10. Steppin' Out Of Line (takes 9 – 15)
11. Almost Always True (takes 1, 2, 4, & 5)
12. Moonlight Swim (takes 1 & 2)
13. Can't Help Falling In Love
(movie version – takes 1 – 5, 7, 14, 15, & 17 – 20)
14. Can't Help Falling In Love (takes 27 & 28)
15. Beach Boy Blues (takes 1 & 2)
16. Rock A Hula Baby (takes 1 – 3)
17. Presentation Of Awards To Elvis
18. Moonlight Swim

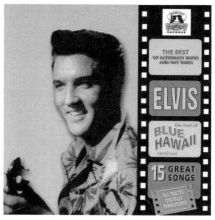

Recording Information:

Tracks 1 – 5 recorded March 21, 1961.
Tracks 6 – 12 recorded March 22, 1961.
Tracks 13 – 16 recorded March 23, 1961.
Tracks 1 – 16 recorded at Radio Recorders, Hollywood for the Paramount Motion Picture "Blue Hawaii".
Track 17 recorded March 25, 1961, Pearl Harbour, Hawaii.
Track 18 is a home recording from 1961.

BLUE HAWAII – THE COMPLETE SESSION VOL. 1 (TRADE SECRETS)

1. Hawaiian Sunset – take 1
2. Hawaiian Sunset – take 2
3. Hawaiian Sunset – take 3
4. Aloha-Oe – takes 1 – 6
5. KU-U-I-PO – take 1
6. KU-U-I-PO – takes 2 – 4
7. KU-U-I-PO – take 5
8. KU-U-I-PO – take 6
9. KU-U-I-PO – take 7
10. KU-U-I-PO – take 8
11. KU-U-I-PO – take 9
12. No More – takes 1 – 6
13. No More – take 7
14. No More – take 8
15. No More – take 9

16. Slicin' Sand – takes 15 & 16
17. Slicin' Sand – take 17
18. Slicin' Sand – take 18
19. Slicin' Sand – take 19
20. Blue Hawaii – takes 1 & 2
21. Blue Hawaii – take 3
22. Blue Hawaii – takes 4 & 6
23. Blue Hawaii – take 7
24. Ito Eats – takes 1 – 4
25. Ito Eats take 5
26. Ito Eats – takes 6 – 8
27. Ito Eats – take 9
28. Ito Eats – track only
29. Hawaiian Wedding Song – take 1
30. Hawaiian Wedding Song – take 2

Recording Information:

Tracks 1 – 19 recorded March 21, 1961.
Tracks 20– 30 recorded March 22, 1961.
All tracks recorded at Radio Recorders, Hollywood for the Paramount Motion Picture "Blue Hawaii".

BLUE HAWAII   THE COMPLETE SESSION VOL. 2 (TRADE SECRETS)

1. Island Of Love – takes 1 – 7
2. Island Of Love – take 8
3. Island Of Love – takes 9 – 12
4. Island Of Love – take 13
5. Steppin' Out Of Line – takes 1 – 7
6. Steppin' Out Of Line – take 8
7. Steppin' Out Of Line – takes 9 – 14
8. Steppin' Out Of Line – take 15
9. Steppin' Out Of line – take 16
10. Steppin' Out Of Line – take 17
11. Steppin' Out Of Line – take 18
12. Steppin' Out Of Line – take 19
13. Can't Help Falling In Love – takes 1 –8
14. Can't Help Falling In Love – take 9

15. Can't Help Falling In Love – takes 1 – 12
16. Can't Help Falling In Love – take 13
17. Can't Help Falling In Love – takes 14 & 15
18. Can't Help Falling In Love – take 16
19. Can't Help Falling In Love – takes 17 – 22
20. Can't Help Falling In Love – take 23
21. Can't Help Falling In Love – take 24
22. Can't Help Falling In Love – takes 25 – 28
23. Can't Help falling In Love – take 29
24. Rock a Hula Baby – takes 1 & 2
25. Rock A Hula Baby – take 3
26. Rock a Hula Baby – take 4
27. Rock A Hula Baby – take 5

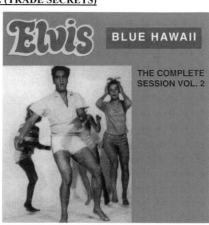

Recording Information:

Tracks 1 – 12 recorded March 21, 1961. Tracks 13 – 27 recorded March 23, 1961.
All tracks recorded at Radio Recorders, Hollywood for the Paramount Motion Picture "Blue Hawaii".

BLUE HAWAII   THE COMPLETE SESSION VOL. 3 (TRADE SECRETS)

1. Beach Boy Blues – take 1
2. Beach Boy Blues – take 2
3. Beach Boy Blues – take 3
4. Almost Always True – takes 1 & 2
5. Almost Always True – take 3
6. Almost Always True – take 4
7. Almost Always True – take 5
8. Almost Always True – takes 6 & 7
9. Almost Always True – take 8
10. Moonlight Swim – take 1
11. Moonlight Swim – take 2
12. Moonlight Swim – take 3
13. Moonlight Swim – take 4
14. Danny
15. Steadfast Loyal And True – take 6
16. As Long As I Have You – take 3
17. As Long As I Have You – take 8
18. Lover Doll – take 7

19. Crawfish – take 7
20. King Creole – take 3
21. King Creole – take 8
22. King Creole – take 1
23. King Creole – take 2
24. King Creole – take 13
25. King Creole – take 14
26. Steadfast Loyal and True – take 1
27. Steadfast Loyal And True – take 3
28. Crawfish – take 11
29. Crawfish – take 13
30. As I Long As I Have You – take 4
31. As Long As I Have You – take 5
32. As Long As I Have You – take 7
33. As Long As I Have You – take 11
34. Lover Doll – take 14
35. Lover Doll – take 15

Recording Information:

Tracks 1– 3 recorded March 23, 1961. Tracks 4 – 13 recorded March 22, 1961.
Tracks 1 – 13 recorded at Radio Recorders, Hollywood for the Paramount Motion Picture "Blue Hawaii".
Tracks 19 – 25, 28 & 29 recorded January 15, 1958. Tracks 16 - 18 & 30 –35 recorded January 16, 1958.
Tracks 15, 26, & 27 recorded January 23, 1958. Track 14 recorded January 28, 1958
Tracks 14 – 35 recorded at Radio Recorders, Hollywood for the Paramount Motion Picture "King Creole".

KEEP ON FOLLOWING THAT DREAM (KWIMPER RECORDS)

1. Follow That Dream (takes 1 & 2)
2. Angel (takes 1 & 2)
3. What A Wonderful Life (takes 1, 2, & 3)
4. Angel (take 4)
5. I'm Not The Marrying Kind (takes 1 – 5)
6. Follow That Dream (take 3)
7. I'm Not The Marrying Kind (takes 6 & 7)
8. Angel (take 5)
9. A Whistling Tune (takes 1 – 3)
10. Follow That Dream (takes 4 & 5)
11. Sound Advice (takes 1 – 5)
12. Angel (take 6)
13. What A Wonderful Life (takes 4 – 6)
14. A Whistling Tune (master take 4)
15. Angel (master take 7)
16. Sound Advice (master take 6)*
17. I'm Not The Marrying Kind (master take 8)*
18. What A Wonderful Life (master take 7)*
19. Follow That Dream (master take 6)*

Recording Information:

All tracks recorded at RCA Studio B, Nashville, July 2, 1961 for the Mirisch United Artists Motion Picture "Follow That Dream".
*It was common practice for the master takes to be cut out of the session reels once the take numbers were decided.
This session was recorded in stereo, but some of the stereo master takes have been lost.
The last four tracks on this disc are mono masters.

KID GALAHAD SESSIONS (RADIO RECORDERS)

1. King Of The Whole Wide World (takes 16 –24)
2. King Of The Whole Wide World (take 25)
3. King Of The Whole Wide World (takes 26 – 28)
4. King Of The Whole Wide World (take 29)
5. King Of The Whole Wide World (takes 30 & 31)
6. King Of The Whole Wide World (version 2 – takes 1 & 2)
7. King Of The Whole Wide World (version 2 – take 3)
8. King Of The Whole World (version 2 – take 4)
9. A Whistling Tune (take 1)
10. A Whistling Tune (take 2)
11. A Whistling Tune (takes 3 –7)
12. Home Is Where The Heart Is (takes 1 – 6)
13. Home Is Where The Heart Is (take 7)
14. Home Is Where The Heart Is (takes 8 & 9)
15. Home Is Where The Heart Is (take 10)
16. Home Is Where The Heart Is (take 11)
17. Home Is Where The Heart Is (take 12)
18. Home Is Where The Heart Is (take 13)
19. Home Is Where The Heart Is (take 14)
20. Home Is Where The Heart Is (takes 15 – 19)
21. Home is Where The Heart Is (take 20)
22. Home Is Where The Heart Is (take 21)

Recording Information:

Tracks 1 – 5 & 9 – 22 recorded October 26, 1961.
Tracks 6 – 8 recorded October 27, 1961.
All tracks recorded at Radio Recorders, Hollywood for the
Mirisch United Artists Motion Picture "Kid Galahad".

ELVIS BY REQUEST – MORE KID GALAHAD SESSIONS (RADIO RECORDERS)

1. Riding The Rainbow (take 1)
2. Riding The Rainbow (takes 2 –3)
3. Riding The Rainbow (take 4)
4. Riding The Rainbow (take 5)
5. Riding The Rainbow (take 6)
6. Riding The Rainbow (take 7)
7. Riding The Rainbow (take 8)
8. Riding The Rainbow (take 9)
9. Riding The Rainbow (version 2 – takes 1 – 5)
10. Riding The Rainbow (version 2 – take 6)
11. Riding The Rainbow (version 2 – take 7)
12. I Got Lucky (take 1)
13. I Got Lucky (takes 2 – 5)
14. I Got Lucky (take 6)
15. I Got Lucky (version 2 – take 1)
16. I Got Lucky (Version 2 – take 2)
17. This Is Living (take 1)
18. This Is Living (take 2)
19. This is Living (take 3)
20. This Is Living (takes 4 – 7)
21. This Is Living (take 8)
22. This Is Living (take 9)
23. This Is Living (take 10)
24. Flaming Star
25. Black Star
26. Summer Kisses, Winter Tears
27. A Cane & A High Starched Collar (2 takes)
28. Britches

Recording Information:

Tracks 1 – 11 recorded October 26, 1961.
Tracks 12 – 23 recorded October 27, 1961.
Tracks 1 – 23 recorded at Radio Recorders, Hollywood for the
Mirisch United Artists Motion Picture "Kid Galahad".
Tracks 25 – 28 recorded August 8, 1960.
Track 24 recorded October 7, 1960.
Tracks 24 – 28 recorded at Radio Recorders, Hollywood for the
20th Century Fox Motion Picture, "Flaming Star".

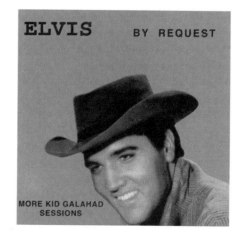

GIRL HAPPY AT THE WORLD'S FAIR (BILKO)

1. Girl Happy (takes 3 & 4)
2. Beyond The Bend (takes 1 & 3)
3. Take Me To The Fair (takes 1, 2, 5, 6 & 7)
4. Cotton Candy Land (takes 1, 2, 3, & 4)
5. Puppet On a String (takes 6 & 7)
6. How Would You Like To Be (take 6)
7. Cross My Heart And Hope To Die (takes 8, 9 & 11)
8. How Would You Like To Be (takes 3 & 2)
9. One Broken Heart For Sale (takes 2, 3 & 1)
10. The Meanest Girl In Town (takes 4, 5, & 6)
11. Relax (takes 12 & 13)
12. I'm Falling In Love Tonight (takes 7 & 6)
13. Do Not Disturb (takes 26 & 27)
14. Spring Fever (takes 2, 3 & 4)
15. They Remind Me Too Much Of You (take 7)
16. Happy Ending (take 9)

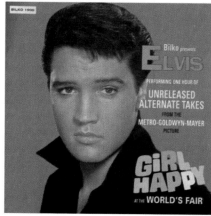

Recording Information:

Tracks 11 & 16 recorded August 30, 1962. Tracks 2, 3, 4, 6, 8, 9, 12 & 15 recorded September 22, 1962.
Tracks 2, 3, 4, 6, 8, 9, 11, 12, 15, & 16 recorded at Radio Recorders, Hollywood for the MGM Motion Picture "It Happened At The World's Fair".
Tracks 1, 5 & 10 recorded June 10, 1964. Tracks 7, 13 & 14 recorded June 11, 1964.
Tracks 1, 5, 7, 10, 13, & 14 recorded at Radio Recorders, Hollywood from the MGM Motion Picture "Girl Happy".

WITH A SONG IN MY HEART (SPEED RECORDS)

1. With A Song In My Heart (excerpt)
2. Frankie And Johnny (take 1)
3. Everybody Come Aboard (takes 1 – 4)
4. Please Don't Stop Loving Me (takes 1 & 4 – 6)
5. Petunia The Gardener's Daughter (take 1)
6. Look Out Broadway (takes 1 – 5)
7. Chesay (take 1)
8. Frankie And Johnny (takes 2 – 4)
9. Shout It Out (takes 1 – 3)
10. Beginners Luck (take 2)
11. Everybody Come Aboard (takes 5 – 10)
12. Please Don't Stop Loving Me (takes 8 & 11 – 14)
13. Petunia The Gardener's Daughter (takes 2 & 3)
14. Look Out Broadway (takes 6, 7, & 11)
15. Chesay (takes 2,.3, 5, & 6)
16. Frankie And Johnny (take 5)
17. Shout It Out (takes 4 – 6)
18. Please Don't Stop Loving Me (takes 15 & 17)
19. Everybody Come Aboard (takes 12 & 13)
20. Frankie And Johnny (movie version – section 1 – take 3)
21. Frankie And Johnny (movie version – section 4 – takes 1 & 2)
22. Frankie And Johnny (movie version – section 5 – take 1)
23. Frankie And Johnny (movie version – sections 6 & 7 – takes 1 & 2)

Recording Information:

Tracks 1 – 9 recorded May 13, 1965. Track 10 recorded May 14 - 15, 1965.
Tracks 11 – 19 recorded May 13, 1965.
Tracks 20 – 23 recorded May 14 – 15, 1965.
All tracks recorded at Radio Recorders, Hollywood for the United Artists Motion Picture "Frankie And Johnny".

HAWAII USA (FLASHBACK)

1. Hawaii USA (GOV takes 2 & 3)
2. Stop Where You Are (DOV takes 2 & 3)
3. Stop Where You Are (D-IOV takes 3 & 4)
4. Sand Castles (KO takes 1 & 9)
5. Queenie Wahine's Papaya (JO takes 1 & 4)
6. Queenie Wahine's Papaya (JOV take 3)
7. Queenie Wahine's Papaya (JIV takes 1 & 2)
8. This Is My Heaven (FOV takes 2 & 4)
9. Scratch My Back (COV take 2)
10. A Dog's Life (EOV take 7)
11. Drums Of The Islands (AOV take 2)
12. Sand Castles (KO takes 2 – 4 & 6 – 8)
13. Sand Castles (KOV take 1)

Recording Information:

Tracks 8, 9, & 11 recorded July 26, 1965.
Tracks 1– 3, 5 – 8, & 10 recorded July 27, 1965.
Tracks 4, 12, & 13 recorded August 2, 1965.
All tracks recorded at Radio Recorders, Hollywood for the Paramount Motion Picture "Paradise Hawaiian Style".

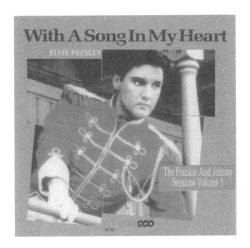

THE COMPLETE FRANKIE AND JOHNNY SESSIONS (FAMOUS GROOVE RECORDS)

"The Complete Frankie And Johnny Sessions" are also available. This collection was released by the Famous Groove label as a double CD packaged in a 10 inch album sleeve.

SPIN IN...SPIN OUT (RMC)

1. Spinout (take 2)
2. Adam And Evil (takes 1 & 2)
3. Smorgasbord (take 1)
4. Adam And Evil (take 6)
5. Am I Ready (takes 3 & 4)
6. Adam And Evil (take 9)
7. Never Say Yes (takes 1 & 2)
8. Adam And Evil (take 10)
9. All That I Am (takes 1 & 2)
10. Adam And Evil (take 11)
11. Stop, Look And Listen (takes 1 – 3)
12. Adam And Evil (take 12)
13. Beach Shack (takes 1 – 3)
14. Adam And Evil (take 13)
15. Am I ready (takes 5 & 6)
16. Adam And Evil (take 14)
17. Smorgasbord (take 4)
18. Adam And Evil (take 15)
19. All That I Am (take 6)
20. Adam And Evil (takes 17 & 18)
21. Adam And Evil (take 16)

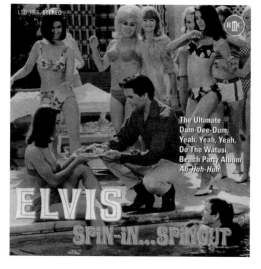

Recording Information:

Smorgasbord/Stop Look And Listen/Am I Ready/Beach Shack – Recorded February 16, 1966.
Never Say Yes/Spinout/All That I Am/Adam And Evil – Recorded February 17, 1966.
All tracks recorded at Radio Recorders, Hollywood for the MGM Motion Picture "Spinout".

EASY COME, EASY GO (AJR RECORDS)

Deleted master recordings:

1. Easy Come, Easy Go
2. The Love Machine
3. Yoga Is As Yoga Does
4. You Gotta Stop
5. Sing You Children
6. I'll Take Love
7. Wild In The Country
8. Angel
9. If You Think I Don't Need You
10. Night Life
11. C'mon Everybody
12. Ask Me
13. It Hurts Me
14. Such A Night
15. I Gotta Know
16. Kiss Me Quick
17. No More
18. (Such An) Easy Question
19. You're A Heartbreaker
20. Suspicion
21. What'd I Say

Recording Information:

Tracks 1, 6, & 5 recorded September 28, 1966.
Tracks 2, 3, & 4 recorded September 29, 1966.
Tracks 1 – 6 recorded at Paramount Studios, Hollywood for the Paramount Motion picture "Easy Come, Easy Go".
Track 19 recorded at Sun Studios, Memphis, December 1954.
Tracks 14 & 15 recorded at RCA Studio B, Nashville, April 4, 1960.
Track 7 recorded at Radio Recorders, Hollywood, November 7, 1960 for the 20th Century Fox Motion Picture "Wild In The Country".
Track 17 recorded at Radio Recorders, Hollywood, March 21, 1961 for the Paramount Motion Picture "Blue Hawaii".
Track 16 recorded at RCA Studio B, Nashville, June 25, 1961.
Track 8 recorded at RCA Studio B, Nashville, July 2, 1961 for the Mirisch United Artists Motion Picture "Follow That Dream".
Track 18 recorded at RCA Studio B, Nashville, March 18, 1962.
Track 20 recorded at RCA Studio B, Nashville, March 19, 1962.
Tracks 9, 10, & 11 recorded at Radio Recorders, Hollywood, July 9, 1963. Track 21 recorded at Radio Recorders, Hollywood, August 30, 1963.
Tracks 9 – 11 & 21 recorded for the MGM Motion Picture "Viva Las Vegas".
Tracks 12, & 13 recorded at RCA Studio B, Nashville, January 12, 1964.
This CD featured the stereo masters from the "Easy Come, Easy Go" soundtrack which were unavailable on CD officially at the time of this release.
"You 're A Heartbreaker" is the original version without added echo, and the remaining tracks are RCA masters that were issued in various counties either
in stereo for the first time, or with one or more of the stereo channels missing.

ELVIS – INTERNATIONAL HEATWAVE (FORT BAXTER)

1. Words (rehearsal)
2. The Next Step Is Love (rehearsal)
3. Crying Time (rehearsal)
4. What'd I Say (rehearsal)
5. Stranger In The Crowd (rehearsal)
6. How The Web Was Woven (rehearsal)
7. I Just Can't Help Believin' (rehearsal)
8. You Don't Have To Say You Love Me (rehearsal)
9. Bridge Over Troubled Water (rehearsal)
10. Mary In The Morning (stage rehearsal)
11. Polk Salad Annie (stage rehearsal)
12. That's All Right Mama (live)
13. Patch It Up (live)
14. Love Me Tender (live)
15. You've Lost That Loving Feeling (live)
16. Sweet Caroline (live)
17. I Just Can't Help Believin' (live)
18. Mystery Train/Tiger Man (live)
21. Bridge Over Troubled Water (live)
22. Heartbreak Hotel (live)
23. One Night (live)
24. Blue Suede Shoes (live)
25. All Shook Up (live)
26. Polk Salad Annie (live)
27. I've Lost You (live)
28. Suspicious Minds (live)
29. Can't Help Falling In Love (live)
30. Closing Tune (live)

Recording Information:

All tracks taken from the soundtrack of the original version of the MGM Motion Picture "Elvis – That's The Way It Is", 1970.

ELVIS ON TOUR (A.J. RECORDS)

1. Dialogue/Johnny B. Goode (rehearsal)
2. See See Rider (live)
3. Polk Salad Annie (live)
4. Separate Ways (studio out take)
5. Proud Mary (live)
6. Never Been To Spain (live)
7. Burning Love (live)
8. The Lighthouse/
Lead Me, Guide Me/
Bosom Of Abraham (rehearsal)
9. Love Me Tender (live)
10. Bridge Over Troubled Water (live)
11. Funny How Time Slips Away (live)
12. An American Trilogy (live)
13. I Got A Woman (live)
14. A Big Hunk O' Love (live)
15. You Gave Me A Mountain (live)
16. Sweet, Sweet Spirit (live)
(Performed by J.D. Sumner & The Stamps Quartet)
17. Lawdy Miss Clawdy (live)
18. Can't Help Falling In Love (live)
19 Memories (studio master)

Recording Information;

All tracks taken from the soundtrack of the MGM Motion Picture "Elvis On Tour", 1972.

Since the first official release of Elvis' early live recordings from the Louisiana Hayride shows on the vinyl album "The First Year" in 1984, these recordings along with a 1956 performance from Little Rock, Arkansas which was first released on a vinyl bootleg album, have appeared on a large number of budget priced CD releases. The CD's featured on this page, along with the album "The Legend Begins" on the next page, are not official releases but cannot be classed as bootleg CD's either, as the material included on them was in the public domain at the time of their release.

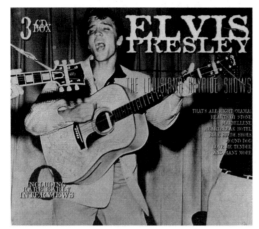

Above: The Hayride Shows (3 CD set – Goldies label)
This collection also included the Little Rock performance,
and additional interviews.

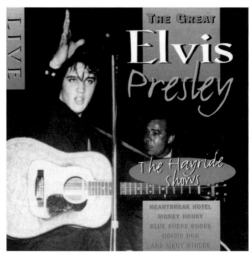

Above: The Great Elvis Presley – The Hayride Shows
(CD – Trace label)

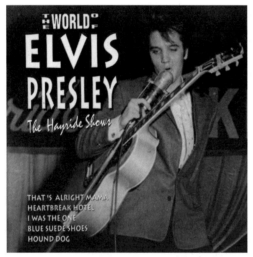

Above: The World Of Elvis Presley – The Hayride Shows
(CD – Trace label)

Below: Elvis Presley Recorded Live (CD – Super gain label)

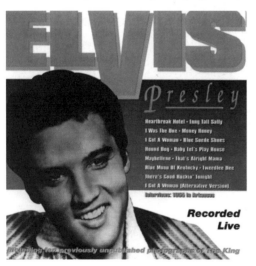

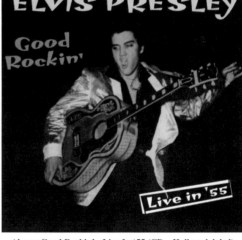

Above: Good Rockin' - Live In '55 (CD – Hallmark label)

Below: Heartbreak Hotel (CD – picture disc)

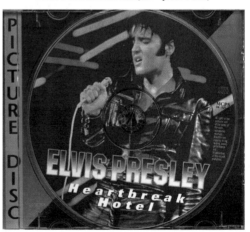

CUTTIN' LOOSE (NO LABEL NAME)

1. Hearts Of Stone
2. Money Honey
3. I Don't Care If The Sun Don't Shine
4. Hound Dog

Recording Information:

Tracks 1 & 2 recorded Saturday , January 15, 1955.
Track 3 recorded Saturday, January 22, 1955.
Track 4 recorded Saturday, December 15, 1956.

THE LEGEND BEGINS (ESSENTIAL GOLD)

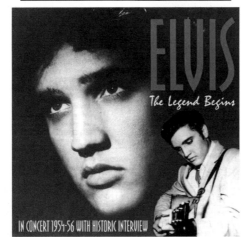

1. That's All Right Mama
2. Blue Moon Of Kentucky
3. Tweedle Dee
4. Good Rockin' Tonight
5. Baby Let's Play House
6. Blue Moon Of Kentucky
7. I Got A Woman
8. That's All Right Mama
9. Baby Let's Play House

10. Maybelline
11. That's All Right Mama
12. Heartbreak Hotel
13. Long Tall Sally
14. I Was The One
15. Money Honey
16. I Got A Woman
17. Blue Suede Shoes
18. Hound Dog
19. TV Guide Interview

Recording Information:

Tracks 1 & 2 recorded live October 16, 1954 at the Louisiana Municipal Auditorium, Shreveport, Louisiana.
Track 3 recorded live during 1955 performance at the Louisiana Municipal Auditorium, Shreveport, Louisiana.
Tracks 4 – 8 recorded live March 19, 1955 at the Eagles Hall, Houston, Texas.
Tracks 9, 10, & 11 recorded live September 24, 1955 at the Louisiana Municipal Auditorium, Shreveport, Louisiana.
Tracks 12 – 18 recorded live May 16, 1956 at the Robinson Memorial Auditorium, Little Rock, Arkansas.
Track 19 interview with journalist Paul Wilder, backstage at the Polk Theatre, Lakeland, Florida, August 6, 1956.

LIVE IN THE 50'S VOLUME ONE (LUCKY RECORDS)

Live recordings from 1956.

1. Heartbreak Hotel
2. Long Tall Sally
3. Introductions & Presentations
4. I Was The One
5. I Want You, I Need You, I Love You
6. I Got A Woman
7. Don't Be Cruel
8. Ready Teddy
9. Love Me Tender
10. Hound Dog
11. Love Me Tender
12. I Was The One

13. I Got A Woman
14. Don't Be Cruel
15. Blue Suede Shoes
16. Baby Lets Play House
17. Hound Dog/Announcements
18. Intro/Shake, Rattle And Roll
19. Heartbreak Hotel
20. Blue Suede Shoes
21. Comedy Skit/Blue Suede Shoes
(with Milton Berle)
22. Hound Dog/Dialogue
23. I Want You, I Need You, I Love You
24. Presentation of Billboard Award

Recording Information:

Tracks 1 – 10 recorded live at the Alabama Fair and Dairy Show, September 26, 1956, Afternoon Show.
Tracks 11 – 17 recorded live at the Alabama Fair and Dairy Show, September 26, 1956, Evening Show.
Tracks 18 – 21 recorded for The Milton Berle Show, San Diego, April 3, 1956.
Tracks 22 – 24 recorded for the Milton Berle Show , Hollywood, June 5, 1956.

LIVE IN THE 50'S VOLUME TWO (LUCKY RECORDS)

1. Shake, Rattle & Roll/Flip, Flop & Fly
2. I Got A Woman
3. Baby Lets Play House
4. Tutti Frutti
5. Tutti Frutti
6. I Was The One
7. Blue Suede Shoes
8. Heartbreak Hotel
9. Blue Suede Shoes
10. Heartbreak Hotel
11. Money Honey

12. Heartbreak Hotel
13. Good Rockin' Tonight
14. Baby Let's Play House
15. Blue Moon Of Kentucky
16. I Got A Woman
17. That's Al Right
18. Heartbreak Hotel
19. Long Tall Sally
19. Blue Suede Shoes
20. Money Honey
21. Interview – Hy Gardner Calling

Recording Information:

Tracks 1 – 12 from The Dorsey Brothers Stage Show:
Tracks 1 & 2 recorded January 28, 1956 at CBS Studios, New York.
Tracks 3 & 4 recorded February 4, 1956 at CBS Studios, New York.
Tracks 5 & 6 recorded February 11, 1956 at CBS Studios, New York.
Tracks 7 & 8 recorded February 18, 1956 at CBS Studios, New York.
Tracks 9 & 10 recorded March 17, 1956 at CBS Studios, New York.
Tracks 11 & 12 recorded March 24, 1956, CBS Studios, New York.
Tracks 13 – 17 recorded at live March 19, 1955 at the Eagles Hall, Houston, Texas.
Tracks 18 – 20 recorded live May 6, 1956 at the New Frontier Hotel, Las Vegas, Nevada.
Track 21 recorded July 1, 1956.

LIVE IN THE 50'S VOLUME THREE (LUCKY RECORDS)

1. Don't Be Cruel
2. Love Me Tender
3. Ready Teddy
4. Hound Dog
5. Don't Be Cruel
6. Love Me Tender
7. Love Me
8. Hound Dog
9. Medley:
Hound Dog
Love Me Tender
Heartbreak Hotel

10. Don't Be cruel
11. Too Much
12. When My Blue Moon Turns To Gold Again
13. Peace In The Valley
14. Intro/I Want You, I Need You, I Love You
15. Hound Dog
16. Comedy Skit
17. Ed Ripley Interview
18. Every Once In A While I Like To Talk To Somebody

Left: original cover art.

Below: alternate cover art.

Recording Information:

Tracks 1 –13 recorded for The Ed Sullivan Show:
Tracks 1 – 4 recorded September 9, 1956 at CBS Studios, Hollywood.
Tracks 5 – 8 recorded October 28, 1956 at CBS Studios, New York.
Tracks 9 – 13 recorded January 6, 1957 at CBS Studios, New York.
Tracks 14 – 16 recorded for the Steve Allen Show:
Tracks 14 – 16 recorded July 1, 1956 at the Hudson Theatre, New York.
Tracks 17 & 18 recorded 1956.

LIVE IN THE 50'S VOLUME FOUR (LUCKY RECORDS)

1. That's All Right
2. Blue Moon Of Kentucky
3. Tweedle Dee
4. Baby Let's Play House
5. Maybelline
6. That's All Right
7. I Was The One
8. Love Me Tender
9. Hound Dog
10. Heartbreak Hotel
11. Long Tall Sally
12. I Was The One
13. Money Honey
14. I Got A Woman
15. Blue Suede Shoes
16. Hound Dog
17. Radio Interview
18. Introduction/It's Nice To Go Travelling
19. Fame And Fortune
20. Stuck On You
21. Witchcraft/Love Me Tender
(duet with Frank Sinatra)
22. Introduction To Nancy Sinatra

Recording information:

Tracks 1 – 9 from KWKH's Louisiana Hayride:
Tracks 1 & 2 recorded live October 16, 1954 at the Municipal Auditorium, Shreveport, Louisiana.
Track 3 recorded live during a 1955 performance at the Municipal Auditorium, Shreveport, Louisiana.
Tracks 4 – 6 recorded live September 24, 1955 at the Municipal Auditorium, Shreveport, Louisiana
Tracks 7 – 9 recorded live September 15, 1956 at the Hirsch Memorial Coliseum, Shreveport, Louisiana.
Tracks 10 – 17 recorded live May 16, 1956 at the Robinson Memorial Auditorium, Little Rock, Arkansas.
Tracks 18 – 22 recorded live March 26, 1960, at the Fountianbleau Hotel, Miami, for ABC Television's "Frank Sinatra Timex Show" .

PEARL HARBOUR SHOW 1961 (GOLDEN ARCHIVES SERIES)

1. Heartbreak Hotel
2. All Shook Up
3. A Fool Such As I
4. I Got A Woman
5. Love Me
6. Such A Night
7. Reconsider Baby
8. I Need Your Love Tonight
9. That's All Right Mama
10. Don't Be Cruel
11. One Night
12. Are You Lonesome Tonight
13. It's Now Or Never
14. Swing Down Sweet Chariot
15. Hound Dog

Recording Information:

All tracks recorded live March 25, 1961 during a benefit performance for the U.S.S. Arizona Memorial Fund at the Bloch Arena, Pearl Harbour, Hawaii.

THE COMPLETE BURBANK SESSIONS VOL. 1 (AUDIFON)

1. Dialogue
2. That's All Right
3. Heartbreak Hotel
4. Love Me
5. Baby What You Want Me To Do
6. Dialogue
7. Blue Suede Shoes
8. Baby What You Want Me To Do
9. Dialogue
10. Lawdy Miss Clawdy
11. Are You Lonesome Tonight
12. When My Blue Moon Turns To Gold Again
13. Blue Christmas
14. Trying To Get To You
15. One Night
16. Baby What You Want Me To Do
17. Dialogue
18. One Night
19. Memories

Recorded live June 27, 1968 during the 6 p.m. "Sit Down" show at Burbank Studios, Burbank, California, for the NBC TV Special "Elvis".

THE COMPLETE BURBANK SESSIONS VOL. 2 (AUDIFON)

1. Dialogue
2. Heartbreak Hotel
3. Baby What You Want Me To Do
4. Dialogue
5. That's All Right
6. Are You Lonesome Tonight
7. Baby What You Want Me To Do
8. Blue Suede Shoes
9. One Night
10. Love Me
11. Dialogue
12. Trying To Get To You
13. Lawdy Miss Clawdy
14. Dialogue
15. Santa Claus Is Back In Town
16. Blue Christmas
17. Tiger Man
18. When My Blue moon Turns To Gold Again
19. Memories

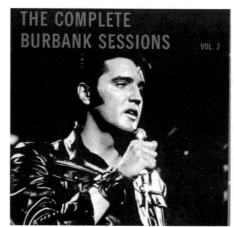

Recorded live June 27, 1968 during the 8 p.m. "Sit Down" show at Burbank Studios, Burbank, California, for the NBC TV Special "Elvis".

THE COMPLETE BURBANK SESSIONS VOL. 3 (AUDIFON)

6 p.m. Stand Up Show:

1. Intro & Dialogue
2. Heartbreak Hotel/One Night
3. Medley: Heartbreak Hotel/
Hound Dog/All Shook Up/
4. Can't Help Falling In Love
5. Jailhouse Rock
6. Don't Be Cruel
7. Blue Suede Shoes
8. Love Me Tender
9. Dialogue
10. Trouble
11. Dialogue
12. Baby What You Want Me To Do
13. If I Can Dream

8 p.m. Stand Up Show:

1. Intro & Dialogue
2. Medley: Heartbreak Hotel/
Hound Dog/All Shook Up
3. Can't Help Falling In Love
4. Jailhouse Rock
5. Don't Be Cruel
6. Blue Suede Shoes
7. Love Me Tender
8. Dialogue
9. Trouble
10. Dialogue
11. Trouble/Guitar Man
12. Dialogue
13. Trouble/Guitar Man
14. Dialogue
15. If I Can Dream

Both shows recorded live June 29, 1968 at Burbank Studios, Burbank, California, for the NBC TV Special "Elvis".

OPENING NIGHT 1969 (FORT BAXTER – ALL STAR SHOWS)

Recorded live at the International Hotel, Las Vegas, August 1969*
Source: sound board recording.

1. Blue Suede Shoes
2. I Got A Woman
3. All Shook up
4. Love Me Tender
5. Jailhouse Rock/Don't Be Cruel
6. Heartbreak Hotel
7. Hound Dog
8. Memories
9. Mystery Train/Tiger Man
10. Life Story (Dialogue)

11. Baby What You Want Me To Do
12. Are You Lonesome Tonight
13. Yesterday
14. Hey Jude
15. Band Introductions
16. In The Ghetto
17. Suspicious Minds
18. What'd I Say
19. Can't Help Falling In Love

* Although the sleeve of this album states that these performances are from Elvis' Opening Night performance, (July 31, 1969) this show was actually recorded on August 3, 1969.

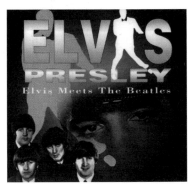

The performance featured on
"Opening Night 1969"
has also been issued on the following CD's:

"Elvis Meets The Beatles"
and
"Elvis Live Unlicensed"

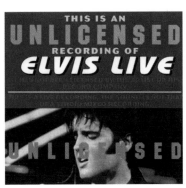

HERE I GO AGAIN (DIAMOND ANNIVERSARY EDITIONS)

Recorded live at the International Hotel, Las Vegas, August 23, 1969, Midnight Show, Dinner Show*
Source: sound board recording.

1. Opening Theme
2. Blue Suede Shoes
3. I Got A Woman
4. All Shook Up
5. Monologue
6. Love Me Tender
7. Jailhouse Rock/Don't Be Cruel
8. Heartbreak Hotel
9. Monologue
10. Hound Dog
11. I Can't Stop Loving You
12. Johnny B. Goode

13. Monologue (Life Story)
14. Baby What You Want Me To Do
15. Runaway
16. Are You Lonesome Tonight
17. Words
18. Yesterday/Hey Jude
19. Introductions
20. In The Ghetto
21. Suspicious Minds
22. What'd I Say
23. Can't Help Falling In Love

* The sleeve of this album states that this show was recorded during the Dinner Show on August 23, 1969.
However, this show was actually recorded during the Midnight Show on August 24, 1969.
The recording ended during "Suspicious Minds". The second part of "Suspicious Minds" and the last two songs on this disc have been taken from Fort Baxter's "Opening Night 1969" album.

WALK A MILE IN MY SHOES (FORT BAXTER)

Recorded live at the International Hotel, Las Vegas, February 1, 1970*
Source: sound board recording.

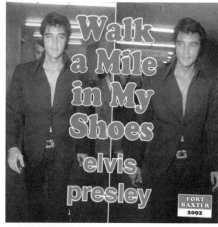

1. All Shook Up
2. That's All Right
3. Proud Mary
4. Don't Cry Daddy
5. Teddy Bear/Don't Be Cruel
6. Long Tall Sally
7. Let It Be Me
8. I Can't Stop Loving You
9. Walk A Mile In My Shoes
10. In The Ghetto

* The correct date of this performance is January 26, 1970.
This was the opening Show of Elvis' second Las Vegas Season.
This CD features the first half of this performance.

ON STAGE – TRUE LOVE TRAVELS ON A GRAVEL ROAD CUPIDO RECORDS)

Recorded live at the International Hotel, Las Vegas, February 21, 1970 & January 26, 1970.*
Source: sound board recording.

1. Introduction
2. All Shook Up
3. I Got A Woman
4. Long Tall Sally
5. Don't Cry Daddy
6. Dialogue
7. Everybody Loves Somebody (Excerpt)
8. Hound Dog
9. Love Me Tender (Elvis Kissed Priscilla)
10. Kentucky Rain
11. Let It Be Me

12. I Can't Stop Loving You
13. C.C. Rider
14. Dialogue:
Elvis Talks About His Memphis Album
15. True Love Travels On A Gravel Road
16. Sweet Caroline (the first live version)
17. Polk Salad Annie (the first live version)
    Group Introductions
18. Kentucky Rain (the first live version)
19. Suspicious Minds
20. Can't Help Falling In Love (incomplete)

* This CD features the first half of Elvis' Closing Show from February 23, 1970 and the second half of the Opening Show from January 26, 1970.
 (The first half of this show can be found on "Walk A Mile In My Shoes")
The performances from January 26, 1970 start at track 14.

DOUBLE DYNAMITE (ROCK LEGENDS)

Recorded live at the International Hotel, Las Vegas, August 19, 1970 - Dinner and Midnight Shows.
Source: audience recording.

Disc One: Dinner Show

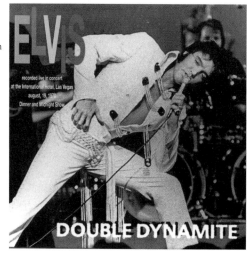

1. Tiger Man
2. I Got A Woman/Amen/I Got A Woman
3. Elvis Talks
4. You Don't Have To Say You Love Me
5. You've Lost That Lovin' Feelin'
6. Polk Salad Annie
7. The Wonder of You
8. Heartbreak Hotel
9. One Night
10. Blue Suede Shoes
11. Along Came Jones (1 line)
12. Hound Dog
13. Bridge Over Troubled Water
14. Suspicious Minds
15. Can't Help Falling In Love

Disc Two: Midnight Show

1. Introduction
2. That's All Right
3. I Got A Woman
4. Tiger Man/
5. Elvis Talks
6. Love Me Tender
7. I've Lost You
8. I Just Can't Help Believin'
9. You've Lost That Lovin' Feelin'
10. Polk Salad Annie
11. Band Introductions
12. Johnny B. Goode
13. Band Introductions
14. The Wonder Of You
15. Heartbreak Hotel
16. One Night
17. All Shook Up
18. Blue Suede Shoes
19. Hound Dog
20. Bridge Over Troubled Water
21. Suspicious Minds
22. Can't Help Falling In Love
23. Closing Vamp

A DINNER DATE WITH ELVIS (LIVE ARCHIVES)

Recorded Live at the International Hotel Las Vegas, August 20, 1970, Dinner Show.
Source: audience recording.

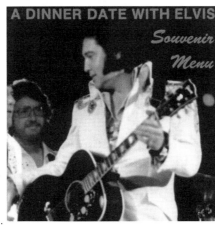

1. Opening Overture
2. That's All Right
3. I Got A Woman/Ave Maria
4. Tiger Man
5. Monologue
6. I've Lost You
7. I Just Can't Help Believin'
8. Polk Salad Annie
9. Sweet Inspiration
10. The Wonder Of You
11. Heartbreak Hotel
12. Memphis Tennessee
13. One Night
14. Blue Suede Shoes
15. Hound Dog
16. Bridge Over Troubled Water
17. Can't Help Falling In Love
18. Closing Vamp

Above:
this CD has now been re-released with the same sleeve as
the original vinyl issue.

STANDING ROOM ONLY (NO LABEL NAME)

Recorded live at the International Hotel, Las Vegas, August 20, 1970, Midnight Show.
Source: audience recording.

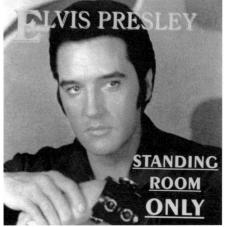

1. That's All Right Mama
2. I Got A Woman/Ave Maria
3. Tiger Man
4. Love Me Tender
6. I've Lost You
7. You've Lost That Lovin' Feelin'
8. Polk Salad Annie
9. Sweet Inspiration
10. Johnny B. Goode
11. Band Introductions
12. The Wonder Of You
13. Heartbreak Hotel
14. Blue Suede Shoes
15. Hound Dog/More
16. Bridge Over Troubled Water
17. Suspicious Minds
18. Can't Help Falling In Love
19. Closing Theme
20. Interview At Shrine*

* Track 20 is a bonus track featuring an interview with Elvis recorded at the
Shrine Auditorium, Los Angeles in June 1956.

FROM VEGAS TO MACON (ROCK LEGENDS)

Recorded live at the International Hotel, Las Vegas, August 21, 1970, Dinner Show & Recorded live in Macon, Georgia, April 24, 1975*.
Source: disc one: audience recording – disc two: sound board recording.

Disc One: Las Vegas

1. That's All Right
2. I Got A Woman – slow ending
3. Tiger Man
4. Love Me Tender
5. I Just Can't Help Believin'
6. Sweet Caroline
7. You've Lost That Lovin' Feelin'
8. Polk Salad Annie
9. Introductions
10. Johnny B. Goode/
Happy Birthday to James Burton/
Introductions Continued/
Elvis Introduces Neil Diamond/
Elvis Introduces His Grandmother
11. The Wonder Of You
12. Heartbreak Hotel
13. One Night
14. Blue Suede Shoes/Whole Lotta Shakin' Goin' On
15. Hound Dog
16. Bridge Over Troubled Water
17. Suspicious Minds
18. Can't Help Falling In Love

Disc Two: Macon

1. Dialogue
2. Love Me
3. If You Love Me Let Me Know
4. You Don't Have To Say You Love Me
5. Big Boss Man
6. It's Midnight
7. Promised Land
8. Fairytale
9. Burning Love
10. Introductions
11. My Boy
12. T-R-O-U-B-L-E
13. I'll Remember You

*This is not a complete performance. The beginning and the end of this show are missing.
The sleeve of this CD states that the complete show was not recorded by the engineer.

ALL THINGS ARE POSSIBLE (DIAMOND ANNIVERSARY EDITIONS)

Recorded live at the International Hotel, Las Vegas, January 27, 1971, Midnight Show.
Source: sound board recording.

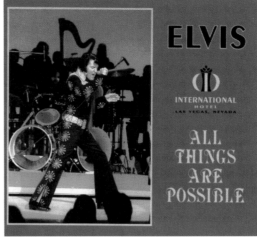

1. 2001: A Space Odyssey
2. That's All Right Mama
3. You Don't Have To Say You Love Me
4. Love Me Tender
5. There Goes My Everything
6. Sweet Caroline
7. You've Lost That Lovin' Feelin'
8. Polk Salad Annie
9. Only Believe
10. How Great Thou Art
11. Introductions

12. Johnny B. Goode
13. The Wonder Of You
14. Something
15. Make The World Go Away
16. Love Me
17. One Night
18. Blue Suede Shoes
19. Hound Dog
20. Mystery Train/Tiger Man*
21. Love Me Tender*
22. Can't Help Falling In Love*

* The sound board recording from January 27, 1971 is incomplete.
The last three songs on this disc have been added from an additional sound board recording made on January 26, 1971.
This was the Opening Night of Elvis' fourth Las Vegas Season.

LEAN, MEAN AND KICKIN' BUTT (FORT BAXTER)

Recorded live at the International Hotel, Las Vegas, January 28, 1971, Midnight Show.
Source: sound board recording.

1. Opening Vamp
2. That's All Right
3. I Got A Woman
4. Love Me Tender
5. You Don't Have To Say You Love Me
6. Sweet Caroline
7. You've Lost That Lovin' Feelin'
8. Polk Salad Annie
9. Johnny B. Goode
10. Something
11. The Wonder Of You
12. Heartbreak Hotel
13. Blue Suede Shoes
14. Hound Dog
15. One Night
16. Teddy Bear
17. Suspicious Minds
18. The Impossible Dream

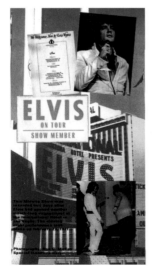

This disc was packaged in the long box
digi-pack format, and the cover art
featured photographs and memorabilia
from the time.

**I DON'T WANNA SING THESE SONGS
(THE ELVIS PRESLEY LIVE COLLECTION)**

Recorded live at the Hilton Hotel, Las Vegas, August 12, 1971,
Midnight Show.
Source: audience recording.

1. Introduction/That's All Right Mama
2. Proud Mary
3. Jailhouse Rock
4. You Don't Have To Say You Love Me
5. You've Lost That Lovin' Feelin'
6. Polk Salad Annie
7. Johnny B. Goode
8. It's Over
9. Love Me
10. Whole Lotta Shakin' Goin' On/Blue Suede Shoes
11. Heartbreak Hotel
12. Teddy Bear/Don't Be Cruel
13. Love Me Tender
14. I Don't Wanna Sing That Song/Hound Dog
15. Suspicious Minds
16. I'm Leaving
17. Lawdy Miss Clawdy
18. Bridge Over Troubled Water
19. Can't Help Falling In Love

'71 SUMMER FESTIVAL VOLUME 2 (CHIPS)

Recorded live at the Hilton Hotel, Las Vegas,
August 14, 1971, Midnight Show.
Source: audience recording.

1. 2001 Theme
2. That's All Right
3. Proud Mary
4. You Don't Have To Say You Love Me
5. You've Lost That Lovin' Feelin'
6. Polk Salad Annie
7. Johnny B. Goode
8. It's Over (with 2 false starts)
9. Love Me
10. Blue Suede Shoes/Whole Lotta Shakin' Goin' On/Blue Suede Shoes
11. Heartbreak Hotel
12. Teddy Bear/Don't Be Cruel
13. Rip It Up (one verse)
14. Hound Dog
15. I Need Your Lovin' Everyday
16. Suspicious Minds
17. Band Introductions
18. I'm Leaving
19. Lawdy Miss Clawdy
20. Bridge Over Troubled Water (with reprise)
21. Can't Help Falling In Love

I Don't Wonna Sing These Songs

71 SUMMER FESTIVAL (CHIPS)

Recorded live at the Hilton Hotel, Las Vegas,
August 23, 1971, Dinner Show.
Source: audience recording.

1. 2001 Theme
2. That's All Right
3. Proud Mary
4. I Got A Woman/Amen
5. Sweet Caroline
6. Polk Salad Annie
7. Johnny B. Goode
8. It's Impossible
9. Love Me
10. Blue Suede Shoes/Whole Lotta Shakin' Goin' On
11. Heartbreak Hotel
12. Teddy Bear/Don't Be Cruel
13. Hound Dog
14. Love Me Tender
15. Suspicious Minds
16. Band Introductions
17. I'm Leaving
18. Lawdy Miss Clawdy
19. Can't Help Falling In Love

ELVIS IN PERSON – THE POWER OF ZHAZAM! (CAPTAIN MARVEL J,R. RECORDS)

Recorded Live in Boston, November 10, 1971.
Source: sound board recording.

1. Without A Song… (Introduction)*
2. 2001 Opening Overture
3. That's All Right Mama
4. I Got a Woman/Amen
5. Proud Mary
6. You Don't Have To Say You Love Me
7. You've Lost That Lovin' Feelin'
8. Polk Salad Annie
9. Coming Home Baby (Instrumental Intermezzo)
10. Love Me
11. Heartbreak Hotel
12. Blue Suede Shoes
13. One Night
14. Hound Dog
15. How Great Thou Art
16. Introductions
17. I'm Leavin'
18. Bridge Over Troubled Water
19. I Can't Stop Loving You
20. Love Me Tender
21. Suspicious Minds
22. Coming Home Baby (Instrumental Intermezzo)
23. Funny How Time Slips Away
24. Can't Help Falling In Love
25. Closing Vamp
26. The Image, The Man… (Press Conference Excerpts)*
27. I'm So Lonesome I Could Cry*

*The spoken introduction used on track 1 of this disc is taken from Elvis' acceptance speech from the Jaycees Awards Ceremony in Memphis, January 16, 1971.
Track 26 is an excerpt from a Press Conference Elvis held at the New York Hilton Hotel on June 8, 1972 that preceded his shows at New York's Madison Square Garden.
Track 27 is home recording made at the Memphis home of Sam Thompson in 1974.

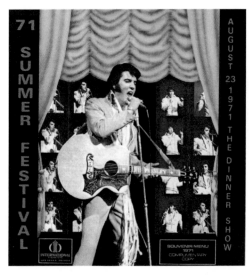

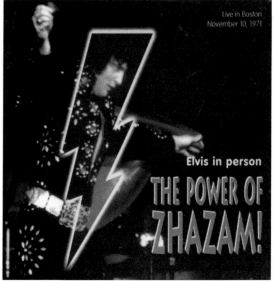

Left: the CD artwork included a montage of photographs from the Boston concert .

OPENING NIGHT, JAN. 26, 1972 (2001)

Recorded live at the Hilton Hotel, Las Vegas, January 26, 1972, Opening Show.
Source: sound board recording.

1. See See Rider
2. Proud Mary
3. Never Been To Spain
4. You Gave Me A Mountain
5. Until It's Time For You To Go
6. Polk Salad Annie
7. Love Me
8. Little Sister/Get Back
9. All Shook Up
10. Teddy Bear/ Don't Be Cruel
11. One Night
12. Hound Dog
13. Big Hunk O' Love
14. Bridge Over Troubled Water
15. Lawdy Miss Clawdy
16. An American Trilogy
17. Band Introductions
18. I'll Remember You
19. Suspicious Minds
20. Can't Help Falling In Love
21. Closing Vamp

THE HAMPTON CONCERT (LUNA RECORDS)

Recorded live at the Coliseum, Hampton, Roads, Virginia, April 9, 1972, Evening Show.
Source: sound board recording*

1. CC Rider
2. Until It's Time For You To Go
3. Polk Salad Annie
4. Love Me
5. All Shook up
6. Teddy Bear
7. Don't Be Cruel
8. Are You Lonesome Tonight
9. I Can't Stop Loving You
10. Hound Dog
11. Bridge Over Troubled Water
12. Suspicious Minds
13. For The Good Times
14. Band Introductions
15. American Trilogy
16. Love Me Tender
17. A Big Hunk O' Love
18. How Great Thou Art
19. Sweet, Sweet Spirit*
20. Lawdy Miss Clawdy
21. Can't Help Falling In Love

* Recorded for the MGM motion picture "Elvis On Tour".
Sweet, Sweet Spirit is performed by J.D. Sumner and the Stamps Quartet.

CARRY ME BACK TO OLD VIRGINIA (VICKY RECORDS)

Recorded live at the Coliseum, Richmond, Virginia, April 10, 1972.
Source: sound board recording*

1. See See Rider
2. Proud Mary
3. Never Been To Spain
4. You Gave Me A Mountain
5. Until It's Time For You To go
6. Polk Salad Annie
7. Love Me
8. All Shook Up
9. Bridge Over Troubled Water
10. Love Me Tender
11. It's Over
12. Group Introductions
13. For the Good Times
14. American Trilogy
15. Funny How Time Slips Away
16. Can't Help Falling In Love
17. Closing Theme

*Recorded for the MGM motion picture "Elvis On Tour".

Unofficial Releases: Live & Rehearsal Recordings

SWEET CAROLINA (VICKY RECORDS)

Recorded live at the Coliseum, Greensboro, North Carolina, April 14, 1972, Evening Show.
Source: sound board recording*

1. 2001 Theme
2. See See Rider
3. Proud Mary
4. Never Been To Spain
5. You Gave Me A Mountain
6. Until It's Time For You To Go
7. Polk Salad Annie
8. Love Me
9. All Shook Up
10. Teddy Bear/Don't Be Cruel
11. Hound Dog
12. Heartbreak Hotel
13. A Big Hunk O' Love
14. Bridge Over Troubled Water
15. Suspicious Minds
16. Love Me Tender
17. Group Introductions
18. For The Good Times
19. American Trilogy
20. Burning Love
21. Release Me
22. Funny How Time Slips Away
23. Can't Help Falling In Love/ Closing Vamp

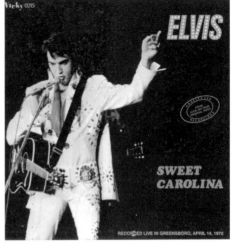

* Recorded for the MGM Motion Picture "Elvis On Tour".

WELCOME IN SAN ANTONE (VICKY RECORDS)

Recorded live at the Convention Centre, San Antonio, Texas, April 18, 1972.
Source: sound board recording*

1. 2001 Theme
2. See See Rider
3. Proud Mary
4. Never Been To Spain
5. You Gave Me A Mountain
6. Until It's Time For You To Go
7. Polk Salad Annie
8. Love Me
9. All Shook Up
10. Teddy Bear/Don't Be Cruel
11. Heartbreak Hotel
12. Hound Dog
13. How Great Thou Art
14. I Can't Stop Loving You
15. Love Me Tender
16. Suspicious Minds
17. Group Introductions
18. For The Good Times
19. Burning Love
20. American Trilogy
21. Funny How Time Slips Away
22. Can't Help Falling In Love

*Recorded for the MGM Motion Picture "Elvis On Tour"

BLAZING INTO THE DARKNESS (PREMIER)

Recorded live at the Hilton Hotel, Las Vegas,
August 11, 1972, Dinner Show.
Source: sound board recording.

1. 2001 Theme
2. See See Rider
3. Proud Mary
4. Until It's Time For You To Go
5. You Don't Have To Say You Love Me
6. You've Lost That Loving Feeling
7. Polk Salad Annie
8. What Now My Love
9. Fever
10. Love Me
11. Blue Suede Shoes
12. One Night
13. All Shook Up
14. Teddy Bear/Don't Be Cruel
15. Heartbreak Hotel
16. Hound Dog
17. Love Me Tender
18. Suspicious Minds
19. Band Introductions
20. My Way
21. American Trilogy
22. Can't Help Falling In Love

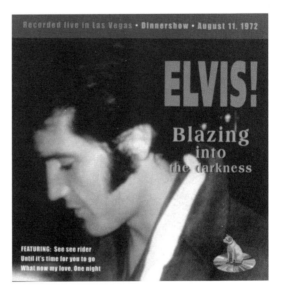

ELVIS AT FULL BLAST (FORT BAXTER)

Recorded live at the Hilton Hotel, Las Vegas, August 11, 1972, Midnight Show.
Source: sound board recording.

1. 2001/CC Rider
2. I Got A Woman
3. Proud Mary
4. Until It's Time For You To Go
5. You've Lost That Lovin' Feelin'
6. Polk Salad Annie
7. What Now My Now Love
8. Fever
9. Love Me
10. All Shook Up
11. Teddy Bear/ Don't Be Cruel
12. Heartbreak Hotel
13. Blue Suede Shoes
14. Little Sister/Get Back
15. Hound Dog
16. It's Over
17. Suspicious Minds
18. Band Introductions
19. My Way
20. A Big Hunk O' Love
21. American Trilogy
22. Can't Help Falling In Love/Closing Vamp

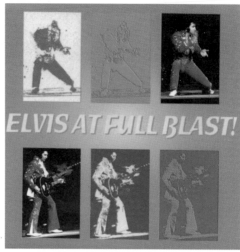

I'LL REMEMBER YOU (ROCK LEGENDS)

Recorded live at the Hilton Hotel, Las Vegas, August 15, 1972, Midnight Show.
Source: sound board recording.

1. Opening Theme
2. See See Rider
3. Johnny B. Goode
4. Until It's Time For You To Go
5. You Don't Have To Say You Love Me
6. Polk Salad Annie
7. Elvis Walks And Talks
8. What Now My Love
9. Fever
10. Love Me
11. Blue Suede Shoes
12. Heartbreak Hotel
13. All Shook Up
14. Love Me Tender

15. Teddy Bear/Don't Be Cruel
16. Little Sister/Get Back
17. Hound Dog
18. I'll Remember You
19. Walk That Lonesome Road*
20. Suspicious Minds
21. Band Introductions
22. For The Good Times
23. A Big Hunk O' Love
24. You Gave Me A Mountain
25. Can't Help Falling In Love
26. Closing Vamp
27. Rock My Soul*
28. You Better Run*

*Walk That Lonesome Road is performed by J.D. Sumner and the Stamps Quartet.

*Tracks 27 & 28 are recordings from a performance in Alexandria, Louisiana, March 29, 1977.

THE ALTERNATE ALOHA (SP)

Recorded live at the Honolulu International Centre, Honolulu, Hawaii, January 12, 1973.
Source: sound board recording.

Recorded 12 January 1973 - Previously Unreleased

1. The Aloha Interview*
2. Also Sprak Zarathustra
3. C.C. Rider
4. Burning Love
5. Something
6. You Gave Me A Mountain
7. Steamroller Blues
8. My Way
9. Love Me
10. It's Over
11. Blue Suede Shoes
12. I'm So Lonesome I Could Cry
13. Hound Dog
14. What Now My Love

15. Fever
16. Welcome To My World
17. Suspicious Minds
18. Band Introductions
19. I'll Remember You
20. An American Trilogy
21. A big Hunk O' Love
22. Can't Help Falling In Love
23. Blue Hawaii*
24. Early Morning Rain*
25. Hawaiian Wedding Song*
26. KU-U-I-PO*
27. No More*

This was the dress rehearsal performance for Elvis' "Aloha From Hawaii Via Satellite" broadcast which took place on January 14, 1973.

*The first track is an excerpt from a Press Conference given by Elvis and the Colonel in September 1972 to announce their plans for the satellite broadcast.

The last five songs on this disc were recorded after the live performance. These performances were taped for inclusion in the American version of the special which was aired in April 1973.

DON'T THINK TWICE (MADISON)

Recorded Live at the Hilton Hotel, Las Vegas, January 29, 1973.
Source: sound board recording.

1. 2001 Theme
2. See See Rider
3. I Got A Woman/Amen
4. Until It's Time For You To Go
5. Sweet Caroline
6. Steamroller Blues
7. You Gave Me A Mountain
8. Fever
9. Love Me
10. Blue Suede Shoes
11. Love Me Tender
12. Johnny B. Goode
13. Hound Dog
14. What Now My Love
15. Suspicious Minds
16. Introductions
17. I Can't Stop Loving You
18. An American Trilogy
19. Can't Help Falling In Love
20. Closing Vamp
21. Don't Think Twice It's All Right (longer version)*

* Track 21 is an extended version of a previously released studio master.

IT'S A MATTER OF TIME (FORT BAXTER)

Recorded live at the Hilton Hotel, Las Vegas, February 5, 1973, Dinner Show.
Source: sound board recording.

1. 2001 A Space Odyssey
2 C.C. Rider
3. I Got A Woman/Amen
4. Until It's Time For You To Go
5. You Don't Have To Say You Love Me
6. Steamroller Blues
7. You Gave Me A Mountain
8. Fever
9. Love Me
10. Blue Suede Shoes
11. Love Me Tender
12. Johnny B. Goode
13. Hound Dog
14. What Now My Love
15. Suspicious Minds
16. Band Introductions
17. I'll Remember You
18. I Can't Stop Loving you
19. American Trilogy
20. Can't Help Falling In Love
21. It's A Matter Of Time*

* Track 21 is a good quality audience recording taken from Elvis' Dinner Show at the Las Vegas Hilton on August 23, 1973.

RETURN TO LAKE TAHOE (NO LABEL NAME)

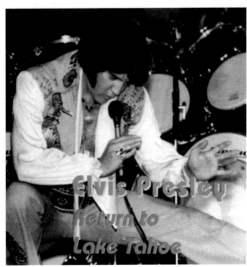

Recorded live at the Sahara Tahoe Hotel, Lake Tahoe, Nevada, May 10, 1973, Midnight Show.
Source: audience recording.

1. 2001 Theme
2. C.C. Rider
3. I Got A Woman/Amen
4. Love Me Tender
5. Steamroller Blues
6. Help Me Make It Through The Night
7. You Gave Me A Mountain
8. Love Me
9. Blue Suede Shoes
10. Long Tall Sally/ Whole Lotta
 Shakin' Goin' On/Flip, Flop, And Fly
11. I'm Leaving
12. Hound Dog
13. Fever
14. What Now My Love
15. Suspicious Minds
16. Band Introductions
17. I'll Remember You
18. I Can't Stop Loving You
19. Bridge Over Troubled Water
20. Big Hunk O' Love
21. Can't Help Falling In Love
22. Closing Vamp
23. Presentation*

* Track 23 is a bonus track featuring Elvis' presentation of the Potomac yacht to US comedian Danny Thomas on behalf of the St. Judes Children's Hospital, Memphis.

EVENT NO. 8 (MADISON)

Recorded live at the Houston Astrodome, Houston, Texas, March 3, 1974, Afternoon Show.
Source: sound board recording.

1. Opening Riff/See See Rider
2. I Got A Woman/Amen
3. Love Me
4. Trying To Get To You
5. All Shook Up
6. Love Me Tender
7. Johnny B. Goode
8. Hound Dog
9. Fever
10. Polk Salad Annie
11. Why Me Lord
12. Suspicious Minds
13. Introduction Of The Band
14. I Can't Stop Loving You
15. Help Me
16. How Great Thou Art
17. Let Me Be There
18. Funny How Time Slips Away
19. Elvis Talks
20. Can't Help Falling In Love
21. Closing Riff

HELLO MEMPHIS (ROCK LEGENDS)

Recorded live at the Midsouth Coliseum, Memphis, March 16, 1974.
Source: sound board recording.

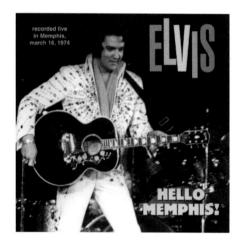

1. Opening Theme 2001
2. C.C. Rider
3. I Got A Woman/Amen
4. Love Me
5. Trying To Get To You
6. All Shook Up
7. Steamroller Blues
8. Teddy Bear/Don't Be Cruel
9. Love Me Tender
10. Johnny B. Goode
11. Hound Dog
12. Fever
13. Polk Salad Annie
14. Why Me Lord
15. Suspicious Minds
16. Introductions
17. I Can't Stop Loving You
18. Help Me
19. An American Trilogy
20. Let Me Be There
21. Funny How Time Slips Away
22. Can't Help Falling In Love
23. Closing Theme

This was Elvis' first live performance in Memphis, Tennessee since his February 25, 1961 at the Ellis Auditorium.

GUARANTEED TO BLOW YOUR MIND (LUXOR)

Recorded live in Richmond, Virginia, March 18, 1974.
Source: sound board recording.

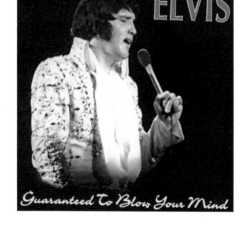

1. Opening Theme "Love Me Tender"*
2. Keep It Going*
3. Going Back To Memphis Tomorrow*
4. Announcements/Warm up*
5. Also Sprach Zarathustra
6. See See Rider
7. I Got A Woman/ Amen
8. Love Me
9. Trying To Get to You
10. All Shook Up
11. Steamroller Blues
12. Teddy Bear/Don't Be Cruel
13. Love Me Tender
14. Long Tall Sally/Whole Lotta Shakin' Goin' On'/ Mama Don't Dance/ Flip, Flop & Fly/Jailhouse Rock/ Hound Dog
15. Fever
16. Polk Salad Annie
17. Why Me Lord
18. Suspicious Minds
19. Introductions
20. I Can't Stop Loving You
21. Help Me
22. American Trilogy
23. Let Me Be There
24. Funny how Time Slips Away
25. Can't Help Falling In Love
26. Closing Vamp
27. Announcements

*Tracks 1 – 4 were recorded during the warm up acts before Elvis' performance in Memphis, Tennessee, June 10, 1975.

STEAMROLLER BLUES (FORT BAXTER)

Recorded live at the Midsouth Coliseum, Memphis, March 20, 1974.
Source: sound board recording.

1. 2001/C.C. Rider
2. I Got A Woman (with reprise)
3. Love Me
4. Trying To Get To You
5. All Shook Up*
6. Steamroller Blues*
7. Teddy Bear/Don't Be Cruel*
8. Love Me Tender*
9. Long Tall Sally/
Whole Lotta Shakin' Goin' On/
Mama Don't Dance/
Flip, Flop & Fly/
Jailhouse Rock/
Hound Dog
10. Fever*
11. Polk Salad Annie*

12. Why Me Lord
13. How Great Thou Art
14. Suspicious Minds*
15. Band Introductions*
16. Blueberry Hill/I Can,t Stop Loving You
17. Help Me
18. An American Trilogy
19. Let Me Be There
20. My Baby Left Me
21. Lawdy Miss Clawdy
22. Funny How Time Slips Away*
23. Can't Help Falling In Love/Closing Vamp

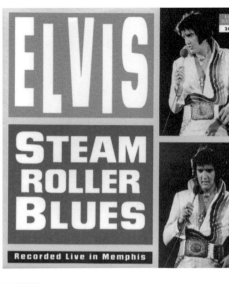

An edited version of this show was officially released by RCA in 1974 on the album
"Elvis Recorded Live On Stage in Memphis"
*Not included on the original RCA release

SPANISH EYES (FORT BAXTER)

Recorded live at the Sarah Tahoe Hotel, Lake Tahoe, Nevada, May 24, 1974, Midnight Show
Source: sound board recording.

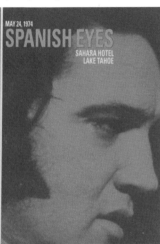

1. C.C. Rider
2. I Got A Woman/Amen
3. Love Me
4. Trying To Get To You
5. All Shook Up
6. Love Me Tender
7. You Don't Have To Say You Love Me
8. Hound Dog
9. Fever
10. Polk Salad Annie
11. Why Me Lord

12. Suspicious Minds
13. Band Introductions
14. I Can't Stop Loving You
15. Help Me
16. Bridge Over Troubled Water
17. Let Me Be There
18. Spanish Eyes
19. Big Boss Man
20. Funny How Time Slips Away
21. Can't Help Falling In Love

AND THE KING FOR DESSERT (FORT BAXTER)

Recorded live at the Sarah Tahoe Hotel, Lake Tahoe, Nevada,
May 25, 1974, Dinner Show.
Source: sound board recording.

1. C.C. Rider
2. I Got A Woman /Amen
3. Love Me
4. Tryin' To Get To You
5. All Shook Up
6. Love Me Tender
7. You Don't have to Say
You Love Me
8. Hound Dog
9. Fever
10. Polk Salad Annie
11. Why Me Lord

12. Suspicious Minds
13. Band Introductions
14. I Can't Stop Lovin' You
15. Help Me
16. An American Trilogy
17. Let Me Be There
(incomplete – 1st part only)
18. Funny How Time Slips Away
(incomplete – 2nd part only)
19. Big Boss Man
20. It's Now Or Never
21. Can't Help Falling In Love

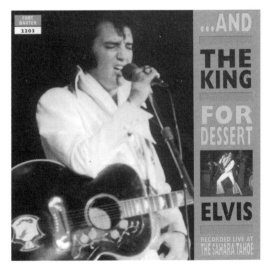

Unofficial Releases: Live & Rehearsal Recordings

IF YOU TALK IN YOUR SLEEP (FORT BAXTER)

Recorded live at the Hilton Hotel, Las Vegas, August 19, 1974, Opening Night.
Source: sound board recording.

1. Big Boss Man
2. Proud Mary
3. Down In The Alley
4. Good Time Charlie's Got The Blues
5. Never Been To Spain
6. It's Midnight
7. If You Talk In Your Sleep
8. I'm Leaving
9. Let Me Be There (with reprise)
10. Softly As I Leave You
11. If You Love Me, Let Me Know
12. Love Me Tender
13. Polk Salad Annie
14. Band Introductions
15. Promised Land
16. Introducing Telly Savalas
17. My Baby Left Me
18. Bridge Over Troubled Water
19. Fever
20. Hound Dog
21. Can't Help Falling in Love

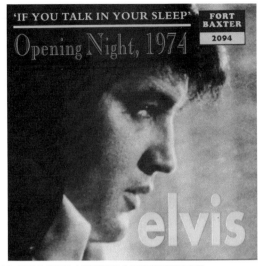

FROM SUNSET BOULEVARD TO PARADISE ROAD (DIAMOND ANNIVERSARY EDITIONS)

Recorded at RCA Studios, Hollywood, California, August 16, 1974.
Recorded at the Hilton Hotel, Las Vegas, August 19, 1974, Opening Night.
Source: sound board recording.

Disc One:

1. If You Love Me (Let Me Know)
2. If You Love Me (let Me Know
3. Promised Land
4. Promised land
5. Down In The Alley
6. Down In The Alley
7. It's Midnight
8. It's Midnight
9. Your Love's Been A Long Time Coming
10. Good Time Charlie's Got The Blues
11. Softly As I Leave You
12. Softly As I Leave You
13. I'm Leavin'
14 The First Time Ever I Saw Your Face
15. Proud Mary
16. If You Talk In Your Sleep
17. If You Love Me (Let Me Know)

Disc Two:

1. The Twelfth Of Never
2. Faded Love
3. Just Pretend
4. The Twelfth Of Never*
5. Big Boss Man
6. Proud Mary
7. Down In The Alley
8. Good Time Charlie's Got The Blues
9. Never Been To Spain
10. It's Midnight
11. If You Talk In Your Sleep
12. I'm Leavin'
13. Let Me Be There
14. Softly As I Leave You
15. If You Love Me (Let Me Know)
16. Love Me Tender
17. Polk Salad Annie
18. Introductions
19. Promised Land
20. Introduction of Telly Savalas
21. My Baby Left Me
22. Bridge Over Troubled Water
23. Fever
24. Hound Dog
25. Can't Help Falling In Love

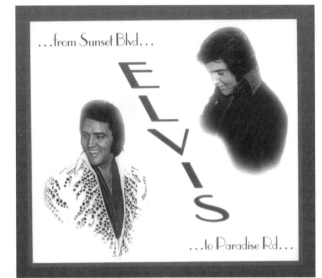

Above: the CD artwork featured a selection of candid photographs from the period.

All tracks on Disc One along with tracks 1-4 on Disc Two were recorded during Elvis' August 16, 1974, rehearsals at RCA Studios, Hollywood.
The remainder of Disc Two features the same live performance originally released on Fort Baxter's "If You Talk In Your Sleep" CD.
* Track 4 on Disc Two is an overdubbed version produced by David Briggs.

BREATHING OUT FIRE (MADISON)

Recorded live in Dayton, Ohio, October 6, 1974, Evening Show.
Source: sound board recording,.

1. See See Rider
2. I Got A Woman/Amen
3. Love Me
4. If You Love Me Let Me Know
5. Fever
6. Big Boss Man
7. Love Me Tender
8. Hound Dog
9. The Wonder Of You
10. Blue Suede Shoes
11. Band Introductions
12. Lawdy Miss Clawdy
13. Band Introductions
14. All Shook Up
15. Teddy Bear/Don't Be Cruel
16. Heartbreak Hotel
17. Why Me Lord? (with reprise)
18. That's All Right
19. Blue Christmas
20. Let Me Be There (with reprise)
21. Hawaiian Wedding Song (with reprise)
22. Johnny B. Goode
23. Can't Help Falling In Love
24. Closing Vamp

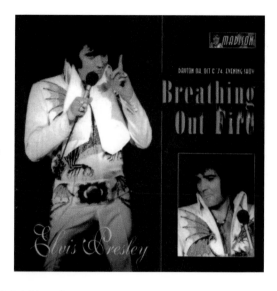

NIGHT FEVER IN VEGAS (ROCK LEGENDS)

Recorded live at the Hilton Hotel, Las Vegas, August 30, 1974, 3 a.m. Show.
Source: sound board recording.

Disc One:

1. See See Rider
2. Dialogue
3. I Got A Woman/Amen
4. Dialogue
5. Love Me
6. If You Love Me
7. It's Midnight
8. Big Boss Man
9. Fever
10. All Shook Up
11. Dialogue
12. Softly As I Leave You
13. Hound Dog/Introduction
14. Hound Dog
15. An American Trilogy
16. Dialogue
17. Suspicious Minds

Disc Two:

1. Karate Introduction
2. If You Talk In Your Sleep
3. Karate Speech
4. Help Me
5. Let Me There (with reprise)
6. Dialogue
7. How Great Thou Art (with reprise)
8. Dialogue
9. Hawaiian Wedding Song
10. Dialogue
11. You Gave Me A Mountain
12. Can't Help Falling In Love

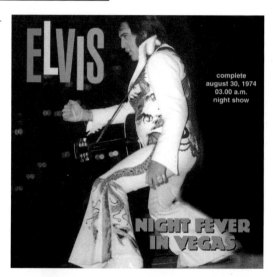

DESERT STORM (FORT BAXTER)

Recorded live at the Hilton Hotel, Las Vegas, September 2, 1974, Closing Show.
Source: sound board recording.

Disc One:

1. Microphone Dialogue
2. I Got A Woman/Amen
3. Karate Dialogue
4. Until It's Time For You To Go
5. If You Love Me Let Me Know
6. It's Midnight
7. Big Boss Man
8. You Gave Me A Mountain
9. Priscilla Dialogue
10. Softly As I Leave You
11. Hound Dog
12. An American Trilogy
13. It's Now Or Never

Disc Two:

14. Band Introductions
15. Bringing It Back*
16. Aubrey*
17. Band & Celebrity Introductions
18. It's Now Or Never
19. Let Me Be There
20. If You Talk In Your Sleep
21. Drugs Dialogue
22. Hawaiian Wedding Song
23. Jewellery Dialogue
24. Can't Help Falling In Love
25. Closing Vamp

*"Bringing It Back" was performed by Elvis' vocal group Voice and featured Elvis singing some of the bass parts.
"Aubrey" was also performed by Voice and featured a spoken narration from Elvis.

The opening number "See See Rider", and the song "Without You" (also performed by Voice) were not recorded by the engineer.

ROCKIN' WITH ELVIS APRIL FOOL'S DAY (NO LABEL NAME)

Recorded live at the Hilton Hotel, Las Vegas, April 1, 1975, Dinner Show.
Source: audience recording.

1. C.C. Rider
2. Dialogue
3. I Got A Woman/Amen
4. Dialogue
5. I Got A Woman
6. If You Love Me Let Me Know
7. And I Love You So
8. Big Boss Man
9. The Wonder Of You
10. Burning Love
11. Introductions
12. Introductions (continues)
13. Introduction of Roy Clark and the owner of the Las Vegas Hilton
14. My Boy
15. I'll Remember You
16. Let Me Be There
17. Elvis introduces actor Hugh O'Brian
18. How Great Thou Art
19. Hound Dog
20. Fairytale
21. Can't Help Falling In Love*
22. Closing Vamp*

PLACE: Hilton Hotel, Las Vegas
DATE: April First 1975, (April Fool's Day)
TIME: 9:00 p.m. Dinner Show
CONTENT: The Entire Show

* Tracks 21 & 22 were recorded at the Midsouth Coliseum, Memphis Tennessee, March 20, 1974, and originally issued by RCA on the album "Elvis Recorded Live On Stage In Memphis".

A DAMN FINE SHOW (VICKY)

Recorded live at the Veterans Memorial Coliseum, Jacksonville, Florida, April 25, 1975, 8.30 p.m.
Source: sound board recording.

1. If You Love Me Let Me Know
2. You Don't Have To Say You Love Me
3. Big Boss Man
4. It's Midnight
5. Burning Love
6. Introductions/What'd I Say/Introductions/Hail! Hail! Rock 'n' Roll
7. My Boy
8. T.R.O.U.B.L.E.
9. I'll Remember You
10. Let Me There
11. An American Trilogy
12. Funny How Time Slips Away

This is an incomplete performance.
The beginning and end of this show are missing from the source tape.

SOLD OUT IN DIXIE (ROCK LEGENDS)

Recorded live in Mobile, Alabama, June 2, 1975, Evening Show.
Source: sound board recording.

1. Opening Theme
2. See See Rider
3. I Got A Woman/Amen
4. Love Me
5. If You Love Me (Let Me Know)
6. Love Me Tender
7. All Shook Up
8. Teddy Bear/Don't Be Cruel
9. Hound Dog
10. The Wonder Of You
11. Burning Love
12. Introduction
13. Johnny B. Goode
14. Band Introductions
15. School Days
16. Bridge Over Troubled Water
17. T.R.O.U.B.L.E.
18. I'll Remember You
19. Let Me There
20. An American Trilogy
21. Funny How Time Slips Away
22. Little Darlin'
23. Mystery Train/Tiger Man
24. Can't Help Falling In Love
25. Closing Vamp

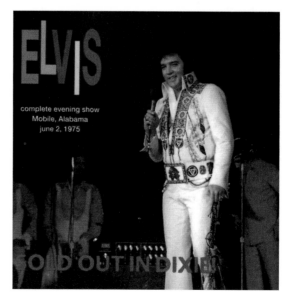

DEEP DOWN SOUTH (KING RECORDS)

Recorded live at the Memorial Auditorium, University Of Alabama,
Tuscaloosa, Alabama, June 3, 1975.
Source: sound board recording.

1. Also Sprach Zarathustra
2. C.C. Rider
3. I Got A Woman/Amen
4. Love Me
5. If You Love Me Let Me Know
(with repeat)
6. Love Me Tender
7. All Shook Up
8. Teddy Bear/Don't Be Cruel
9. Hound Dog
10. The Wonder Of You
11. Introductions
12. Johnny B. Goode
13. Hail, Hail Rock 'n' Roll
14. Bridge Over Troubled Water
15. T.R.O.U.B.L.E.
16. Hawaiian Wedding Song
17. Let Me Be There
18. American Trilogy
19. Funny How Slips Away
20. Little Darlin'
21. Mystery Train/Tiger Man
22. Can't Help Falling In Love
23. Closing Vamp

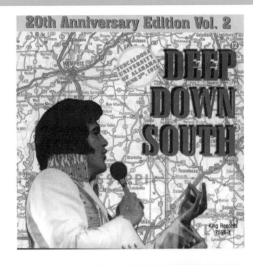

CUT 'EM DOWN TO SIZE (PEGASUS)

Recorded live at the State Fair Coliseum, Jackson, Mississippi, June 9,1975, 8.30 p.m.
Source: sound board recording.

1. Also Sprach Zarathustra*
2. C.C. Rider*
3. I Got A Woman/Amen/I Got A Woman*
4. Love Me
5. If You Love Me (Let Me Know)
6. All Shook Up
7. Teddy Bear/Don't Be Cruel
8. Hound Dog
9. The Wonder Of You
10. Polk Salad Annie
11. Introductions by Elvis:
James Burton Solo:
Johnny B. Goode
Jerry Scheff Solo
Glenn D. Hardin Solo:
Joe Guercio Orchestra Solo:
Hail! Hail! Rock 'n' Roll
12. T.R.O.U.B.L.E.
13. Why Me Lord
14. Let Me Be There
15. An American Trilogy
16. Funny How Time Slips Away
17. Jambalaya*
18. Elvis cuts the security down to size
19. Mystery Train/Tiger Man
20. Help Me Make It Through The Night
21. Can't Help Falling In Love

*The original source tape used for this release was incomplete.
Tracks 1 & 2, and also the first part of track 3 are taken from Elvis June 10, 1975
performance in Memphis. Track 17 was recorded in Lake Charles on May 4, 1975 .

LET ME TAKE YOU HOME
(DIAMOND ANNIVERSARY EDITIONS)

Recorded live at the Midsouth Coliseum, Memphis, Tennessee, June 10, 1975.
Source: sound board recording.

1. Also Sprach Zararthustra
2. See See Rider
3. I Got A Woman/Amen
4. Love Me
5. If You Love Me (Let Me Know)
6. Love Me Tender
7. All Shook Up
8. Teddy Bear/Don't Be Cruel
9. Hound Dog
10. Fairytale
11. Burning Love
12. Introductions
13. Johnny B. Goode
14. Introductions
15. Hail, Hail Rock 'n' Roll
16. Introductions of Vernon and Dr Nick
17. T.R.O.U.B.L.E.
18. Why Me Lord?
19. How Great Thou Art
20. Let Me Be There
21. Funny How Time Slips Away
22. Little Darlin'
23. American Trilogy*
24. Mystery Train/Tiger Man*
25. Can't Help Falling In Love*
26. Closing Vamp *

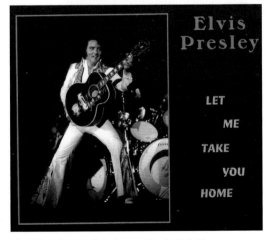

*The original source tape was incomplete. Tracks 23 & 24 were taken from Elvis' June 9, 1975 performance in Jackson, and tracks 25 & 26
were recorded in Shreveport on June 7, 1975.

Unofficial Releases: Live & Rehearsal Recordings

AMERICA'S OWN (GENEVA RECORDS)

Recorded live at the Nassau Coliseum, Uniondale, New York, July 19, 1975, Afternoon Show.
Source: audience recording.

1. 2001
2. See See Rider
3. I Got A Woman/Amen
4. Big Boss Man
5. Love Me
6. If You Love Me, Let Me Know
7. Love Me Tender
8. All Shook Up
9. Teddy Bear
10. Don't Be Cruel
11. Hound Dog
12. The Wonder Of You
13. Trying To Get To You

14. Burning Love
15. School Days
16. T.R.O.U.B.L.E.
17. Heartbreak Hotel
18. Killing Me Softly (Sherrill Nielsen)
19. Let Me There
20. Bosom Of Abraham
21. You Better Run
22. You Gave Me A Mountain
23. Little Darlin'
24. Mystery Train/Tiger Man
25. Funny How Time Slips Away
26. Can't Help Falling In Love
27. Closing Vamp

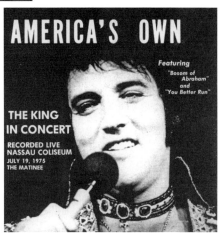

AMERICA'S OWN VOLUME 2 (CLAUDIA RECORD COMPANY)

Recorded live at the Nassau Coliseum, Uniondale, New York, July 19, 1975, Evening Show.
Source: audience recording.

1. Opening Vamp
2. See See Rider
3. I Got A Woman/Amen
4. Big Boss Man
5. Love Me
6. If You Love Me (Let Me Know)
7. Love Me Tender
8. All Shook Up
9. Teddy Bear/Don't Be Cruel
10. Hound Dog
11. The Wonder Of You
12. Polk Salad Annie
13. Introductions by Elvis
14. Green Onions*
15. Johnny B. Goode

16. Solos by: James Burton,
Ronnie Tutt, Jerry Scheff,
Glen D. Hardin
17. School Days
18. T.R.O.U.B.L.E.
19. Why Me Lord
20. How Great Thou Art
21. Let Me There
22. You'll Never Walk Alone
23. Funny How Time Slips Away
24. Little Darlin'
25. I'm Leavin'
26. Can't Help Falling In Love
27. Closing Vamp

*Performed by Elvis' TCB band during the introductions.

ELVIS BY SPECIAL REQUEST (LIVE ARCHIVES)

Recorded live at the Hilton Hotel, Las Vegas, August 20, 1975, Dinner Show.
Source: audience recording.

1. See See Rider
2. I Got A Woman/Amen
3. Hound Dog
4. It's Now Or Never
5. And I Love You So
6. Blue Suede Shoes
7. Green Green Grass Of Home
8. Fairytale
9. Softly As I Leave You
10. Band Introductions
11. Johnny B. Goode/School Days
12. T.R.O.UB.L.E.
13. Why Me Lord
14. Until It's Time For You To Go
15. Burning Love
16. Can't Help Falling Love
17. Loving You*
18. Crying In The Chapel*
19. Wooden Heart*
20. Blue Christmas *

* Tracks 17 – 20 are bonus songs recorded at the Las Vegas Hilton,
December 13, 1975, Dinner Show.

JUST PRETEND (FORT BAXTER)

Recorded live at the Hilton Hotel, Las Vegas, December 13, 1975, Midnight Show.
Source: sound board recording.

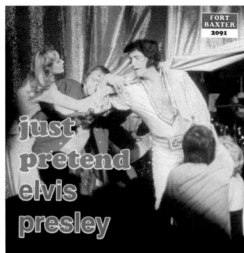

1. C.C. Rider
2. I Got A Woman/Amen
3. Love Me
4. Trying To Get To You
5. And I Love You So
6. All Shook Up/Teddy Bear/Don't Be Cruel
7. You Gave Me A Mountain
8. Help Make It Through The Night
9. Polk Salad Annie
10. Band Introductions/Johnny B. Goode/Hail, Hail Rock 'n' Roll
11. Just Pretend
12. How Great Thou Art
13. Burning Love
14. Hound Dog/Welcome To My World
15. Softly As I Leave You
16. America
17. It's Now Or Never/O Sole Mio
18. Little Darling
19. Little Sister
20. Can't Help Falling In Love

PHOENIX OVER TENNESSEE (JR)

Recorded live at the Freedom Hall, Johnson City, Tennessee,
March 17, 1976, 8.30 p.m.
Source: audience recording.

1. Opening Riff
2. See See Rider
3. I Got A Woman/Amen
4. Love Me
5. You Gave Me A Mountain
6. Trying To Get To You
7. All Shook Up
8. Teddy Bear/Don't Be Cruel
9. Until It's Time For You To Go
10. Hurt
11. Polk Salad Annie
12. Introductions/What'd I Say
13. And I Love You So
14. How Great Thou Art
15. Love Me Tender
16. Let Me Be There
17. America, The Beautiful
18. Heartbreak Hotel
19. Hound Dog
20. Hawaiian Wedding Song
21. Mystery Train/Tiger Man
22. Can't Help Falling In Love
23. Closing Vamp
24. Announcements

RUNNING FOR PRESIDENT (KING RECORDS)

Recorded live at the Coliseum, Charlotte, North Carolina,
March 20, 1976, Evening Show.
Source: sound board recording.

1. Also Sprach Zarathustra
2. Amen
3. Let Me Be There
4. You Gave Me A Mountain
5. Steamroller Blues
6. All Shook Up
7. Teddy Bear
8. Hound Dog
9. Polk Salad Annie
10. Band Introductions
11. And I Love You See
12. Hurt
13. Burning Love
14. America
15. Funny How Time Slips Away
16. Fairytale
17. How Great Thou Art
18. Can't Help Falling In Love
19. Closing Vamp

The songs "See See Rider" and "I Got A Woman" were not recorded by the engineer.

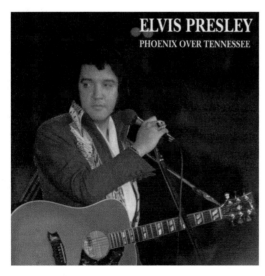

HOLDING BACK THE YEARS (DIAMOND ANNIVERSARY EDITIONS)

Recorded live in Cincinnati, Ohio, March 21, 1976.
Source: sound board recording.

1. Also Sprach Zarathustra
2. See See Rider
3. I Got A Woman/Amen
4. Love Me
5. Let Me Be There
6. Love Me Tender
7. Steamroller Blues
8. All Shook Up
9. Teddy Bear/Don't Be Cruel
10. You Gave Me A Mountain
11. Polk Salad Annie
12. Introductions
13. Hail, Hail Rock 'n' Roll
14. And I Love You So
15. Hurt
16. Hurt
17. Announcement by Elvis
18. Burning Love
19. America, The Beautiful
20. Hound Dog
21. Funny How Time Slips Away
22. Can't Help Falling In Love
23. Closing Vamp

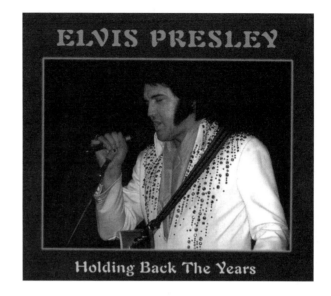

ONE HELLUVA NIGHT (NO LABEL NAME)

Recorded live at the Memorial Auditorium, Buffalo, New York,
June 26, 1976, 8.30 p.m.
Source: audience recording.

1. Also Sprach Zarathustra
2. See See Rider
3. I Got A Woman/Amen
4. Love Me
5. If You Love Me, Let Me Know
6. You Gave Me A Mountain
7. All Shook Up
8. Teddy Bear/Don't Be Cruel
9. And I Love You So
10. Jailhouse Rock
11. Fever
12. America, The Beautiful
13. Polk Salad Annie
14. Introductions: Early Morning Rain/What'd I Say
15. Love Letters
16. Introductions: Hail, Hail Rock 'n' Roll
17. Hurt
18. Hurt
19. Burning Love
20. Happy Birthday
21. Funny How Time Slips Away
22. Can't Help Falling In Love
23. Closing Vamp

HURT (SUNSET)

Recorded live in Largo, June, 1976, Evening Show.*
Source: sound board recording.

1. Theme 2001
2. See See Rider
3. I Got A Woman
4. Amen
5. Love Me
6. If You Love Me
7. You Gave Me A Mountain
8. Medley: All Shook Up/Teddy Bear/Don't Be Cruel
9. And I Love You So
10. Jailhouse Rock
11. Fever
12. Love Letters
13. School Days
14. Hurt
15. Hurt
16. Hound Dog
17. Funny How Time Slips Away
18. Can't Help Falling in Love

*The performance on this CD is actually taken from a concert in
Charleston, West Virginia, July 24, 1976, Evening Show.

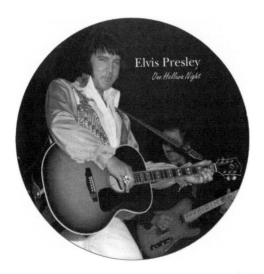

MY IT'S BEEN A LONG, LONG TIME (LUXOR)

Recorded live in Greensboro, North Carolina, June 30, 1976, 8.30 p.m.
Source: sound board recording.

1. Sweet Inspiration*
2. The Last Time I Saw Him*
3. Introductions*
4. Also Sprach Zarathustra
5. See See Rider
6. I Got A Woman/Amen
7. Love Me
8. If You Love Me, Let Me Know
9. You Gave Me A Mountain
10. All Shook Up/Teddy Bear/Don't Be Cruel
11. And I Love You So
12. Blue Suede Shoes
13. Fever
14. America, The Beautiful
15. Introductions
16. Early Morning Rain
17. What'd I Say
18. Johnny B. Goode
19. Introductions
20. Love Letters
21. Introductions
22. Hail Hail Rock 'n' Roll
23. Love Me Tender
24. Hurt
25. Hurt
26. Funny How Time Slips Away
27. Hound Dog
28. Can't Help Falling In Love
29. Closing Vamp
30. Announcements

*Tracks 1 – 3 were performed by the Sweet Inspirations, and are taken from a later performance in Duluth, Minnesota, October 16, 1976, 8.30 p.m.

GOODBYE MEMPHIS (FORT BAXTER)

Recorded live in Memphis, Tennessee, July 5, 1976 & Toledo, Ohio, April 23, 1977.
Source: sound board recording.

Disc One:

1. Also Sprach Zarathustra
2. See See Rider
3. I Got A Woman/Amen
4. Love Me
5. Fairytale
6. You Gave Me A Mountain
7. All Shook Up
8. Teddy Bear/Don't Be Cruel
9. And I Love You So
10. Jailhouse Rock
11. Fever
12. America, The Beautiful
13. One Night
14. That's All Right
15. Blue Christmas
16. Band Introductions
17. Early Morning Rain
18. What'd I Say
19. Johnny B. Goode
20. Band Solos
21. Love Letters
22. Band Introdctions
23. School Days
24. Hurt
25. Hurt (full reprise version)

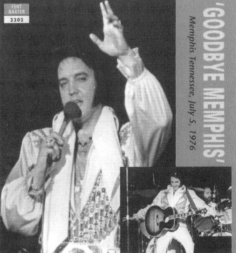

Disc Two:

1. Hound Dog
2. Funny How Time Slips Away
3. Help Me
4. How Great Thou Art
5. Softly As I Leave You
6. Polk Salad Annie
7. Jambalaya (one line only)
8. It's Now Or Never
9. Can't Help Falling In Love
10. Closing Vamp
11. O Sole Mio/It's Now Or Never
12. Little Sister
13. Teddy Bear/Don't Be Cruel
14. And I Love You So
15. Fever .
16. Polk Salad Annie
17. My Way
18. Band Introductions
19. School Days
20. Hurt
21. Hound Dog
22. Can't Help Falling In Love
23. Closing Vamp
24. Baby What You Want Me To Do*
25. Spanish Eyes*

All tracks on Disc One and tracks 1 – 10 on Disc Two were recorded at the Memphis show.
Tracks 11 – 23 on Disc Two were recorded at a later concert in Toledo, Ohio, April 23, 1977.
* The last two tracks on Disc Two are home recordings from 1974.
The Memphis recording was Elvis' last live performance in his home town.

THE BICENTENNIAL ELVIS EXPERIENCE (FORT BAXTER)

Recorded live at the Coliseum, Hampton Roads, Virginia, August 1, 1976.
Source: sound board recording.

1. 2001/C.C. Rider
2. I Got A Woman/Amen
3. Love Me
4. If You Love Me, Let Me Know
5. You Gave Me a Mountain
6. All Shook Up
7. Teddy Bear/Don't Be Cruel
8. And I love You So
9. Jailhouse Rock
10. Fever
11. America, The Beautiful
12. Return To Sender
13. Band Introductions
14. Early Morning Rain
15. What'd I Say
16. Johnny B. Goode
17. Band Introductions
18. Love Letters
19. Band Introductions/
Hail, Hail Rock 'n' Roll
20. Hurt (with reprise)
21. Hound Dog
22. Funny How Time Slips Away
23. Can't Help Falling In Love/
Closing Vamp

OLD TIMES THEY ARE NOT FORGOTTEN (DIAMOND ANNIVERSARY EDITIONS)

Recorded live at the Memorial Coliseum, Tuscaloosa, Alabama, August 30, 1976.
Source: sound board recording.

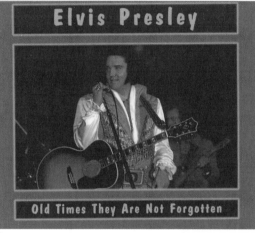

1. Also Sprach Zarathustra
2. See See Rider
3. I Got A Woman/Amen
4. Love Me
5. If You Love Me Let Me Know
6. You Gave Me A Mountain
7. All Shook Up
8. Teddy Bear/Don't Be Cruel
9. And I Love You So
10. Jailhouse Rock
11. Fever
12. America, The Beautiful
13. Introductions
14. Early Morning Rain
15. What'd I Say
16. Johnny B. Goode
17. Introductions
18. Love Letters
19. Introductions
20. Hail, Hail Rock 'n' Roll
21. Hurt
22. Hound Dog
23. Heavenly Father*
24. Mystery Train/Tiger Man
25. Can't Help Falling In Love
26. Closing Vamp

*Performed by Kathy Westmoreland

SOUTHBOUND (LUXOR)

Recorded live in Macon, Georgia, August 31, 1976, 8.30 p.m.
Source: sound board recording.

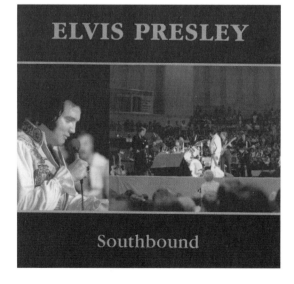

1. Also Sprach Zarathustra
2. See See Rider
3. I Got A Woman/Amen
4. Elvis Talks
5. Love Me.
6. If You Love Me, Let Me Know
7. You Gave Me A Mountain
8. All Shook Up
9. Teddy Bear/Don't Be Cruel
10. And I Love You So
11. Jailhouse Rock
12. Fever
13. America, The Beautiful
14. Introductions
15. Early Morning Rain
16. What'd I Say
17. Johnny B. Goode
18. Introductions
19. Love Letters
20. Introductions
21. Hail Hail Rock 'n' Roll
22. Hurt
23. Hound Dog
24. That's All Right Mama
25. Blue Christmas
26. Mystery Train/Tiger Man
27. Can't Help Falling In Love
28. Closing Vamp
29. Trying To Get To You*
30. Hurt (first live version ever)*

* Tracks 29 & 30 are bonus songs recorded live in Johnson City, Tennessee,
March 17, 1976.

STILL ROCKING THE NATION! (DISC 'LE ROI')

Recorded live at the Von Braun Civic Centre, Huntsville, Alabama, September 6, 1976, 8.30 p.m.
Source: sound board recording.

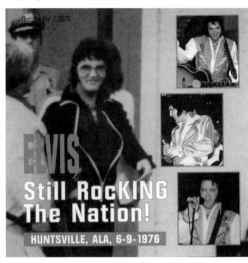

1. Also Sprach Zarathustra
2. See See Rider
3. I Got A Woman/Amen
4. Love Me
5. Fairytale
6. You Gave Me A Mountain
7. All Shook Up
8. Teddy Bear/Don't Be Cruel
9. And I Love You So
10. Jailhouse Rock
11. Fever
12. America (with reprise)
13. Band Introductions
14. Early Morning Rain
15. What'd I Say
16. Johnny B. Goode
17. Ronnie Tutt Drum Solo
18. Jerry Scheff Bass Solo
19. David Briggs Piano Solo
20. Love Letters
21. School Days
22. Hurt (with reprise)
23. Hound Dog
24. Danny Boy (Sherrill Nielsen)
25. That's All Right
26. Blue Christmas
27. Mystery Train/Tiger Man
28. Funny How Time Slips Away
29. Can't Help Falling In Love
30. Closing Vamp

CHICAGO BEAT (LIVE ARCHIVES)

Recorded live at the Chicago Stadium, Chicago, Illinois, October 14, 1976.
Source: sound board recording.

1. 2001
2. See See Rider
3. I Got A Woman/Amen
4. Love Me
5. If You Love Me, Let Me Know
6. You Gave Me A Mountain
7. Jailhouse Rock
8. All Shook Up
9. Teddy Bear
10. And I Love You So
11. Fever
12. Polk Salad Annie
13. Band Intro's
14. Early Morning Rain
15. What'd I Say
16. Johnny B. Goode
17. Ronnie Tutt Solo
18. Jerry Scheff Solo
19. Tony Brown Solo
20. David Briggs Solo
21. Love Letters
22. School Days
23. Hurt
24. Hurt (full reprise)
25. Love Me Tender
26. Hound Dog
27. Funny How Time Slips Away
28. Mystery Train/Tiger Man
29. Can't Help Falling In Love
30. Closing Theme

AMERICA THE BEAUTIFUL (KING RECORDS)

Recorded live at the Cow Palace, San Francisco, November 28, 1976.
Source: sound board recording.

1. Also Sprach Zarathustra
2. I Got A Woman/Amen
3. Love Me
4. If You Love Me, Let Me Know
5. You Gave Me A Mountain
6. Jailhouse Rock
7. It's Now Or Never
8. All Shook Up
9. Teddy Bear
10. Don't Cruel
11. And I Love You So
12. Fever
13. America
14. Polk Salad Annie
15. Introductions
16. Early Morning Rain
17. What'd I Say
18. Johnny B. Goode
19. Love Letters
20. Hurt
21. Hound Dog*
22. Can't Help Falling In Love*
23. Closing Vamp

*Due to a technical fault tracks "Hound Dog" and "Can't Help Falling In Love" were not recorded.
The versions included on this CD are from a performance in Tuscaloosa, Alabama on August 30, 1976.

PRESLEY AT THE HILTON (J.R.)

Recorded live at the Hilton Hotel, Las Vegas, December 5, 1976.
Source: audience recording.

1. Announcement
2. Also Sprach Zarathustra
3. See See Rider
4. I Got A Woman/Amen
5. Monologue
6. Blue Christmas
7. That's All Right
8. Monologue
9. Are You Lonesome Tonight?
10. Monologue
11. Sweet Caroline
12. You Gave Me A Mountain
13. Jailhouse Rock
14. O Sole Mio/It's Now Or Never
15. Monologue
16. Trying To Get To You

17. Fever
18. America, The Beautiful
19. Introductions
20. Early Morning Rain
21. What'd I Say
22. Johnny B. Goode
23. Introductions
24. Love Letters
25. Hail Hail Rock 'n' Roll/
Introductions
26. Hurt
27. Hound Dog
28. Monologue
29. How Great Thou Art
30. Can't Help Falling In Love
31. Closing Vamp

RUN ON (FRONT ROW PRODUCTIONS)

Recorded live at the Hilton Hotel, Las Vegas, December 7, 1976.
Source: sound board recording.

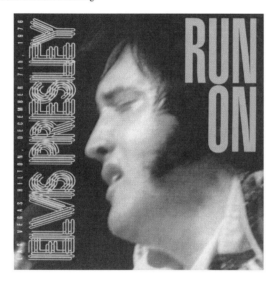

1. C.C. Rider
2. I Got A Woman/Amen
3. Love Me
4. If You Love Me Let Me Know
5. You Gave Me A Mountain
6. O Sole Mio/It's Now Or Never
7. Blue Christmas
8. That's All Right
9. Are You Lonesome Tonight?
10. Softly As I leave You
11. Fever
12. All Shook Up/Teddy Bear/Don't Be Cruel
13. Introductions
14. Early Morning Rain
15. What'd I Say
16. Love Letters
17. Hail, Hail, Rock 'n' Roll
18. Hurt
19. Hound Dog
20. The Hawaiian Wedding Song
21. You'd Better Run
22. Rock My Soul
23. Can't Help Falling In Love/Closing Theme
24. Christmas Souvenir Announcement

BLACK DIAMOND (GENERATIONS)

Recorded live at the Hilton Hotel, Las Vegas, December 12, 1976, Closing Show.
Source: audience recording.

Disc One:

1. 2001 Theme
2. CC Rider
3. I Got A Woman/Amen
4. Love Me
5. My Way
6. Fairytale
7. You Gave Me A Mountain
8. Elvis Talks To The Audience
9. Jailhouse Rock
10. Little Sister
11. O Sole Mio/It's Now Or Never
12. Trying To Get To You
13. Happy Birthday Charlie Hodge
14. Blue Suede Shoes
15. Elvis Talks About His Birthstone
16. Blue Christmas
17. Softly As I Leave You
18. Are You Lonesome Tonight
(laughing with the audience)
19. That's All Right Mama
20. Bridge Over Troubled Water

Disc Two:

1. Band Introductions (including)
Early Morning Rain
What'd I Say
Johnny B. Goode
2. Drum Solo – Ronnie Tutt
3. Fender Bass Solo – Jerry Scheff
4. Piano Solo – Tony Brown
5. Electric Piano Solo – David Briggs
6. Love Letters
7. Band Introductions/School Days
8. Hurt
9. Such A Night
10. Sweet Caroline
11. Can't Help Falling Love/Closing Vamp
12. If I Loved You*
13. Baby What You Want Me To Do*
14. Separate Ways*
15. Snowbird*
16. Little Egypt*
17. Burning Love*
18. For The Good Times*
19. Wearin' That Loved On Look*

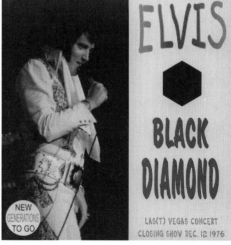

* Additional recordings originally released by RCA/BMG in
the USA on a series of "Time Life" albums.

A HOT WINTER NIGHT IN DALLAS (FORT BAXTER)

Recorded live in Dallas, Texas, December 28, 1976.
Source: sound board recording.

1. 2001
2. C.C. Rider
3. I Got A Woman/Amen
4. Love Me
5. Fairytale
6. You Gave Me A Mountain
7. Jailhouse Rock
8. O Sole Mio/It's Now Or Never/O Sole Mio
9. Trying To Get To You
10. Blue Suede Shoes
11. My Way
12. Polk Salad Annie
13. Band Introductions
14. Early Morning Rain
15. What'd I Say

16. Johnny B. Goode
17. Ronnie Tutt Drum Solo
(Elvis sings "Hey Bo Diddley")
18. Jerry Scheff Bass Solo
19. Tony Brown Piano Solo
20. David Briggs Electric
Piano Solo
21. Love Letters
22. School Days
23. Hurt (with reprise)
24. Unchained Melody
25. Can't Help Falling In Love
26. Closing Vamp

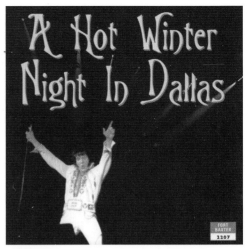

BURNING IN BIRMINGHAM (2001)

Recorded live in Birmingham, Alabama, December 29, 1976.
Source: sound board recording.

1. See See Rider
2. I Got A Woman/Amen
3. Love Me
4. Fairytale
5. You Gave Me A Mountain
6. Jailhouse Rock
7. O Sole Mio/It's Now Or Never
8. Trying To Get To You
9. My Way
10. Polk Salad Annie
11. Band Introductions
12. Early Morning Rain (full version)
13. What'd I Say

14. Johnny B. Goode
15. Band Solos
16. Love Letters
17. School Days
18. Funny How Time Slips Away
19. Hurt (with reprise)
20. Hound Dog
21. For The Good Times
22. The First Time Ever I Saw Your Face
23. Unchained Melody
24. Mystery Train/Tiger Man
25. Can't Help Falling In Love
26. Closing Vamp

AULD LANG SYNE (LIVE ARCHIVES)

Recorded live in Pittsburgh, P.A., December 31, 1976.
Source: audience recording.

Disc One:

1. 2001 Theme
2. CC Rider
3. I Got A Woman
4. Amen
5. Big Boss Man
6. Love Me
7. Fairytale
8. You Gave Me A Mountain
9. Jailhouse Rock
10. Presentation of the Liberty Bell
11. It's Now Or Never
12. My Way
13. Funny How Time Slips Away
14. Auld Lang Syne
15. Introductions of Vernon &
Lisa Marie Presley
16. Blue Suede Shoes
17. Trying To Get To You

Disc Two:

1. Polk Salad Annie
2. Introductions
3. Early Morning Rain
4. What'd I Say
5. Johnny B. Goode
6. Ronnie Tutt Drum Solo
7. Jerry Scheff Solo
8. Tony Brown Solo

9. Love Letters
10. Hail, Hail Rock 'n' Roll
11. Fever
12. Hurt
13. Hound Dog
14. Are You Lonesome Tonight?
15. Reconsider Baby
16. Little Sister
17. Unchained Melody
18. Rags To Riches
19. Can't Help Falling In Love
20. Closing Vamp

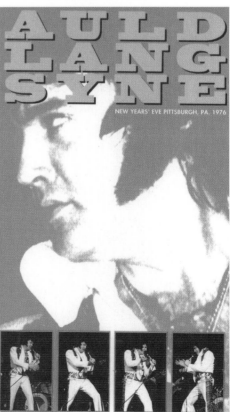

Above: the original double vinyl album
Right: the CD digi-pack version

Unofficial Releases: Live & Rehearsal Recordings

COMING ON STRONG (SOUTHERN STYLE)

Recorded live in West Palm Beach, Florida, February 13, 1977 & Montgomery, Alabama, February 16, 1977*
Source: sound board recordings.

West Palm Beach:

1. Little Sister (incomplete)
2. You Gave Me A Mountain
3. Blue Suede Shoes
4. O Sole Mio/It's Now Or Never
5. My Way
6. All Shook Up
7. Teddy Bear/Don't Be Cruel
8. And I Love You So
9. Fever
10. Blueberry Hill
11. Hurt
12. Hound Dog
13. Jailhouse Rock
14. Can't Help Falling In Love

Montgomery:

1. You Gave Me A Mountain
2. O Sole Mio/It's Now Or Never
3. Little Sister
4. Teddy Bear/Don't Be Cruel
5. My Way
6. Polk Salad Annie
7. Hurt
8. Hound Dog
9. Where No Stands Alone
10. Unchained Melody
11. Can't Help Falling In Love

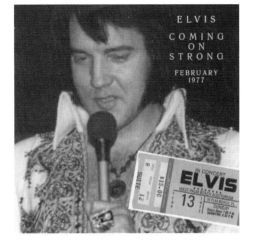

*Both of these shows are incomplete recordings. The beginning of each show and the band introductions were not recorded by the sound engineer. Two solos by Sherill Nielsen were also cut from the West Palm Beach show due to bad sound distortion.

RIOT IN CHARLOTTE (CHIPS RECORDS)

Recorded live in Charlotte, North Carolina, February 21, 1977.
Source: audience recording.

1. 2001 Theme
2. CC Rider
3. I Got A Woman/Amen
4. Are You Lonesome Tonight?
5. Reconsider Baby – That's All Right
6. Love Me
7. Moody Blue
8. You Gave Me A Mountain
9. Jailhouse Rock
10. O Sole Mio/It's Now Or Never
11. Little Sister
12. Teddy Bear/Don't Be Cruel
13. My Way
14. Release Me
15. Early Morning Rain
16. What'd I Say
17. Johnny B. Goode
18. Chickin' Pickin' (James Burton)
19. Drums Solo (Ronnie Tutt)
20. Bass Solo (Jerry Scheff)
21. Piano Solo (Tony Brown)
22. Piano Duet (Tony Brown & Elvis)
23. Love Letters
24. Hail! Hail! Rock 'n' Roll
25. Hurt
26. Why Me Lord (J.D. Sumner)
27. Can't Help Falling In Love

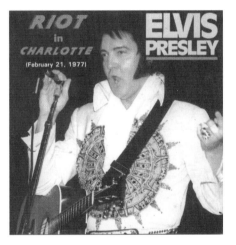

MOODY BLUE AND OTHER GREAT PERFORMANCES (FORT BAXTER)

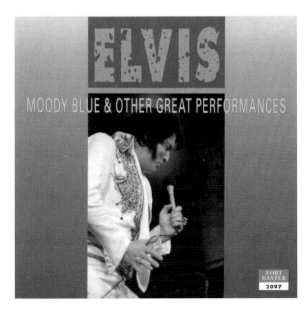

Recorded live in Charlotte, North Carolina, February 21, 1977.
Source: sound board recording.

1. Are You Lonesome Tonight?
2. Reconsider Baby
3. Love Me
4. Moody Blue
5. You Gave Me A Mountain
6. Jailhouse Rock
7. It's Now Or Never
8. Little Sister
9. Teddy Bear
10. Don't Be Cruel
11. My Way
12. Release Me
13. Hurt
14. Why Me Lord
15. Polk Salad Annie*
16. Where No One Stands Alone*
17. Unchained Melody*
18. Can't Help Falling In Love*

This CD includes an incomplete sound board recording of the audience recorded show which was first released on the "Riot In Charlotte" CD.
* Tracks 15 – 18 were recorded in Montgomery, Alabama on February

BY SPECIAL REQUEST – FROM LOUISIANA TO TENNESSEE (ROCK LEGENDS)

Recorded live at the Rapides Parish Coliseum, Alexandria, Louisiana, March 30, 1977
Source: sound board recording.

1. Love Me
2. If You Love Me Let Me Know
3. You Gave Me a Mountain
4. Jailhouse Rock
5. O Sole Mio/It's Now Or Never
6. Little Sister
7. Teddy Bear/Don't Be Cruel
8. And I Love You So
9. Fever
10. Love Me Tender
11. Hurt
12. Hound Dog
13. Danny Boy

14. Walk With Me
15. Blue Suede Shoes
16. Can't Help Falling In Love
17. Closing Theme
18. Help Me*
19. My Boy*
20. Loving Arms*
21. It's Midnight*
22. If You Talk In Your Sleep*
23. Thinking About You*
24. Good Time Charlie's Got Away*
25. Talk About The Good Times*
26. Girl Of Mine *

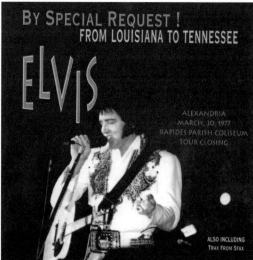

The complete performance was not recorded by the engineer.
Tracks 13 & 14 were performed by Sherill Nielsen.
*Tracks 18 – 26 are alternate and undubbed masters from Elvis' 1973
sessions at Stax Studios, Memphis, Tennessee.

MEMORIES FROM KALAMAZOO (VAVAVOOM RECORDS)

Recorded live at the Wings Stadium, Kalamazoo, Michigan, April 26, 1977, 8.30 p.m.
Source: sound board recording.

1. Love Me
2. Fairytale
3. If You Love Me Let Me Know
4. You Gave Me A Mountain
5. Jailhouse Rock
6. O Sole Mio/It's Now Or Never
7. Big Boss Man
8. Heartbreak Hotel
9. Blue Suede Shoes
10. And I Love You So (false start & microphone problems)
11. And I Love You So
12. My Way

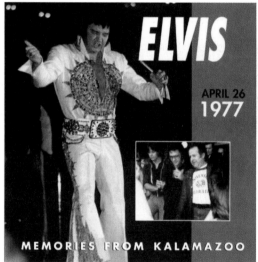

The start and end of this performance were not recorded by the engineer.

ELVIS PRESLEY...TONIGHT 8.30 P.M. (J.R.)

Recorded live at the Capitol Centre, Largo, Maryland, May 22, 1977, 8.30 p.m.
Source: audience recording.

1. Also Sprach Zarathustra
2. See See Rider
3. I Got A Woman/Amen
4. Love Me
5. Fairytale
6. You Gave Me a Mountain
7. Jailhouse Rock
8. Funny How Time Slips Away
9. O Sole Mio/It's Now Or Never
10. Little Sister
11. Monologue
12. Teddy Bear/Don't Be Cruel

13. My Way
14. Introductions
15. Early Morning Rain
16. What'd I Say
17. Johnny B. Goode
18. Introductions
19. Hail, Hail Rock 'n' Roll
20. Danny Boy*
21. Walk With Me*
22. Hound Dog
23. Can't Help Falling In Love
24. Closing Vamp

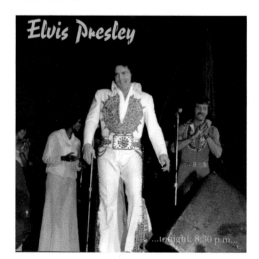

*Tracks 20 & 21 were performed by Sherill Nielsen

UNCHAINED ELVIS (KRYPTON MASTERSOUND)

Recorded live in Binghamton, New York, May 26, 1977, 8.30 p.m.
Source: audience recording.

1. 2001 Theme/See See Rider
2. I Got A Woman/Amen
3. Love Me
4. If You Love Me Let me Know
5. You Gave Me A Mountain
6. Jailhouse Rock
7. O Sole Mio/It's Now Or Never
8. Little Sister
9. Teddy Bear/Don't Be Cruel
10. And I Love You So
11. Why Me Lord
12. Polk Salad Annie
13. Introductions of:
The Sweet Inspirations
J.D. Sumner And The Stamps Quartet
Kathy Westmoreland

14. Early Morning Rain
15. What'd I Say/Johnny B. Goode
16. Ronnie Tutt's Solo
Jerry Scheff's Blues
Tony Brown's Piano Solo
Bobby Ogden's Solo
17. School Days
18. Hurt
19. Hound Dog
20. Can't Help Falling In Love
21. Closing Vamp
22. Heartbreak Hotel*
23. Bridge Over Troubled Water*
24. Unchained Melody*

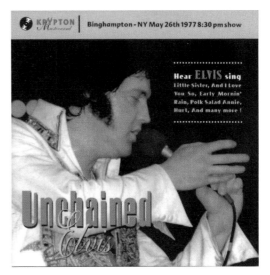

* Tracks 22 – 24 recorded live in Binghamton, New York, May 27, 1977, 8.30 p.m.

JAILHOUSE ROCK MAN IN CONCERT GREAT DANE RECORDS)

Recorded live in Rochester, New York, May 25, 1977.
Source: audience recording.

1. Introduction
2. C.C. Rider
3. I Got A Woman/Amen
4. Love Me
5. If You Love Me Let Me Know
6. You Gave Me A Mountain
7. Jailhouse Rock
8. O Sole Mio/It's Now Or Never
9. Little Sister
10. Medley: Teddy Bear/Don't Be Cruel
11. Trying To Get To You
12. Danny Boy
13. Walk With Me
14. One Night
15. My Way
16. Medley: Early Morning Rain/What'd I Say/Johnny B. Goode/
Hail, Hail Rock 'n' Roll
17. Hurt
18. Hound Dog
19. Can't Help Falling In Love
20. Carol Channing presents pure Elvis in "Spanish Eyes"*
21. The United States Airforce presents: the Wolfman Jack Radio Show:
Elvis in "Steamroller Blues" *

Tracks 12 & 13 were performed by Sherill Nielsen.
The Medley listed at track 16 is actually the songs performed during the band introductions.
* Tracks 20 & 21 are bonus songs. These are taken from US radio broadcasts.
The "Pure Elvis" reference indicates that the version of "Spanish Eyes" included here is the undubbed version first released by RCA on the
"Our Memories Of Elvis" album in 1979.

AS I LEAVE YOU (ECOLORADO)

Recorded live in Omaha, Nebraska, June 19, 1977.
Source: sound board recording.

1. See See Rider
2. I Got A Woman/Amen
3. That's All Right Mama
4. Are You Lonesome Tonight?
5. Love Me
6. Fairytale
7. Teddy Bear
8. Don't Be Cruel
9. And I Love You So
10. Jailhouse Rock
11. How Great Thou Art
12. Band Introductions

14. Early Morning Rain
15. What'd I Say
16. Johnny B. Goode
17. Band Introductions
18. I Really Don't Want To Know
19. Band Introductions
20. Hurt
21. Hound Dog
22. O Sole Mio/It's Now Or Never
23. Can't Help Falling In Love
24. Closing Theme
25. Rapid City Interview*

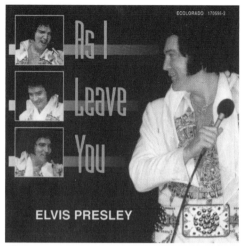

ELVIS PRESLEY

This performance is one of two concerts filmed by CBS television for Elvis' 3rd and final TV special, "Elvis in Concert".
*Track 25 is actually a presentation to Elvis of the Medallion of Life, by the Mayor of Rapid City, and a young girl from the Sioux Indian community.
This was also filmed by the CBS cameras along with Elvis concert in Rapid City, South Dakota, on 21 June, 1977.

SINCE CINCINNATI (AJR RECORDS)

Recorded live at the Riverfront Stadium, Cincinnati, Ohio, June 25, 1977.
Source: audience recording.

1. Gospel*
2. Gospel*
3. Hot Hot Sunday*
4. If You Leave Me Now*
5. Also Sprach Zarathustra
6. C.C. Rider/Dialogue
7. I Got A Woman/Amen
8. Love Me
9. If You Love Me Let Me Know
10. Lord, You Gave Me A Mountain
11. Jailhouse Rock
12. O Sole Mio
13. Little Sister
14. Teddy Bear/Don't Be Cruel

15. And I Love You So
16. My Way
17. Introductions
18. Early Morning Rain
19. What'd I Say
20. Johnny B. Goode
21. I Really Don't Want To Know
22. Introductions: Vernon On Stage
23. Unchained Melody
24. Hound Dog
25. Can't Help Falling Love

*Tracks 1& 2 are performed by J.D. Sumner and the Stamps Quartet.
Tracks 3 & 4 are performed by the Sweet Inspirations.

ADIOS – THE FINAL PERFORMANCE (MYSTERY TRAIN/A.J. RECORDS)

Recorded live at the Market Square Arena, Indianapolis, Indiana, June 26, 1977, 8.30 p.m.
Source: audience recording

1. 2001 Theme
2. C.C. Rider
3. I Got A Woman/Amen
4. Love Me
5. Fairytale
6. You Gave Me A Mountain
7. Jailhouse Rock
8. It's Now Or Never
9. Little Sister
10. Teddy Bear
11. Don't Be Cruel
12. Please Release Me
13. I Can't Stop Loving You
14. Bridge Over Troubled Water
15. Band Introductions
16. Early Morning Rain
17. Johnny B. Goode
18. I Really Don't Want To Know
19. Hurt
20. Hound Dog
21. Can't Help Falling In Love
22. Closing Theme

This was Elvis Presley's last live appearance.

A PROFILE – THE KING ON STAGE (FORT BAXTER)

Disc One:

Recorded live at the Hilton Hotel, Las Vegas, August 20, 1973, Dinner Show.
Source: sound board recording.

1. 2001
2. CC Rider
3. I Got A Woman
4. Love Me
5. Steamroller Blues
6. You Gave Me A Mountain
7. Trouble
8. Blue Suede Shoes
9. Rock 'n' Roll Medley
10. Love Me Tender
11. Fever
12. What Now My Love
13. Suspicious Minds
14. Band Introductions
15. My Boy
16. Release Me
17. An American Trilogy
18. Mystery Train/Tiger Man
19. Help Me Make It Through The Night
20 How Great Thou Art
21. Can't help Falling In Love
22. Closing Vamp

Right: the Profile box set.

Disc Two:

Recorded live in Kansas City, June 29, 1974, Evening Show.
Source: sound board recording.

1. Stagger Lee*
2. I Got My Mojo Working*
3. Alla' En El 'Rancho Grande (long version)*
4. Cotton Fields*
5. CC Rider
6. When My Blue Moon Turns To
Gold Again/Blue Christmas
7. I Got A Woman
8. Love Me
9. Trying To Get To You
10. All Shook Up
11. Love Me Tender
12. Hound Dog
13. Fever
14. Polk Salad Annie
15. Why Me Lord
16. Suspicious Minds
17. Band Introductions
18. I Can't Stop Loving You
19. Help Me
20. Bridge Over Troubled Water
21. Let Me Be There
22. Johnny B. Goode*
23. Can't Help Falling In Love*

Right: disc one.

Bottom right: disc two.

* Tracks 1 – 4 were recorded in July 1970 during rehearsals at MGM Studios,
Culver City, California.
Tracks 22 & 23 were recorded live in Dayton, Ohio, October 6, 1974.

A PROFILE – THE KING ON STAGE (FORT BAXTER) Continued

Disc Three:

Recorded Live in Lake Charles, Louisiana, May 4, 1975, Evening Show.
Source: sound board recording.

1. Jambalaya
2. Love Me
3. If you Love Me Let Me Know
4. Love Me Tender
5. All Shook Up
6. Teddy Bear/Don't Be Cruel
7. The Wonder Of You
8. Polk Salad Annie
9. Band Introductions
10. Johnny B. Goode
11. Steamroller Blues
12. T.R.O.U.B.L.E.
13. I'll Remember You
14. Why Me Lord
15. Let Me Be There
16. An American Trilogy
17. Hound Dog
18. Funny How Time Slips Away
19. Little Darlin'
20. Can't Help falling In Love

The opening two songs from this show: CC Rider & I Got A Woman/Amen were not recorded by the engineer.

Right: the box set included an illustrated booklet featuring photographs and memorabilia from the concert years.

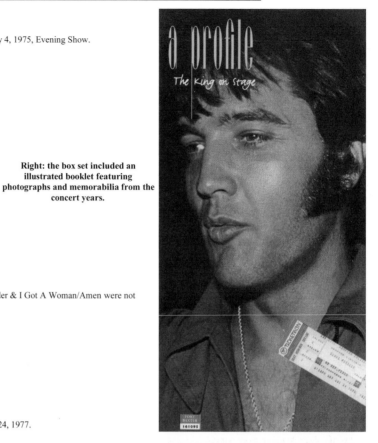

Disc Four:

Recorded Live in Ann Arbor, Michigan, April 24, 1977.
Source: sound board recording.

1. If You Love me Let Me Know
2. You Gave Me A Mountain
3. Trying To get To You
4. It's Now Or Never
5. Little Sister
6. Teddy Bear/Don't Be Cruel
7. Help me
8. My Way
9. Polk Salad Annie
10. Hurt
11. Blueberry Hill*
12. Danny Boy*
13. Walk With Me*
14. Unchained Melody
15. Can't Help Falling In Love

Right: disc three.

Bottom right: disc four.

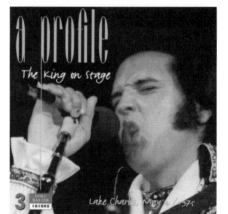

The complete show was not recorded by the engineer.
* Track 11 recorded in West Palm Beach, Florida, February 13, 1977.
Tracks 13 & 14 recorded in St. Petersburg, Florida, February 14, 1977.
Vocal on tracks 12 & 13 by Sherril Nielsen.

A PROFILE – THE KING ON STAGE VOLUME 2 (FORT BAXTER)

Disc One:

Recorded live at the Sahara Tahoe Hotel, Nevada, May 27, 1974,
Special 3 a.m. Closing Show.
Source: sound board recording.

1. See See Rider
2. I Got a Woman/Amen
3. Love Me
4. Trying To Get To You
5. All Shook Up
6. Love Me Tender
7. You Don't Have To Say You Love Me
8. Hound Dog (with two reprises)
9. Fever
10. Polk Salad Annie
12. Suspicious Minds
13. Band Introductions
14. I Can't Stop Loving You
15. Help Me
16. Bridge Over Troubled Water (with reprise)
17. Let Me Be There
18. The Wonder Of You
19. Big Boss Man
20. The First Time Ever I Saw Your Face
21. An American Trilogy*
22. It's Now Or Never*
23. Can't Help Falling In Love*
24. Closing Vamp*

Right: the Profile Vol. 2 box set.

*Tracks 21 – 24 recorded in Lake Tahoe during May 1974 – exact date unknown.

Disc Two:

Recorded live in College Park, Maryland, September 28, 1974.
Source: sound board recording.

1. See See Rider
2. Dialogue
3. I Got A Woman/Amen
4. Love Me
5. If You Love Me Let Me Know
6. It's Midnight
7. Big Boss Man
8. Fever
9. Dialogue
10. Love Me Tender
11. Hound Dog
12. Band Introductions
13. Blue Christmas
14. All Shook Up
15. Teddy Bear/Don't Be Cruel
16. Trying To Get To You
17. Killing Me Softly*
18. When It's My Time*
19. Heartbreak Hotel
20. Let Me Be There (with reprise)
21. How Great Thou Art

Right: disc one.

Bottom right: disc two.

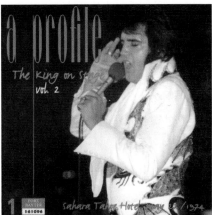

* Track 17 performed by Voice.
Track 18 performed by J.D. Sumner and the Stamps Quartet.
The concert concludes on disc three.

A PROFILE – THE KING ON STAGE VOLUME 2 (FORT BAXTER) Continued

Disc Three:

Recorded live in Dayton, Ohio, October 6, 1974, Matinee Show.
Source: sound board recording.

1. Hawaiian Wedding Song*
2. Blue Suede Shoes*
3. Dialogue*
4. Can't Help Falling In Love*
5. Closing Vamp*
6. See See Rider
7. I Got A Woman/Amen
8. Love Me
9. If You Love Me Let Me Know (with reprise)
10. It's Midnight
11. Big Boss Man
12. Fever
13. Love Me Tender
14. Hound Dog (with reprise)
15. Band Introductions
16. Lawdy Miss Clawdy
17. Band Introductions
18. All Shook Up
19. Teddy Bear/Don't Be Cruel
20. Heartbreak Hotel
21. Why My Lord
22. Promised Land
23. You Gave Me A Mountain
24. Let Me Be There (with reprise)
25. Hawaiian Wedding song (with reprise)
26. Can't Help Falling In Love
27. Closing Vamp

Right: a replica concert poster for Elvis' Lake Tahoe concerts was included with this collection.

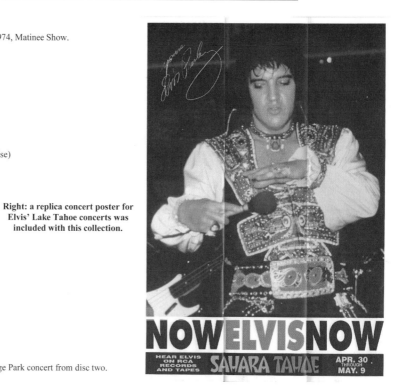

* Tracks 1 – 5 is the conclusion of the College Park concert from disc two.

Disc Four:

Recorded live at the Hilton Hotel, Las Vegas, March 22, 1975, Midnight Show.
Source: sound board recording.

1. Also Sprach Zarathustra
2. See See Rider
3. I Got A Woman/Amen
4. Love Me
5. If You Love Me Let Me Know
6. And I Love You So
7. Big Boss Man
8. It's Midnight
9. Promised Land
10. Green Green Grass Of Home
11. Fairytale
12. Band Introductions
13. My Boy
14. I'll Remember You
15. Let Me Be There (with reprise)
16. Teddy Bear/Don't Be Cruel
17. Hound Dog
18. You're The Reason I'm Living
19. Can't Help Falling In Love
20. Closing Vamp
21. How The Web Was Woven*
22. I'll Take You Home Again Kathleen*

Right: disc three.

Bottom right: disc four.

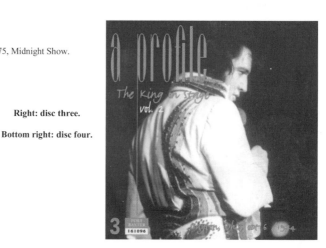

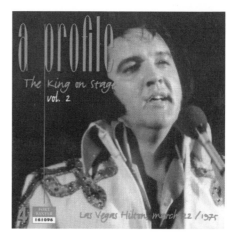

* Tracks 21 & 22 feature Elvis at the piano: recorded July 16, 1970 during rehearsals at MGM Studios, Culver City, California.

THE LEGEND LIVES ON (P.C.S.)

Live and studio out takes 1969 – 1972.

1. Elvis Talks About His Career
2. Yesterday/Hey Jude
3. Introductions By Elvis/Happy Birthday To James Burton
4. In The Ghetto
5. Suspicious Minds
6. What'd I Say
7. Can't Help Falling In Love
8. Yesterday/Hey Jude
9. Proud Mary
10. Let It Be Me
11. Sweet Caroline
12. Release Me
13. Walk A Mile In My Shoes
14. Bridge Over Troubled Water (undubbed master)
15. A Big Hunk O' Love
16. It's Impossible
17. The Impossible Dream
18. It's Over

Recording Information:

Tracks 1 – 7 recorded live August 21, 1969, Midnight Show.
Track 8 recorded live August 25, 1969.
Tracks 9 & 11 recorded live February 16, 1970.
Track 10 recorded live February 17, 1970.
Track 12 recorded live February 18, 1970.
Track 13 recorded live February 19, 1970.
Tracks 1 – 13 recorded at the International Hotel, Las Vegas.
Track 14 recorded June 5, 1970 at RCA Studio B, Nashville.
Track 15 recorded live February 15, 1972.
Tracks 16 & 17 live recorded February 16, 1972.
Track 18 recorded live February 17, 1972.
Tracks 15 – 18 recorded at the Hilton Hotel, Las Vegas

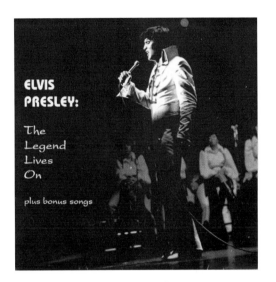

GOOD TIMES NEVER SEEMED SO GOOD (CAPTAIN MARVEL JR. RECORDS)

Live and rehearsal recordings 1969 – 1970.

1. Elvis Talks About The Elvis Presley Show
2. See See Rider
3. I Got A Woman
4. Don't Cry Daddy
5. Walk A Mile In My Shoes
6. Release Me
7. Kentucky Rain
8. Polk Salad Annie
9. Sweet Caroline
10. Proud Mary
11. Let It Be Me
12. Walk A Mile In My Shoes #2
13. Yesterday
14. The Wonder Of You
15. Runaway
16. Polk Salad Annie #2
17. Let It Be Me
18. Don't Cry Daddy
19. I Just Can't Help Believin'
20. You've Lost That Lovin' Feeling

Recording Information:

Track 1 excerpt from a press conference in Houston, Texas. Recorded February 27, 1970.
Track 3 recorded live August 24, 1969.
Track 15 recorded live August 24, 1969, Dinner Show.
Track 13 recorded live August 25, 1969.
Track 11 recorded live February 15, 1970.
Tracks 9 & 10 recorded live February 16, 1970.
Tracks 4, 16, & 17 recorded live February 17, 1970.
Tracks 2, 6, 7, 8, & 14 recorded live February 18, 1970.
Tracks 5 & 12 recorded live February 19, 1970.
Tracks 18 – 20 recorded July 24, 1970 during rehearsals at MGM Studios, Culver City, California.

THE LOST PERFORMANCES 1970/72 (MYSTERY TRAIN)

Live and rehearsal out takes 1970 – 1972.

1. Introduction
2. Walk A Mile In My Shoes
3. The Wonder Of You
4. Don't Cry Daddy
5. In The Ghetto
6. There Goes My Everything
7. Make The World Go Away
8. Just Pretend
9. Heartbreak Hotel
10. Twenty Days And Twenty Nights
11. Love Me
12. Hound Dog
13. Don't Be Cruel
14. I Washed My Hands In Muddy Water
15. I Was The One
16. Cattle Call
17. Baby Lets Play House
18. Don't
19. Money Honey
20. All Shook Up
21. Teddy Bear
22. Don't Be Cruel
23. Are You Lonesome Tonight
24. I Can't Stop Loving You
25. How Great Thou Art
26. Release Me
27. I Can't Stop Loving You
28. The End – A New Beginning

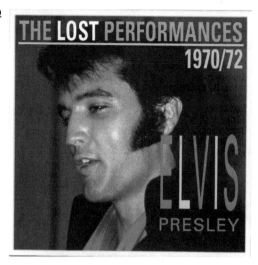

Recording Information:

Track 27 recorded July 15, 1970 during rehearsals at MGM Studios, Culver City, California.
Track 14 – 19 recorded July 29, 1970 during rehearsals at MGM Studios, Culver City, California.
Tracks 2, 6, 8, 11, 12, & 13 recorded live August 11, 1970, Midnight Show.
Tracks 10 recorded live August 12, 1970, Midnight Show.
Tracks 3, 4, 5, 7 recorded live August 13, 1970, Dinner Show.
Track 9 recorded live August 13, 1970, Midnight Show.
Tracks 2 – 13 recorded at the International Hotel, Las Vegas.
Tracks 20 – 25 recorded live April 9, 1972 at the Coliseum, Hampton Roads, Virginia, Evening Show.
Track 26 recorded live April 14, 1972 at the Coliseum, Greensboro, North Carolina, Evening Show.
All tracks taken from the soundtrack of the Warner Brothers home video "Elvis The Lost Performances".
Tracks 1 & 28 are instrumentals from the opening and closing title sequences.
Track 1 includes some dialogue from "Elvis On Tour".
Tracks 1 – 19 & 27 are out takes from "Elvis – That's The Way It Is".
Tracks 20 – 26 are out takes from "Elvis On Tour".

COMMAND PERFORMANCE (VIK)

Live audience recordings 1970 – 1974.

1. See See Rider
2. Mystery Train/Tiger Man
3. Little Sister/Get Back
4. My Babe
5. Reconsider Baby
6. Trouble
7. My Boy
8. Spanish Eyes
9. Oh Happy Day
10. The First Time Ever I Saw Your Face
11. Big Boss Man
12. It's Midnight
13. If You Talk In Your Sleep
14. Hawaiian Wedding Song
15. Softly As I Leave You
16. It's Now Or Never
17. Never Been To Spain
18. You Gave Me A Mountain
19. Proud Mary
20. Love Me
21. Hound Dog
22. A Big Hunk O' Love

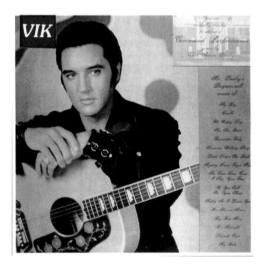

Recording Information:

Track 9 recorded August 14, 1970 at the International Hotel, Las Vegas, Midnight Show.
Tracks 1 – 4 recorded August 4, 1972, 10 p.m. Show.
Tracks 17 – 22 recorded February, 1972.
Tracks 6 & 7 recorded September 2, 1973, Dinner Show.
Track 8 recorded February 7, 1974, Midnight Show.
Tracks 10 – 12 & 16 recorded August 21, 1974, Dinner Show.
Tracks 13 – 15 recorded August 23, 1974, Midnight Show.
Tracks 1 – 4, 6 – 8, & 10 – 22 recorded at the Hilton Hotel, Las Vegas.
Track 5 recorded June 10, 1972 at Madison Square Garden, New York, Afternoon Show.

THE REQUEST BOX SHOWS (BILKO)

Live audience recordings 1975.

1. See See Rider
2. Bathroom Story (dialogue)
3. Blue Suede Shoes
4. Young And Beautiful
5. Are You Lonesome Tonight
6. If You Love Me Let Me Know
7. Softly As I Leave You
8. It's Now Or Never
9. Polk Salad Annie
10. Introducing The Righteous Brothers
11. My Boy
12. And I Love You
13. Green, Green Grass Of Home
14. Fairytale
15. T.R.O.U.B.L.E.
16. Why Me Lord
17. Until It's Time For You To Go
18. Burning Love
19. Can't Help Falling In Love

Recording Information:

Tracks 1– 11 recorded August 19, 1975.
Tracks 12 – 19 recorded August 20, 1975.
All tracks recorded live at the Hilton Hotel, Las Vegas.

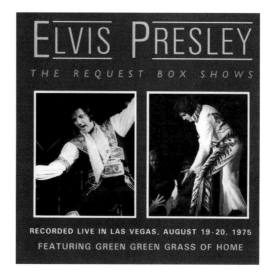

OLD ONES, NEW ONES AND IN BETWEEN ONES (GROTI RECORDS)

Unreleased sound board and rare RCA recordings 1969 – 1977

1. 2001 Theme/See See Rider/I Got A Woman/Amen
2. I'll Remember You
3. Polk Salad Annie
4. In The Ghetto
5. Sweet Caroline
6. Are You Lonesome Tonight
7. Kentucky Rain
8. My Babe
9. You've Lost That Lovin' feeling
10. Little Sister/Get Back
11. Yesterday
12. An American Trilogy
13. Unchained Melody
14. What'd I Say
15. Don't Cry Daddy
16. I Will Be True/
It's Still Here/
I'll Take You Home Again Kathleen
17. A Big Hunk O' Love

Recording information:

Track 1 recorded at the Cow Palace, San Francisco, November 28, 1976.
Track 2 recorded at the Municipal Auditorium, Mobile, Alabama, June 2, 1975, Afternoon Show.
Tracks 3 – 12 live out takes first released on the 1980 album "Elvis Aron Presley".
Track 13 overdubbed live recording first released as a 1978 single and included on the 1980 album "Elvis Aron Presley".
Tracks 14, 15, & 17 live out takes first released on the 1981 album "Greatest Hits Volume 1" in the US and "The Sound Of Your Cry" in the UK.
Track 16 undubbed masters first released on the 1980 album "Elvis Aron Presley".

FROM BURBANK TO VEGAS (MOON)

Rehearsal and live recording 1968 – 1972.

1. I Got A Woman
2. Blue Moon/Young Love/Happy Day
3. Guitar Boogie
4. When It Rains It Really Pours
5. Blue Christmas
6. Are You Lonesome Tonight/That's My Desire
7. That's When Your Heartaches Begin
8. Baby What's Wrong/Peter Gunn/Guitar Boogie
9. Love Me
10. When My Blue Moon Turns To Gold Again
11. Blue Christmas/Santa Claus Is Back In Town
12. An American Trilogy
13. Never Been To Spain
14. You Gave Me A Mountain
15. A Big Hunk O' Love
16. It's Impossible
17. The Impossible Dream
18. It's Over

Recording Information:

Tracks 1 – 11 recorded June 24, 1968 during dressing room rehearsals for the NBC TV Special, "Elvis" at Burbank Studios, Burbank, California.
Tracks 13 – 16 recorded live February 16, 1972.
Track 17 recorded live February 17, 1972.
Track 12 recorded live February 1972.
Tracks 12 – 18 recorded at the Hilton Hotel, Las Vegas.

INHERIT THE WIND (TIGER)

Live, rehearsal and studio recordings 1969 – 1975.

1. Inherit The Wind
2. Baby What You Want Me To Do
3. Polk Salad Annie
4. Polk Salad Annie
5. Patch It Up
6. Something
7. Sweet Caroline
8. I've Lost You
9. I Just Can't Help Believin'
10. You've Lost That Lovin' Feelin'
11. You Don't Have To Say You Love Me
12. You Don't Have To Say You Love Me
13. Mary In The Morning
14. Kentucky Rain (remake)
15. Bridge Over Troubled Water (undubbed master)
16. Burning Love
17. Polk Salad Annie

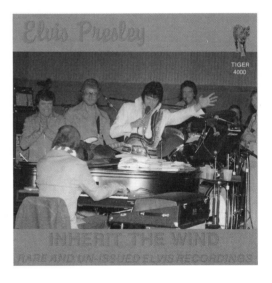

Recording Information:

Track 14 recorded February 19, 1969 at American Sound Studios, Memphis.
New overdubs for track 14 recorded October 16, 1980 at Young 'un Sound, Nashville.
Track 1 recorded live August 26, 1969, Dinner Show.
Track 2 recorded live August 26, 1969, Midnight Show.
Track 3 recorded live August 1970. Exact date unknown.
Tracks 1, 2, & 3 recorded at the International Hotel, Las Vegas.
Track 15 recorded June 5, 1970 at RCA Studio B, Nashville.
Tracks 6 , 7, & 8 recorded August 6, 1970.
Tracks 4, 5, & 9 – 13 recorded August 7, 1970.
Tracks 4 – 13 recorded during stage rehearsals at the International Hotel, Las Vegas.
Track 16 recorded live in Greensboro, North Carolina, April 14, 1972, Evening Show.
Track 17 recorded live at the Hilton Hotel, Las Vegas, December 13, 1975, Midnight Show.

GET DOWN AND GET WITH IT! (FORT BAXTER)

1. Stagger Lee
2. Got My Mojo Working
3. I've Lost You
4. Stranger In The Crowd
5. The Next Step Is Love
6. You Don't Have To Say You Love Me
7. Sweet Caroline
8. Yesterday
9. Hey Jude
10. I Can't Stop Loving You
11. It's Your Baby, You Rock It
12. Crying Time
13. Ghost Riders In The Sky
14. Runaway
15. It's Now Or Never
16. Peter Gun Theme
17. Love Me
18. One Night
19. Alla En El Rancho Grande
20. That's All Right
21. Twenty Days And Twenty Nights
22. Patch It Up
23. Cotton Fields
24. Sylvia
25. Stranger In The Crowd
26. How The Web Was Woven
27. I'll Take You Home Again, Kathleen

Recorded July 16, 1970 during rehearsals at MGM Studios, Culver City, California.

ELECTRIFYING! (BILKO)

Live & rehearsal recordings, 1970.

1. That's All Right
2. Twenty Days And Twenty Nights
3. Patch It Up
4. Love Me
5. Yesterday
6. Hey Jude
7. I Can't Stop Loving You
8. It's Your Baby, You Rock It
9. Ghost Riders In The Sky
10. Peter Gun Theme
11. Hound Dog
12. Don't Cry Daddy
13. Let It Be Me
14. Polk Salad Annie
15. The Lord's Prayer
16. My Country Tis Of Thee
17. Havana Gila
18. My Baby Left Me
19. You Don't Have To Say You Love Me
20. Stranger In The Crowd
21. Blueberry Hill
22. Lawdy Miss Clawdy
23. Heartbreak Hotel
24. One Night
25. It's Now Or Never

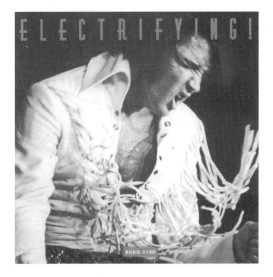

Recording Information:

Tracks 1– 10 recorded July 16, 1970 during rehearsals at MGM Studios, Culver City, California.
Tracks 15 – 20 recorded July 29, 1970 during rehearsals at MGM Studios, Culver City, California.
Tracks 11– 14 & 21 – 25 recorded live February 23, 1970, Closing Show at the International Hotel, Las Vegas.

THE BRIGHTEST STAR ON SUNSET BOULEVARD VOLUME 1 (FORT BAXTER)

1. That's All Right
2. I Got A Woman
3. The Wonder Of You
4. I've Lost You
5. The Next Step Is Love
6. Stranger In The Crowd
7. You've Lost That Loving Feeling
8. Something
9. Don't Cry Daddy
10. Don't Cry Daddy (reprise)
11. You Don't Have To Say You Love Me
12. Polk Salad Annie
13. Bridge Over Troubled Water
14. I Can't Stop Loving You
15. Just Pretend

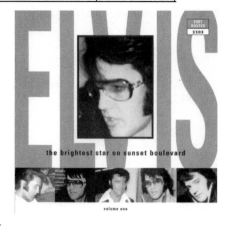

Recorded July 24, 1970 during rehearsals at RCA Studios, Hollywood, California..

THE BRIGHTEST STAR ON SUNSET BOULEVARD VOLUME 2 (FORT BAXTER)

1. Sweet Caroline
2. Words
3. Suspicious Minds
4. I Just Can't Help Believin'
5. I Just Can't Help Believin' (reprise)
6. Tomorrow Never Comes/
Running Scared (few lines)
7. Mary In The Morning
8. Twenty Days And Twenty Nights
9. You've Lost That Lovin' Feeling
10. I Just Can't Help Believin'
11. Heart Of Rome (x rated version)
12. Memories
13. Johnny B. Goode
14. Make The World Go Away
15. Stranger In The Crowd (x rated version)
16. I Washed My Hands in Muddy Water

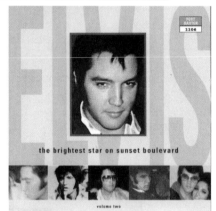

Recorded July 24, 1970 during rehearsals at RCA Studios, Hollywood, California.

HANG LOOSE (BILKO)

1. Polk A Little Sock Salad (Polk Salad Annie)
2. Sweet Caroline
3. Polk Salad Annie
4. I've Lost You
5. I've Lost You #2
6. I Just Can't Help Believin'
7. You Don't Have To Say You Love Me
8. You Don't Have To Say You Love Me #2
9. Bridge Over Troubled Water
10. You've Lost That Lovin' Feeling
11. Patch It Up
12. Something
13. Can't Help Falling In Love
14. Folsom Prison Blues/I Walk The Line
15. Portrait Of My Love

Recording Information:

Tracks recorded August 6, 1970 during stage rehearsals at the International Hotel, Las Vegas.
Track recorded live August 14, 1970, during the Midnight Show at the International Hotel, Las Vegas. (audience recording)
Track 15 recorded during a stage rehearsal in Las Vegas. Exact date unknown.

ELVIS ON TOUR – CAMERA AND MICROPHONE REHEARSAL (RISING SUN)

1. Burning Love
2. For The Good Times
3. The First Time Ever I Saw Your Face
4. A Big Hunk O' Love
5. See See Rider
6. For The Good Times
7. You Better Run
8. Lead Me, Guide Me
9. Sweet, Sweet Spirit
10. Turn Your Eyes Upon Jesus

Recorded March 30, 1972 during rehearsals at RCA Studio C, Hollywood.

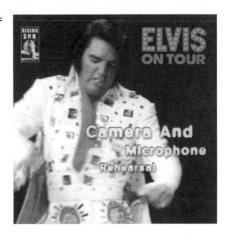

THE REHEARSAL FOR THE HAMPTON CONCERT (LUNA RECORDS)

1. Don't Be Cruel
2. Love Me/All Shook Up
3. Heartbreak Hotel
4. Teddy Bear/Don't Be Cruel
5. Hound Dog
6. Lawdy Miss Clawdy
7. Burning Love
8. For The Good Times
9. See See Rider
10. Never Been To Spain/
Help Me Make It Through The Night (excerpt)/
The First Time Ever I Saw Your Face (excerpt)
11. For The Good Times
12. For The Good Times
13. For The Good Times
14. Vernon Presley Interview

Recording Information:

Tracks 7, 8, & 11 – 13 recorded March 30, 1972 during rehearsals at RCA Studio C, Hollywood.
Tracks 1 – 6, 9, & 10 recorded March 31, 1972 during rehearsals at RCA Studio A, Hollywood.
Track 14 recorded April 1972.

KICKIN' BACK AND FORTH (MOON)

1. Monologue: Elvis talks about a paternity suit filed against him.
   Monologue: Elvis speaks out on drugs.
   Hawaiian Wedding Song
2. If You Love Me Let Me Know
   If You Love Me Let Me Know (2)
   Promised Land (x rated version)
3. Promised Land (2)
4. Aubrey
5. True Love Travels On A Gravel Road
   The First Time Ever I Saw Your Face
   Dialogue
   My Way
   Fever
   Portrait Of My Love

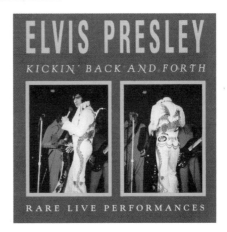

Recording Information:

Tracks 1 & 4 recorded live September 2, 1974, during the Closing Show at the Hilton Hotel, Las Vegas. (audience recording)
Tracks 2 & 3 recorded August 16, 1974 during rehearsals at RCA Studios, Hollywood, California.
Track 5 recorded during rehearsals at the Las Vegas Hilton. Exact date unknown. These songs may actually be from more than one rehearsal recording.

Acknowledgements

I would like to thank the following people for their help, contributions, and support:

Shaun Livesey for providing additional cover artwork, advice on Elvis' record releases, and help with the original concept for this publication.

Edward Christie & Alan Parker (for making this possible), Mum & Dad, Arnold, Chris & Amy, Gaz, Joanne, Mick & Marie, Ste and all at the Witton, Monika Leone & The Sound of Elvis Fan Club of South Australia, Henrik Knusden & Elvis Unlimited.

Cover artwork and page layout by David Parker, Bij and Rob Green.

Bootlegs: It is illegal to manufacture, distribute or sell bootleg or counterfeit recordings. Bootleg CD or vinyl pictured in this publication is owned by the author, but in no way were they or Abstract Sounds Ltd. involved in the manufacture, distribution or sale of these recordings.

Bootlegs are illegal. Pressing and selling them is illegal.

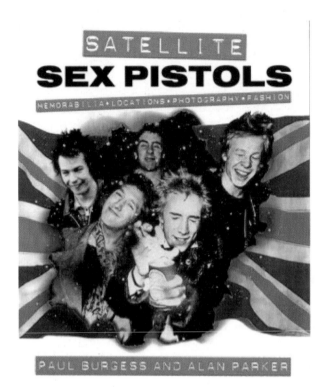

"SATELLITE" - SEX PISTOLS PRESS QUOTES

"Not just another rock n' roll swindle then; but thorough enough to be the last word on the Sex Pistols"
(*The Times Metro*)

"This book is alive with the band's incendiary beauty"
(*Select Magazine*)

"It's enough to make you want to pogo, gob and rip your T-shirt to shreds"
(*Front Magazine*)

"Gobs all over the opposition, The definitive visual document of the life and times of the Sex Pistols"
(*Record Collector*)

"Enough Sex Pistols memorabilia to shake a pogo stick at.."
(*Esquire Magazine*)

"Book Of The Month- Contains page after page of extraordinary Images"
(*Record Mart & Buyer*)

"An exhaustive, interesting work,and a must for your lists"
(*Metal Hammer*)

"In some ways the definitive book about the band"…KKKK

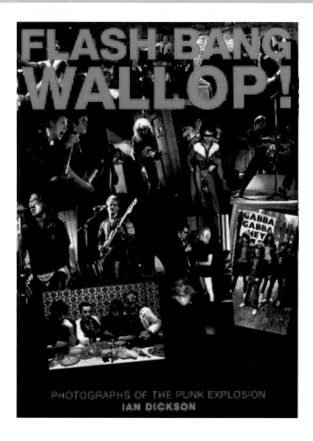

"…A superb collection of photographs of icons from every
branch of the gurning, gobbing family tree of punk, *"Flash
Bang Wallop!"* is nothing less than a masterpiece…"
(Record Collector #257, January 2001)

"…Dickson fast became *the* lens on the scene throughout
the formative punk years…"
(Guitar Magazine, September 2000)

"…All the usual suspects are here in this definitive photographic
record of the punk era (the perfect accompaniment to Jon Savage's
untouchable tome *"England's Dreaming")*…"
(Melody Maker, 1-7 November 2000)

"…It's brilliant!"
(Ramones UK Fan Club, November 2000)